JAVA™
BY ABSTRACTION
A CLIENT-VIEW APPROACH

HAMZEH ROUMANI

THIRD EDITION

Learning Solutions

New York   Boston   San Francisco
London   Toronto   Sydney   Tokyo   Singapore   Madrid
Mexico City   Munich   Paris   Cape Town   Hong Kong   Montreal

Cover art courtesy of Hamzeh Roumani

Pearson Learning Solutions, 501 Boylston Street, Suite 900, Boston, MA 02116
A Pearson Education Company
www.pearsoned.com

Printed in Canada

2 3 4 5 6 7 8 9 10 XXXX 15 14 13 12 11

000200010270568166

MHB

ISBN-10: 0-558-81983-4
ISBN-13: 978-0-558-81983-5

To Souad, Hamdi, and Adib—my family.

Thank you for your encouragement,
and for putting up with my "affair with the book."

Contents at a Glance

Table of Contents

Preface

This textbook is intended for a first course on object-oriented programming (OOP) in an undergraduate program in computer science, computer engineering, or information systems. The text uses the "objects-first" model[1] to present the fundamentals of OOP and software engineering, but it does so in a unique way.

Approach

Abstraction is used extensively in computer science education (CSE) and, starting with the client view rather than the implementer's view, has proven successful in several areas, such as computer organization and networking. In fact, CSE research[2,3] has long recognized the importance of the separation of concerns in CS1 and has called for "An Exodus from Implementation-Biased Teaching."[4] Many instructors prefer to start with the client view but are unable to find textbooks that embrace this approach. This book is meant to fill that void.

Java by Abstraction adopts the client view by writing main programs that only use existing classes. Given the large number of ready-made classes in the Java standard library and elsewhere, the book can cover key OOP concepts, such as encapsulation, aggregation, inheritance, generics, and polymorphism, without ever writing a class. It tackles merging lists, finding medians, and removing duplicates without ever using arrays. Delaying the implementation to CS2 allows students to grasp the true meaning of encapsulation and contracts, and promotes system thinking. In fact, it is my belief that the perceived complexity of teaching OOP in CS1 is due, to a large extent, to mixing the implementer and the client views.

Students who learn the client view in CS1 can "look under the hood" in CS2 and selectively implement some of the ready-made components used in CS1. With the key OOP concepts and software engineering practices out of the way, CS2 can focus on such implementer concerns as class implementation, data structures, recursion, and the events/callback model. At the end of CS2, students who were taught using the client-view-first approach will have the same body of knowledge as those who have followed the conventional approach, except they will find OOP easier and will be better prepared to deal with black-box components.

Certain aspects of *constructivist pedagogy* have influenced the writing of this book: for students to construct knowledge, we must explicitly teach a viable model even if it lies beneath the abstraction level.[5] I make it a point, for example, to "explain" the behaviour of assignment, the new operator, the equality of references, and the passing of parameters by value through a memory model complete with addresses. The model does not break the encapsulation because it does not expose or dictate any particular implementation; it is simply a cover story that allows us to reason about things in an implementation-independent fashion.

Labs

I believe that labs constitute an integral component of CS1, not as evaluation tools, but as teaching instruments that complement the coverage in lecture.[6] Using Felder's terminology for classifying learning styles,[7] active students (who like to "try it out and see how it works") should do the lab before reading the chapter, whereas reflective students should read the chapter first and then do the lab. The first six labs are exploratory in nature, and the remaining six are more like mini projects.

eCheck

Each chapter is followed by four exercises that can be auto-checked using eCheck, a unique program on the book's website. eCheck acts like a test harness and an oracle: it sends carefully randomized test cases to the student's program, captures its output, and compares it with the oracle. If the student's program fails to produce the expected output for a particular test case, eCheck identifies the test case and displays both outputs. In that case, the student needs to investigate, fix the problem, then recheck. In addition to playing the role of a tutor, this program can also be used for marking: When a student successfully completes a checked exercise, eCheck connects to the departmental server and sends the student's data. Departments that adopt the book will be supplied with a server-side package that receives and records the incoming data. The server-side package enables instructors to insert additional exercises (beyond the basic 48) so that checked exercises will vary from one term to the next.

Pedagogical Features

The following features are used consistently throughout this textbook:

- **Key concepts** within the text are in bold, and they appear at the end of each chapter in the Summary of Key Concepts.
- Each chapter begins with a list of **objectives**, a **motivational paragraph**, and an **outline**. It ends with a **summary**, **review questions**, a **lab**, **exercises**, and exercises to use with eCheck.
- Additional material appears in three types of text boxes: the **Programming Tips**, which list common errors and pitfalls; the **In More Depth** boxes, which provide further details about the topic at hand; and **Java Details**, which address issues peculiar to Java and not central to OOP. These boxes can be selectively skipped without any loss of continuity.

Acknowledgments

The Department of Computer Science and Engineering at York University has a three-course introductory sequence ($CS101_0$-103_0 using the ACM *Computing Curricula 2001* terminology). The client-view approach of this textbook emerged[8] after years of teaching this sequence and observing how students progress through it. I am therefore grateful to the many colleagues who taught these courses over the years and shared their experiences with me. They include Professors Eshrat Arjomandi, Melanie Baljko, Michael Jenkin, Gordon Turpin, Vassilios Tzerpos, and Franck van Breugel. In particular, I am indebted to Franck whose clarity of thought, strict adherence to principles, and deep understanding of abstraction were a source of guidance and encouragement and provided a firm ground when things were shaky.

H. Roumani
Toronto, Ontario
Canada

[1] IEEE-CS/ACM Joint Task Force. *Computing Curricula 2001, Computer Science, Final Report (2001)*. http://www.acm.org/sigcse/cc2001/cc2001.pdf.

[2] Bucci, P., Long, T., and Weide, B. "Do We Really Teach Abstraction?" In *Proc. 2001 ACM SIGCSE Symposium* (2001), pp. 26–30.

[3] Long, T., et al. "Providing Intellectual Focus to CS1/CS2." In *Proc. 1998 ACM SIGCSE Symposium* (1998), pp. 252–256.

[4] Long, T., et al. "Client View First: An Exodus from Implementation-Biased Teaching." In *Proc. 1999 ACM SIGCSE Symposium* (1999), pp. 136–140.

[5] Ben-Ari, M. "Constructivism in Computer Science Education." In *Proc. 1998 ACM SIGCSE Symposium* (1998), pp. 257–261.

[6] Roumani, H. "Design Guidelines for the Lab Component of Objects-First CS1." In *Proc. 2002 ACM SIGCSE Symposium* (2002), pp. 222–226.

[7] Soloman, B., and Felder, R. *Learning Styles and Strategies.* http://www.ncsu.edu/felder-public/ILSdir/styles.htm.

[8] Roumani, H. "Practice What You Preach: Full Separation of Concerns in CS1/CS2", In *Proc. 2006 ACM SIGCSE Symposium* (2006), pp. 491–495.

To the Student

This course is probably your first postsecondary exposure to the discipline of computing, and consequently, you need to know that you cannot study and prepare for it the same way you do for a course in math or physics. Even if you feel you understand the ideas presented in lecture or covered in a particular chapter, you still need to dedicate time to writing programs, as well as compiling and running them, before you fully grasp the material. Initially, this might be frustrating, because you may spend hours wrestling with the compiler; but once you master how it works, programming becomes fun. You will enjoy being able to create your own unique applications, and you will take pride in them.

Developing programming skills requires extended practice, and this means that you have to start as early as the first week of classes. Here is a proven weekly strategy:

1. Read the chapter (preferably before going to your lecture).
2. Do the Lab that follows the chapter.
3. Do as many of the exercises as you can.
4. Do at least one eCheck exercise, and do not give up until it passes eCheck.

If you find it easier, reverse tasks 1 and 2. The Labs are a hands-on application of the theoretical material covered in the chapter. The exercises test your understanding of the material as well as your ability to write programs. eCheck is an "acid test": for it to deem your program correct, you must understand the material, write syntactically correct code, and meet exact specifications.

All the software packages and tools needed to develop and test Java programs, including the unique eCheck, are available for free download from this book's web site. You will learn how to download, install, and use these packages and tools in Labs 1 and 2. Here is the URL of the book's web site: `http://www.cse.yorku.ca/~roumani/jba`

```
tic void main(String[] args)

String SHIFT = "00AM12PM"

output.print("Enter h:
String entry = input.n
```

Introduction to Programming

n this chapter, you will learn how to identify and name the key components of a Java program and the steps needed to execute it. We look in-depth at Java's primitive types, variable declaration and its implication on memory, and arithmetic operators and data conversion.

Learning Objectives

1. *Identify the lexical elements of Java™ and the key features of its programs*

2. *Become familiar with the edit-compile-run process*

3. *Learn to code with style using widely accepted conventions*

4. *Recognize Java's primitive types and their literals*

5. *Gain a solid understanding of declaration and the memory model*

6. *Evaluate arithmetic expressions*

7. *Learn about promotion and type casting*

Chapter Outline

1.1 Anatomy of a Program

This section explores the Java programming language by examining a simple program. The objectives are to learn how to recognize and name the elements of the language and to become familiar with the development process.

1.1.1 A Quick Tour

We start our exploration by looking at the program shown in Fig. 1.1. This program exposes features common to all Java programs. At this stage, we are not concerned with how the program was put together. We just want to be able to identify its elements, learn their technical names, and understand the roles they play.

Imports

The **import** statement on line 1 tells us that this program plans to use the System class which resides in the `lang` **subpackage** of the `java` **package**. A **class** is the smallest building block in Java. To make finding classes easier and to avoid naming conflicts, classes are often organized in subpackages, which, in turn, are organized in packages. A package hierarchy may have no subpackages, just classes in a package, or it may have several levels of subpackages. The hierarchy of the `java` package is shown, in part, in Fig. 1.2.

To uniquely specify a class in a package hierarchy, the import statement uses the **fully qualified class name**, a sequence of dot-delimited names. The sequence begins with the package name, ends with the class name, and lists in between all the intermediate subpackages (if any). The fully qualified name of the System class is thus

```
java.lang.System
```

Since our program apparently needs the System class (it refers to it on line 11), it had to import it, using its fully qualified name, on line 1.

Figure 1.1
This Java program computes the area of a rectangle. The line numbers to the left are not part of the program; they were added so that we can refer to statements as we explain the program.

```
001    import java.lang.System;
002
003    public class Area
004    {
005        public static void main(String[] args)
006        {
007            int width;
008            width = 8;
009            int height = 3;
010            int area = width * height;
011            System.out.println(area);
012        }
013    }
```

Figure 1.2 In this package hierarchy `lang` and `util` are two of the sub-packages of the `java` package.

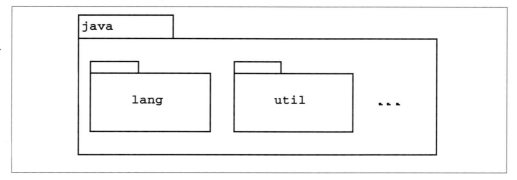

Java is a **case-sensitive** language; "Import" is not the same as "import". As a rule, words that are part of the Java language must always be written in lowercase. For other words (e.g., a package name), we follow a **coding style** that has guidelines for every category of words. For package and subpackage names, the guideline is to use lowercase. We will present these guidelines as we encounter them in the program. (They are all listed in Appendix C.)

If you plan to use more than one class in your program, you will need one import statement per class, but there are two shortcuts. The first shortcut is that all classes in the same subpackage can be imported with one import statement by replacing the class name with an asterisk. For example,

```
import java.util.*;
```

makes all classes in `java.util` available to your program (whether you plan to use all of them or not). The other shortcut is that the subpackage `java.lang`, which contains commonly used classes, is automatically imported; that is, you can assume that the following statement is implicitly added to every program you write:

```
import java.lang.*;
```

Hence, we really did not need the first statement in the program in Fig. 1.1. The program will function exactly the same with or without it.

Class Definition

The statement on line 3 indicates the beginning of a class named `Area`. This statement is called the **class header** and is followed by two braces (an opening brace on line 4 and a closing brace on line 13) that enclose the **class body**. Any group of consecutive statements surrounded by braces is called a **block**. As a matter of style, the two braces of a block must align vertically, and all statements in between must be left justified and indented to the right by one tab position relative to the opening brace. Also a matter of style is the usage of *title case* for the class name. Title case means only the first letter of the name is capitalized unless the name is an acronym, in which case all letters are capitalized. For multiword names, capitalize the first letter of every word. For example, `Area`, `Math`, `URL`, and `StringTokenizer` are properly named classes.

Programming Tip   1.1

Pitfall: Replacing a subpackage name by an asterisk

There is no way to import all classes in "`java.util`" *and* in "`java.io`" with one import statement. Importing "`java.*`" will not work because the asterisk means "all classes," not "all subpackages." The import "`java.*.*`" would also not work because it is illegal to use more than one asterisk.

Pitfall: Assuming that asterisks have an impact on performance

Using an asterisk has no effect on the execution speed or the size of your program. It may take a bit longer for the compiler to find the imported classes, but the end result is the same with or without asterisks.

Java Details   1.1

Life Without Imports

You can use a class without importing it provided you fully qualify its name wherever it is used. For example, we could remove the import statement from our program provided we rewrite line 11 as

```
java.lang.System.out.println(area);
```

In a typical program, however, an imported class is used on several lines, and it would be a nuisance to fully qualify its name every time it is used.

Method Definition

The statement on line 5 indicates the beginning of the `main` method. This statement is the **method header** and is followed by a block that constitutes the **method body**. We use lower-case letters for method names, but for multiword names we capitalize the first letter of each subsequent word. In this style, `main`, `equals`, `toString`, and `isLeapYear` are properly named methods.

Statements

The body of the `main` method contains five statements. A variable named `width` is declared as an integer (`int`) on line 7 and is assigned the value 8 on line 8. In our coding style, variables are named using the same case convention as methods. Java is a **strongly typed language**, which means every variable must be declared before being used. On line 9, a second variable, `height`, is declared as an integer and is assigned the value 3. This line could have been written as two separate statements:

Style: An alternative layout for braces

Instead of having braces that are vertically aligned, some prefer to place the opening brace of a block on the same line as the header:

```
public class Area {
   public static void main(String[] args) {
      ...
      ...
   }
}
```

In this textbook we will adhere to vertically aligned braces.

```
int height;
height = 3;
```

However, it is a convenient and commonly used shortcut to combine declaration with assignment. The statement on line 10 uses the same shortcut to declare a third integer variable, `area`, and assign it the product of the previous two variables. Note that this variable will not be confused with the class name, `Area`, thanks to Java's case sensitivity. The last statement outputs the computed area on the screen. It does so by delegating the printing work to other classes. Whenever you see dot-delimited words in a statement, think of the words as stages in a communication process. For example, the last statement in the program,

```
System.out.println(area);
```

is analogous to making a phone call: It first dials the phone number of a company, `System`, and then dials the extension of a department within the company, `out`. Finally, it requests a service from an employee in the company, `println`.

Layout

Java is **freeform**. Freeform means that statements can begin in any column, and you can add **whitespace** (spaces, carriage returns, tabs) to any statement. For example, you can make a statement span two lines, or you can write two statements on a line. The only thing you have to observe is the **semicolon rule**, which states that every statement must end with a semicolon unless it is a header whose body follows (this is why class and method headers do not end with semicolons). For example, you can rewrite the method's body in our example program as follows:

```
{int width; width=8; int height=3; int
area = width * height; System.out.println(
area);}
```

However, instead of misusing freeform, we use it to make the code easier to read and understand by adding whitespace here and there. As a matter of style, a statement should be written on one line unless it is too wide, in which case we break it (ideally after a comma) and continue it indented on the next line. Feel free to insert blank lines to separate parts of your code. Within a statement, add no more than one space in between tokens, for example, between `int` and `width`. The precise guideline for token spacing is presented in Section 1.1.2.

Comments

Comments are nonexecutable notes that you add to your program, and they come in two categories: **documentation comments**, which explain what the program does and how to use it, and **internal comments**, which explain (to a programmer) how the program works internally. You can add a **multiline** internal comment to your program by prefixing the comment with `/*` and ending with `*/`. For example, you can add the following lines before line 3:

```
/*
A first program for Chapter 1
Author: JBA
First Created: June 2004
Last Modified: September 2010
*/
```

For a short internal comment, you can use a **one-line** comment, which begins with `//` and ends with a carriage return. For example, you can insert the following line before line 3:

```
// This is my first Java program!
```

These comments do not have to start at the beginning of the line; you can also use them inline. For example, you can add a comment to line 8:

```
width = 8; // in cm.
```

We will not write documentation comments in this book, but we mention, for completeness, that they start with `/**` (two asterisks) and end with `*/`.

1.1.2 Language Elements

Establishing the correctness of a sentence written in English (or any other human language) is a multistage process. In the first stage, we examine each word in the sentence and attempt to classify it according to the rules of the language, for example, as a verb, noun, proper name,

---

Programming Tip   1.3

Pitfall: Delaying comments until the code is finalized

Code is never finalized; if it were, comments would no longer be needed. Comments should be written as the program is being developed so that they capture your state of mind at the time.

Pitfall: Adding a comment that restates a statement

The comment

```
int area = width * height; //multiply width by height
```

is not only useless, but it is worse than no comments at all. This is because it is normal for programs to change, and comments like this cannot keep up with the changes. For example, `width` may later be renamed to `length`, but the comment may continue to refer to `width`, which is confusing. When you write internal comments, assume that the reader is an experienced programmer; explain only the subtle parts of your code.

preposition, and so on. Similarly, the first stage in determining the correctness of a Java program is to break each of its statements into tokens and to classify each token as one of the **lexical elements** of Java. A program that passes this stage is not necessarily correct because it may violate Java's **syntax**, which determines how the lexical elements can be combined. Similarly, a lexically and syntactically correct Java statement may not be allowed in certain contexts, and it is the **semantics** that determines this. We will cover the syntax and semantics of statements as we encounter them. In this section, we look at the lexical elements of Java: keywords, identifiers, literals, operators, and separators.

Keywords

Keywords are words that have predefined meanings in Java, and they are listed in Fig. 1.3. (Notice that they are all in lowercase.) Since these words cannot be used except for their intended purpose, they are part of Java's **reserved words**, which also include the literals `true`, `false`, and `null`. In our program, we can see that `import` and `public` are two keywords.

Identifiers

Identifiers are names that programmers choose to use in their programs; they have no predefined meaning in Java. For example, `Area` (a class name), `main` (a method name), and

Documentation Comments

These comments are written in helper classes, ones that are used by programs, to explain to program writers how to use these classes. The *javadoc* utility that comes with Java can extract these comments from classes and produce HTML files.

Figure 1.3 Java reserves these keywords in addition to the literals: `true`, `false`, and `null`.

abstract	assert				
boolean	break	byte			
case	catch	char	class	const	continue
default	do	double			
else	enum	extends			
final	finally	float	for		
goto					
if	implements	import	instanceof	int	interface
long					
native	new				
package	private	protected	public		
return					
short	static	strictfp	super	switch	synchronized
this	throw	throws	transient	try	
void	volatile				
while					

width (a variable name) are identifiers. Note that `lang`, `System`, and `println` are also identifiers. We did not choose them, but the developer of an imported class did. You can use any name you like for an identifier as long as it is not a reserved word, it begins with a letter, and it consists only of letters, digits, the characters $ and _ (dollar and underscore), or any combination thereof. Note, in particular, that no spaces are allowed. In terms of style, we must choose names that are meaningful to the reader and that follow the case guideline: title case for class names and lowercase (with a special multiword treatment) for package, method, and variable names.

Literals

Literals are constant values. For example, the number 3 that appears on line 9 is an integer literal. Like variables, literals have types associated with them yet they do not need to be declared. You can easily recognize a literal because it is either a number, a character surrounded by single quotes, characters surrounded by double quotes, or one of the reserved words `true`, `false`, or `null`. We will learn later in this chapter how to determine the type of a literal just by looking at it.

Operators

An **operator** is like a mathematical function because it takes one or more arguments (known as *operands*) and produces a result. The multiplication asterisk on line 10 is an operator that takes two operands, `width` and `height`, and produces a result (being their product). Java's operators are made of certain combinations of the following characters:

```
= > < ! ~ ? : & | + - * / ^ %
```

For example, ++ and != are operators. Java's operators are either **unary** (they take a single operand), **binary** (they take two operands), or **ternary** (they take three operands). The unary operands are either **prefix** (the operator is placed before its operand) or **suffix** (the operator is placed after its operand). The binary operators are all **infix** (the operator is placed between its operands). There is only one ternary operator in Java. We will meet most of Java's operators in the coming chapters. A complete list is available in Appendix B.

Separators

Separators are characters that separate various parts of your code. They are similar to punctuation symbols in human languages. Java's separators are

```
.  ,  ;   ...   ( )  [ ]  { }
```

(The three-dot separator is the ellipsis.) We have already seen some of these separators in action, as semicolons separating statements and as braces separating blocks.

The lexical elements of Java are summarized in Fig. 1.4. Given any Java statement, one can always parse it, that is, resolve it, and expose its lexical elements. But for parsing to reproduce the elements that the programmer intended, whitespace sometimes has to be inserted. For example, if you do not insert a space between the two keywords `public` and `class`, the parser will treat "`publicclass`" as one identifier, which is probably not what you had in mind. On the other hand, the statement "`width=8`" will still be parsed correctly (as identifier, operator, literal), even though it contains no spaces, because = cannot be part of an identifier. It is clear that for successful parsing, keywords and identifiers must not "touch," that is, there must be whitespace or a separator between any two. In our coding style, the spacing guideline can be stated as follows:

Leave exactly one space

- between otherwise touching keywords or identifiers
- before and after a non-unary operator
- after the comma separator

Figure 1.4 The lexical elements of Java

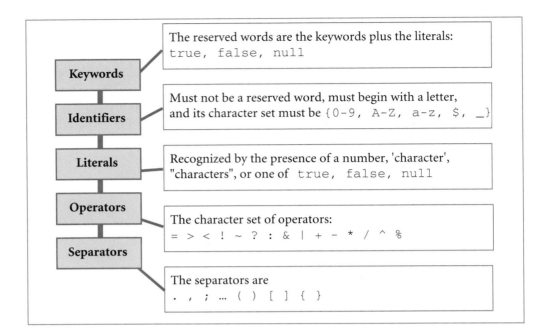

Keywords — The reserved words are the keywords plus the literals:
`true, false, null`

Identifiers — Must not be a reserved word, must begin with a letter, and its character set must be `{0-9, A-Z, a-z, $, _}`

Literals — Recognized by the presence of a number, 'character', "characters", or one of `true, false, null`

Operators — The character set of operators:
`= > < ! ~ ? : & | + - * / ^ %`

Separators — The separators are
`. , ; ... ( ) [ ] { }`

Java Details   1.3

Statement Categories

In addition to looking at statements in terms of what they are made of, one can also look at them semantically, that is, in terms of what they do. From that perspective, one can divide Java statements into five categories (aside from comments):

1. **Declaration** Used to specify types and serve as headers for classes and methods
2. **Assignment** Enables us to give a value to a variable
3. **Usage of Other Classes** Allows us to access features from imported classes
4. **Flow Control** There are four subcategories:

   - conditional: `if-else, switch-case`
   - iteration: `for, while, do-while`
   - branching: `break, return, continue`
   - exception: `try-catch-finally, throw`

5. **Other Statements** `synchronized, assert,` and the empty statement

1.1.3 Program Execution

Three steps are needed to execute (run) a program:

- **Edit** We use an editor to write the program and save it in a file. A program containing a class named `Area` *must* be saved in a file named `Area.java`. This file is known as the **source file**.
- **Compile** We use a **compiler** to translate our program from Java, a **high-level language**, to **bytecode**, a language that is intermediate between Java and **machine language**, the native language of the processor. The compiler reads the source file, translates it, and stores the translation in a file called the **class file**. The file is so named because it has the same name as the source but with a *class* extension; for example, the source `Area.java` compiles into `Area.class`. If the compiler is not able to translate the program, it will issue a list of **compile-time errors**. In that case, we must go back to the editor, correct the reported errors, save the file, and recompile. Figure 1.5 depicts this **edit-compile cycle**, which must be repeated until the source compiles successfully.

- **Run** We use a **virtual machine (VM)** to execute the bytecode in the class file. The VM is a program that simulates a real processor: it translates the bytecode, one instruction at a time, to machine language and forwards the translation to the real processor (see Fig. 1.6).

Figure 1.5 The edit-compile cycle culminates in the production of the class file.

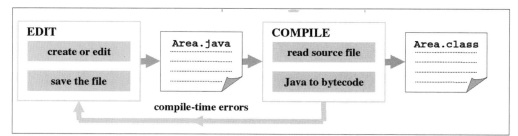

Programming Tip   1.6

Pitfall: Forgetting to recompile after a modification

When the compiler detects errors in your program, it will not create a class file, *but it will not erase an existing one*. This can lead to the following scenario: You run a program and then decide to make a modification in it. The modified program generates errors so you go back to the editor and fix them but forget to recompile. When you run the program, the old class file will run, and it appears as though the VM is ignoring any changes you make to the program.

Figure 1.6 The VM executes the class file.

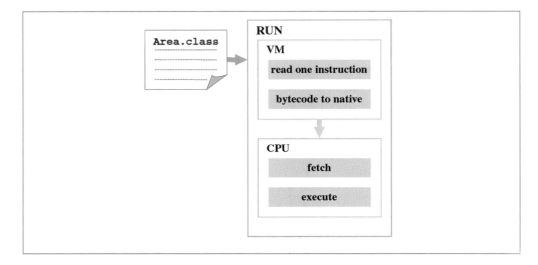

When the program runs, the VM locates the very first statement in the `main` method, translates it, and asks the processor to execute it. That statement becomes in control of the computer, and we say that it has received **control**. Afterward, the next statement in the method receives control, and so on. This is called the **sequence flow** because control *flows* from one statement to the next in sequence; that is, the execution order is the same as the physical order of statements in the program. Once the last statement is executed, control is returned to whatever program was in control before the VM was launched.

In More Depth   1.1

Languages and Translation

Programming a computer means issuing instructions to its central processing unit (CPU), and this must be done in its native language, *machine language*. To do so, we must somehow cross the vast divide that separates human and machine languages. The challenge here is not one of representation—that we use letters whereas machines use 0s and 1s—rather, it is the very fabric of language that is different. Machine language has three important characteristics that can be summarized and contrasted as follows:

- **Direct Data Referencing** Machine language instructions must use the actual memory address in which data is stored rather than merely the name of the data. Human languages, on the other hand, are based on names (symbols) that denote objects.
- **Primitive Data Manipulation** Albeit fast, processors can execute only a few primitive operations. Almost any process that we, humans, perceive as "simple" must be broken down to several machine operations before the processor can execute it.
- **Context-Free** Statements made in machine language have definite unambiguous meanings. The meanings of human sentences, however, are dependent on the context in which they are said.

Take, for example, the computation of a sales amount. It can be expressed in human-readable terms using only one statement:

```
sales = quantity × price
```

In machine language, you cannot use names but must specify addresses. Let us assume that the quantity is stored in memory at address 24, the price at 40, and the sales amount at 60. With these addresses, we can now refer to the data in a way that the CPU accepts, but this is only the first hurdle. The CPU cannot multiply data in memory; the data must first be fetched to registers within the CPU. Only then can it be manipulated. Hence, we need to break down the computation into primitive steps:

```
Fetch data from address 24 to register A
Fetch data from address 40 to register B
Set register C to the product of registers A and B
Store data in C at address 60
```

As you can see, it is daunting to write programs in machine language. Worse yet, once the program is written, it cannot be ported to a machine with a different CPU because different processors have different machine languages. Even if all the computers you use are from the same vendor, a minor change in the operating system may require a change to the program. Thus, writing programs in machine language is not the way to go.

An alternative approach is to write programs in a language we like, for example, English, and then have the program translated to machine language by a program written in machine language. This is not feasible because all human languages are heavily context-sensitive, making them "too loose" to be used for programming: a sentence said in one context can mean something else if said in another. Even grammar, which we rely on for clarification, is sometimes context-sensitive itself. For example, the word *time* in the sentence *time flies like an arrow* can be thought of as a subject, a verb, or an adjective, depending on the context.

As you can see, human languages are unsuitable and machine languages are lacking. Therefore, *high-level languages* were invented, for example, Fortran, Pascal, and C. High-level languages share the symbolism and richness of human languages but are unambiguous enough to make their automatic translation to machine language possible. Each such language comes with a translator, called a *compiler*, that translates source files into executable, machine language files. Note that since different processors have different machine languages, you will need a separate executable file per platform. Hence, compiled languages are *not* platform-independent.

The Virtual Machine and Platform Independence

Compiling to native code is like shooting at a moving target, because processors (and their machine languages) are always in a state of change. Rather than adapting to a changing world, we can target a fixed machine (the *virtual machine*) and create a compiler that translates Java source files to it. The machine language of the virtual machine is called *bytecode*. Bytecode is chosen so that it is easy and fast to translate from Java to it; it is also relatively fast to translate from bytecode to any genuine machine language (see Fig. 1.7).

Java is platform-independent because its compiled programs can be executed on any machine that can simulate the VM. The simulator is a program that reads the class file one instruction at a time, translates it to machine language, and executes it. This instant translation process is called *interpretation*. Java is known as an *interpreted-compiled* language because of this feature.

The interpretive aspect of Java accounts for its lower performance compared with compiled languages. Modern VMs compensate for this by storing the translated code in memory, a technique called *just in time* (jit) compilation.

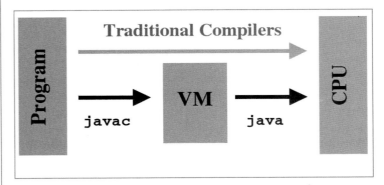

Figure 1.7 The Java compiler translates Java source code into an intermediate bytecode, which can be deployed on any platform with a VM. The VM translates each bytecode instruction into machine language and executes it.

Example 1.1

Consider the program shown in Fig. 1.8. Provide a critique of how the program is written by examining each statement and commenting on its lexical structure, compile-time errors, and style (naming, indentation, and spacing). Assume that the name of the program's source file is "Example11.java".

Answer:
The first statement contains the `import` keyword, three identifiers delimited by the dot separator, and the semicolon separator. It is syntactically correct. In terms of naming, the package, subpackage, and class names were not chosen by the writer of this program, so we will not comment on their appropriateness. In terms of spacing, one space is correctly inserted between the keyword and the first identifier, but another is incorrectly inserted before the semicolon. Hence, the first statement has one style violation. The next

Figure 1.8 A
Java program
that contains
compile-time
errors and style
violations

```
001    import java.util.Date ;                    syntactically correct
                             ↑ style
                               violation
002    import javax.swing.JOptionPane;

003

004    public class example1.1
                     └─┬─────┘ identifier cannot contain a dot
005    {
006        public static void main(String[] args)
007        {              ↓ variables
                           should be lowercase
008            int Height = 2;
009            int          } should be one line
010              width;     }
011            width=3;        ↓ operator
012            intlength = 4;
       was    └────────┘
       not
       declared
013            int v = width * Height * length;
014            System.out.println(v);
015        }
016    }
```

statement is similar to the first, and it has no errors or style violations. We note, however, that the class it imports is never used in the program. Note that there is nothing wrong with that; perhaps the class is scheduled to be used in a later release.

The statement on line 4 contains two keywords followed by an identifier and a literal delimited by a dot. We can see that it is intended to be a class header but with an illegal class name (an identifier cannot contain a dot). The compiler, however, will interpret "example1" as the class name and will expect to see it followed by an opening brace. When it does not, the compiler issues the compile-time error:

```
Example11.java:4: '{' expected
```

Notice how this error does not make any sense to the programmer, since there is a brace on the following line, but it makes perfect sense from the compiler's perspective. Even if the dot were removed, there would still be a compile-time error because a class with a source file `Example11.java` has to be named `Example11`. The tokens in this statement are correctly spaced.

For the rest of the program, we will only point out errors and style violations.

■ Line 8 contains a style violation because lowercase letters should be used for a variable name.

■ Line 9 contains a style violation because such a statement should not span two lines.

■ Line 11 contains a style violation because no spaces were inserted around the `=` operator.

■ Line 12 contains an error because, in the eyes of the compiler, the variable `intlength` is being used even though it was not declared.

■ Line 13 contains an error and a style violation. The error is that the variable `length` is being used even though it was not declared. The style violation is in not using a meaningful name for the variable `v`. If it represents a volume, then `volume` should have been used.

1.2 The Declaration Statement

Every variable in the program must be declared before it is used. The **declaration statement** has the following form:

```
type variableName;
```

In this statement, the programmer is indicating that a variable with the specified name will be used later in the program and that its future value will be of the specified **type**. The statement does *not* assign a value to the variable; it merely prepares it to hold a value of a particular type. For example, the following statement declares that the programmer intends to use a variable named `width` and store integers in it:

type → `int width;` *variable*

A declaration must appear before the variable is used in the program; otherwise, the compiler will report an error. Specifically, the variable is available for usage starting from the statement that follows the declaration and ending at the end of the block that encloses the declaration (the one whose opening brace appears first before the declaration). This area is known as the **scope** of the variable, and it is an error to use a variable outside its scope. The terms "**in scope**" and "**out of scope**" refer to areas in the program in which the variable can and cannot be used, respectively.

To fully understand this statement, three questions must be answered:

- How should the name of the variable be chosen?
- What are the allowed types?
- What really happens behind the scenes when the compiler sees this statement?

The following sections provide the answers.

1.2.1 Variable Names

You can use any name for your variable as long as it is an identifier (as defined in Section 1.1.2) and provided you are not in the scope of another variable with the same name. To make the program self-documenting—and hence easier to understand—choose a name that is indicative of what the variable represents. If the variable is going to hold the width of a rectangle, call it `width`. Avoid using single-letter names such as `w` (as done in algebra) unless the context is generic, and, in general, avoid using any nonstandard abbreviation (such as `prc` for price). For example, `quantity`, `taxRate`, and `isPrime` are properly named variables.

1.2.2 The Integer Types

These types are intended for variables whose values are whole numbers, no decimal point. The most common integer type is called **int**; int incorporates values whose range is about ±2 billion. This type is typically used when the variable represents a count of some sort, for example, the number of students in a course, the number of repetitions of a loop, or the amortization period of a mortgage (measured in years). The range of int accommodates most practical applications unless a very small measuring unit is chosen. For example, the number

Programming Tip

1.7

Pitfall: Assuming that a declared variable is automatically initialized to zero

Not in Java. You cannot even ask the question, What is the value of the variable right after its declaration? You may be tempted to write a program that prints out this value, but such a program will not compile.

Pitfall: Declaring all variables at the top

This is inevitable in some languages but should be avoided in Java programs. A variable is only accessible inside its scope, so the smaller the scope, the smaller the risk of an accidental change. Declare a variable just before you intend to use it.

of seconds that have elapsed since 1970 until now is well within the int range (there are only about $\pi \times 10^7$ s in one year), but if you choose to measure this duration in milliseconds, it will not fit. For applications in which a bigger range is needed, use the **long** integer type whose range is about $\pm 10^{19}$.

Integer Literals

Any whole number literal appearing in a program is considered by default to be of the type int unless it is suffixed by (1) or (L), in which case its type is considered long. For example, the type of 3 is int whereas that of 3L is long.

We mention, for completeness, that Java defines two more integer types, **byte** and **short**, with ranges that are smaller than the int. There are no literals associated with these types. All four types are summarized in Fig. 1.9. The size column indicates the number of bytes needed to store one value of each type. We will see in the next section the role that this number plays.

Figure 1.9 The integer types in Java

Type	Range (approximate)	Size (bytes)
byte	$\pm 1 \times 10^2$	1
short	$\pm 3 \times 10^4$	2
int	$\pm 2 \times 10^9$	4
long	$\pm 9 \times 10^{18}$	8

In More Depth

1.3

How Is the Range Computed?

If N is the number of bytes associated with an integer type, then the range of its values is from -2^{8N-1} to $+2^{8N-1} - 1$. For example, if N is 1 (corresponding to the byte type), then the above computation leads to the range -128 to $+127$.

Java Details   1.4

Number System

By default, all integer literals are assumed to be in the decimal system. If you want to express an integer in hexadecimal, prefix it by 0x or 0X, the digit 0 followed by the letter x or X. This prefix can be combined with the L suffix. For example, 0x13 is an int literal with decimal value 19, and 0X21L is a long literal with decimal value 33.

1.2.3 Declaration and Memory

When we declare a variable, we are asking the compiler to set aside an area of memory to hold its future values. Declaration is thus closely related to storage, and in order to develop a deeper understanding of declaration, we need to take a look at computer memory.

Memory can be viewed as a one-dimensional arrangement of cells, each of which is called a **memory byte** (see Fig. 1.10). The total number of bytes is the size of memory in the computer, and since it is typically quite large, it is expressed in multiples of byte: a **kilobyte** (KB) is 1024 bytes; a **megabyte** (MB) is 1024 KB; and a **gigabyte** (GB) is 1024 MB. The bytes are numbered sequentially, starting from 0, and the number assigned to a byte is called its **address**. What you store in a byte becomes its **content**, and it is important to distinguish content from address. If you need to store something that does not fit in a byte, use a **memory block**, a group of consecutive bytes.

Figure 1.10 A memory diagram with 4 bytes reserved for width

Bytes can be considered as analogous to seats in a theatre and addresses as tickets, a piece of paper with a seat number printed on it. If you purchase ticket number 6, then you are entitled to sit in seat number 6. The operating system (O/S) is analogous to the box office of the theatre: when the computer is turned on, the O/S is in possession of all tickets, but then it gives them to programs upon request. Specifically, when the compiler encounters a declaration such as

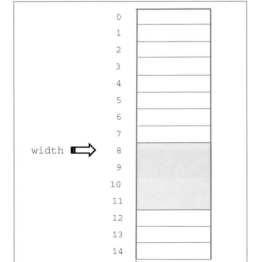

```
int width;
```

it realizes that 4 bytes of memory are needed, so it requests a block of four tickets from the O/S. Assume that the O/S responded by delivering tickets 8, 9, 10, and 11. In that case, the compiler would consider the declaration successful and would add the following entry to its **symbol table** (a notebook in which it keeps track of all declarations):

Identifier	Type	Block Address
width	int	8

The memory diagram in Fig. 1.10 depicts this declaration by showing an arrow emanating from the variable and pointing to

---

In More Depth   1.4

What Are Bytes Made Of?

Each byte is made up of eight **bits**. The **bit** is the ultimate storage location, but, ironically, you cannot "store" anything in a bit. It is merely a switch that can be toggled one way or the other, up or down. These two positions are labelled "1" and "0." Hence, storing the binary sequence 11110000 at address 24 amounts to setting the eight switches in that byte as follows: up, up, up, up, down, down, down, down. This setting is said to *represent* the binary sequence. Hence, the act of storing something in memory amounts to finding a *representation* of it. Terms like *storage* and *content* are widely used, but they can be misleading. These terms conjure up images of shelves or bins in which you store something by physically placing it there, and this is *not* how memory works. To ensure that you are using the correct mental model when you think of memory, examine the following points:

■ Can you tell which memory bytes are used and which are empty? No. Nothing is "empty" or "blank" when it gets to memory. Each byte has eight switches, and each switch is either up or down.

■ Can you store two things in the same byte? No. Storing anything in a byte resets its switches and, hence, overwrites the previous setting.

■ Can you store the same thing in more than one place? Yes. We do not place "the thing" in memory; we merely find a representative for it.

---

the beginning of the allocated memory block. By definition, the address of a block is the address of the first byte in it.

This interpretation of the declaration statement allows us to give a precise meaning to a term toward which we have been taking a cavalier attitude: "**variable**." We define a variable as the memory block reserved for it, and we define its name as a symbolic representation of the address of that block. In the theatre analogy, a variable is a seat, its name is the ticket, and its value is whoever sits in the seat. (By lifting the arms in between seats, you can create a multi-byte seat.)

1.2.4 Other Data Types

In addition to integers, Java has built-in support for other types. The basic concepts that we have learned for integers—declaration, memory allocation, and the notion of a variable—apply as is to all other types; only the nature of the data is different. The remaining types are the following.

The Real Types

Real types are intended for variables whose values have a decimal point. The most common real type is called **double**; double incorporates values that have up to 15 significant digits and are in the range of about $\pm 10^{308}$. This type is typically used when the variable represents an amount (dollar and cent) or a scientific measurement. If a value has more than 15 significant digits, then it will not be reproduced exactly; we say that a **round-off** will take place. Dealing

The IEEE-754 Standard

Java represents real numbers by adopting the IEEE-754 standard in which numbers are expressed in scientific-like notation: a fractional part multiplied by a power. The exponent of the power determines the order of magnitude of the number, and, being an integer, it can be reproduced without problems. The fractional part, however, may not be exactly reproducible because it may have more decimal places than space permits. This is why real types have a finite number of significant digits. The problem may be obvious for an irrational value like π, but even an innocent-looking value like 0.3 will not reproduce exactly. This is because computers use the binary system internally, and in that system, 0.3 has infinitely many bits after the binary point.

with, and avoiding, round-off is beyond the scope of this textbook, but it should be stated that its presence makes real types "risky" when compared with the infinite precision of all other types in Java. Java supports a second, less precise real type called **float**. The type float incorporates values that have up to 7 significant digits and are in the range of about $\pm 10^{38}$. The names *double* and *float* were adopted in Java for historical reasons; the standard names are *double precision* and *single precision*.

Real Literals

A number with a decimal point and no suffix is considered to be of the type `double`. If the suffix d or D is present, then the type is also considered `double` regardless of the presence of a decimal point. On the other hand, if the suffix f or F is present, then the type is considered `float` regardless of the decimal point. If you want to express a real literal in exponential notation, which is handy if it is very big or very small in absolute value, then type an e (or E) before the exponent. For example, `2.5E3` is of the type `double`, and its value is 2.5×10^3, or `2500.0`, whereas `1e-4f` is of the type `float` and its value is 1×10^{-4}, or `0.0001`.

The Boolean Type

When we write programs, we often need to test whether a certain condition is met. In addition, we sometimes need to store the outcome of such a test. Since conditions are either met or not met, we seek a type that can have only two possible values: `true` and `false`. Such a type is supported in Java under the name: **boolean**.

Boolean Literals

There are only two such literals: `true` and `false`. Note that these are reserved words and must be written in lowercase.

The Character Type

The character type in Java is called **char**, and each of its values corresponds to a single character. Most programming languages use the **ASCII** character set, which contains 2^8, or 256,

Java Details 1.5

Booleans Are Not Integers

Java does not specify how a `boolean` is actually represented in binary; it leaves this to implementation. One can imagine that each `boolean` is stored in one byte as an integer, perhaps with 0 being `false` and -1 being `true`, but this cannot be verified because Java does not allow us to compare (or convert) a `boolean` to an integer.

characters. ASCII provides adequate support for the English-speaking world. Java, on the other hand, uses the **Unicode** character set, which contains 2^{16}, or 65 536, characters. Unicode provides support for all human languages (historic and modern) and various specialized fields. Unicode assigns integer codes (from 0 to 65 535) to all these characters, and to maintain backward compatibility, the codes assigned to English characters are the same as they are in ASCII. You do not need to memorize these codes, but it is helpful to keep two general features in mind: consecutive digits have consecutive codes, and consecutive letters have consecutive codes. (See Fig. 1.11.)

It should be noted that this type is not really different from integer types because, behind the scenes, Java does not store the character itself, only its code, and the code is an integer. The only difference is that character codes cannot be negative. If we classify the values of the four integer types we met earlier as **signed integers**, and those of <u>char as **unsigned integers**</u>, we can indeed treat them all as integers. We will see in Section 1.3.3 that one can indeed operate on characters as if they were integers.

Character Literals

Java recognizes character literals by the presence of *single* quotes surrounding them, for example, `'A'`. This works well for most characters, but what if you cannot type the character between the quotes? Perhaps it is in a language that your keyboard does not support, or it may have a special meaning when typed (e.g., carriage return). To address such cases, Java allows you to put an **escape sequence** between the quotes, which denotes the intended character. For example, `'\t'` is the TAB character. Figure 1.12 lists these escape sequences.

1.2.5 Primitive and Nonprimitive Types

The eight data types introduced thus far (four integer, two real, one character, and one boolean) are known as Java's **primitive types** because they are internally supported by it; that is, their names are reserved words, their value sets are predefined, and their operations (like adding and subtracting) are built into the operators of the language. Figure 1.13 recaps the properties of all primitive types. Note that since `char` is merely an unsigned integer, we can say that there are seven numeric types and one boolean primitive type.

Java also supports three nonprimitive types: *class*, *interface*, and *array*. The nonprimitive types are meant to accommodate programmer-defined types, that is, the programmer chooses

Figure 1.11
Character codes

Code	Character
0	
· · ·	
32	space
· ·	
48–57	'0'–'9'
· ·	
65–90	'A'–'Z'
· ·	
97–122	'a'–'z'
· ·	
65535	

Figure 1.12 The escape sequences

Escape	Meaning
\uxxxx	The character whose code is (hex) xxxx
\'	Single quote
\"	Double quote
\\	Backslash
\n	New line
\r	Carriage return
\f	Form Feed
\t	Tab
\b	Backspace

their names, selects their data, and defines their operations. One of them is the String class, and it encapsulates strings (sequences of characters). We mention it here because it is the only nonprimitive type that has literals.

String Literals

Any sequence of characters surrounded by double quotes is taken to be of the type String. For example, "Java by Abstraction" is a string literal. If one of the characters in the string cannot be typed in, then its corresponding escape sequence (see Fig. 1.12) can be

Programming Tip   1.8

Pitfall: Using double quotes for a char literal

The literal "A" is not the same as 'A'; in fact, it is not a char literal.

Pitfall: Enclosing more than one character in single quotes

A char value must have exactly one character. Something like 'AB' is not a char literal and will, in fact, lead to a compile-time error. (If a String literal were intended, then double quotes should have been used.)

Figure 1.13
Java's primitive types. S.D. indicates the number of significant digits.

PRIMITIVE TYPES		Type	Size (bytes)	Approximate Range		S.D.
				min	max	
N U M B E R	**I N T E G E R** — **S I G N E D**	byte	1	-128	$+127$	∞
		short	2	$-32,768$	$+32,767$	∞
		int	4	-2×10^9	$+2 \times 10^9$	∞
		long	8	-9×10^{18}	$+9 \times 10^{18}$	∞
	I N T E G E R — UNSIGNED	char	2	0	$65,535$	∞
	R E A L — SINGLE	float	4	-3.4×10^{38}	$+3.4 \times 10^{38}$	7
	R E A L — DOUBLE	double	8	-1.7×10^{308}	$+1.7 \times 10^{308}$	15
BOOLEAN		boolean	1	true/false		N/A

embedded instead. For example, "One\nTwo" will appear on two lines if printed because \n means new line.

Example 1.2

Consider the program shown in Fig. 1.14. State any style violations or errors in it.

Figure 1.14
A Java program that contains syntax errors and style violations

```
001    import java.lang.System;
002
003    public class Example12
004    {
005       public static void main(String[] args)
006       {
007          int width;
008          int base = 5;
009          {
010             int height = 3;        out of scope?
011             int length;       → out of scope
012             System.out.println(base);
013          }
014          int length = 2;    ok. to redeclare
015          int volume = width * height * length;
016          System.out.println(volume);
017       }
018    }
```

Answer:

Let us start by identifying style-related issues. In terms of statement layout, the program conforms to the indentation guidelines: the class and method bodies are indented by one tab position relative to their headers, and the block on lines 10 through 12 is indented relative to its opening brace. The program is apparently using a tab size of 3 (skipping two positions per indentation). Note that any tab size is acceptable as long as it is applied consistently in all blocks. There are no violations in whitespace usage or in naming.

In terms of errors, there are two, and they both occur on line 15: the variable `width` is declared but not initialized, and the variable `height` is not declared (the declaration on line 10 is out of scope). Note that there is nothing wrong with line 12: the variable `base` is in scope and can be used. There is also nothing wrong with line 14: it is OK to redeclare `length` because its earlier declaration is out of scope. Admittedly, the block within the method's body (lines 9 through 13) is artificial (and is clearly useless in this case), but we will see later that several Java statements come with their own blocks, and hence, they do create scope issues similar to the one simulated here.

◻

Programming Tip   1.9

Pitfall: Using real types when an exact answer is sought

Real types provide reasonably high precision for scientific computations, but they are not suitable for business applications that use a large number of monetary values, such as accounting. This is because cent amounts like 0.01 cannot be represented exactly. For such applications, either express all amounts in cents and use integers (if possible), or use a nonprimitive type such as `java.math.BigDecimal`.

In More Depth   1.6

What Is a "Type"?

The word *type* encompasses not only a set of values but also the operations that can be performed on these values. For example, the `int` type in Java specifies integers in a certain range as well as several arithmetic operations and relational comparisons.

Sometimes it is the operations that dictate the appropriate type to use, not the set of values. For example, the value 224 can be thought of as an integer or as a sequence of three characters. Both types will reproduce the data correctly, but only one will facilitate the kinds of operations that are typically applied on it. For example, if 224 represents a quantity, then it should be stored as an integer so that we can add to it, multiply it by a price, or do other arithmetic operations on it. If it represents, say, a telephone prefix, then it should be stored as a string so that we can perform string operations on it, such as finding its middle digit or searching for a substring in it.

1.3 The Assignment Statement

The **assignment statement** has the following general form:

```
variableName = value;
```

The left-hand-side (LHS) must be the name of an in-scope variable. The term **value** on the right-hand-side (RHS) refers to anything that culminates in a value, and there are three things that do: a literal, a (declared and initialized) variable, and an expression. When this statement is executed, the following three steps are performed:

1. Evaluate the RHS.
2. Ensure the RHS and the LHS are type-compatible or else stop.
3. Store the value of the RHS in the memory block of the LHS.

For example, consider the following two statements:

```
int quantity;
quantity = 25;
```

The first reserves a 4-byte block in memory and associates its address with the name `quantity`. The second evaluates the RHS and determines (easily in this case) that its value is 25 and that its type is `int`. Since the LHS and the RHS have the same type, they are compatible; therefore, we store 25 in the memory block reserved for `quantity`.

As a convenience, you can combine declaration with assignment in one statement as shown in the following examples:

```
int quantity = 25;
char grade = 'B';
boolean isFound = false;
```

When the value is a literal, one can easily evaluate it and determine its type. If it is a variable that has been declared and initialized, then the value and type of the RHS would be the value and type of the variable. Here is an example:

```
int quantity = 25;
int stock = quantity;
```

The variable `quantity` appearing in the RHS of the last assignment has been assigned the value 25 and is of the type `int`. We thus have compatibility, and 25 will be stored in the block reserved for `stock`.

This leaves the case where the RHS is an expression, which is explored in the following sections.

1.3.1 The `int` Arithmetic Operators

The `int` type defines 11 operations that can be performed on its values. One of them is the infix binary plus operator, and it represents addition. Given any two `int` values a and b, the result of a + b is also an `int` value and is equal to the sum of a and b. In general, when the result of an operator belongs to the same set as the operands, we say that the set is closed under

| In More Depth | 1.7 |

Assignment versus Equality

The assignment statement is a process that involves doing things: evaluate, check, store. It is therefore imperative or prescriptive in nature. Algebraic equality, on the other hand, is descriptive in nature, for it merely states that two things are equal; it does not make them equal. Writing

```
x = x + 1
```

is quite meaningful as an assignment but is false as an equality: x cannot possibly be equal to x + 1.

---

this operator, or that the **closure property** is satisfied. Thanks to closure, we can now have a sum on the RHS of an assignment (rather than a literal or a variable) and still maintain type compatibility. Here is an example:

```
int stock = 100;
int order = 15;
int total = stock + order;
```

But how is closure guaranteed given that int values have a finite range? Is it not possible that the sum will be outside the range? To ensure this does not happen, the designers of Java defined the plus operator such that it wraps around when the range is exceeded. In other words, if you add 1 to the most positive int, you get the most negative int. As an analogy, think of the numbers written on the face of a clock: if you add 1 hour to 11 o'clock, you get 12, but if you add 1 hour to 12 you go back to 1.

In addition to ensuring type compatibility, closure allows us to form complex expressions by cascading the operation, for example,

```
int total = stock + order + 1;
```

But this raises a question: Should we compute stock + order first (and then add 1) or compute order + 1 first and then add it to stock? In mathematics, addition is associative, which means it does not matter which sum is computed first. However, in computing, it generally does matter, and one must adopt a consistent **association rule**. The rule for addition is left to right, so the above expression would be evaluated as if it were parenthesized as follows:

```
int total = (stock + order) + 1;
```

Figure 1.15 lists all 11 operations of the int type. As you can see, 5 of them are binary and 6 are unary. The involved operations are straightforward except perhaps for the following three peculiarities.

- **Division** (/) The / operator yields the quotient of the two operands. It is computed such that the division result is rounded toward zero. Hence 5 / 3 yields 1 and (-5) / 3 yields -1.

■ **Remainder** (%) The % operator yields the remainder of the (implied) division. It is computed such that the result of a % b is equal to a - (a / b) * b. This implies that the sign of the remainder is the same as that of the dividend regardless of the sign of the divisor. Hence, 5 % (-3) yields 2 and (-5) % 3 yields -2.

■ **Auto-Increment** (++) and **Auto-Decrement** (--) The difference between the prefix and the postfix versions is in whether incrementing (or decrementing) is done before (pre) or after (post) evaluating the result. For example, if x is 5, then z = ++x leads to z being 6, while z = x++ leads to z being 5. Both of them lead to x becoming 6.

All operators satisfy the closure property by interpreting the range as circular. The only exception is when the divisor of / or % is zero. Division by zero is undefined, so in that case, the program will terminate with a so-called arithmetic exception.

Figure 1.15 indicates that each operator has a **precedence** level and an association rule. The precedence level is a negative number, and when an expression is evaluated, operators with a higher precedence level are evaluated before ones with a lower level. For example, to evaluate the expression

    a + b * c

we must multiply b with c first and then add the result to a because multiplication has a higher precedence (−4) than addition (−5). The association rule is indicated in Fig. 1.15 by an arrow, which is either left to right or right to left. It plays a role when evaluating an expression with operators of the same precedence level. For example, to evaluate the expression

    a + b - c

we must add a to b first and then subtract c from the sum because + and − have the same precedence level (−5) and their association is left to right.

Figure 1.15 The arithmetic operators in Java. The precedence (a negative number) determines which operator acts first when operators of different precedence appear in an expression. The association (indicated by the arrow) determines which operator acts first when operators of the same precedence are to be evaluated.

Precedence	Operator	Kind	Syntax	Operation
-5 ➡	+	infix	x + y	add y to x
	-	infix	x - y	subtract y from x
-4 ➡	*	infix	x * y	multiply x by y
	/	infix	x / y	divide x by y
	%	infix	x % y	remainder of x / y
-2 ➡	+	prefix	+x	identity
	-	prefix	-x	negate x
	++	prefix	++x	x = x + 1; result = x
	--	prefix	--x	x = x - 1; result = x
-1 ➡	++	postfix	x++	result = x; x = x + 1
	--	postfix	x--	result = x; x = x - 1

Programming Tip.   1.10

Pitfall: Omitting the multiplication sign

You cannot write 2x instead of 2 * x, even though math allows you to do so.

Pitfall: Using brackets or braces in expressions

In math, you use brackets and braces for parentheses nesting. In programs, only parentheses may be used. Here is an example that illustrates both pitfalls: the mathematical expression

```
3a[2 - b(c + d)]
```

should be coded in Java as

```
3 * a * (2 - b * (c + d))
```

Example 1.3

Evaluate the expression

```
5 + (4 - 3) / 5 - 2 * 3 % 4
```

Answer:
The expression contains parentheses, which override the default precedence. Therefore, they must be evaluated first. This leads to

```
5 + 1 / 5 - 2 * 3 % 4
```

This expression has three operators of the same precedence, so we start with the left-most (which is /):

```
5 + 0 - 2 * 3 % 4
```

Multiplication is next:

```
5 + 0 - 6 % 4
```

Then the remainder:

```
5 + 0 - 2
```

Again, we have two operators of the same precedence so we start with the left-most:

```
5 - 2
```

Finally, we subtract and end up with 3.   ☐

To enhance program readability and to reduce the risk of errors, use parentheses in complex expressions.

1.3.2 Other Arithmetic Operators

The int type is not the only primitive type that defines arithmetic operators. Indeed, each of the long, float, and double types provides 11 operators, and all of them satisfy the closure property over the range of its values. Interestingly, these four sets of 11 share the same symbols. In fact, the contents of Fig. 1.15 apply as is to each of the four types. The term "**overloaded**" refers to operators that share the same symbol. Therefore, we can say Java has 11 overloaded arithmetic operators that operate on four types or that it has 44 operators.

It should be emphasized that overloading does not imply that the operations are the same. The overloaded + operator, for example, operates differently (and uses different hardware circuits) when its operands are integers than when they are reals. Even within integers it has to wrap around differently based on the range. In particular, the following three differences are noteworthy:

- **Division** (/) The / operators provided by int and long yield the quotient, whereas the ones provided by the real types (float and double) yield the division. For example, 2 / 5 is 0 whereas 2. / 5. is 0.4.
- **Handling Closure** Operators provided by int and long ensure closure by treating the range as circular. Those provided by the real types (float and double) manage closure by adding a fictitious value to the allowed range: **Infinity**. If the result of a real operation is greater than the most positive value in the range (or less than the most negative), it is set to Infinity (or -Infinity); hence, it effectively stays in the allowed range. Further computations on such a result, for example, adding 5 to Infinity or multiplying it by 3, proceed normally.
- **Handling Undefined Operations** For int and long, the only undefined operation is division by zero (occurs with / and %), and it is handled by throwing an arithmetic exception. For float and double, undefined operations include division by zero and certain manipulations of Infinity, for example, subtracting two infinities or multiplying infinity by zero. Rather than throwing exceptions, real types handle such operations by assigning a second fictitious value, NaN (Not a Number), to the result.

As long as we do not mix types (i.e., all operands on the RHS as well as the variable on the LHS have the same type), evaluation will proceed cleanly without any need for data conversion. The next section deals with situations in which types are mixed.

You may have noticed that three integer types (byte, short, and char) were not mentioned at all in the above discussion. This is because they do *not* define any operator. We will see in the next section how to operate on them using operators from other types.

Example 1.4

Consider the fragment

```
double x = 12.5;
double y = 2.25;
double z;
```

In More Depth   1.8

Expression Trees

We write expressions in one dimension and use parentheses to express the evaluation order. Expression trees provide an elegant two-dimensional representation in which the order of evaluation is readily visible without parentheses. An expression tree is based on a three-node structure consisting of a root node (the one at the top) and two children nodes below the root, as shown in Fig. 1.16. A binary operator is placed in the root node, and its two operands are placed in children nodes. It is understood that once the operator operates on its operands, the tree structure is replaced by a single node containing the result of the operation. Evaluating an expression represented by a complex tree reduces to repeatedly removing such three-node structures until the entire tree becomes one node. That node will contain the value of the expression.

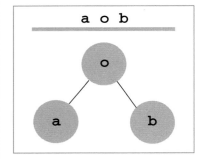

Figure 1.16 An expression tree

Consider now the tree shown on the left side of Fig. 1.17. The + operator cannot operate because its right child is itself an operator. One must first evaluate 3 * 4 and then replace the lower structure by the node 12. At this stage the + operator can operate. Contrast this order with that of the expression tree on the right. In this case, the + operator has to be done first.

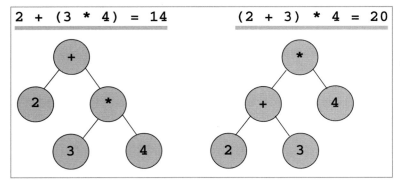

Figure 1.17
Different evaluation orders lead to different trees.

Add an assignment statement that computes z as follows:

$$z = \frac{17x - 6(1 - y^2)}{2x}$$

Answer:

```
z = (17. * x - 6. * (1. - y * y)) / (2. * x);
```

Note that to avoid mixing types, all literals are made explicitly double.

___

Programming Tip   1.11

Pitfall: Applying algebraic laws and identities to evaluate expressions

Our experience in algebra is largely based on dealing with real numbers that have an infinite range and an infinite precision. This experience leads us to believe (incorrectly) the following:

- `(a * b) / c` is equal to `a * (b / c)`. The two expressions can actually be different: if the operands were integers, we could select `a = 2, b = 3, c = 4`, and the first would yield `1`, while the second would yield `0`. If the operands were real, we could select `a = 2` and `b = c =` the largest allowed value. The first expression would yield `Infinity`, while the second would yield `2`.
- `(a + b) - c` is equal to `a + (b - c)`. These two can also be different for real operands (due to round-off). For an example that uses `double` operands, select `a = 1` and `b = c = 1.0E308`. The first expression would yield `0`, while the second would yield `1`.

1.3.3 Mixed Types and Casting

Ideally, all elements of an assignment statement share the same type, but there are situations in which either the operands on the RHS have mixed types or the type of the RHS is different from that of the LHS, or both. In such situations Java must perform conversions on the values. There are two kinds of conversions.

1. **Widening Conversions or Promotions** Widening conversions or **promotions** involve converting a value of a *lower* type to one of a *higher* type, where low and high are defined as shown in Fig. 1.18. For example, converting a `char` to an `int`, or a `long` to a `double` is a promotion. Even though such promotions may cause loss of precision (when converting an integer to a real), they are reasonably safe because the magnitudes of the values are preserved. Because of this, the Java compiler performs such promotions automatically when needed.

2. **Narrowing Conversions or Demotions** Narrowing conversions or **demotions** involve converting a value of a *higher* type to one of a *lower* type. For example, converting a `float` to a `byte`, or a `double` to an `int`, is a demotion. These demotions may lead not only to loss of precision but also to total loss of the numerical value (because the value could be outside the range of the lower type). Hence, the Java compiler does *not* demote values, even if needed.

Note that Fig. 1.18 leaves out one primitive type: `boolean`. This is because conversion to or from this type is *not* allowed, neither automatically nor manually.

Figure 1.18 The hierarchy of numeric types

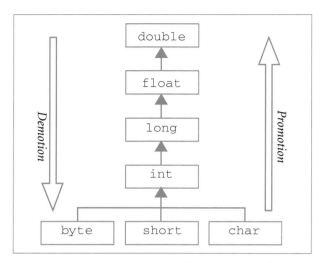

The compiler detects the need for conversion in three situations:

■   when the two operands of an operator are not the same
■   when both operands are of the type byte, or
■   when the type of the RHS is different from that of the LHS.

If the required conversion involves promotion, it is done automatically; but if it involves a demotion, then a compile-time error is triggered.

If you are willing to take responsibility for the possible consequences, you can manually cast a value from one numeric type to another with the **cast operator**. The cast operator is a unary prefix operator (precedence level: –3; association: right to left) whose symbol is the name of the type sandwiched between two parentheses. For example, you can take responsibility for the conversion in the last assignment of Example 1.5 by rewriting it as

```
int result = (int) (100 * dVar);
```

Example 1.5

Provide a critique of the following fragment:

```
int iVar = 15;
long lVar = 2;
float fVar = 7.6f - iVar / lVar;
double dVar = 1L / lVar + fVar / lVar;
int result = 100 * dVar;
System.out.println(result);
```

Answer:
The first assignment involves a single type and is straightforward. The second has an int RHS and a long LHS. The compiler will auto-promote the RHS to long; that is, the compiler will proceed as if the RHS contains 2L. The third assignment involves a mixed expression, and the computation will begin with the / operator. Since its two operands are not of the same type, one of them will be auto-promoted to the other. This will resolve the overloaded operator to the one offered by the long type. The quotient of 15L and 2L is 7L. Still in the same statement, we see a second mixed expression involving a float and a long, so we convert the long to a float and subtract 7F from 7.6F. This yields 0.6F, and its type is the same as that of the LHS. The next assignment involves two divisions. The left one has same-type operands (long) and yields 0L. The right one requires a promotion from long to float, and it yields 0.3F. To complete the assignment, this value is auto-promoted to

> double so that it matches the LHS. The very last assignment involves an `int` and a `double`, and its RHS evaluates to the `double` value 30.0. Completing the assignment requires demoting this value to an `int`, and this leads to a compile-time error.

In this case, the fragment will compile. Pay special attention to the way casting was done. Had we written

```
int result = (int) 100 * dVar;
```

the error would have persisted. This is because the cast operator has a higher precedence than multiplication so it will cast the 100, not the product, and this is not what we wanted.

The output generated by the fragment may surprise you: it is 29, *not* 30. If you consider this difference significant, then you should not have casted.

Casting up the hierarchy of Fig. 1.18 is safe but unneeded since the compiler does it automatically. Casting down, however, should generally be avoided, or used with caution, except for one common (and safe) situation: to select the real / operator instead of the integer one. For example, to compute the average number of hits per second, we may write something like

```
hits / seconds
```

where both operands are `long`. This will not compute the sought average (due to truncation) so we cast

```
(double) hits / seconds
```

This will cast `hits` to `double`, which forces a promotion of `seconds` to `double`, thereby selecting the / of the type `double`. Note that the following two casting variations also result in a `double`, but only one of them (the second) will lead to the sought result:

```
(double) (hits / seconds)
hits / (double) seconds
```

Assignment Shortcuts

We conclude our coverage of the assignment statement by mentioning a shortcut: any assignment of the form

```
variable = variable operator expression;
```

can be abbreviated as

```
variable operator= expression;
```

Here are some examples:

```
hits += 6;       is short for  hits = hits + 6;
hits *= count;   is short for  hits = hits * count;
```

Assignment is treated in Java as an operator with the symbol =, precedence level -15, and right-to-left association. Appendix B contains a precedence table of all operators in Java, and at level −15, assignment has the lowest precedence. This is precisely how assignment is meant to work: evaluate all operators in the expression on the RHS before the assignment operation is carried out. The **assignment shortcuts** are also operators, and they have the same level and association rule as the assignment operator.

Example 1.6

Provide a critique of the following fragment:

```
char letter = 'D';
letter = (char) (letter + 1);
System.out.println(letter);
int code = letter;
System.out.println(code);
int offset = letter - 'A';
System.out.println(offset);
```

Answer:

In the first assignment, the types are compatible (both are `char`) so the code of `'D'` will be stored in `letter`. (According to Appendix A, this code is `68`, but we do not need to know this in order to reason about this fragment.) The second assignment contains the expression

```
letter + 1
```

The two operands have different types (`char` and `int`), so we auto-promote the `char` and use the `+` of the `int` type. The result is an `int`, and in order to store it in `letter`, we must demote it by a manual cast. This leads to the code of the character that follows `'D'`, which is `'E'`. The first output will thus be E. What happened behind the scene is that `'D'` was converted to `68`, `68` was incremented to `69`, and then `69` was converted to `'E'`.

The next assignment,

```
int code = letter;
```

assigns a `char` to an `int`. Since the RHS is *lower*, it gets auto-promoted to an `int`. The end result is to store the code of `'E'` in `code`. The second output will thus be the code of code of `'E'` (which is `69`).

The next statement includes the expression

```
letter - 'A'
```

Both operands are of the type `char`, but this type has no operators. Hence, both must be promoted up the hierarchy (Fig. 1.18) to `int`. This leads to subtracting the code of A from the code of E, and since alphabetically consecutive letters have consecutive codes, this difference is the `int` `4`. The third output will thus be 4.

Example 1.6 demonstrates how type casting is used to manipulate values whose type does not provide operator support. The values are first cast to `int`, where they can be manipulated, and then cast back.

Summary of Key Concepts

1. The **class** is the smallest building block in Java. Classes are often organized in package hierarchies: related classes are placed in a **subpackage**, and related subpackages are placed in a **package**. The **fully qualified name of a class** begins with its package name, ends with its class name, and lists all its intermediate subpackages in between delimited by dots. To be able to use a class in your program, you must **import** it.

2. When we write programs, we adhere to the **coding style** described in Appendix C, which provides rules for naming identifiers and formatting statements.

3. A **class definition** consists of a **class header** followed by a **class body**. A **method definition** consists of a **method header** followed by a **method body**. A **block** is a group of consecutive statements sandwiched between braces.

4. The **semicolon rule** states that every statement must end with a semicolon unless it is a header whose body follows.

5. Program comments are either **documentation** or **internal**. Internal comments are either **one-line** or **multiline**.

6. Java is **case-sensitive**. Even though the words *for* and *For* are the same, Java treats them differently because of the case difference. Java is **freeform**; whitespace can be added anywhere within its statements. Spaces, carriage returns, and tabs are collectively known as **whitespace**. Java is a **strongly typed language** because every variable must be assigned a type before being used.

7. The building blocks of a language are its **lexical elements**. The **syntax** of a language provides rules for combining its lexical elements. **Keywords** and **reserved words** have special meanings in Java. **Identifiers** are programmer-defined names; they have no predefined meaning in Java. **Literals** are constant values; they have types. An **operator** acts on one or more operands and produces one result. A **binary** operator has two operands. It is placed between two operands if it is **infix**. A **unary** operator has one operand. A unary is placed before (after) the operand if the unary is **prefix** (**postfix**). A **ternary** operator has three operands. There is one such operator in Java. Characters whose role is to separate parts of code are known as **separators**.

8. A Java **compiler** reads the Java program from the **source file** and produces a **bytecode** program in the **class file**. The compiler produces **compile-time errors** when a statement contains **syntax** or **semantics** errors. The **edit-compile cycle** occurs when errors detected by the compiler force a return to the editor in order to have them fixed. The **virtual machine (VM)** is a program that behaves like a real machine: it reads one bytecode instruction at a time, translates it to **machine language**, and executes it. **Sequence flow** refers to the order in which statements in a program receive **control**.

9. A **byte** is the smallest addressable unit of memory. It has a **content** and an **address**. Commonly used multiples of bytes are **kilobytes** (KB), **megabytes** (MB), and **gigabytes** (GB). A **memory block** is a group of consecutive bytes (contiguous addresses).

10. A **type** is a specification of allowed data values and their associated operations. A **variable** has a name, value, and a type. A **declaration statement** reserves a memory block for a variable, associates the block address with the variable name, and assigns a type for its future value. The compiler keeps track of all declarations in its **symbol table**.

11. The **scope** of a variable is an area of the program between the variable declaration and the closing brace of the smallest block that encloses the declaration. A reference to a variable within its scope is said to be **in scope**. A reference to a variable

outside its scope is said to be **out of scope**. An out-of-scope variable leads to a compile-time error.

12. The integer types are `byte`, `short`, `int`, and `long`; they are all **signed**. The real types are `float` and `double`. **Round-off** refers to the inherent error in real number representation. The boolean type is `boolean`. The character type is `char`. Its values are **unsigned integers**, and they represent codes of characters. The codes are based on the **Unicode** standard, an international extension of the English-only **ASCII** code. Characters that cannot be typed in are entered through an **escape sequence**.

13. **Primitive types** are types whose names are keywords and whose operations are operators.

14. A **value** is either a literal, a variable, or an expression. An **assignment statement** evaluates the value of its right-hand side and stores it in the memory block of its left-hand side if the two sides are type compatible.

15. Operators with a higher **precedence** are evaluated before operators with a lower precedence. Operators with equal precedence are evaluated according to their **association rule**.

16. Two or more operators that have the same symbol are **overloaded**. An operator whose result belongs to the same set as its operands is said to satisfy the **closure property**. Integer types ensure closure by wrapping the range. For real types, **Infinity** and **NaN** were added to ensure closure.

17. The **cast operator** allows the programmer to force a type conversion. **Demotions** or **narrowing conversions** may lead to information loss. They can only be done through a programmer-forced type cast. **Promotions** or **widening conversions** are done automatically by the compiler. **Assignment shortcuts** are operators that combine an operation with assignment.

Review Questions

1. What is a package, and how is it different from a subpackage?
2. Is `lib` an acceptable package name in terms of style?
3. Is it possible to import more than one class with one `import` statement?
4. Is there a semicolon at the end of a class header?
5. Is `String` an acceptable class name?
6. What does "strongly typed" mean?
7. Why is it inappropriate to make statements span multiple lines?
8. How does a compiler distinguish between a comment and an executable statement?
9. How do you know whether a word is a Java keyword?
10. How do you know whether a word is a Java reserved word?
11. What are the syntactical rules for naming identifiers?
12. What are the style guidelines for naming identifiers?
13. Can you determine the type of a literal just by looking at one?
14. What is the difference between a source and a class file?
15. What is a memory block?
16. How does the compiler remember the type of a declared variable?
17. Name Java's primitive types. Why are they primitive?
18. A value can be a literal. Name the other two things that a value can be.
19. What is the closure property, and how does integer type satisfy it?
20. What is the difference between the precedence level and the association rule of an operator?

21. If the symbol used for an operator is overloaded, how does the computer know which operator to use?

22. Is converting a `long` value to `double` a promotion or a demotion?

23. What is the difference between automatic and manual casts?

24. Can a `boolean` value be converted to any other type?

25. Why is conversion needed? Specify a case that would be impossible if conversion were not allowed.

The Computing Environment on Campus

LI.I   A Guided Tour

The objective of this task is to familiarize you with the computing environment on campus. (The home environment is covered in Lab 2.) Search your course web page for a link to this tour. The tour's details will of course vary from one campus to another, but the key points are common. Specifically,

1. Obtain a username (a login ID) and a password.
2. Become familiar with the O/S on campus. In particular, you should be able to do the following: identify your home directory and the current working directory; create subdirectories (folders) and switch from one to another; and list, copy, and rename files. You will also need to know how to launch a web browser and how to print files to a printer on campus.
3. Learn how to use one of the editors available on campus. You will find that most of your time at the computer is spent with the editor. Hence, you should become comfortable with an editor and learn how to use its features. Even if you plan to work mostly from home, there will be times when you will need to modify a program while on campus, so this skill will be needed.
4. Learn how to compile and run a Java program. All the needed development tools are already installed in your campus environment. Some environments provide a text-based terminal window (also known as a console or a command prompt) in which you issue (type in) commands for compiling and running. Other environments provide a graphical window that integrates editing, compiling, and running. Either way, you should be able to easily switch from editing to compiling and running.

LI.2   A eCheck Tutorial

Each chapter in this textbook ends with a section entitled eCheck, which contains programming projects. Each project asks you to write a program named CheckxxL, where xx is the chapter number (01, 02,...) and L is the project code (A, B,...). To ensure that your completed project is correct, have it tested by eCheck, a program that comes with this textbook. It generates a large number of semi-randomly chosen test cases and runs your project under each. If your project did not produce the expected output, eCheck reports the problem and asks you to fix it.

1. Launch your editor and create a new program named Check00A with the following statements in its main method:

```
System.out.println("******************");
System.out.print("> ");
```

```
System.out.print("Good Afternoon");
System.out.println(" <");
System.out.println("******************");
```

The difference between `print` and `println` is that `print` does not append a carriage return, that is, the next output continues on the same line.

2. Compile and run the program. You should see the following output:

```
******************
> Good Afternoon <
******************
```

3. Modify the program, if need be, so that it prints the proper salutation based on the actual time of your lab session. Specifically, if you are going to eCheck your program between 6:00 in the morning and 12:00 noon, inclusive, then make it print "Good Morning" instead. If you will be eChecking past 6:00 p.m. but before 6:00 a.m., then make the program print "Good Night". For all other times keep your program unchanged. Note that in all cases, the message should be separated from the left and right angular brackets by a single space and that the rows of asterisks should align with the angular brackets. This means you may have to change the first and last statements in your program, in addition to the middle one. *(Note that no "if statements" are involved here; we are simply writing a different program based on when we will eCheck it.)*

4. Once you are convinced the program is working as specified, test it by eCheck. Issue the command

```
java eCheck 00A
```

Note that you provide only the program number, `00A` in this case. If your campus environment is integrated, you can launch eCheck as a Java tool using the same command as above.

5. eCheck will determine the correct output, based on the actual time of day, and compare it with your output. In this case, eCheck will determine that your output is incorrect and will produce a report. Here is a capture of the key part of the report:

Specifically, the following line caused the mismatch

```
(position 0 contains Unicode 62 instead of 42):
Expected: * Good Afternoon *
Your App: > Good Afternoon <
```

Your report may be different, due to the time of day, but the problem is the same: eCheck expects the message to be surrounded by asterisks, not angular brackets.

6. Modify your program to factor in the changed requirement. Re-run and ensure it is working as expected and then re-eCheck. Repeat this process until eCheck prints

```
Your program passed all tests :-)
```

Note that, by definition, the correctness of a program is based solely on whether it meets its specification. You cannot say a program is "essentially or mostly correct." For example, your program may produce the correct numeric result, but if the result had the wrong format, eCheck would consider the whole program incorrect.

7. Note that the eCheck report refers to *terminated statements* or *TS*. This is a measure of the executable size of your program; it is simply a count of how many semicolons are in it. A good program must not only meet its external specification but it must also adhere to internal guidelines in terms of how it is written. Proper usage of language constructs, correct style, and delegation to existing classes are signs of internal correctness. Our example program had TS = 5 but it can be written in less. Can you make TS 3?

8. Modify your program one last time to make TS 12. (Hint: Use `print`.)

9. Your program now has twice as many statements as eCheck expects. eCheck it and examine the produced report. eCheck cannot claim that the program is incorrect but it generates a warning:

```
Your program cannot be handled by eCheck because
its TS count is too high. High TS may be indicative
of inadequate usage of language constructs. Please
re-think your implementation or speak with your TA,
and then re-eCheck your program before its deadline.
```

LI.3 Using the eCheck Server

eCheck is designed primarily to be a tool that helps you practise programming and build self-confidence by providing instant feedback. In addition, it can be used as a grading and recording tool. When a program passes all tests, eCheck can connect (over HTTP) to your departmental server and record that you have successfully completed this task.

1. Check your course web page to determine whether the server feature is enabled. If so, you will need to obtain the following pieces of information:

   ■ the URL of the eCheck server

   ■ your login ID

   ■ your password

2. Launch the eCheck Options program by issuing the command

   `java Options`

   Enter the information obtained in the previous step and click *Apply*. You do not need to repeat these steps unless you changed your password.

3. eCheck your 00A project (the correct one). You will find that after a successful check, eCheck will connect to the server, upload your program, and then print a message that your name has been recorded. It may, however, encounter one of the following situations:

   ■ **eChecking Deadline** has Passed Refers to your course web page to see the deadlines for submitting these programs. Make sure you eCheck well before the deadline.

   ■ **Authentication Failure** Your password is probably mistyped. Re-enter the Options.

   ■ **Communication Failure** eCheck could not connect to its server. Either you do not have an Internet connection or the server is down. Retry later.

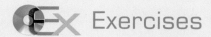 Exercises

Programming exercises are indicated with an asterisk.

1.1 Do you see a similarity between package hierarchies (class, subpackage, package) and directory structures (file, subdirectory, directory)? Is the notion of *fully qualified* names present in both? What is the rationale behind introducing directories?

1.2 How can you tell if a language is case-sensitive? Consider the operating system of your computer. How can you prove, or disprove, that it is case-sensitive?

1.3 The package bag contains the two classes Key and Pen and the subpackage purse; purse contains the two classes ID and Money. Identify the classes that are imported by the following statement:

```
import bag.*;
```

1.4 Examine the identifiers shown below, and identify the ones that are syntactically correct.

```
Table4
utility-4
date
compareTo
Set
equals
extends
set
```

1.5 Based on letter case, determine whether each of the identifiers in Exercise 1.4 is acceptable, in our coding style, as a class name, a variable name, or a method name. You can exclude the ones that are syntactically incorrect.

1.6 Here is the body of the main method of a program:

```
int period = 12; // in minutes
/*
Express the answer in seconds:
answer = 60 * period;
System.out.println(answer);
/*
Output also in minutes
*/
System.out.println(period);
```

Some argue that this program has a compile-time error; others believe that there is nothing wrong with it and that it will produce two lines of output. Show that both are incorrect.

1.7 Parse each of the following statements, that is, identify its lexical elements, and specify the type of any literal element. Note that we are not concerned with syntactical correctness in this question.

```
double balance = 34e3;
boolean isValid = false;
```

```
long count = System.out.readLong();
booleanIsValid = 'F';
String address = new String("Toronto");
number = Integer.parseInt(input);
public static void main(String[] command)
System.out.printf("%,.2f", amount);
```

1.8 Suppose that a machine with bytecode as its native language were invented. How will this machine execute a Java program? Will we still need a compiler? How does the performance of such a machine compare with a VM running on a conventional machine?

1.9 Estimate the memory needed to store this textbook. Ignore figures and formatting, and assume that each page contains, on average, 35 lines, and each line contains, on average, 80 Unicode characters. Express your answer in megabytes.

1.10 You have 1000 seven-digit telephone numbers. Would you store each telephone number as a short, an int, a long, or a seven-character string?

1.11 An argument states that the number 15 000 000 000 cannot be accurately represented in a float since it contains 11 digits, whereas a float is limited to 7. Show that this argument is incorrect.

1.12 An application generates financial statements for banks. The developer of the application decided to use float to represent the amounts. The developer's rationale is that no amount can exceed 10^{38} dollars even for the biggest of banks. Do you agree with the decision?

1.13 Determine the type and the number of storage bytes of each of the following literals:

```
145
71L
1500f
1.425e2
"The file \"Sales.txt\" is stored in:\n\\Revenue"
```

1.14 The following declaration resulted in allocating a memory block at address 80:

```
double sum = 12.5;
```

Draw a memory diagram that depicts the allocated block, sum, and the value 12.5.

1.15 Which of the following statements is correct in light of the memory allocation of Exercise 1.14?

```
sum is 12.5.
sum is 80.
sum is the memory block at 80.
```

1.16 Some argue that the following code fragment has a compile-time error; others believe that there is nothing wrong with it and that its output is BBCBB. Show that both are incorrect. (The difference between print and println is that print does not append a carriage return; i.e., the next output continues on the same line.)

```
char grade = 'B';
System.out.print(grade);
```

```
{
    System.out.print(grade);
    {
        grade = 'C';
        System.out.print(grade);
    }
    System.out.print(grade);
}
System.out.println(grade);
```

1.17 Explain the compile-time error in the following fragment. Show that by deleting one statement from the inner block, the program will compile and will produce 123 as output.

```
long speed = 1;
int size = 7;
{
    boolean even = false;
    long speed = 5;
    size = 2;
}
int even = 3;
System.out.print(speed);
System.out.print(size);
System.out.println(even);
```

1.18 Is it true that the expression

```
a * b * c / d
```

is evaluated as

```
((a * b) * (c / d))
```

Justify your answer.

1.19 A program needs to declare a variable x, store 5 in it, and then increment x. Here are four different ways for achieving this, each made up of a pair of statements:

```
int x = 5;
x = x + 1;

int x = 5;
x++;

int x = 5;
x = x + 1 / 2 + 1 / 2;

int x = 5;
x += 1;
```

Which statement pair correctly performs the required operation? There may be more than one correct pair.

1.20 The following fragment is meant to compute the average (arithmetic mean) of three variables:

```
int x = 6;
int y = 1;
int z = -3;
double mean = x + y + z) / 3;
```

Identify the compile-time error in it and correct it. Will the fragment accomplish its goal after the error is corrected?

1.21* Consider the fragment

```
int i = 6;
long l = 4;
double d = 12;
l = i + i;
d = i + i;
i = l + l;
l = d + d;
```

Which assignments require a cast? Validate your answers by creating a program and compiling it.

1.22* Consider the fragment

```
int x = 3;
int y = 14;
double pie = x + y / 100.0;
int z = (5 % 4) + 6 / 8;
System.out.println(pie);
System.out.println(z);
```

Is there a compile-time error in it? If not, predict its output. Validate your answers by creating a program and running it.

Note: If your Java version is earlier than 5.0, then skip the following exercises. You will learn in Section 2.2.5 how to handle features that became available in 5.0.

1.23* Write a program with the following code in its main method:

```
double price = 12.7;
System.out.printf("%.2f", price);
```

This printf service allows you to specify the desired output format through a string literal. Run the program and examine its output. Change the literal from ".2" to ".3" and run again. Repeat the process several times until you determine the role that this literal plays in formatting the output.

1.24* Write a program with the following code in its main method:

```
double price = 12.7;
System.out.printf("%,f", price);
```

This `printf` service allows you to specify the desired output format through a string literal. Run the program and examine its output. Change the value of `price` to a number greater than 1000 and run again. Repeat this process several times until you determine the role that this literal plays in formatting the output.

1.25* Write a program with the following code in its `main` method:

```
double price = 12.7;
System.out.printf("%10f", price);
```

This `printf` service allows you to specify the desired output format through a string literal. Run the program and examine its output. Change the literal from "10" to "15" and run again. Repeat the process several times until you determine the role that this literal plays in formatting the output.

1.26* Exercises 1.23, 1.24, and 1.25 show three different ways for formatting the output. Is it possible to combine these formats? Experiment by concatenating the literals into one:

```
System.out.printf("%,10.2f", price);
```

eCheck

Check01A (TS = 6)
Perform the following tasks:

1. Write the program `Check01A` so that it outputs:

       My Account Number is ???

   where `???` is your login ID (as recorded in Options).

2. Save the program, compile it, and then run it and examine its output. Compare the output to the one shown above and ensure that you reproduced the blanks, letter case, and spelling.

3. If your output is different in any way from the above (except of course for the login), repeat the above two steps until you are satisfied that your program is correct.

4. eCheck your program. There will be a problem here because the above output has a deliberate omission.

5. Correct the problem and try eCheck again.

Check01B (TS = 6)
Create the program `Check01B` that computes the value of `x` which is defined as follows (assume that all variables are of type `int`):

```
x = 1 - 2 * y / z
y = 2 - z * z / 2
z = 1 - 'A' / 2 + 1 % 2
```

The output of your program should be:

```
The value of x is: ?
```

where ? is the computed value of x. eCheck your program.

Check01C (TS = 6)

Create the program Check01C whose output is exactly as shown below. Note, in particular, that the two output lines have the same number of characters:

```
The string "//" consists of two slashes whereas
the string "\\" is made up of two back slashes.
```

eCheck your program.

Check01D (TS = 11)

Create the program Check01D that computes the value of x which is defined as follows (assume that all variables are of type double):

```
x = 1.0 - 2.0 * y / z
y = 2.0 - z * z / 2.0
z = 1.0 - 'A' / 2.0 + 1.0 % 2.0
```

The output of your program should be:

```
The value of x is: ?
```

where ? is the computed value of x *rounded to two decimals*. See Exercise 23 for formatting support. eCheck your program.

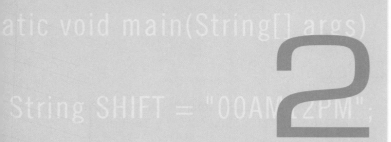

2
Programming by Delegation

Learning Objectives

1. *Explore paradigms that offer varying levels of delegation*

2. *View software construction as an assembling of components*

3. *Learn about delegation and contracts.*

4. *Become familiar with software engineering guidelines*

A ll computers, whether desktop or embedded in other systems, are controlled by software. Software is inherently complex, and its complexity grows superlinearly with its size. Delegation is an abstraction strategy that allows us to confront this complexity. This chapter explains delegation and shows how it can be used to reduce complexity.

Chapter Outline

2.1 What is Delegation?

In the previous chapter we looked at a program (Fig. 1.1) that computes the area of a rectangle. Aside from I/O (input and output), the program contained the following statements:

```
int width = 8;
int height = 3;
int area = width * height;
```

We note that the program allocates memory for its data and performs a computation, and that it does all that on its own without relying on other programs. This is possible in such a "toy program" because it has very few variables (just three), one functionality (computing the area), and a trivial computation (multiplying two integers). Real life programs are far more complex, and hence, they can only be built by delegating some of their work to other programs. The following sections show two different ways through which we can delegate.

2.1.1 Delegating to a `static` Method

The Body Mass Index (BMI) is a number used by healthcare professionals to assess a person's risk of developing health problems. It is believed that an index between 19 and 25 is good whereas an index outside this range indicates a higher risk. For example, a 170 lb person of height 5'9 (five feet and nine inches) has a BMI of about 25. We like to create a program that computes the BMI given the weight in pounds and the height in feet. Rather than do everything ourselves, we look for a program that does that. The `ToolBox` class in the `type.lib` package has a method named `getBMI`. If we delegate to it, the sought program can be developed quickly and easily, as follows:

```
double weight = 170.0;
String height = "5'9";
double bmi = ToolBox.getBMI(weight, height);
```

Compare this code fragment with the one above and you will quickly appreciate the power of delegation. The two fragments are remarkably similar even though the latter involves in fact more complexity than the former. This power stems from the fact that our program does not need to know how the BMI is computed; it delegates this to a method in a different class.

What Is a Method?

A method (known in other programming languages as *procedure, subroutine,* or *function*) is a member of a class. Its job is to perform an action, which is why its identifier is often a verb or a complete predicate. In this section, we will concentrate on a certain kind of methods known as `static` methods. When a program delegates to a `static` method in some class, we say that it is **invoking it on** that class. The syntax rules require that the class/method names be separated by a dot and that the method name be followed by a pair of parentheses. The parentheses enclose any data that the method needs in order to perform its action. This data appears as a sequence of comma-separated values called **parameters**. The program is said to **pass** these parameters to the method. Using this terminology, we say: "Our program invokes the `getBMI` method on the `ToolBox` class passing the person's weight and height as parameters".

The Characteristics of a Method

A method is characterized by its signature and return. The **signature** of a method is defined as its name together with the types of parameters it accepts. The signature of the method used in our example is

```
getBMI(double, String)
```

Methods in a class have unique signatures; i.e. a class cannot have two methods with the same signature. When a method completes its action, it culminates in a value (a result). That value gets sent back to the program that invoked it. The type of the returned value is called the **return** of that method. The return of the `getBMI` method is `double`.

It is important to note that some methods do not take parameters. When you invoke such a method, you still need to follow its name by a pair of parentheses (with nothing in between) because this is how the compiler recognizes it as a method. Note also that some methods do not return anything to the caller. Such methods are said to have a **void** return.

The Mechanics of Method Invocation

When the compiler encounters a method invocation, it searches for its signature in the class on which it was invoked. The compiler then treats each parameter as the RHS of an imaginary assignment statement whose LHS has the type indicated in the signature. In other words, each parameter must be a value (literal, variable, or expression) whose type is compatible with the corresponding type in the signature. If any of these steps cannot be completed, the compiler will generate a compile-time error.

When we run the program and the VM encounters a method invocation, it evaluates the parameters and then executes the invoked method after providing it with the parameter values. In our example, upon encountering the statement:

```
double bmi = ToolBox.getBMI(weight, height);
```

the VM starts by determining the values of the two parameters. It will then suspend the execution of our program and start executing the `getBMI` method using 170 and "5'9" as the values of its parameters. When the method completes its action, the VM resumes executing our program after replacing the invocation expression (the dot-separated names and parameters) with the returned value. In our example, the returned value is 25.1 so the VM will resume the execution of our program as if the above invocation were replaced with the assignment:

```
double bmi = 25.1;
```

Invocation is analogous to making a phone call: You first dial a phone number (the class name) and then an extension (the method name). Then you make a request (the parameters). Afterward, the party at the other end gives a response (the return). This analogy explains why invocation is sometimes referred to as *sending a message,* or *calling*.

Example 2.1

For each of the following fragments, provide a critique of how invocation is done.

(a) `double bmi = ToolBox.getBMI(170.0, "5'9");`

(b) `double weight = 170.0;`
`    int height = 175;`
`    double bmi = ToolBox.getBMI(weight, height);`

(c) `int weight = 170;`
`    String height = "5'9";`
`    double bmi = ToolBox.getBMI(weight, height);`

(d) `double weight = 170.0;`
`    String height = "5'9";`
`    ToolBox.getBMI(weight, height);`

Answer:

(a) This invocation is effectively the same as the original because parameter evaluation yields the same values and types as before.

(b) The compiler will search the `ToolBox` class looking for the signature:

`getBMI(double, int);`

Since no such signature exists in that class, the compiler will issue a compile-time error.

(c) This invocation is effectively the same as the original because the involved conversion is widening. The compiler will auto-promote the `int` value to `double`.

(d) This invocation will compile without problems, but it is useless because the return is trashed; that is, the method did compute and return the BMI, but the calling program did not store or display the return. (This mode of invocation would have been appropriate had the return been `void`.)

Complexity Reduction

Delegating to a `static` method clearly reduces the complexity of the calling program because the program does not need to know how the computation is done. In our particular example, the computation involves parsing the height string in order to extract the feet and inches parts and then determining the height in meters. It also involves converting the weight to kilograms and, finally, dividing the weight by the square of the height. Delegation shields our program from all this, thus keeping it short and easy to understand and maintain.

Programming Tip   2.1

Pitfall: Using a void method in an expression

While it is odd to trash the return of a nonvoid method, it is a compile-time error to use a void method where a value is expected. For example, consider the following statement:

```
int width = System.out.println(4);
```

This statement leads to a compile-time error because the `println` method is void yet it is placed where a value is expected (on the RHS of an assignment).

Unified Modelling Language

We can depict the fact that a class contains a particular method by drawing a class diagram, as shown in Fig. 2.1. The class is depicted as a box with two compartments: the top compartment contains the name of the class, and the bottom compartment contains a list of the methods it provides, one per line. The name of the class is optionally fully qualified, but with double colons rather than dots as the delimiter, and is optionally preceded by a stereotype («utility» in this example). The role of the stereotype will become clear shortly. Each method is specified by its signature and return, separated by a colon. The class diagram is an example of **UML** (**Unified Modelling Language**), which we will cover in Chapter 7.

In addition to `static` methods, a utility class may contain a few constants that may be useful to someone using that class. The `Math` class of the `java.lang` package, for example, contains the `double` value of the constant π. Such constants are known as `static` **attributes**. An attribute is characterized by its name and type. Attributes in a class have unique names. The type of an attribute determines the type of data it can hold. The compiler and the VM treat the attributes the same as local variables except for one difference: an attribute is declared and initialized by its class, not by the program that accesses it. Because of this, the notion of scope does not apply to attributes.

If present, attributes appear in the UML class diagram in a compartment between the name and the method compartments, as shown in Fig. 2.2. The name of the constant (`PI` in this case) and its type (`double`) are separated by a colon. You can access static attributes the same way you invoke static methods; namely, on the class. The only difference is that attribute names are *not* followed by parentheses. For example, the following statement accesses and outputs the value of π:

```
System.out.println(Math.PI);
```

Figure 2.1
The UML class
diagram of
`ToolBox`

```
        « utility »
     type::lib::ToolBox
  getBMI(double, string): double
```

Example 2.2

Write a fragment that uses the `sqrt` method of the `Math` class to compute and display the square root of the number 32.75. The UML class diagram is shown in Fig. 2.2.

Answer:

```
double number = 32.75;
double root = Math.sqrt(number);
System.out.println(root);
```

| « utility » |
java::lang::Math
PI: double
sqrt(double): double

Figure 2.2 Diagram of the `Math` class

In More Depth 2.1

Delegation Within a Class

You may have had a previous programming experience in which methods (you may have called them functions or procedures) reside in the same class as the caller and you may be wondering if this too is a form of delegation. The answer is yes, but such delegation does not provide full separation between the requester of a service (the client) and its provider (the implementer).

2.1.2 Delegating to an Object

Suppose that we want to create a program that deals with rectangles. Each rectangle is fully specified by two attributes (width and height) and possesses a host of properties such as area, circumference, and diagonal length. If our program were to keep track of all these variables for each rectangle, it would quickly become complicated, especially if it has to handle several rectangles simultaneously. Wouldn't be nice if each rectangle "knew" how to keep track of its own data? In that case, we would only need to keep track of one variable per rectangle. This is what delegating to objects affords us. To start, we look for a class that manufactures rectangles on demand, and we find the `Rectangle` class in the `type.lib` package. We use it as follows:

```
Rectangle r = new Rectangle(3, 4);
Rectangle s = new Rectangle(2, 5);
System.out.println(r.getArea());
System.out.println(s.getCircumference());
```

The first statement creates a rectangle object of width 3 and height 4 and refers to it as `r`. The second creates a 2×5 rectangle object and refers to it as `s`. The third asks `r` for its area and outputs the result, while the fourth asks s for its circumference and outputs the result. Note how a program with only two variables (r and s) and no computation whatsoever can capture all the attributes and properties of two rectangles. This is the power of object-based delegation.

What Is an Object?

An object is a software entity that is capable of storing data as well as performing computations. It stores data in its attributes and performs computations in its methods. The first object that the above fragment created stores 3 in its width attribute and 4 in its height attribute. It has several methods, such as getArea, and getCircumference, that allow it to compute (and return to us) everything we need to know about the rectangle it represents. The variable that we use to refer to an object, such as r, is known as the object reference. Hence, an object has *four* things: **attributes**, **methods**, **state** (the values of the attributes), and **reference**.

Invoking the object's method is very similar to invoking static methods except we do it **on the reference** rather than on the class. Specifically, we follow that object reference by a dot and then the method's name. Parameter passing and return handling are done using the same mechanics as in static methods.

The Mechanics of Object Creation

All rectangle objects have the same attributes and the same methods; they differ only in state and reference. They derive their common qualities (attributes and methods) from the factory that made them, the Rectangle class, and they pick up their distinct qualities (state and reference) upon their construction. Hence, we can view any class as a place where attributes are defined (i.e. declared) and methods are specified. We will use the word **feature** to refer generically to an attribute or a method, and hence, we can say that a class is a collection of features.

A very useful model for reasoning about classes and objects is the copying model: when an object is created, we imagine that the class gets copied, and that each copy would have its own values for the attributes and its own reference. The copying process is also known as an **instantiation**, and an object can thus be referred to as an **instance** of a class.

UML

Fig. 2.3 shows part of the UML class diagram of Rectangle. It is made of a top compartment containing the (fully qualified) class name (without the Utility stereotype), a middle compartment listing the attributes and their types, and a bottom compartment listing the available methods.

Fig. 2.4 introduces the UML **object diagram** and the **instance-of** relationship. The object diagram is similar to the class diagram except it focuses on the object's characteristics, namely: identity and state. Hence, it specifies the identity together with the class name in the top compartment, underlined and with a colon separator, and indicates the state using "attribute = value" entries. The types of the attributes and the entire method compartment are not reproduced here because they are identical to the ones in the class diagram. The dashed line with the arrowhead at the class diagram indicates that this object is an instance of this class.

Figure 2.3 The UML class diagram of `Rectangle`

type::lib::Rectangle
width: int
height: int
getArea(): int
getCircumference(): int
getDiagonal(): double
getWidth(): int
setWidth(int): void

Figure 2.4 The object diagrams of two instances of `Rectangle`

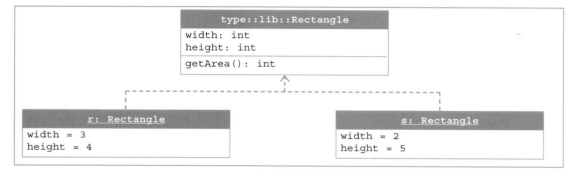

Example 2.3

Write a fragment that outputs the length of the diagonal in a 7×9 rectangle.

Answer:

```
Rectangle x = new Rectangle(7, 9);
double d = x.getDiagonal();
System.out.println(d);
```

2.1.3 A Unified View of Delegation

The previous two sections presented two different ways of delegating, and in this section, we contrast the two and present a way to view them as different degrees of the same process.

The first scheme delegates work to `static` methods. The method takes our data through its parameters, processes the data, and then returns the result to us. This delegation can thus be considered *procedural* because we keep our data and let some other program process the data. In the second scheme, we delegate both data and its processing to objects so our role reduces to creating the needed objects and choreographing their actions.

We can unify our view of the two schemes by generalizing the class copying model that was introduced for object-based delegation so it can also model procedural delegation. Recall that in this model, a program that wishes to delegate to an object must start by copying the class and then using the copy. Method invocation is done *on the copy* and state is held by the copy. We can extend this model to the procedural scheme by assuming that utility classes *cannot* be copied; i.e. they are static. If we cannot copy these classes then we must use the methods in the class itself. This explains why static invocation is done *on the class* rather than on the copy. Furthermore, it explains why the first scheme does not support states.

Example 2.4

Write a program that outputs the return of the getTime and toString methods of the Date class whose UML class diagram is shown in Fig. 2.5.

Figure 2.5
Diagram of the
Date class

java::util::Date
getTime(): long
toString(): String

Answer:

```
import java.util.Date;
public class Example2_4
{
    public static void main(String[] args)
    {
        Date d = new Date();
        System.out.println(d.getTime());
        System.out.println(d.toString());
    }
}
```

Here is the generated output:

```
1081449925012
Thu Apr 08 14:45:25 EDT 2004
```

The getTime method returns the number of milliseconds that elapsed since midnight (GMT) of January 1, 1970. The toString method returns the current date and time.

An Object to a Class Is Like a Value to a Type

Classes that can be instantiated behave very much like the primitive types we met in Chapter 1. Each type represents a set of values and a set of operators, and if a value is of a particular type, then it can participate in the operations provided by that type. A class that can be copied represents a set of attributes and a set of methods. An object of that class has a particular set of values for the attributes, and the methods of the class can be invoked on it. Such a class can be viewed as a generalization of primitive types, one whose instance involves several values.

Delegation as an Abstraction

Delegation is one example of a well-established divide-and-conquer strategy called *abstraction*. Abstraction is the single-most recurring theme in the computing field; in fact, the ability to build and represent abstractions and to view things at different abstraction levels is a hallmark of computer science. Abstraction allows you to replace something complex with something simpler by discarding distracting details. And by abstracting the abstraction, a process called layering the abstraction, you obtain higher-level abstractions.

2.1.4 CASE STUDY

Procuring Bread

In this section, we strengthen our understanding of delegation by applying it in a context outside programming. Suppose you want a piece of bread, but you are not inclined to solicit the help of others. You want to be 100% self-sufficient. You can do this by planting some wheat in the backyard, grinding the wheat kernels into flour, and then baking the flour into bread. This may work, but by the time you learn how to perfect all these traits, you will be very hungry.

A better approach would be to buy some wheat from a farmer, take it to a mill to turn it into flour, and then take the flour to a baker. You would have to use your own car to transport the wheat from the farm to the mill and the flour from the mill to the bakery, but you no longer need to learn the intricacies of each task.

This is procedural delegation: data is allocated centrally while tasks are delegated to external methods.

The above approach does shield you from task-related problems but leaves you exposed to material-related risks. If the farmer changed the packaging of wheat; e.g. used boxes instead of bags, you may need to buy a bigger car. Furthermore, you may have to empty the boxes in bags if the mill insisted on bag delivery. Hence, your non-delegation of data leaves you vulnerable to changes in data structure. A better approach would be to deal with a company that takes care of the entire process: it deals with all three parties and handles transportation. You can still choose the kind of wheat you like, or your preferred baking method, but all the inner details are hidden from you. This is the equivalent of an object based delegation.

Abstraction in General

The process of selectively removing details from something and replacing them with a simpler representative is called **abstraction** (from the verb *abstract*, which means to separate or to consider apart from). The outcome of this process (the representatives) is also called an abstraction. The process is driven by an **abstraction criterion**. The abstraction criterion determines what is essential (to be retained in the extracted representative) and what is not (to be discarded). The obtained abstraction is simpler than the original because it has fewer details and is said to provide an *abstract* view of it (used here as an adjective).

The abstraction process can be repeated by abstracting the abstraction, that is, by selecting a new criterion or widening the scope of the original one, and applying it to the obtained abstraction. Cascaded abstractions are called **layered abstractions**, and each is said to have a level defined such that the more features you discard, the higher the level. Hence, a very high-level abstraction reveals the big picture because it captures a few key features and discards most of the details. A set of consecutively layered abstractions is called an **abstraction hierarchy**.

As a non-programming example of abstraction, consider the cars shown at the top of Fig. 2.6. If we ignore the fact that these cars are different physical objects (i.e. have different identities), and the fact that they have different makes and colours (i.e. different states), then they all look like the generic, abstract car shown at the bottom of the figure. This car represents the class from which the top cars were created.

Delegation by Abstraction

Imagine that you were given a nondelegating program and were asked to maintain it; that is, correct an error in it or make a modification to how it works. To do this, you must first understand the program, but given the size of typical programs today, this is immensely complex. Software complexity is superlinear in its size. Measured in number of lines, software size is typically in the millions (about half a million for a pacemaker, five million for a word processor, and fifty million for an operating system). How do you confront something this complex?

Abstraction enables you to cope as follows: examine the code and look for patterns. Whenever you see a code fragment that is performing some computation, remove it from the code and replace it with a note that describes briefly *what* the fragment does, *not how it does it*. Continue along this line until the entire program reduces to notes and variable declarations. This abstraction is equivalent to a procedural delegation with the notes being method invocations. Next, the process is layered by discarding variable declarations and amending the notes accordingly. This leads to the equivalent of a modular delegation. Further layering involves replacing notes that differ only by state with a single note, resulting in the equivalent of an object-oriented delegation.

Delegation in programming can thus be viewed as an abstraction whose criterion is to extract notes about what things are to be done and to discard the details about how the things are done.

Figure 2.6 By ignoring identity and state, abstraction enables us to replace many car objects with one `Car` class. The process can be reversed by instantiation.

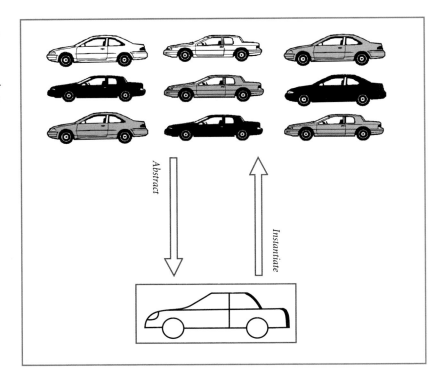

Java Details   2.1

Paradigms in the Standard Library

The overwhelming majority of classes in the Java standard library adopt the object-oriented paradigm because it offers the most flexibility and delegation. In the case of the `java.lang.Math` class, which provides mathematical utilities and constants, a procedural paradigm is used because no data delegation is involved. The designers could have used an object-oriented methodology, but it does not make sense to incur the copying overhead when all copies would have the same data. This is an example of a tradeoff between regularity (all classes are object oriented) and performance. The `Arrays` and `Collections` classes in `java.util` and the class `URLEncoder` in `java.net` are examples of other utility classes in the standard library.

 ## 2.2 Application Development

The possibility of delegation opens up a whole new way for developing applications. Rather than thinking about a linear progression of processing steps that transform input to output, you can think of intelligent software agents whose interaction manifests the desired functionality of the application. And rather than building applications from scratch, you can think of assembling them from ready-made components. This vision is presented in the following sections.

2.2.1 Application Architecture

The delegation framework leads us to define a Java **application** not as a single class but as a set of classes that work together to fulfill the requirement of the application. The word **system** is also used to refer to an application because it, too, implies several pieces cooperating to achieve a goal. One of the classes in the set is special and is called the **main class**. The remaining classes are called **helper classes** or **components**. An application is thus made up of a main class and one or more components. Note that the words *class* and *program* are used to refer generically to any building block (i.e., to the smallest compilation unit); they do not distinguish a main class from a component.

When the application is launched, it is the main class that receives control, and it implements the logic of the application by sequencing the delegation to components. If you think of the application as an orchestra playing a symphony, then the main class would be the conductor, and the helper classes would be the musicians. The conductor does not play any instrument yet the symphony cannot be played without him/her. Similarly, it is the main class that embodies the particular character of the application, and because of this, the application is named after its main class. Helper classes, on the other hand, are often generic and can be reused in other applications.

The main class has to satisfy a particular requirement that depends on the environment in which the application will run. For desktop applications, which run by typing a command at the operating system level, the main class has to have a method with the header

```
public static void main(String[] args)
```

In this case, the main class is often referred to as an **app**. In this textbook, we will only deal with desktop applications; hence, we will use the terms *main class* and *app* interchangeably.

The multiclass application architecture is depicted in Fig. 2.7 using UML diagrams. A dashed line from one class to another indicates that the former **uses** the latter. We saw in Fig. 2.4 that this line is also used to express an instance-of relation, but this overloading should not lead to ambiguity since the earlier usage involves an object diagram (with an underlined title) connected to a class diagram.

It should be noted that Fig. 2.7 is not meant to suggest that delegation takes place only between the app and the components because the components may also delegate among themselves. Furthermore, the diagram should not imply that all these classes must reside in the same

Java Details   2.2

The Main Class Jargon

- ◼ The main class of a Java application running within a web browser is referred to as an *applet*. It has to extend the `Applet` class.
- ◼ The main class of a Java application running within a web server is referred to as a *servlet*. It has to implement the `Servlet` interface.
- ◼ We are using the term *app* to refer to the main class of a desktop application. Others refer to this very class as an *application* (thereby overloading the term *application*).

rint("Enter h:m:AM or PM >

machine. It is possible that some are remote, for example, web services. Hence, the application can be thought of as a collection of services from several providers running on different machines.

Figure 2.7 An application consists of a main class (App) and several helper classes (components).

This architecture enables software construction to become component- or service-oriented. As more and more ready-made components become available, we can envision a stage in which developing an application reduces to developing its main class, that is, to an assembly line. This has enormous implications for the time and cost needed to develop software and, more importantly, on reliability, because reused components are continually tested and corrected. The skills needed for developing software are therefore shifting from bottom-up thinking to top-down system thinking, from algorithm-centric to organization- and communication-centric. These issues are explored in the next sections.

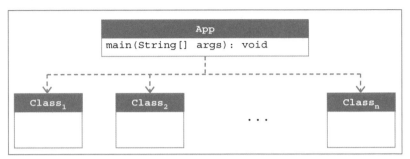

2.2.2 The Client View

We will use the word **client** to refer to the developer of the main class of an application and the word **implementer** to refer to the developer of a component in that application. This textbook adopts the client's view throughout: it teaches you how to write the main class, how to look for components, and how to interact with these components but not how to implement them. Once you master the client's role, you will be able to do the following:

Figure 2.8 The client of a class sees only the interface. The "how" details are encapsulated inside.

1. Create any application you want as long as you can find ready-made components. The number of such components is steadily increasing.
2. Even if you cannot find a particular component, you can specify it formally and write the main class as if it existed.
3. Being a good client prepares you to become a good implementer because an implementer is a client too, one that uses other components.

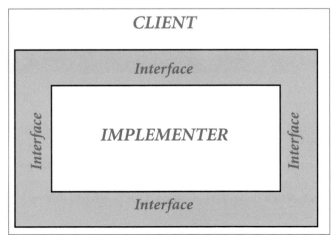

How do you go shopping for components? Each component advertises its services through a document called the **interface**, also called the **Application Programming Interface (API)**. The interface document describes *what* the component does but not *how* it does it. The "how" details are irrelevant to the client, and they stay within the component. As shown in Fig. 2.8, the component can be depicted as an opaque enclosure with the "how" details inside and the "what" details on the outer surface. Looking from the outside, the client sees the class as a capsule with the interface written on it. This gives rise to the

Fallacy: The client Is inferior to the implementer

The usual argument for this statement, "the client is inferior to the implementer," is that the client knows only what something does, whereas the implementer knows what it does and how it does it. This argument makes you inferior if you plug your appliance in a wall outlet not knowing how the electricity was generated. The fact is that the two parties have different concerns, and it is meaningless to subordinate one to the other.

definition of a class as an **encapsulation**. An attempt by a client to see how a component works is called **breaking the encapsulation**.

The client view of a component is analogous to your view of a product you buy, such as a digital camera. The camera is an enclosure (a physical one) with controls on it, for example, push buttons. The camera comes with a warranty and an instruction booklet, which tells you how to use the controls. The controls and the booklet constitute the interface, and they do indeed explain everything there is to know about using the camera. However, they do not reveal how the camera actually captures pictures. If you tried to find out, say, by opening the enclosure and looking inside, the camera's warranty becomes void.

Note that not every attribute or method of the camera has an associated control. The camera has a method that determines the aperture of its lens, but it may not have a corresponding control that enables the user to set or read the aperture. Similarly, a component may have attributes and methods that are used internally, as part of the implementation, and should not be shared with the client. Such features are said to be **private**, and they are invisible to the client. **Public** features, however, are visible, and they appear in the interface. For example, the buttons that allow you to select the picture resolution and control the flash are public features of the digital camera. The camera's abilities to control the aperture and change shutter speed are private features (in most cameras). A public attribute is called a **field**. Hence, the interface of a class documents its fields and public methods. This terminology is summarized in Fig. 2.9.

A second, very useful analogy is to imagine that you are a manager and that you need to hire someone. You advertise the position by posting a job description (what the prospective

Figure 2.9 A class has features, which are attributes and methods. Only public features appear in the interface.

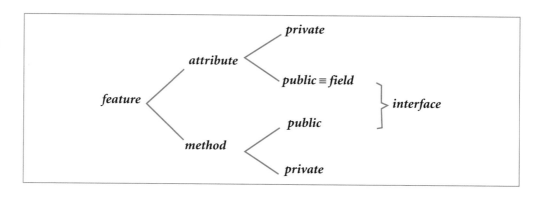

employee will do); this will be the interface. When an individual applies for the position and gets hired, the two of you sign the job description and it becomes a contract. You expect the employee to abide by the contract, but by the same token, you should not micromanage. In other words, the employee should perform all duties listed in the contract, and you should trust the work done by the employee without asking how it was done.

Java Details   2.3

Access Modifiers

To support the client/implementer separation of concerns, Java provides four access modifiers to allow the implementer to exercise precise control over what appears in the interface and what stays encapsulated:

- `public`: A **public** feature is placed in the interface. The client can see it and can use it.
- `private`: A **private** feature stays encapsulated. The client cannot use it and does not even know that it exists.
- none (no access modifier): A feature with no access modifier is odd: it acts as `public` for classes that reside in the same package as it resides and as `private` for all other classes.
- `protected`: A **protected** feature acts as `public` for classes that extend it (extension is covered in Chapter 9) and classes in the same package. All other classes can see that it exists but cannot use it.

All the examples in this textbook involve writing a client that uses a class in a different package, and hence, features with no access modifier will appear as private to us, that is, will be invisible. And since we will not write programs that extend classes, `protected` features, albeit visible, cannot be used by us. Hence, we will be dealing exclusively with `public` features.

In More Depth   2.4

"What" and "How" in Hardware Design

"What" superseding the "how" is elevated to new heights in hardware engineering: hardware description languages such as Verilog and VHDL allow engineers to describe what a circuit should do, push a button, and literally see a chip that implements the description come out the other end of a synthesizer!

How the interface document is written has profound implications and is one of the most important concepts in software engineering. At one extreme, it can be written in terms that are so loose that it can mean whatever you want. At the other, it can be written in an executable form that can be validated by the compiler and the VM. We will see in Section 2.3.3 how this document can be expressed as a contract between the implementer of a program and its clients.

Example 2.5

Consider the `computeArea` method of the `type.lib.Rectangle1` class (Section 2.1.1). It appears in the API of the class as follows:

```
int computeArea(int width, int height)
Returns the product of the two passed parameters.
```

Provide a critique of the API.

Answer:
The first line indicates the method's return followed by its signature (but with types and names for the parameters instead of just types). This specification is almost precise: it tells the client unambiguously how to invoke the method, the type of parameters, and the type of the return, but it leaves the roles of the parameters implicit (the choice of names is not explicit enough). The API should have stated the following:

```
Parameters:
width - the width of a rectangle
height - the height of a rectangle
```

With these added lines, the client knows exactly and unambiguously how to invoke the method. The second line is meant to explain what the method does but it is obviously incorrect: it breaks the encapsulation. As client, all I need to know is that the area of my rectangle will be computed, not how it is computed. A possible correction is this:

```
Returns the area of a rectangle with the passed sides
```
□

We have been insisting that the interface discloses information on a need-to-know basis, and this has benefits to both the client and the implementer.

1. Complexity
   Both parties have less to learn and worry about. The client can ignore how each component works, and the implementer can ignore what the component will be used for.
2. Accountability
   If you do not know something, you cannot be held responsible if it does not work. We will see in the next section how to assign liability.
3. Substitutability
   The client can replace a component by another, and the implementer can modify the internals of a component, without violating the interface.

The last point is practised in everyday life: you drive a rented car without having to learn anew because all cars have more or less the same interface. Your bank may hire a new teller without asking for your approval because the teller's name is not in the account opening agreement; that is, as long as the teller does what a teller is supposed to do, the client has no say in who the teller is because this would break the encapsulation.

The fact that it is the interface, not the class, that affects the client is particularly useful in situations where a component is not yet available. Java provides support for this idea through a nonprimitive type called, not surprisingly, "Interface." Like a class, it has an API, and we can design a client that delegates to it, but we cannot compile or run until someone provides a class that implements the interface.

We conclude this section with an observation: the question of what constitutes a client is actually dependent on the abstraction level. We have been taking the view that the main class personifies the client, but if we were developing a component, we would consider ourselves clients too because we invariably delegate to some class (perhaps to one in the standard library). Hence, we should think of applications as layered systems in which everyone, starting from the person running the application and ending in the hardware, is a client. In situations where we want to refer to the real human client at the top level, we will use the word **end-user**, or just **user**.

In More Depth   2.5

The Client/Implementer Mix-Up

You may, in a later course, learn about class implementation, and you may find yourself having to write the main class as well as some of its components (typical in very small projects). Even though you will be playing the client and implementer roles, it is essential that you consciously put on the hat of each; that is, do not mix roles tweaking the design of each as the need arises, but be fully consumed in one role at a time. Your client-only training in this course will make you insist on an interface for any delegation. A missing or a "jelly" interface often leads to circular delegation: class A delegating to B and class B delegating to A. This makes the overall system entangled and difficult to maintain, and leaves its components nonreusable in a later project.

2.2.3 Post-Compilation Errors

Components we acquire for our application are class files, and as mentioned in Section 1.1.3, these are generated after the edit-compile cycle has filtered out all compile-time errors. It would be ideal if these were the only types of errors, but a component may still contain errors even after it compiles successfully. When a program asks the VM to do something impossible, like dividing an integer by zero or determining the sixth letter in the word *Java*, it protests by **throwing an exception**, and this leads to a **runtime error**. The underlying mechanics of this process is covered in Chapter 11. Runtime errors are so named because they depend on what happens while the program is running, such as when the user supplies an input. For example, the statement

```
int y = 1 / x;
```

could lead to a runtime error even though there is nothing wrong with it as far as the compiler is concerned. If the user entered zero for x, execution of the application would halt, and an error message would be displayed on the console. The first line of the message would be

```
java.lang.ArithmeticException: / by zero
```

The remaining lines would provide a **stack trace**, a trail of all invocations, starting (backward) from the component in which the error occurred, all the way up to the main class. The location of the error is specified exactly: the name of the component, the name of the method, and the line number. Since a runtime error causes the application to suddenly "die," it is known informally as a **crash**.

If the error occurred in our own class, we would go back to the editor and examine the source in light of the error message and the circumstances that led to it. Examining code for the purpose of locating any post-compilation error is called **debugging**. After correcting the source, it is resaved and recompiled, and any compile-time errors (introduced by the debugging progress) are corrected. The process is repeated as needed, and this expands the edit-compile cycle into the **edit-compile-run** cycle.

Even after correcting all runtime errors, there is no guarantee that our class is error-free: it may still contain **logic errors** (also called **bugs**). These are the worst kinds of errors because they do not manifest themselves through messages; everything appears normal, the program does produce output, but the output is wrong. For example, if you computed the area of a rectangle like this:

```
int area = width + height;
```

then neither the compiler nor the VM will detect that you added instead of multiplied. Not all logic errors are caused by the programmer; some are caused by the end-user. A program may prompt for one thing, but the user may enter another, and this will lead to a "garbage-in/garbage-out" logic error. Testing techniques (Chapter 7) can eliminate some logic errors but cannot prove their absence. Software engineering (Section 2.3) provides innovative techniques for exposing post-compilation errors. Once a logic error has been exposed, extensive debugging needs to be done to locate its source. If it occurred in the main class, then the source is corrected, and the cycle is retraversed. The full edit-compile-run cycle, with all three types of errors, is depicted in Fig. 2.10.

But what if the post-compilation error surfaced not in the main class but in a component? At first glance, it seems that the proper course of action in this case would be to throw away the component and replace it with one that has the same interface. After all, we did not want to know how components are written, let alone how to debug them. This course of action, however, is simplistic and unfair because it presumes a component guilty just because the error occurred in it. Yes, the VM may indicate a runtime error in a component, but this could be because some other component, or even our main class, has passed erroneous information to it. Replacing the component in this case will not solve the problem. The situation is equally indeterminate in the case of logic errors. Given that a typical application involves hundreds of components, how do you determine the guilty party when a problem occurs?

Figure 2.10 The edit-compile-run cycle and the three kinds of errors

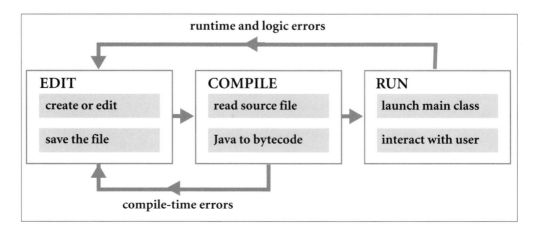

An analogy may help throw some light on the solution. When you work on a project as part of a team, the same problem often occurs: things are misunderstood, the project ends up late, and everyone blames everyone. This occurs because people often use subjective or context-sensitive phrases to describe what they expect, and this leads to misunderstandings and lack of accountability. The solution in the business world is to have lawyers draw contracts because legal terms are more precise. This is not a perfect solution (legal terms are sometimes subject to interpretation), but it minimizes the number of times we need to resort to courts to resolve contract disputes.

We can adopt a similar approach for establishing guilt: each component should come with an electronic contract embedded in its interface. Any time the contract is violated, either because wrong information is sent to the component or because the component behaved contrary to its specifications, the VM would crash the application and identify the guilty party. Turning the interface from an informational document to an actionable contract is explored in Section 2.3.3.

2.2.4 CASE STUDY

The Java Standard Library

Sun Microsystems is the maker of Java, and its web site at *java.sun.com* is like a wonderland for a client: thousands and thousands of classes complete with API and covering a multitude of subject areas. The major subjects are **J2SE** (Java 2 Standard Edition) for developing desktop applications, **J2EE** (Java 2 Enterprise Edition) for developing enterprise-wide and server applications, and **J2ME** (Java 2 Micro Edition) for developing consumer space applications (smart cards, phones, set-top boxes, etc.).

Lab 2 guides you through the installation and setup of the **JDK** (J2SE Development Kit), which was known as the **SDK** (Software Development Kit) in earlier versions of Java. If you need specialized packages, for example, web services, speech, or media, you can download them from the above site, and they will co-exist with the J2SE classes and tools. The JDK consists of two things:

- **The J2SE Runtime Environment** This **JRE** contains all that is needed to run, *not* develop, Java applications. Most notably, this includes the VM and the class library.
- **Tools** This refers to programs needed to develop Java applications. Most notably, this includes the compiler.

A developer needs the full JDK directory, but an end-user (who only runs compiled programs) needs only the JRE. End-users can download the JRE by itself from the above site.

Overview of the JDK Files

The JDK will install in a directory named "jdk..." where ... is the JDK edition. Under Windows, you will find this directory in \Program Files\Java. The JDK edition consists of several parts; for example,

```
jdk1.5.0_01
```

refers to release 1.5, minor release 0, and update 01. People usually drop the initial "1." and the final update number when they refer to a release. Hence, the above JDK may be referred to as "Release 5.0."

The directory structure under the above directory is shown in Fig. 2.11 (only the key subdirectories are shown). bin and lib contain the development tools. These tools were themselves developed using a client-component architecture. The client of each tool is stored in bin and its components in lib. Because of this, the bin directory is often added to the PATH environment variable so that the tools can be accessed from anywhere. The tools include the compiler javac and the VM's main program java.

The third directory, jre, contains the JDK's JRE, and it, too, has a bin and a lib. These subdirectories contain the VM and the class library. Of particular importance is the ext subdirectory under lib. It is called the **extension directory** because any class file stored in it becomes part of the library; that is, it extends the library. Most vendors bundle all classes in one **jar** file (Java ARchive), and they ask you to simply drop it in ext. This makes its content (packages and classes) importable to your class.

Overview of the Class Library

The classes are organized in packages and subpackages. The top-level packages are shown in Fig. 2.12.

Figure 2.12 describes very briefly the service provided by the subpackages and classes of each top-level package. It also explains some of the acronyms that you are likely to encounter when you browse the library. Chapter 3 explains how further details about each package can be obtained.

Figure 2.11 Part of the JDK directory structure

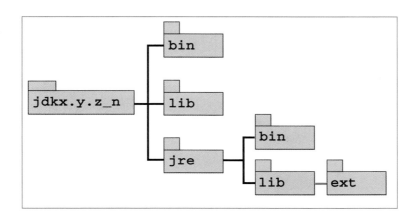

Programming Tip   2.3

Pitfall: Confusing the JRE with the JDK's JRE

The JRE that comes with the JDK is known as the private JRE, and it appears as a subdirectory named *jre* under the JDK1.5.0_01 directory. The other JRE is known as the public JRE, and it appears as a directory named JRE1.5.0_01 on the same level as the JDK. There is nothing wrong with having two JREs in the same machine as long as you are aware of their existence and distinctiveness. The following two scenarios highlight situations in which you must distinguish the two:

- Using the wrong extension directory
  If you need to install a jar file in the lib\ext extension directory, make sure you use the private JRE, the one whose path starts with jdk, not jre. If you used the wrong JRE, you would get the compile-time error: "package not found in import."
- The ordering of entries in PATH
  If you chose to use the command prompt as console, you would be asked to include the JDK's bin directory in your PATH. In that case, make sure you include it before any other; that is, make it the first entry in your PATH. Otherwise, you will end up compiling using the private JRE and running using the public JRE, and this will create problems if the two are not 100% identical in edition 4 and extensions. You can detect this problem if you import a class X and can successfully compile yet you get the runtime error: "NoClassDefFoundError X."

Pitfall: Confusing CLASSPATH with `import`

The `import` statement allows the compiler to identify a class you plan to use in your program because it specifies its package. It is not meant to help the compiler locate files on your hard disk. For that, the environment variable CLASSPATH is used. Hence, these two mechanisms work in tandem: `import` specifies the package, and CLASSPATH specifies where the package (or its `jar` file) is stored. Note that the location of the standard library (and its extension directory) does not have to be set in CLASSPATH.

2.2.5 Ready-Made Input and Output Components

I/O is an excellent example of delegation to ready-made components. The Java standard library comes with many ready-to-use components that enable our program to communicate with the end-user, disk files, other programs, or even other computers. In this section we will look at components that facilitate communicating with the end-user through the console, a process called **console I/O**.

Figure 2.12
Some top-level packages in the standard library

`java.awt`	Provides support for drawing graphics AWT = Abstract Windowing Toolkit
`java.beans`	Provide support for Java Beans
`java.io`	Provides support for file and other I/O operations
`java.lang`	Provides the fundamental Java classes This package is auto-imported by the compiler
`java.math`	Provides support for arbitrary-precision arithmetic
`java.net`	Provides support for network access
`java.rmi`	Provides support for RMI RMI = Remote Method Invocation
`java.security`	Provides support for the security framework
`java.sql`	Provides support for databases access over JDBC JDBC = Java Database Connectivity SQL = Structured Query Language
`java.text`	Provides formatting for text, dates, and numbers
`java.util`	Miscellaneous utility classes including JCF JCF = Java Collection Framework
`javax.crypto`	Provides support for cryptographic operations
`javax.servlet`	Provides support for servlet and JSP development JSP = Java Server Pages
`javax.swing`	Provides support for GUI development GUI = Graphical User Interface
`javax.xml`	Provides support for XML processing XML = eXtensible Markup Language

Keyboard Input

To capture entries made by the end-user, we need a component that knows how to communicate with the keyboard and how to translate keystrokes to typed data. The class

```
java.util.Scanner
```

is such a component. It has methods that transform keystrokes made by the user into primitive types or strings. This class is not a utility; hence, we must first obtain an instance of it before invoking methods. To do that, and assuming the above-mentioned package is imported, we write

```
Scanner input = new
        Scanner(System.in);
```

We are not in a position at this stage to fully understand the details of this statement. All that we need to know is that it creates an instance of the `Scanner` class and provides us with an object reference input on which we can invoke methods. We need to write this statement once in our program (*not* once per input), and we will do so immediately after the main method header, viz.

```
public static void main(String[] args)
{
    Scanner input = new Scanner(System.in);
    ...
```

This way, the object reference input would be in scope throughout the method, which means we can use it whenever needed. The name input is just an identifier that we chose; you can of course choose a different one. The left side of Fig. 2.13 depicts the object diagram of this instance as well as the associated class diagram.

Here is an example of how a program can read input:

```
System.out.println("Enter the width...");
int width = input.nextInt();
```

Before using any input method, we must first prompt the user by printing a message, and that is what the first statement does. When the next statement is executed, the program is suspended (i.e., its execution is halted) until the user presses ENTER. At that point the method captures the keystrokes that the user typed before pressing ENTER, interprets them as an int, and returns that int to us. At that point, the execution of our program resumes. Note that if the keystrokes cannot be interpreted as an int, a runtime error will occur.

There is a nextP() method for every primitive type p, for example, P=Long. In addition, there is a nextLine() method for reading a line of text and a next() method for reading a word (characters without embedded whitespace).

Screen Output

To display output, we need a component that knows how to transform typed data into characters and how to send these characters to the screen. The class

```
java.io.PrintStream
```

is such a component. This class is not a utility; we must first obtain an instance of it before invoking methods. Fortunately, the VM automatically makes an instance of this class for us and stores its object reference in the static field out of the System utility class. Let us give a name to this object reference:

Figure 2.13
Objects used for console I/O

```
PrintStream output = System.out;
```

The right side of Fig. 2.13 depicts the object diagram of this instance as well as the associated class diagram.

Here is an example of how a program can generate output:

```
int height = 12;
output.println(height);
```

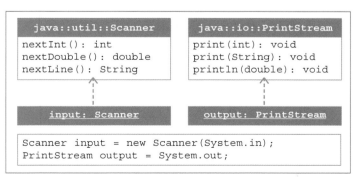

java::util::Scanner	java::io::PrintStream
nextInt(): int	print(int): void
nextDouble(): double	print(String): void
nextLine(): String	println(double): void

input: Scanner   **output: PrintStream**

```
Scanner input = new Scanner(System.in);
PrintStream output = System.out;
```

Notice that this is not different from what we have been using so far to generate output; the above statement is equivalent to

```
System.out.println(height);
```

We prefer to use the new way, however, because it exposes the symmetry between input and output, and makes redirecting output to a disk file much easier as we shall see later. Based on this, we will make it a habit to declare both object references at the top of our programs so that both will be in scope whenever needed. The template shown in Fig. 2.14 will be assumed throughout the remainder of this textbook.

2.3 Software Engineering

If you were a civil engineer about to undertake a construction project, you would have at your disposal a highly structured process that guides you through every step of the way, from estimating and bidding to planning and execution. This is because over the long history of that discipline, many projects were monitored and studied. From these studies emerged patterns, and these patterns have led to guidelines that ensure mistakes are not repeated. In comparison, software development is very young and **software engineering** (S/E), the study of software projects and their progress, is even younger. Nevertheless, a number of areas have already been identified as critical, and a number of guidelines are in place. These guidelines are not to be observed *after* the software is constructed, to undo bad decisions, but *during* development so that bad decisions are not made in the first place. Generally speaking, the guidelines are themed around mitigating risks, enhancing readability, and defining software correctness. They form the basis of our style guide and are explored in the following sections.

Figure 2.14 Use this template as a starting point for all programs. If you do not have J2SE 5.0, make the two changes indicated in Java Details 2.4.

```java
import java.util.Scanner;
import java.io.PrintStream;

public class Template
{
    public static void main(String[] args)
    {
        Scanner input = new Scanner(System.in);
        PrintStream output = System.out;

        ...

        // use input.nextInt for input
        // use output.println for output

        ...

    }
}
```

Java Details   2.4

Handling Console I/O in Earlier Releases of Java

The `Scanner` class and the enhanced `PrinStream` class were introduced in release 5 of J2SE. If you do not have access to this release, you can still run all the examples in this textbook provided you make two changes to the template in Fig. 2.14:

```
import type.util.*;

public static void main(String[] args)
{
   Scanner input = new Scanner(System.in);
   PrintStream2 output = new PrintStream2(System.out);
   ...
```

This template uses two classes in the `type` package that mimic the overall behaviour of console I/O in release 5. This includes console input, formatted output, and file I/O. You will learn how to install the `type` package in Lab 2.

2.3.1 Risk Mitigation by Early Exposure

A recurring theme in S/E is the mitigation of certain risks by early exposure. If you are not sure about something, do not delay finding out about it; face it as early as possible.

For example, if a runtime or logic error could be turned into a compile-time error, then its uncertainty risk would be mitigated. If a programmer accidentally assigned a real value to an integer variable, the value would be truncated, and this could lead to a serious logic error. Java mitigates this early by flagging it as a compile-time error. Similarly, generics prevent you from adding the wrong type to a collection (as we shall see later) at the compilation level rather than at runtime.

A second group of examples will be seen in Chapter 7 in which several risks are exposed early by developing the project iteratively, one requirement at a time. The next section gives a further example of this theme.

2.3.2 Handling Constants

Code readability is one of the key software engineering guidelines, and proper naming of variables goes a long way toward achieving that. Indeed, the statement:

```
amount = quantity * price;
```

is self-documenting. But even with proper naming, things can become ambiguous when literals appear. Consider the statement:

```
rate = price / 12;
```

Why are we dividing the price by 12? Perhaps it represents an annual amount and we want to compute it per month. Or is it because the price is per foot and we want it per inch? You may say that the context would make the reason evident, or you may add a comment to clarify, but either way, this code contains a **magic number** (a literal whose significance cannot be positively determined). Such numbers are a violation of the readability guide.

You will appreciate this issue the most if you imagine being hired to maintain a program containing such numbers; for example, modify some computation to make it biweekly instead of monthly. A statement like the one above must divide by 24 instead of 12. You cannot mechanically find and replace every occurrence of 12 by 24 because some of the 12s in the code may refer to something else and should not be modified. Over a trillion dollars were spent on the infamous Y2K problem to modify software so that it would interpret the year "05" as 2005 rather than 1905. A significant portion of the cost went into locating code in which hard-coded numbers like 19 and 1900 were used in century computations. An obvious solution is to do what we did for variables; use meaningful identifiers:

```
int monthPerYear = 12;
rate = price / monthPerYear;
```

This is a significant improvement since the code is now self-documenting. Furthermore, if it were decided one day to switch to biweekly rates, only one statement would need to be changed.

This approach, however, introduces a new problem: the number 12 is no longer a constant. If the variable that holds the literal were inadvertently changed, the whole computation would be wrong, which is a logic error. The solution is to flag such an inadvertent change as a compile-time error, an example of mitigation by early exposure. This way, we reap the benefit of an identifier, and the compiler will ensure the value is constant. To do this, prefix the declaration of the variable that holds the literal with the keyword **final**:

```
final int MONTH_PER_YEAR = 12;
```

This constant can now be used in the program like any other variable, for example,

```
rate = price / MONTH_PER_YEAR;
```

But if you try to modify it, as in

```
MONTH_PER_YEAR = 6;
```

the compiler will generate a compile-time error.

As a matter of style, we name constants using digits and uppercase letters. If the name is made up of more than one word, our earlier scheme of capitalizing the first letter of each word to make it stand out no longer works, so we use the underscore as a delimiter. Our style guide states that, aside from zero, ± 1, and ± 2, no magic numbers may appear.

Ideally, even string literals should not appear in prompts and messages (among other advantages, this makes translating them to foreign languages, and thus internationalizing the software, easier), but we will not enforce that in this textbook.

Java Details   2.5

Blank Finals

It is possible to omit the initialization suffix in a constant declaration:

```
final int MONTH_PER_YEAR;
```

This leads to a so-called *blank final*. This is typically employed when the user, not the programmer, sets the constant value. Such a final must be initialized later in the program, but this can be done once and only once.

2.3.3 Contracts

We saw in Sections 2.2.2 and 2.2.3 that a lot is hanging on the interface document. In this section, you will learn how to read this document as a **contract**. Contracts allow us to not only document components but also assign liability when a problem occurs.

The contract must start by stating the fully qualified name of the class and describing what is being encapsulated by this component. Keep in mind that no reference should be made to how the component works. Next, a feature contract as shown in Fig. 2.15 must be written for each public feature in the class.

We will start with methods. The header of a method shows its return followed by the signature. To facilitate referencing parameters in the documentation, the signature gives a dummy name for each in addition to stating its type. The header is followed by a textual description of *what* the method does. An example header is

```
int max(int a, int b)
Returns the greater of two int values. If the arguments have the
same value, the result is that same value.
```

You can write the description using either second- or third-person form, but be consistent. As you can see in this example, the description leaves no doubt as to what the method does and covers all cases. The next section, client responsibility, states the significance of each parameter:

```
Parameters:
a - an argument
b - another argument
Precondition:
true
```

Figure 2.15 The contract of a feature

Feature's Header
Textual Description
Client's Responsibility ❑ Zero or more parameters ❑ A precondition
Implementer's Responsibility ❑ Zero or one return ❑ A postcondition

The words *argument* and *parameter* can be used synonymously in the contract. The parameters of this method are generic and so are their descriptions. The **precondition** (or pre for short) is a proposition, a sentence or predicate that is either true or false. It is the responsibility of the client to ensure, prior to invoking a method, that its precondition is true. In our example, the precondition is set to the literal "true," and this means the client need not ensure anything; that is, this method has no precondition. Here is the remainder of the contract for this method:

```
Returns:
the larger of a and b.
Postcondition:
the return is as stated under "Returns".
```

The **postcondition** (post) is also a proposition, and the implementer warrants that it will be true upon return from the method. In this example, the implementer undertakes to return the larger of the two passed parameters.

You can think of the method's contract as follows: the client brings some parameters to the implementer and guarantees that the precondition is met. In return, the implementer delivers a return to the client and guarantees that the postcondition is met. The responsibility of one party is the right of the other. Hence, it is the right of the implementer to have a true precondition and the right of the client to have a true postcondition. We mentioned earlier that nothing in the contract should break the encapsulation, and this applies, in particular, to pre and post.

Liability is assigned as follows: If the precondition is false, the client is at fault (this is so regardless of the state of the postcondition). On the other hand, if the precondition is true and the postcondition is false, then the implementer is at fault. In the remaining case (both conditions are true), the two parties would have fulfilled their obligations.

Based on this, we can see that the client of the above method, max, can never be at fault. You may argue that if the values of the passed parameters were not integers, the client should be held accountable, but this case would be a compile-time error. As mentioned in Section 2.3.1, Java turns several potential problems into compile-time errors and leaves it to contracts to address post-compilation errors.

Example 2.6

Write a contract for the `squareRoot` method, which takes a positive real number (a `double`) and returns its positive square root (also a `double`).

Answer:
The answer is shown in Fig. 2.16.
If the client invoked this method passing -9 for x, the contract would have been violated (pre is false), and the client would be the culprit. And if it were invoked with x being 9 and the return were 4, the contract would also have been violated (post is false), and the implementer would be the culprit.

It should be noted that if the client in Example 2.6 ignored the precondition and passed a negative value, anything can happen. The implementer may, for example, take one of the following actions:

■ return the square root of the absolute value of x
■ return some random number not related to x
■ return NaN
■ trigger a runtime error

Figure 2.16 A contract with pre not equal to true

```
double squareRoot(double x)
```

Returns the square root of the given argument.

Parameters:
  x - an argument.
Precondition:
  x > 0
Returns:
  the positive square root of x.
Postcondition:
  the return is as stated under "Returns".

Figure 2.17 Instead of relying on the client, the implementer in this contract checks the sign and acts accordingly.

```
double squareRoot(double x)
```

Returns the square root of the given argument

Parameters:
  x - an argument
Precondition:
  true
Returns:
  the positive square root of x
Postcondition:
  x > 0 and the return is as stated under "Returns"
  or
  x ≤ 0 and the return is NaN.

The client cannot even assume that the implementer will consistently choose one action or another because such an assumption would break the encapsulation; namely, it would be based on information not in the interface. If the implementer chose to disclose the action in the interface, then the situation would be different, as shown in Fig. 2.17. In this case, the client can never be wrong, because pre is true in the contract, and it is the implementer who checks for the non-positive case and takes a consistent and documented action. The client can now rely on the implementer taking this action.

We encounter preconditions and postconditions in everyday life. For example, some transit systems operate on the honour system. Before riding a train you are supposed to have purchased a ticket. This is the precondition. The postcondition is that the train will take you along the route indicated on your ticket. The implementer here is the company that operates the trains, and it determines how the precondition should be handled. They may decide not to check it or to randomly do so. The point is this: the company does not disclose its handling policy, or the corresponding penalty, in the contract.

Example 2.7

Let us pursue the transit example further and discuss the postcondition. Sometimes, the company is forced to cancel a route, and since this is a postcondition violation, the company takes responsibility and arranges alternative transportation for ticket holders. Most cancellations occur because of power failures, so to avoid restitution it was proposed to amend the precondition as follows:

```
Precondition:
passenger has ticket
and
power is available
```

Provide a critique of this cost-cutting measure.

Answer:

This contract is unacceptable because it breaks the encapsulation. As client, I am not involved in how the train moves. For all I know, it might be pulled by horses. Another way to see the problem is to note that the precondition must be something that the client controls.

Note: The proper way of handling the additional cost would be to recoup it from the company that delivers power. It acts as an implementer for the transit company, and its contract must specify a penalty for a postcondition violation.

From now on, we will simplify the writing of the contract by adopting the implicit condition convention for writing contracts:

- ■ If the precondition is the literal "true," omit it.
- ■ Create a new section called "Throws" if the post involves an exception.
- ■ Fuse the postcondition with the "Returns" and "Throws" sections.

In other words, the precondition will be explicit only if it is not the literal "true." The postcondition will no longer appear explicitly in the contract. The part of it that does not involve an exception is absorbed in the "Returns" section, and the other part, if any, appears under the new "Throws" section. The following example demonstrates the usage of the new conventions.

Example 2.8

Write a contract for the same method of Example 2.6 except it throws an exception if the argument is not positive. Use the implicit condition convention.

Answer:

Since the implementer has specified the action that will be taken both if the argument is positive (return the square root) and if not (throw an exception), there is nothing for the client to ensure; that is, the precondition is "true"; hence, it will be omitted. The postcondition is

```
Postcondition:
x > 0 and the return is as stated under "Returns".
or
x <= 0 and throw an exception
```

The top part can be fused with the "Returns" section. The bottom one will be left by itself in the new "Throws" section, as shown in Fig. 2.18.

Comparing the contract in Fig. 2.18 to those in Fig. 2.16 and Fig. 2.17, you could argue that the former is "friendlier" because its precondition is true, and, hence, it asks less of its client. (You could also label it as "mistrusting," but the idea is the same.) Classes in the Java standard library adopt this "pre=true" approach and use the implicit condition convention throughout.

Figure 2.18
A contract with implicit pre and post

```
double squareRoot(double x)
```
Returns the square root of the given argument.

Parameters:
   x - an argument.
Returns:
   the positive square root of x.
Throws:
   an exception if x ≤ 0.

The contract for fields (public attributes) is simpler since no parameters or returns are involved. Furthermore, since the client has direct access to fields, the notion of pre and post does not apply. This leaves only the field header (type and name) and the textual description.

In More Depth   2.6

The Case for Private Attributes

The fact that fields cannot have preconditions or postconditions is a strong indication of their risk. If a client set a field to a value inconsistent with its meaning, for example, a negative count, it would not be possible to detect the problem. As we shall see later, a good component does *not* expose any attribute; instead, it makes all of them private and provides methods for (indirectly) accessing them. This restores the benefits of contracts. The only exception to this all-attributes-private rule is when an attribute is `final`, since making it a field poses no danger.

2.3.4 CASE STUDY

Meet the Managers

In this section, we apply everything we learned about delegation and contracts to a nonprogramming problem. This will help us strengthen our understanding of the concepts presented in Chapters 1 and 2, and will also give us a glimpse of how this challenging and important problem is tackled.

The problem can be stated as follows: Recall that the declaration

```
int quantity;
```

leads to allocating a block of memory big enough to hold an `int` and associating its address with `quantity`. But how do we know where in memory the allocation should be done? We must somehow ensure that no two variables have overlapping blocks. Furthermore, when the variable is initialized, for example,

```
quantity = 25;
```

then the number 25 must be expressed in binary in 4 bytes (or 32 bits since each byte contains 8 bits), and these bytes must be written to the memory block reserved for this variable. But how do we know how to express something in so many bits or bytes? Furthermore, as the program runs, control may exit the scope of the variable, and this means we must somehow free the reserved block so that other variables can use it. But how do you unreserve a block of memory?

This storage management problem is indeed complex, and if we were to worry about all these details as we write our application, we would never be able to create sophisticated applications. We must obviously delegate this work and focus on our own work. We identify two separate issues:

Figure 2.19
Delegating declaration to SM and MM

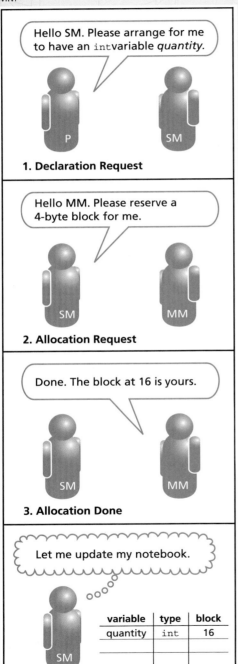

1. **Declaration Request**

2. **Allocation Request**

3. **Allocation Done**

4. **Declaration Done**

1. Keeping track of used and free cells in memory
2. Associating identifiers with types and blocks

The first requires that someone look after memory regardless of what is being stored in it. We therefore post a position entitled "Memory Manager" (MM), with a job description: "Keep track of the contents of all cells in memory and distinguish free from used ones." MM does not need to have any expertise in the binary system or in data types.

The second issue requires someone with expertise in data representation and who knows how to keep the symbol table of Section 1.2.3, a mapping between addresses and identifiers. Let us call this employee the Symbol Manager (SM).

Finally, we perfect these two abstractions by layering them: we introduce MM to SM. This way, the running program does not need to speak with MM directly; that is, it is a client of SM, and SM is a client of MM. Let us see how the two managers can enable the running program, P, to solve the storage problem; see Fig. 2.19.

The figure depicts a scenario in which we (program P) request that memory be set aside for storing the int variable quantity. When the request was received, SM knew that int needs 4 bytes so it contacted MM and requested a block of 4. Upon receiving this, MM searched memory for any free (unused) 4 consecutive bytes, and found that the ones at 16, 17, 18, and 19 are. It marked them as used and sent 16, the block address, back to SM. SM updated its symbol table accordingly.

Note that all the gory details about memory and addresses are completely hidden from us. We do not see addresses and do not worry about representations. All we know is that the int quantity has a place reserved for it in memory. This not only simplifies our program, but it also makes us more adaptable to change. For example, if one day it were decided to move to a 64-bit architecture in which 8 bytes are optimal for an int, no change would be needed in our program. All we need to do is to replace (or retrain) SM.

Two other scenarios are depicted in Fig. 2.20. In one, we ask SM to assign 25 to quantity, and in the other we ask SM to look up the value of quantity. It is evident from the figure that we are shielded from details relating to binary numbers, representation, and addresses.

To draw a contract for SM, we must agree on its features:

- **declare** Given an identifier and its data type, allocate a block for it. Return nothing.

- **assign** Given an identifier and a value, store the value in the block of the identifier. Return nothing.

Figure 2.20 The delegation of two tasks: assignment (left) and evaluation (right)

Figure 2.21
Meet the
managers.

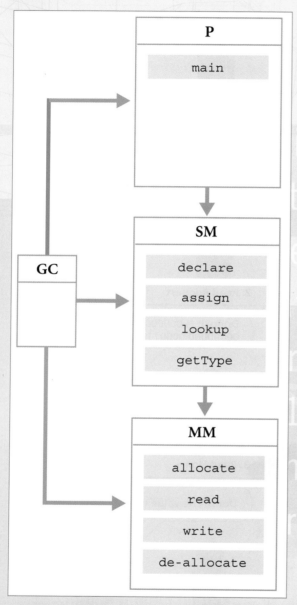

- **lookup** Given an identifier, return the value stored in its block.
- **getType** Given an identifier, return its type.

Recall from Section 1.2.3 that a variable is defined as a block; hence, the above language is consistent with the notion that SM encapsulates a variable. Note, in particular, that no reference is made to how the block size is determined, how the value was converted to binary, or to the symbol table. These are "how" details that should not be in the interface.

The public methods in MM are

- **allocate** Given a size, reserve a memory block of that size and return its address.
- **read** Given the size and address of a memory block, return its content (a binary sequence).
- **write** Given the address of a memory block and a binary sequence, write the sequence in the indicated block. Return nothing.
- **de-allocate** Given the size and address of a used memory block, mark it as free. Return nothing.

The details of the contracts are left as an exercise. The overall architecture is shown in Fig. 2.21 using basic UML diagrams in which method names are shown but without a return or a full signature.

You may have noticed an anomaly related to de-allocation. If our program is no longer interested in a variable, there is no way for it to return its block to the pool of free cells. Even though MM is capable of de-allocating, SM has no corresponding task. This is one area in which Java is different from other languages. It does not rely on the programmer remembering to return unwanted stuff; it provides automatic garbage collection. A new manager, named **Garbage Collector** (or **GC**), is hired to snoop around P to see if any variable is no longer usable, because, for example, it has exited its scope. If one is found, it deletes it from the symbol table of SM and requests MM to de-allocate its

block (see Fig. 2.21). The job of GC is different from those of MM and SM in that it is asynchronous: rather than reacting to requests, GC lives in its own world and operates at its own pace.

In terms of actual implementation, the "read" and "write" tasks of MM are implemented in hardware, whereas "allocate" and "de-allocate" are implemented in the operating system. The "declare" task of SM is implemented in the compiler, whereas its remaining tasks are implemented in the virtual machine. GC is implemented in the virtual machine too. As you can see, it is irrelevant from the client's view whether an interface is implemented in hardware or software. In fact, the client should not be able to tell (and does not really care) where software ends and hardware begins.

Summary of Key Concepts

1. Today's application must **delegate** some or all of its work to other classes.

2. In the **procedural** paradigm, the program **invokes** methods **on** their class.

3. A **method** has a **signature** (name and parameter types) and a **return** (type of the returned value). If a method is **void**, then it has no return. Data is **passed** to a method through its **parameters**.

4. In the **modular** paradigm, the program **accesses** attributes and invokes methods **on** their class. An **attribute** has a name and a type and allows data to **persist**. Attributes and methods are known collectively as **features**.

5. In the **object-oriented** paradigm, the program **instantiates** the class and uses the created **object** rather than the class. This paradigm is also known as **OOP** (for object-oriented programming). While a class has only attributes and methods, its **instance** also has an **object reference** and a **state** (the values of all attributes).

6. A **class diagram** in **UML** (**Unified Modelling Language**) depicts a class as a rectangle with one or more compartments. The top one is mandatory and contains the class name (possibly qualified) and an optional **stereotype**. The next two are optional: one for attributes and one for methods.

7. A **utility class** is one that cannot be instantiated. In a utility class, all features are said to be **static**, and they are accessed/invoked on the class name. UML identifies such a class by using the stereotype: «utility».

8. An **object diagram** in UML depicts the object's identity in the top compartment and its state in the bottom one.

9. A **dashed line** between two class diagrams indicates that one class delegates to the other. Such a line between an object and a class diagram indicates that the object is an instance of the class.

10. **Abstraction** is a strategy for replacing complex features by simpler ones based on an **abstraction criterion**. **Layered abstractions** give rise to **abstraction hierarchies** in which **higher-level** abstractions have fewer details.

11. A Java **application** (or **system**) consists of a **main class** (or **app**) and one or more **helper classes** (or **components**). The main class is a **client** that uses services; components are **implementers** that provide services.

12. A component class is an **encapsulation**. The "how" details are encapsulated, while the "what" details are posted in the **interface** (also known as the **API**). Any attempt to learn something about a class beyond what is in the API is known as **breaking the encapsulation**.

13. A component class is itself a client of other components, and this leads to a view in which the application consists of a series of layers that begins with the human **user** (also known as the **end-user**) and ends in the hardware.

14. Java provides several **access modifiers** for each feature in a class. The ones that appear in the interface are **public** and **protected**, but only the public ones can be used in a main class. A public attribute is called a **field**.

15. When a program asks the VM to do something impossible, the VM **throws** an **exception**. This manifests itself through a **runtime error** (a **crash**). The program is terminated, and an error message and a **stack trace** are displayed.

16. A **logic error** (a **bug**) in a program leads to wrong results but has no otherwise visible manifestation.

17. When a post-compilation error is detected, one must **debug** the source to determine the cause and then traverse the **edit-compile-run cycle**.

18. J2SE, J2EE, and J2ME are the three main categories of tools and libraries that Sun Microsystems offers. Each has a **JDK** (Software Development Kit) for developing applications and a **JRE** (Java Runtime Environment) to run them.

19. Packages are often deployed in zipped archives called **jar** files. If a jar file is placed in Java's **extension directory**, all its classes become an extension to the standard library and, hence, can be imported.

20. **Console I/O** (input and output) refers to the program's ability to read keyboard input and generate text output on the screen. We will use the object reference `input` (an instance of `java.util.Scanner`) for `input`, and the object reference `output` (an instance of `java.io.PrintStream`) for `output`.

21. **Software engineering** (S/E) is the study of software projects and their progress. Its guidelines for developing software are meant to mitigate risks, enhance readability, and define correctness.

22. Rather than using magic numbers that are hard-coded, a program must declare **final** variables.

23. A **contract** spells out the client and the implementer responsibilities as **pre** and **post** conditions, respectively. The client guarantees that the precondition is true prior to making a call. The implementer guarantees that the postcondition will be true upon return from a call.

24. In the **implicit condition convention** for writing contracts, the following items are specified per method: header (signature and return), a brief description of each parameter and of the return, any non-"true" precondition, any thrown exception.

25. The **development environment** (covered in the Lab) consists of a JDK, APIs, an editor, and a **console**.

Review Questions

1. What is a method, and what are its two characteristics?
2. Can a method have no parameters? Can a method have no return?
3. Two methods have the same signature but different returns. Can they reside in the same class?
4. What is the invocation syntax?
5. What happens if a program invokes a nonexistent method on a class?
6. A passed value is said to resemble the right-hand side of an assignment statement. What are the similarities?
7. What is an attribute, and what are its two characteristics?
8. Two attributes have the same name but different types. Can they reside in the same class?
9. Attributes are said to resemble variables. What are the similarities?
10. Do attributes need to be declared or initialized before being used?
11. What determines the scope of an attribute?
12. How is an object related to a class, and what is meant by state?
13. Do all instances of a class have the same set of attributes and methods?
14. Is it possible for two instances of the same class to have different values for one of the static attributes?
15. How is the fully qualified class name in UML different from that of Java?
16. How are attributes and methods specified in the UML class diagram?
17. Show that a UML object diagram does not duplicate information present in its class diagram.
18. What is abstraction, and what is it used for?
19. How is an app different from an application?
20. What is the responsibility of the client?
21. What does an API mean?
22. Driving a car requires knowing how to signal a left turn. Does this knowledge break the encapsulation?

23. Is encapsulation designed to make the client's life easier or the implementer's?

24. Can a client be an implementer? Can an implementer be a client? Is the end-user a client or an implementer?

25. When a program crashes, does the virtual machine identify where the problem occurred? When a program contains a bug, does the virtual machine identify where the bug is?

26. Explain the difference between correcting a compile-time error and debugging.

27. Can the end-user be the culprit when a runtime error occurs in the main class?

28. Can the main class be the culprit when a runtime error occurs in a component?

29. Can a bug in a component lead to a runtime error in the main class?

30. What is software engineering?

31. Give an example of a risk that is mitigated by early exposure.

32. Explain how the **final** keyword enables us to eliminate magic numbers.

33. Who guarantees that the precondition is met? Who guarantees that the postcondition is met?

34. Whose fault is it if both pre and post are not met?

35. Does a false precondition always lead to a runtime error?

The Development Environment

L2.1 What Is a Development Environment?

A **development environment** is made up of all the tools and documents needed to develop applications. It consists of six elements; the first three are platform-independent, and the last three are not.

A Working Directory This is where all your programs are stored.

API You will need easy and quick access to the API of Java and TYPE.

TYPE This refers to the family of programs and packages that come with this textbook. It is bundled in one *type.jar* file that installs as an extension of the standard library.

The JDK The JDK for your particular platform must be installed.

An Editor An editor is a program that allows you to create, modify, and save source programs.

A Console A console is a window through which you can run, and interact with, your programs.

L2.2 Setting Up the Development Environment

You can find everything you need to set up a development environment on your home computer on the book's web site:

```
http://www.cse.yorku.ca/~roumani/jba
```

There is a separate section for each operating system. Read the one that pertains to the O/S of the machine on which you want to install the environment.

L2.3 Testing the Environment

- Launch the editor and the console.
- In the editor, open the file *Demo.java* in your working directory.
- Compile it in the console.
- Verify that *Demo.class* was created.
- Run the created class.

If the above test failed, you should examine the reported error message and determine the source of the problem accordingly. Visit the book's web site for help.

L2.4 Configuring eCheck

- ■ Open the console.
- ■ Issue the command *java Options*.
- ■ Set your login data.
- ■ Set the eCheck URL given by your instructor.
- ■ Click *Apply*.

eCheck uses the above data to communicate with a server at your department and record that you have successfully completed assigned programs. If your course does not use the eCheck server, or if you want to eCheck your programs off-line, click the "Offline" check box. This way, you can still benefit from eCheck as a learning tool.

L2.5 Measuring Elapsed Time

We like to write a program that figures out how long it takes for the end-user to respond to a prompt. Specifically, it prompts the user to press ENTER and outputs the number of milliseconds that have elapsed between printing the prompt and receiving the input.

Start by creating a program based on the template of Fig. 2.14. It is a good idea to save the file under the name Template.java, so that you can reuse it in future projects, and then to resave it (using the save as menu) under the name Lab2_1.java.

We will delegate keeping track of time to a class in java.lang called System. One of its methods is static and has the following API:

```
long currentTimeMillis()
```

Returns: the difference, measured in milliseconds, between the current time and midnight, January 1, 1970.

The header indicates that the method returns a long value and that it takes no parameters (evidenced by the empty parenthesis pair in the signature). Since this method is static, we invoke it on the class as in the following example:

```
long now = System.currentTimeMillis();
```

To measure a time interval, we invoke the method just before and just after the interval, and then subtract the two returns. Here is a template:

```
output.println("Press ENTER");
long start = System.currentTimeMillis();
input.nextLine();
...
```

We used the nextLine() method because it can read any entry, including an empty one (generated when the user presses ENTER without typing anything). Notice that we trashed the return (rather than store it in a variable) because we are not interested in it, only that it took place. Continue the development and create the class `Lab2_1` such that its I/O is similar to the following sample run:

```
Press ENTER
Pressing ENTER took you 443 milliseconds.
```

In particular, your output must have one space before and after the shown duration.

> **Note:** the `nanoTime()` method was added to the `System` class in Java 5.0. It is similar to the one used above, but it is more precise because it returns the time in nanoseconds.

L2.6 Approximating Today's Date

We saw in Section 2.1.3 that one can use the `Date` class to obtain today's date, and we will see in Chapter 7 that one can use the `Calendar` class to express a date in various locales and time zones. In this section, and as an exercise, we will figure out today's date from the number of milliseconds between January 1, 1970 and now. We will ignore leap years and assume 365 days per year.

To avoid magic numbers (which would be a style violation), our program starts by naming a couple of constants:

```
final int BASE_YEAR = 1970;
final long MS_PER_YEAR = 1000 * 3600 * 24 * 365;
```

As a start, let us compute and display today's year:

```
long now = System.currentTimeMillis();
long year = now / MS_PER_YEAR;
output.println(BASE_YEAR + year);
```

Create the program `Lab2_2`, compile it, and run. Did you get the result you expect? Why not? Our program does in fact have a logic error in it. Spend some time debugging it so that you can determine what is wrong. The best debugging tool is printing: simply print each and every intermediate value that your program uses. Ironically, *the error can be fixed by inserting one character only*.

After correcting the problem, and obtaining the correct year, continue the development so that today's month and day are also displayed. You may want to add two more constants:

```
final long MS_PER_MONTH = MS_PER_YEAR / 12;
final long MS_PER_DAY = MS_PER_YEAR / 365;
```

You should benefit from the built-in remainder operator. For example,

```
long left = now % MS_PER_YEAR;
```

yields the number of milliseconds that remain left over after the years are accounted for. Note that since leap years were ignored, it should not be surprising if the computed date is off by 10 days or so. (Why?)

L2.7 Retrieving System Information

The System class has a second static method:

```
String getProperty(String key)
```

This method takes a string that specifies the name of a property of the computer system on which the program is running, and it returns the value of that property. For example, this statement

```
output.println(System.getProperty("java.version"));
```

outputs the version of the JRE that is executing the statement. Several properties can be accessed through this method, and some of them are shown in Fig. 2.22. Create the program Lab2_3 that outputs all properties whose names are shown in the figure.

Examine the output of your program. Does it correctly specify the name of the extension directory (where type.jar was stored)? It should also correctly indicate the name of your working directory (where the program was stored).

L2.8 Integrated Development Environments (*optional*)

The environment that was set up in this Lab requires that you switch back and forth between the editor and the console as you go through the edit-compile-run cycle. This is not a problem given that today's operating systems are multitasking: you can run the console without closing the editor, see both windows on the screen, and switch between them with

Figure 2.22
Some of the system properties that can be passed to the getProperty of the java.lang. System class

java.version	Java Runtime Environment version
java.vendor	Java Runtime Environment vendor
java.vendor.url	Java vendor URL
java.home	Java installation directory
java.class.path	Java class path
java.ext.dirs	Path of extension directory
os.name	Operating system name
os.version	Operating system version
user.name	User's account name
user.home	User's home directory
user.dir	User's current working directory

a mouse click or a press of a button. The main advantage of this environment is that it does not put a layer between you and the operating system; hence, it is reliable and available wherever you go.

This environment, however, is not integrated. The editor, albeit aware of Java and able to highlight keywords and library classes, cannot detect compile-time errors. You will have to write the program, save it, switch to the console, and compile before detecting that you used a variable outside its scope or invoked a nonexistent method. In contrast, an *integrated development environment* (IDE) integrates these tasks: the program is compiled as you type; when you try to invoke a method on a class, a menu will pop up that shows all available methods and their signatures. Hence, editing, compiling, and API lookups are all integrated. Running is also integrated because when a runtime error occurs, the statement that triggered it is highlighted, and you can inspect the values of variables just before the crash.

It is up to you whether you use an IDE or a console-based environment in this course. But for follow-up courses, the debugging, refactoring, and testing capabilities of an IDE will more than offset its steep learning curve. The IDE that we highly recommend is *Eclipse* because it is extensible (evolves with plug-ins) and, thus, will grow with your needs. You can start by using only its editor and console and gradually explore its other features. It is available on virtually all platforms and is free.

Installing Eclipse

Eclipse is written in Java and hence you can install it in Windows, Linux, or Mac OS. Follow the instructions in the book's web site to install and configure Eclipse.

Eclipse has many features (and can be extended by plug-ins), but it is essential that you first become comfortable with its basic features and then explore other features as needed. As such, it is recommended that you always use the Java Perspective, and in it expose only the following views: editor, console, and navigator. It is recommended that you position the views as shown in Fig. 2.23: the navigator as a left frame, the editor in the upper right, and the console in the bottom right. Close any other view that Eclipse shows. Once you become comfortable with the basic features, you can explore the more sophisticated ones, for example, debugging, javadoc generation, JUNIT, and Re-Factoring.

You type your program in the editor, and the program is compiled incrementally, that is, as you type it. You can run your program by clicking the "running person" icon. The first time you do so, you must specify that it should run "As an Application." Afterward, you will find its name listed under that icon.

You can run eCheck or Options from the next icon (it shows a red toolbox). Again, the first time you run it, you must drop down the menu, choose External Tools, and click the "Run" button. Afterward, you will find its name listed in the red tool icon.

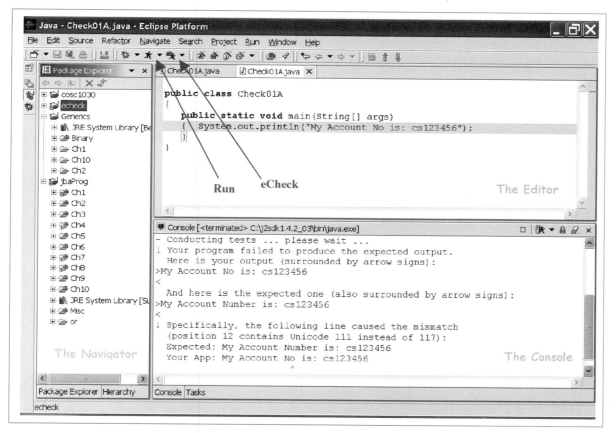

Figure 2.23 A snapshot of the Eclipse IDE showing the relevant icons and the key windows

L2.9 Using UniCon *(optional)*

The `type.jar` file that you have installed contains an application called *UniCon*. UniCon simulates a very simple console, and since it is written in Java, it runs as is on all platforms. You can launch this application by switching to the `bin` directory of the JDK and issuing the command

```
javaw UniCon
```

Alternatively, you can create a shortcut on your desktop and make it point to the `javaw` file in the `bin` directory of the JDK, and then add `UniCon` to the command line.

Once UniCon launches, change its current directory to your working directory. You can use the `cd` command to change directories and `pwd` to determine the current directory. You can then compile programs and run them using `javac` and `java` as usual.

UniCon is meant for a first course on Java because it supports only a very small set of commands. Its advantage is that it requires no installation or path setup.

Exercises

2.1 The factorial method computes the factorial of its int argument and returns it as a double. (a) What is the signature of this method? (b) What is its return? (c) Some argue that based on the definition of factorial, the return should be int; others argue that it should be long or else only very small arguments can be accommodated. Provide a critique of these arguments.

2.2 Assume that the method of the Exercise 2.1 resides in the Math class of the (hypothetical) package extra. Assume further that the Math class cannot be instantiated. (a) Argue that factorial must be a static method. (b) Draw the UML diagram of the Math class.

2.3 An app plans to use the services of a class whose UML diagram is shown in Fig. 2.24. Which of the following statements enables the app to do that? There may be more than one correct answer.

(a) import Orbit;

Figure 2.24
A UML class diagram

« utility » jba::Orbit
payBack(double, int): double

(b) import jba.Orbit;
(c) import jba:Orbit;
(d) import jba.*;
(e) import utility.jba.Orbit;
(f) import jba.Orbit.payBack;

2.4 The following fragment uses a method in a class whose UML diagram is shown in Fig. 2.24. Assuming that the class has been properly imported, do you see any compile-time errors in the fragment?

```
double amount = 2500;
int period = 4;
double pay = Orbit.payBack(amount, period);
```

2.5 This exercise is the same as Exercise 2.4 except for the following fragment:

```
int amount = 2500;
int period = 4;
double pay = Orbit.payBack(amount, period);
```

2.6 This exercise is the same as Exercise 2.5 except for the following fragment:

```
float amount = 2500;
int period = 4;
double pay = Orbit.payBack(amount, period);
```

2.7 This exercise is the same as Exercise 2.6 except for the following fragment:

```
double amount = 2500;
long period = 4;
double pay = Orbit.payBack(amount, period);
```

2.8 This exercise is the same as Exercise 2.7 except for the following fragment:

```
double amount = 2500;
int period = 4;
int pay = Orbit.payBack(amount, period);
```

2.9 Consider the UML class diagram shown in Fig. 2.25. Determine whether the following fragment has any compile-time errors. Assume that the class was properly imported. Note that we are not concerned with semantics or logic errors, only errors that will be detected by the compiler.

Figure 2.25 A UML class diagram

```
      « utility »
      jba::Bond
rating: char
rate: double
estimate(): double
inflate(): void
```

```
Bond.rating = 'C';
Bond.rate = 0.12;
double x = Bond.estimate();
output.println(Bond.inflate());
```

2.10 This exercise is the same as Exercise 2.9 except for the following fragment:

```
Bond.rating = 'C';
Bond.rate = 0.12;
Bond.estimate();
Bond.inflate();
```

2.11 A program, which simulates a person taking a public transit bus, uses three classes: Passenger, Driver, and Bus. Passenger is concerned with getting from one place to another, so its features relate to knowing where the bus stop is, having the correct fare, getting off at the destination station, etc. The Driver is concerned with following the designated route while observing the traffic and transit rules. The Bus is concerned with the vehicle itself, so its features relate to accelerating, turning, and stopping. (a) Identify the client and the implementer. (b) Argue that even though these three classes interact, they have separate concerns. (c) Enumerate three attributes and three methods that might be present in each of the three classes. (d) Identify one feature in each class that should not be made public, that is, one that would break the encapsulation if it were in the interface.

2.12 The following fragment computes the average (arithmetic mean) of three variables:

```
int x = 6 / 2;
int y = 12 / (x - 3);
int z = -3;
double mean = x + y + z) / 3;
```

It contains a compile-time, a runtime error, and a logic error. Identify each.

2.13 An app that converts temperature from Fahrenheit to Celsius involves multiplying by the constant 5/9. To avoid magic numbers, the developer decided to declare this literal as a final and gave it the identifier SCALE_FACTOR. Which of the following declarations does not lead to a logic error? Circle all the correct ones.

```
A.     final double SCALE_FACTOR = 5 / 9;
B.     final double SCALE_FACTOR = 5.0 / 9.0;
C.     final double SCALE_FACTOR = 5 / 9.0;
D.     final double SCALE_FACTOR = (double) (5 / 9);
E.     final double SCALE_FACTOR = (double) 5 / 9;
F.     final double SCALE_FACTOR = 5 / (double) 9;
```

2.14 Rewrite the following fragment so that it is free of magic numbers:

```
output.println("Enter speed in km/h");
double speed = input.nextDouble();
speed = speed * 1000 / 3600;
output.println("Enter distance in ft");
double distance = input.nextDouble();
distance = distance * 0.3048;
double time = distance / speed;
```

2.15 Methods M1 and M2 are similar in that they accomplish the same task, and they take the same parameters. However, the precondition of M1 is much stronger than that of M2. (a) As client, is it easier for you to invoke M1 or M2? (b) If the client is sloppy and does not ensure that preconditions are met, which invocation, M1 or M2, is more likely to crash the app, and which is more likely to make it buggy? Justify your answers.

2.16 The public features of the (hypothetical) Car class include the methods *start*, *accelerate*, *steer*, *addFuel*, and *getFuel*. The precondition of the *accelerate* method is that the tires are not flat (i.e., they have air). Argue that this pre is unacceptable given the interface in today's cars.

2.17 The *declare* method of SM (the symbol manager of Section 2.3.4) takes two parameters: the identifier being declared and its type. What are its precondition and postcondition? Hint: When does a declaration statement lead to a compile-time error?

Figure 2.26 The abstract vending machine

2.18 The *allocate* method of MM (the memory manager of section 2.3.4) takes one parameter: the size of the block to allocate. What are its precondition and postcondition?

2.19 The *de-allocate* task makes MM's job particularly complex. Explain why its job would be significantly simpler if this task were not in the contract.

2.20 It is MM's job to keep track of free and used memory; and it is SM's job to keep a log of every allocated block. It thus seems that both of them are keeping track of used memory. Show that there is no overlap here, that the information kept by the two parties, albeit related, is not identical. Hint: When two programs are running at the same time, there will be two SMs but only one MM.

2.21 A vending machine that dispenses bottled water has seven features in its interface. See Fig. 2.26.

The features consist of three buttons (S, M, L) for selecting the desired bottle size (small, medium, or large), a slot to insert coins, an output tray in which the bottle drops, a hexagonal button (R) for requesting change or coin return, and a red light that flashes once (lights up momentarily) if the machine encounters a problem. To purchase a small bottle, for example, insert 35 cents and press the S, and a small bottle will drop into the output tray. Express these features as methods, complete with signatures and returns.

2.22 Let *selectSmall()* be the method corresponding to pressing the S button of the vending machine in Exercise 2.22. Write its pre and post.

eCheck

Check02A (TS = 16)

The UML diagram of the Math utility class of `java.lang` contains the following two entries in the method compartment:

```
rint(double): double
round(double): long
```

Write the app `Check02A` that explores the difference between these two methods by reading a `double` from the user and outputting the result of invoking each. Here is a sample run of the sought app:

```
Enter any double to test: 12.43
Method Math.rint returns: 12.0
While Math.round returns: 12
```

Here is another sample run:

```
Enter any double to test: 262.5
Method Math.rint returns: 262.0
While Math.round returns: 263
```

Implement your app, test it, and then eCheck it. Keep in mind that your app must work correctly for any input, not just the ones shown above. Note also that your app must adhere to the exact output layout shown above. No number formatting whatsoever is needed; output the returns of the two methods as-is.

There is a subtle difference between the two methods (in addition to the obvious difference in return type): the first method returns the closest integral `double` to the passed parameter (and if two such values are equally close, the even one breaks the tie). The second adds 0.5 to the parameter and returns the floor of the sum as `long`. This algorithmic difference may lead to an observable difference as seen in the second sample run.

Check02B (TS = 16)

The UML diagram of the `Rectangle` class of `type.lib` contains the following two entries in the method compartment:

```
getCircumference(): int
hashCode(): int
```

Write the app `Check02B` that starts by prompting for and reading the width and height of a rectangle, both of type `int`. The app then creates a rectangle object using the `Rectangle` class of `type.lib`. Finally, the app invokes the above two methods and outputs their returns. Here is a sample run:

```
Enter the width: 3
Enter the height: 4
The return of getCircumference is: 14
The return of hashCode is: 95
```

Do not be concerned with the significance of the hash code; our concern now is to become familiar with creating objects and invoking methods on them.

Develop your app, test it, and then eCheck it.

Check02C (TS = 16)

Recall that the UML diagram of the ToolBox utility class of `type.lib` contains the method:

```
getBMI(int, String): double
```

Write the app `Check02C` that prompts for and reads the height and weight of a person and then outputs the corresponding BMI rounded to one decimal. Use the `printf` method to perform the rounding and formatting of the output. Here is a sample run:

```
Height in ft['in]: 5'2
Weight in lb [>0]: 176
The BMI is 32.2
```

Assume as a precondition that the entered height and weight are valid. A height is valid if its feet part is a positive integer and if its (optional) inches part is a non-negative integer less than 12, and if both components are present then they must be separated by a single quote. A weight is valid if it is positive. Note that since these requirements are preconditions, we don't have to do anything at all in our app to check them—if the end user violated them, anything can happen and our app would not be at fault. We will learn later how to be more friendly with the end user.

Develop your app, test it, and then eCheck it.

Check02D (TS = 16)

Write the app `Check02D` that behaves as shown in this sample run:

```
Enter the number of milliseconds since the epoch:
1234567890123
After that many milliseconds, the date is:
Fri Feb 13 18:31:30 EST 2009
```

The user enters a `long` number and the app and outputs the date after that many milliseconds since the epoch (January 1, 1970, 00:00:00 GMT).

Start by creating a date object using the `Date` class of `java.util`. The UML diagram of that class contains the following two entries in the method compartment:

```
setTime(long): void
toString(): String
```

The first allows you to change the date of a `Date` object by specifying a number of milliseconds (since the epoch) as a parameter. The second allows you to retrieve a string representation of the date in the format required by the above specs.

Develop your app, test it, and then eCheck it.

3

Using APIs

Learning Objectives

1. *Learn how to read an API*

2. *Appreciate parameter evaluation and passing*

3. *Explore method binding and over-loading*

4. *Experience the develojment process*

5. *Handle input validation and assertions*

6. *Take an in-depth look at utility classes*

Viewing software development as an assembly of ready-made components requires a catalogue of those components. In this chapter, you will familiarize yourself with this catalogue and learn how to locate information in it. You will also learn how to turn software development into a formal multiphase process with clearly defined deliverables.

Chapter Outline

3.1 Anatomy of an API

As you learned in Chapter 2, everything a client needs to know in order to use a component class is contained in the API of that class. Since component classes are often packaged in an archive (a jar file), their APIs are similarly packaged in one document that acts as the API of the archive. APIs are ideally written in HTML because HTML is universally accessible and provides hyperlinks that make navigating easy within an API as well as across APIs in the same archive. The following sections describe the details of an **archive API** and a **class API**.

3.1.1 Overall Layout

As depicted in Fig. 3.1, an archive API consists of three frames: the frame in the upper-left corner lists all packages in the archive; the frame in the lower-left corner lists the names of all classes; and the large frame on the right contains details. The three frames are individually scrollable and sizable. They are also synchronized: if you select a package in the package frame, its classes will be listed in the class frame; and if you select a class in the class frame, its API will be shown in the details frame. The API of a class consists of four main sections.

The Class Section

The **class section** describes the class in general. It starts with the fully qualified name of the class and its header. The class name allows the client to import the class, and the class header gives finer details about the class, for example, what it extends and what it implements. Later you will learn the significance of these details. The rest of this section describes the encapsulation that the class portrays and provides notes about its usage.

The Field Section

Figure 3.1 The API of an archive is a linked, three-frame document.

The **field section** lists all the fields (i.e., public attributes) that this class has. If the class does not have fields, this section will be absent. We will explore the contents of this section in detail in Section 3.1.2.

Packages	Details
	The class section
	The field section
Classes	The constructor section
	The method section

The Constructor Section

The **constructor section** lists all the public constructors that this class has. For an object-oriented class (not a utility), the constructor allows us to set the initial state of the class instance. For a procedural or modular class (a utility), the class is used without making instances; hence, a constructor is not needed. The constructor section will thus be absent from the API of utility classes.

The Method Section

The **method section** lists all the public methods that this class has. If the class does not have put print("Enter h:m:AM or PM >

Java Details   3.1

An Obligatory Constructor

If the implementer of a class does not specify a constructor, Java automatically creates one; hence, every class must have a constructor. This seems to contradict what was stated earlier about utility classes not having a constructor section in their APIs. The solution to this contradiction lies in public/private access: the implementer of a utility class creates a private constructor in order to thwart Java's obligatory constructor. Since the API lists only the public aspects, this constructor will not appear in it.

methods, this section will be absent. We will explore the contents of this section in detail in Section 3.1.3.

We will be focusing on the APIs of utility classes in this chapter. Nonutility classes are covered in detail in Chapter 4.

3.1.2 Fields

The field section of the API lists all fields in two hyperlinked subsections: the **Field Summary** and the **Field Detail**. The field summary is a two-column table with one row per field, as shown in Fig. 3.2. The left column specifies the field type and whether it is `static`. Note that if a field is not static, you will *not* see the words *not static* in the left column; that is, if the word *static* is absent, then the field is not static. The right column indicates the field's name, and under it, a brief description of what the field is meant to hold.

The field's name is actually a hyperlink that takes us to the Field Detail subsection in which additional information about the field is provided. For example, if we click on the field's name, `PI`, in Fig. 3.2, we will see the details shown in Fig. 3.3.

The line

```
public static final double PI
```

indicates that this field is `public`, which means we are free to use it, `static` (which was stated in the Field Summary), `final` (which we could have guessed based on letter case), and `double` (which was also stated in the summary). The textual part repeats what was stated in the summary and optionally adds more details. In our example, it provides a link to a page that gives the actual numerical value of `PI`.

As we saw in Chapter 2, static fields are accessed on the class; for example, to access the `PI` field of the `Math` class, we write `Math.PI`.

Figure 3.2 Part of the field summary section of the `java.lang.Math` API

Field Summary	
static double	**PI** The double value that is closer than any other to *pi*, the ratio of the circumference of a circle to its diameter.

Figure 3.3 The
field detail sec-
tion of the PI
field in the
Math class API

Field Detail

PI
```
public static final double PI
```

> The double value that is closer than any other to *pi*, the ratio of
> the circumference of a circle to its diameter.
>
> See also: <u>Constant Field Values</u>

Example 3.1

Use the `Integer` class to write a fragment that outputs the minimum value that an `int`
can have.

Answer:
Open the Java API using the link created in Lab 2. All classes of all packages in J2SE are
shown in the class frame. If we click on `Integer,` its API appears in the right pane. The
field summary API is reproduced, in part, in Fig. 3.4.
One of the fields is `MIN_VALUE`, and it is clear from its description that it is the field we
want. Notice that since uppercase letters were chosen for its identifier, it is probably a
`final` field. We can confirm by clicking on its name to see its details. The details, reproduced in Fig. 3.5, confirm that it is `final`.
The sought fragment is thus

```
output.println(Integer.MIN_VALUE);
```

Figure 3.4 Part
of the field sum-
mary section of
the API of the
Integer class

Field Summary

static int	**MAX_VALUE** A constant holding the maximum value an `int` can have, $2^{31} - 1$.
static int	**MIN_VALUE** A constant holding the minimum value an `int` can have, -2^{31}.

Figure 3.5 The
field detail of
the
MIN_VALUE
field of the
Integer
class

Field Detail

MIN_VALUE
`public static final int MIN_VALUE`

A constant holding the minimum value an `int` can have, -2^{31}.

See also: <u>Constant Field Values</u>

Java Details 3.2

Static Imports

Beginning with Java release 5, it is possible to access static fields without specifying the class name if the class was imported using the new static import statement. For example,

```
import static java.lang.Math.*;
```

allows us to use `PI` without having to prefix it by the `Math` class and the dot separator. You can import a particular field by stating its name, or you can import all fields by using an asterisk. Hence, the asterisk denotes "all fields," *not* "all classes," as in the traditional `import` statement. We will not use static imports in this textbook.

3.1.3 Methods

The method section of the API lists all methods in two hyperlinked subsections: the **Method Summary** and the **Method Detail**. The method summary is a two-column table with one row per method, as shown in Fig. 3.6.

Figure 3.6 Part
of the method
summary section
of the API of the
Math class

Method Summary

static double	<u>abs</u>(double a) Returns the absolute value of a double value
static int	<u>abs</u>(int a) Returns the absolute value of an int value
static double	<u>pow</u>(double a, double b) Returns the value of the first argument raised to the power of the second argument

The left column specifies the method's return and whether it is `static`. As with fields, if you do not see the word "static," then the method is not `static`. The right column indicates the method's signature, and under it a brief description of what the method does. The method's name is actually a hyperlink that takes us to the Method Detail subsection in which the method's contract is specified. For example, if we click on the `abs` method of Fig. 3.6, we will see the contract shown in Fig. 3.7.

Example 3.2

Write a fragment that prompts for and reads a real number from the end-user and outputs its absolute value using the `Math` class. Use the API shown in Fig. 3.8 for `Scanner`.

Answer:

```
output.print("Enter a real number: ");
double number = input.nextDouble();
output.println(Math.abs(number));
```

It is assumed that a `Scanner` instance with reference `input` and a `PrintStream` instance with reference `output` have been created earlier in the program (as explained in Section 2.2.5).

Since methods have contracts associated with them and fields do not, classes expose mainly methods in their APIs. As such, we need to develop a deeper understanding of methods, and this is achieved through the following observations.

Figure 3.7 The method detail section of the `abs` Method in the `Math` class API

Method Detail

abs

`public static double abs(double a)`

Returns the absolute value of a `double` value. If the argument is not negative, the argument is returned. If the argument is negative, the negation of the argument is returned. Special cases:
- If the argument is positive zero or negative zero, the result is positive zero.
- If the argument is infinite, the result is positive infinity.
- If the argument is NaN, the result is NaN.

Parameters:
  a - the argument whose absolute value is to be determined
Returns:
  the absolute value of the argument

Figure 3.8 Part of the method summary section of the Scanner class

Method Summary	
double	**nextDouble()** Scans the next token of the input as a double
int	**nextInt()** Scans the next token of the input as an int
String	**nextLine()** Advances this scanner past the current line and returns the input that was skipped
long	**nextLong()** Scans the next token of the input as a long

Parameters Are Passed by Value

We saw in Chapter 2 that a parameter is treated as the right-hand side of an imaginary assignment statement whose left-hand side has the type specified in the signature. Hence, when a method is invoked, each of its parameters is evaluated, its value is promoted if needed, and the final value is then sent to the method. Since it is the value of the parameter that ends up being sent, this mode of parameter passing is known as **pass-by-value**. In contrast, some languages use **pass-by-reference**, which passes the address of the memory block allocated to the parameter, and this allows the method not only to see the value of the parameter but also to change it. For example, if Java allowed passing by reference, then the value of number in Example 3.2 might change upon returning from the abs invocation. All invocations in Java, whether of static or nonstatic methods, are done by value. This promotes software reliability because, as clients, we have the assurance that methods cannot alter the values of our variables, neither deliberately nor inadvertently.

Programming Tip   3.1

Fallacy: Only primitive types are passed by value

Everything is passed by value in Java, including nonprimitive types. An object reference passed to a method cannot be altered by it. (The method *can* alter the state of the object at which the object reference points, but this is not relevant to parameter passing.)

Example 3.3

Write a fragment that computes the value of a mega in decimal. Recall that mega is defined as 2^{20}.

Answer:

```
double base = 2;
double expo = 20;
double mega = Math.pow(base, expo);
```

Overloading

The signature of a method is unique in its class; that is, no two methods in the same class can have the same signature. This rule has two implications: First, it is not possible to have two methods with the same signature even if they have different returns. Second, it is OK to have two methods with the same name as long as they have different parameter lists (regardless of the return). The second implication is manifested in Fig. 3.6, where two methods with the same name, abs, are present, one with signature abs(double) and the other with signature abs(int). When two or more methods in the same class share a name, they are said to be **overloaded**. The word derives from the fact that the name of the method is associated, or loaded, with more than one meaning.

As a second example of overloading, examine the API of the PrintStream class in java.io. Recall from Section 2.2.5 that this is the class that we delegate to for output. Whether you write output.println or System.out.println, you are using the PrintStream API. You can see from the API that the println method is heavily overloaded. There are several versions of it based on the type of the data to be output.

Binding with the Most Specific

When a compiler encounters the invocation

```
C.m(...);
```

it must determine where the invoked method is, and this process is called **binding**, if C is a class and if m is a static method. It takes place during compilation, that is, before the program is run, so it is also called **early binding**. Binding involves the following steps:

1. Find the class

   The class on which the invocation is made appears before the dot separator (for nonstatic methods, it is the declared type of the object reference). If this class is missing (not present or not on the class path or not imported), the compiler issues the error *Cannot find symbol.*

2. Find the method

   Search for a method with a compatible signature within the class found in the previous step. This means the method must have the same name and the same number of parameters as in the invocation, and its parameter types must be the same as, or higher in the type hierarchy than, the types of the passed values. If no such method is found, the error *Cannot resolve symbol* is issued.

Programming Tip   **3.2**

Pitfall: Overloading and type casting

The `println` method of the `PrintStream` class takes one parameter and prints it. It seems to work for any type of parameter: `String`, `int`, `double`, and even `boolean`. Is this an example of automatic promotion? No. Promotion works only among numeric types, and then only in a particular direction (up the hierarchy). The ability of this method to handle all these disparate types is an illusion created by overloading: there are actually many such methods in the `PrintStream` class, but they all share the same name.

3. Select the most specific method

   If the invoked method is overloaded, the previous step may identify several possible targets for the invocation. In this case, the compiler binds to the **most specific** method, that is, to the one requiring the least amount of promotion. If there is no "most specific" method, the compiler produces an "ambiguous invocation" error.

> ### Example 3.4
>
> Bind the following invocation:
>
> ```
> int x = Math.abs(2);
> ```
>
> Can you prove that your binding is correct?
>
> **Answer:**
> The `abs` method is overloaded in the `Math` class with two versions: one accepting an `int` and one a `double`. The literal `2` in the above invocation is compatible with `int` (without any type casting) and with `double` (a widening conversion). Based on the most-specific rule, the compiler will bind this with the `int` method.
> We can prove that this is indeed the binding employed by the compiler by inserting the above statement in a program and compiling. The program does compile, and this proves our reasoning, because had the compiler chosen the `double` method, the return would have been a `double`, and its assignment to an `int` would have been illegal without a cast. □

3.2 A Development Walk-Through

The following sections guide us through the development of our first application. You may have already written a few programs, but now that you understand delegation and contracts and know how to shop for components, you can begin to view software development as a formal process with clearly defined activities and goals.

3.2.1 The Development Process

If you observe a group of software professionals working on a project, you will see that their work goes through five phases, each of which involves certain activities and clearly defined deliverables. In the **analysis** phase (also called the **requirements** phase), you will see **analysts** working closely with the customer in order to define exactly what the sought application is supposed to accomplish. Analysis culminates in two major deliverables: input and validation and output and formatting.

- **Input and Validation** What inputs will the end-user make? For each, what is the **prompt**, and what is the **validation rule**? The prompt is a message that asks the user to make the input and provides any needed details, for example, how to make the entry, what units to use. The validation rule specifies the condition that the input must satisfy and the remedial action that the application should take if the input does not satisfy the condition.

- **Output and Formatting** What output should the application generate, and how should it be **formatted**? The output can be on the screen, on a disk file, or on some other device.

Looking from a very high level of abstraction, the sought application can be viewed as one giant method whose parameters are the application's inputs and whose return is its output. Viewed as such, analysis amounts to describing what this giant method does (not how it does it), and its two deliverables are nothing but the method's contract.

A second phase is **design**, and it involves identifying the needed components and coming up with a series of logical steps for the main class to follow. These steps, called the **algorithm**, activate the components and enable them to achieve the desired output. The algorithm is the deliverable of this phase, and it could be a simple mathematical formula that computes the output from the input or a complex sequence of operations to be carried out by several components. Another phase is **implementation**, in which the algorithm is translated to a main class and the whole application is built. **Testing** and **deployment** are the remaining two phases. We will demonstrate these phases through an example in the following sections, and we will cover them in detail in Chapter 7.

3.2.2 The Mortgage Application

In this section, we simulate a real-world scenario. We are approached by a bank manager, the customer, who is thinking of automating the process of answering queries about mortgages at the branch level. To learn more about the project, our analysts meet with the branch staff and perform a detailed analysis of the requirements.

Analysis

Analysis culminated in the following:

Input

The user supplies the present value (i.e., cash price) of the asset to be mortgaged, the amortization period of the mortgage, and the interest rate. For example, the asset could be a house whose present value is $500 000 and is to be mortgaged over 25 years with an interest rate of 5%. More specifically, analysis revealed the following:

■ The present value must be prompted using the message shown below, and the user's entry (???) should appear one space after it on the same line:

```
Enter the amount... ???
```

■ The entry will be in dollars and cents; hence, it must be represented as a real number. In terms of range, the manager expects the present value to be, in most cases, under $10 000 000. This implies at most 10 significant digits, which is well within the precision of a `double`. When the analysts asked about validation, the manager indicated that the program should not accept a negative entry. No preference toward a particular remedial action was indicated.

■ The amortization period turned out to be fixed at 25 years. The manager said that the bank might decide to change this period in the future, but for the time being, the end-user should not be allowed to change it.

■ The interest rate will be entered as an annual percent; for example, an entry of 2.5 should be interpreted as 2.5% per year. The prompt and input should appear as follows:

```
The annual interest percent... ???
```

In terms of validation, the manager said the program must ensure (in any way it likes) that the entry is positive and less than 100.

Output

The application must output the monthly mortgage payment assuming that the interest is compounded monthly. In terms of formatting, the output should start with a message, as shown below, and should display the payment prefixed with a dollar sign, rounded to the nearest cent, and separated into thousands with commas. For example, if the computed payment were 1522.65945, then the output would be

```
The monthly payment is: $1,522.66
```

This analysis can be expressed formally using the contract language of Chapter 2:

```
Inputs:
amount - the present value
rate - the interest rate as an annual percent
Output:
the formatted monthly payment
Throws:
exception if amount < 0
exception if rate <= 0
exception if rate >= 100
```

Design

We obviously need a formula that connects the input to the output. Our design team came up with the following formula:

$$P = \frac{rA}{1 - \dfrac{1}{(1+r)^n}}$$

where r is the interest rate, A is the present value, and n is the amortization period. In order for P to be a monthly payment and for compounding to be monthly, r has to be the monthly rate, and n has to be measured in months. The formula involves computing a power, and the Math class can handle this. Input is handled using the Scanner class. These two classes, along with the above formula, constitute our algorithm.

Implementation

Rather than implementing all the requirements in one shot, it makes more sense to do so in increments. We will start by ignoring output formatting and input validation and output formatting. Once the program has been tested and is running, we will incorporate these two requirements.

We start by determining the types of the key variables and choosing identifiers for them. The present value is a double, and we will denote it by amount. The interest rate is a double too, and we will denote it by rate. The monthly payment is also a double, and we will denote it by payment. The amortization period (period) is an integer, and as a rule, we always use int for integers unless the range requires a long.

We use the print method to prompt the user for an entry while keeping the cursor on the same line, and we create Scanner and PrintStream instances as per Section 2.2.5:

```
output.print("Enter the amount... ");
double amount = input.nextDouble();
```

The same approach is used for the interest rate:

```
output.print("The annual interest percent... ");
double rate = input.nextDouble();
```

As for the period, we initialize it in the code rather than through user input:

```
int period = 25;
```

Next, we move to computation. To use the formula, we must express the period in months rather than years. Hence we write

```
period = period * 12;
```

Furthermore, the rate must be recognized as a percent (by dividing by 100) and must be made a monthly rate (by dividing by 12). Here are several ways to attempt this:

```
rate = rate / 100 * 12;
rate = rate / (100 / 12);
rate = (rate / 100) / 12;
rate = rate / 100 / 12;
rate = rate / (100 * 12);
```

Convince yourself that the first two attempts are incorrect and that the last three are equivalent. The formula can be computed in one shot, but this makes the computation prone to errors and prevents us from debugging it when things go wrong. Hence, we break the computation into pieces and use temporary (scratch) variables:

```
double numerator = rate * amount;
double denominator = Math.pow(1 + rate, period);
```

```
denominator = 1. - 1. / denominator;
double payment = numerator / denominator;
```

Note that we have included a decimal point to ensure no integer truncation takes place upon division. This is not necessary here because the other operand is real, but in general, be careful whenever / is used. The final task is output:

```
output.print("The monthly payment is: $");
output.println(payment);
```

As written, the program contains a clear violation of a software engineering principle (Section 2.3.2). It uses magic numbers: 25, 12, and 100. We must declare constants and use them instead. The complete app, with properly named finals, is shown in Fig. 3.9.

Here is a sample run of our application:

```
Enter the amount... 285000
The annual interest percent... 3.75
The monthly payment is: $1465.2739188667003
```

Testing and Debugging

Several tests must now be performed, and their results must be compared with computations done on a calculator. If a discrepancy is found, we add print statements to our app so that intermediate results are displayed. This allows us to trace the problem and find its source. Such print statements, called **debugging statements**, do not have to be deleted once the problem is identified; they can simply be turned into a comment (prefixed by two slashes).

3.2.3 Output Formatting

The API of PrintStream lists a method, printf, that can be used to format and output data. We will cover only a subset of the formatting capabilities of this method, and we will stick to this subset throughout. The statements

```
double x = 15.753;
output.printf("%.2f", x);
```

will output 15.75. The first parameter of printf is a string that contains one or more **format specifier**. Each specifier has the form

```
%[flags][width][.precision]conversion
```

The percent sign at the beginning and the conversion letter at the end are mandatory; the elements in between are optional.

- **The Conversion Letter:** The conversion letter can be d, f, s, or n. The letter d is valid if the output is an integer; f is valid if it is a real number; and s is valid if it is a string. We will see the significance of n shortly.
- **The Flag:** The flag can be a comma ',' or a zero '0'. The comma is valid if the output is a number; a comma causes the number to be printed with a thousands separator. The zero is valid if the output is an integer and a width is specified. A zero causes the integer to be right-aligned in a field of zeros.

Figure 3.9 The mortgage application without output formatting or input validation

```java
import java.util.Scanner;
import java.io.PrintStream;

public class Mortgage
{
    public static void main(String[] args)
    {
        Scanner input = new Scanner(System.in);
        PrintStream output = System.out;

        final int AMORTIZATION = 25;
        final int MONTH_PER_YEAR = 12;
        final double PERCENT = 100.0;

        output.print("Enter the amount ... ");
        double amount = input.nextDouble();
        output.print("The annual interest percent ... ");
        double rate = input.nextDouble();

        int period = AMORTIZATION;
        period = period * MONTH_PER_YEAR;
        rate = rate / PERCENT / MONTH_PER_YEAR;
        double numerator = rate * amount;
        double denominator = Math.pow(1 + rate, period);
        denominator = 1. - 1. / denominator;
        double payment = numerator / denominator;

        output.print("The monthly payment is: $");
        output.println(payment);
    }
}
```

- **The Width:** The width specifies the overall number of characters to be printed. If the output requires fewer characters, leading spaces (or zeros if the 0 flag is set) are added and the data is right-aligned in that width.
- **The Precision:** The precision field, which indicates the number of decimals (digits after the decimal point), must be prefixed by a dot. It can be used with f conversions only.

Based on this, the fragment

```java
double x = 12345.255;
output.printf("%,12.2f", x);
```

will output: ■■■12,345.26 (where ■ denotes a space). Note that the output rounds the dropped decimal up if it is greater than or equal to 5.

The specifier `%n` can be used to specify that a new line must be started at this point. For example,

```
output.printf("%,12.2f%n", x);
```

causes a carriage return after the displayed value, similar to `println`. Note that any text that appears before, after, or between specifiers is printed as is. For example,

```
output.printf("Answer:%n(%,.2f)%nDone.", x);
```

leads to the following output:

```
Answer:
(12,345.26)
Done.
```

Back to our project, we refine our app by changing the final output as follows:

```
output.print("The monthly payment is: $");
output.printf("%,.2f%n", payment);
```

The sample run shown earlier becomes

```
Enter the amount... 285000
The annual interest percent... 3.75
The monthly payment is: $1,465.27
```

3.2.4 Relational Operators

Whether arising from validation rules or from the algorithm itself, conditions are quite common in programming, and we need to learn how to express and store them in our programs. We do have a primitive type, `boolean`, capable of storing the result of a condition, but we need a mechanism for expressing conditions, and this is what Java's **relational operators** provide. Each relational operator is a binary infix operator that compares the values of its two operands and culminates in a boolean result. For example,

```
int x = 7;
int y = 5;
boolean z = x < y;
```

The right-hand side of the last assignment includes a relational operator (`<`) and two operands. The operator examines the values of x and y, finds the first not less than the second, and concludes that the result is false. The assignment thus culminates in z having the value `false`. You can add parentheses to the last statement:

```
boolean z = (x < y);
```

but this is not necessary because the assignment operator has the lowest precedence of all operators (its precedence is −15), so it will act after the relational operator. Note that the operator `<` is peculiar compared to operators seen so far in that it does not exhibit closure: its operands are of one type, and its result is of a different type. Java has seven relational operators, and they are shown in Fig. 3.10.

The first four operate on numeric operands only (integers of all sizes, floats, and doubles); the fifth operates on an object reference and a class; and the last two operate on operands of any type (primitive as well as object references). All seven operators culminate in a boolean result.

Programming Tip 3.3

Idiosyncrasy: `printf` precision handling

Keep the following two points in mind when you use the `printf` method:

- **ROUND_HALF_UP instead of ROUND_HALF_EVEN** When a value is to be rounded, we round up if the discarded fraction is greater than 0.5; we round down if the discarded fraction is less than 0.5. What if it is equal to 0.5, that is, halfway in between? In this case, some formatting methods round up (the Round Half Up approach), while others round to the nearest even number (the Round Half Even approach). When rounding a large number of numbers, the latter approach is less likely to change the sum of the numbers because the halfway case is rounded up 50% of the time and rounded down in the other 50%, on average. The `printf` method adopts the Round Half Up approach. For example, if the precision is ".2," then 7.555 and 7.565 become, respectively, 7.56 and 7.57 in `printf`.
- **The case of ".0" precision** In this case, no decimals are printed to the right of the decimal point, but is the decimal point itself printed? The answer is yes if the value being printed has a fractional part; otherwise the answer is no.

In More Depth 3.1

Variable Number of Arguments

Whenever you see the ellipsis separator in the signature of a method, you conclude that you can pass one or more parameters of the same type as the one that has the ellipsis. For example, the hypothetical method

```
int act(double x, int . . . y);
```

takes one parameter of the type `double` and one or more parameters of the type `int`. The API of the `printf` method in J2SE release 5 shows an ellipsis in the second parameter. This implies we can output more than one value with one `printf` statement, that is,

```
int i = 5;
double x = 12.5;
output.printf("i=%d x=%.2f", i, x);
```

The output of this fragment is i=5 x=12.50. This variable argument feature is *not* supported in the `printf` method of the `type.util.PrintStream2`.

3.2.5 Input Validation

Our implementation of the mortgage application ignored **input validation**. Can we leave the program without it? What would happen if one of the inputs were invalid? A close inspection of our program reveals that our program would not crash in that case because the `double` division operator does not trigger an exception. The ensuing logic error would be evident in some cases (the monthly payment is negative or is `NaN`) but would be quite inconspicuous in others. The case below, for example, supplies a negative value for the interest yet the output seems legitimate.

Figure 3.10 The relational operators in Java (the arrow indicates association)

```
Enter the amount... 1000000
The annual interest percent... -5
The monthly payment is: $1,667.02
```

Precedence	Operator	Operands	Syntax	true if
−7→	<	numeric	x < y	x is less than y
	<=	numeric	x <= y	x is less than or equal to y
	>	numeric	x > y	x is greater than y
	>=	numeric	x >= y	x is greater than or equal to y
	instanceof	x instanceof C is true if object reference x points at an instance of class C or a subclass of C.		
−8→	==	any type	x == y	x is equal to y
	!=	any type	x != y	x is not equal to y

Programming Tip   3.4

Pitfall: Testing equality of real numbers

The following statement, attempting to detect the equality of two `double` variables, may *not* work because of round-off errors:

```
boolean equal = x == y;
```

A better approach would be to test whether the two values are close to each other within a small tolerance that depends on the application's context; for example,

```
final double EPSILON = 1.E-5;
boolean equal = Math.abs(x - y) < EPSILON;
```

If the user meant to enter 5 in the above example, then the correct payment would be $5845.90. This example makes it clear that input validation cannot be overemphasized; in fact, the majority of runtime and logic errors in programs arise from inputs that were not properly validated.

But what should a program do if an input is invalid? There are generally three options:

- **Message:** Terminate the program and display a message.
- **Friendly:** Explain the problem and ask the user to re-enter.
- **Exception:** Trigger an appropriate runtime error, that is, crash.

We are not in a position at this time to implement any of these because the first two require selection and loops, covered in Chapter 5, while the last requires exceptions, covered in Chapter 11. Until then, we will delegate to a method that implements the last option; it causes a crash. The crash method of the type.lib.ToolBox class has the following header:

```
static void crash(boolean, String)
```

If the passed boolean is `false`, the method returns without doing anything. Otherwise, it triggers a runtime error whose message is the passed string parameter. For example, the statement

```
ToolBox.crash(amount < 0, "A negative amount!");
```

will throw an exception if `amount` is negative. In that case, the program will terminate, and the displayed error message will include the message "A negative amount!" along with the line number of the statement that invoked the `crash` method.

Now that we know how to take remedial actions, let us refine our mortgage application by incorporating input validation. The validation rules are

```
amount is not negative and rate is in (0,100)
```

In this textbook, we specify an interval that extends from *a* to *b* by writing *a,b* surrounded by square brackets, parentheses, or both. A square bracket at one end means the interval includes that end. A parenthesis at one end, however, means the interval excludes that end. For example, [0,100) includes 0 but excludes 100; [0,100] includes both end values; and (0,100) excludes both end values. Using relational operators, we can express these rules as three conditions:

Java Details 3.3

Throwing Exceptions Using the Standard Java Library

If you prefer to use the standard Java library, you will need to replace

```
ToolBox.crash(condition, message);
```

with

```
if (condition)
{
    throw new RuntimeException(message);
}
```

```
amount >= 0
rate > 0
rate < 100
```

We can therefore validate by adding three statements to our program:

```
ToolBox.crash(amount < 0, "A negative amount!");
ToolBox.crash(rate <= 0, "A non-positive rate!");
ToolBox.crash(rate >= PERCENT, "Invalid rate!");
```

The newer version of the application is shown in Fig. 3.11.

This version is certainly more robust and is in the spirit of Section 2.3.1: early exposure. If an erroneous input can eventually lead to a logic error, turn it into a runtime error. To the end-user, runtime errors may be frustrating, but at least they are visible.

3.2.6 Assertions

An **assertion** is a programming construct that expresses the programmer's conviction that something is true. For example, the last line of the fragment

```
int x = 5;
int y = x;
// I assert that y is equal to 5
```

expresses the programmer's confidence about something. This assertion can be made executable by writing

```
assert y == 5;
```

The `assert` statement does nothing if its condition is met but causes a runtime error if it is not. As usual, the runtime error message will report the line number of the `assert` statement that failed.

From a software engineering point of view, it is a good habit to use the `assert` statement whenever you believe that something is true, either because it is under your control and you arranged for it to be true, or it is not under your control but a contract guaranteed it to be true. If your assumption is correct, you lose nothing by asserting it; if it is not, you would mitigate a risk by exposing it early. If an assertion fails, then either your reasoning was incorrect or a contract that you relied on was broken (it did not meet its postcondition).

In our mortgage application, and after incorporating input validation, it is clear that the computed monthly payment will always be non-negative. Hence, it makes sense to add the following statement to our program:

```
assert payment >= 0;
```

Do not confuse assertion with input validation, or equivalently, `assert` with `crash`. Both can trigger a runtime error but with different implications: `assert` is indicative of an inconsistency in your reasoning or a failure in a delegate, that is, something totally unexpected. `crash` implies that the user made a mistake, that is, something that was foreseen and guarded against.

```java
import java.util.Scanner;
import java.io.PrintStream;
import type.lib.ToolBox;

public class Mortgage
{
    public static void main(String[] args)
    {
        Scanner input = new Scanner(System.in);
        PrintStream output = System.out;

        final int AMORTIZATION = 25;
        final int MONTH_PER_YEAR = 12;
        final double PERCENT = 100.0;

        output.print("Enter the amount ... ");
        double amount = input.nextDouble();
        ToolBox.crash(amount < 0, "A negative amount!");
        output.print("The annual interest percent ... ");
        double rate = input.nextDouble();
        ToolBox.crash(rate <= 0, "A non-positive rate!");
        ToolBox.crash(rate >= PERCENT, "Invalid rate!");

        int period = AMORTIZATION;
        period = period * MONTH_PER_YEAR;
        rate = rate / PERCENT / MONTH_PER_YEAR;
        double numerator = rate * amount;
        double denominator = Math.pow(1 + rate, period);
        denominator = 1. - 1. / denominator;
        double payment = numerator / denominator;

        output.print("The monthly payment is: $");
        output.printf("%,.2f", payment);

    }
}
```

Java Details   3.4

By default, assertions are not enabled by the VM at runtime. Even if the assertion condition is met, the program will not crash. In order to enable assertions you need to add a switch when the app is launched, as follows:

```
java -ea App
```

The switch "ea" stands for "Enable Assertions." The idea here is that during development, the app is run with assertions enabled in order to expose any logical error. Once development is complete and the app reaches production, assertions are disabled (which is the default), and this speeds up execution (because the condition is not checked). Later, if runtime or logic errors are reported, assertions can be re-enabled without the need to recompile.

3.3 General Characteristics of Utility Classes

In the following sections, we take an in-depth look at utility classes, classes that cannot be instantiated. Even though there are very few such classes in the Java standard library, we will find that it is instructive to learn about them.

3.3.1 Memory Diagram

The features of a utility class are all static; hence, they are accessed/invoked on the class. A statement containing the class-dot-feature syntax can be thought of as dialling a phone/extension pair, but what really happens behind the scenes when such a statement is executed?

Programming Tip   3.5

Pitfall: Using `assert` to validate input

You should not use assertion to validate user input. From a theoretical point of view, an assertion is meant for something of which we are 100% certain; input validity does not qualify for that. From a practical point of view, assertions can be turned off, and we certainly do not want input validation in our programs to be skipped.

Java Details 3.5

Errors and Exceptions

The distinction between assertion and input validation manifests itself in the type of runtime error that each triggers. `assert` leads to an `Error`, whereas `crash` leads to an `Exception`. The difference between these two terms will be clarified in Chapter 11.

In More Depth 3.2

Input Validity as a Precondition

We mentioned earlier that one could think of the entire project as a giant method and of analysis as a contract. In this view, the validity of the input becomes a condition that the contract must enforce. We found in Chapter 2 that when the input of a method must satisfy a certain condition, we can either make it a precondition (and thus leave it to the client) or let the implementer check it (and throw an exception if not met). Why did we choose the latter option in our discussion of input validation; that is, why not leave input validity as a precondition?

In a perfect world, where users do not mistype and do not misunderstand prompts, one can indeed skip input validation and trust that the user will always supply valid input. In the real world, however, doing so could lead to terrible consequences and is therefore never adopted. The only time you can entertain relying on preconditions is when the client is a program, not a human being.

Consider an application that computes the area of a circle. It does so by using a field and a method in the `Math` class, as shown in Fig. 3.12.

Class Compilation

When a class such as `Circle` in Fig. 3.12 is compiled, the compiler assumes that it will be loaded one day in memory beginning at address zero. Hence, it assigns an address to every variable and instruction in it based on this zero-offset assumption. The instructions are assigned consecutive addresses based on their order in the program. The `radius` variable, for example, may end up residing in a block that begins at address 16, and every reference to that variable will be replaced with 16. The generated class file is then stored on disk. The same process applies when a component is compiled. For example, when the `Math` class was compiled, everything in it was assigned an address, starting from zero. For example, the `PI` field may have been assigned the address 24, and the `pow` method may have been assigned the address 80.

Class Loading

When the application is launched, the class files are loaded into memory. For each class, the operating system (O/S) (thanks to the Memory Manager of Section 2.3.4) will look for an area

```
import java.util.Scanner;
import java.io.PrintStream;


public class Circle
{
    public static void main(String[] args)
    {
        Scanner input = new Scanner(System.in);
        PrintStream output = System.out;
        output.print("Enter radius: ");
        int radius = input.nextInt();
        output.println(Math.PI * Math.pow(radius, 2));
    }
}
```

Figure 3.12 An application for demonstrating class loading

in memory big enough to hold the class, and populate it with its data and instructions. There is no guarantee where this area might begin, but it most certainly does not begin at zero, as the compiler assumed, because this is where the O/S itself resides. Furthermore, the area may move, from one launch to the next, based on what other programs are in memory. Let us assume that our main class ended up in a block that begins at address 64 and that the Math class was loaded at 800. Figure 3.13 depicts memory after both classes were loaded.

Since neither class was loaded at zero, all compiler-assigned addresses need to be shifted up. For example, the variable radius whose compiler-assigned address is 16 will in fact occupy the block at address 80. Similarly, the PI attribute of the Math class will be associated with the block at address 824. Hence, the expression

Math.PI

should be evaluated by looking up the block at 824, not 24. This example provides insight into the dot syntax. Math.PI means: "go first to address 800 and count 24 cells from there." You can think of the Math class as a page in a book and PI as a line on that page. The dot

Figure 3.13 The memory diagram of an application made up of a main class and a utility. For each class, the compiler adopts a zero-offset convention when assigning addresses.

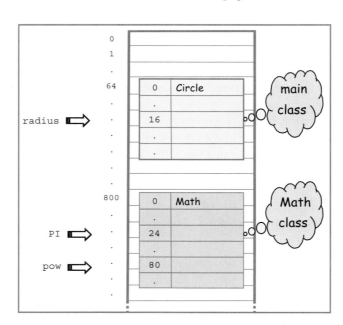

separator translates "page 8, line 24 (assume 100 lines per page)" into "line 824 relative to the beginning of the book." It is this merging of addresses that allows programs written at different times and compiled on different machines to run together and communicate as if they were all written as a single class.

Rather than showing the compiler-assigned address as well as the actual (shifted) address, from now on we will only show the actual address when we draw memory diagrams. Hence, Fig. 3.13 will be redrawn as shown in Fig. 3.14.

Figure 3.14 This is the same diagram as that in Fig. 3.13, but it does not depict compiler-assigned addresses.

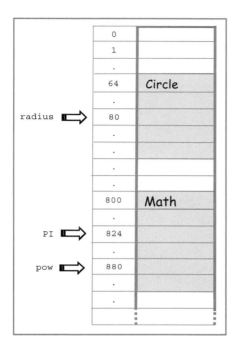

You can think of Fig. 3.14 as a placement of UML class diagrams (introduced in Section 2.1.1) in memory.

3.3.2 Advantages of Utility Classes

We found in Chapter 2 that utility classes are not as versatile as object-oriented classes because all their features are static; hence, they can hold only one state at a time. Nevertheless, it is instructive to learn about these classes because of the following points.

Simplicity

It is simpler to read the API of a utility class because the constructor section is absent. It is also easy to use a utility since all features are invoked on the class. And since there is only one copy of a utility class in memory, it is easier to visualize class loading, and this paves the way to understanding the more elaborate memory diagrams of object-oriented classes.

Suitability

There are situations in which a utility is the natural choice. For example, a group of related methods that do not hold state is ideally placed in a utility because it does not make sense to incur the overhead of instantiation when all the instances are identical. These situations, albeit rare, do occur. For example, the Java standard library includes the following utility classes:

```
java.lang.Math
java.lang.System
java.net.URLEncoder
java.util.Arrays
java.util.Collections
```

Moreover, learning about utilities allows us to understand the static features of object-oriented classes (ones that must be instantiated). These features are common to all instances of an object-oriented class and behave exactly like the features of a utility in terms of access and invocation. For example, the class

```
java.lang.Integer
```

is *not* a utility, yet it has static fields and methods; hence, they can be used without instantiating the class. Two of the fields are

```
static int MAX_VALUE
static int MIN_VALUE
```

The first holds the largest positive integer that an int can hold, and the second holds the smallest such value. As you may have guessed from the letter case, both are final. One of the methods in the class is

```
static int parseInt(String)
```

It takes a string containing an integer, for example, `"123"`, converts it into an `int`, and returns it. We can use this method, for example, as follows:

```
int x = Integer.parseInt("123");
output.println(x);
```

The method's contract states that if the string cannot be converted to an `int`, then an exception will be thrown.

The `Integer` class is called a **wrapper** because it wraps a class around the primitive type `int`. There is a wrapper class for every primitive type (`Byte`, `Short`, etc.). You will find similar `static` features in their APIs.

3.3.3 CASE STUDY

Dialog Input/Output

In addition to console I/O, your application can use dialogs to communicate with the end user. A **dialog** is a window that pops in the middle of the screen and either displays a message for the user to see or asks the user to make an entry or a selection. When a dialog is displayed, the user cannot ignore it and continue interacting with the application through the console. Because of this, dialogs are meant for very important messages only, not as a replacement of console I/O.

The `JOptionPane` class in the `javax.swing` package has several static methods that provide a number of dialogs. We will take a look at two of them as examples of utilities. The remaining dialogs can be used in a similar way. Consult the class API for details.

Displaying a Message

You can display a string by using an invocation similar to this:

```
JOptionPane.showMessageDialog(null,
"Hello!");
```

The first parameter should be `null` for all console applications, that is, applications that do not have a graphical user interface. When this dialog is displayed, the user must click its OK button before the application resumes.

Prompting for and Reading Input

You can display a dialog that contains a prompt and a space in which the user can enter something. The dialog interprets the user's entry as a string and returns it as such. If you want to re-interpret the entry as some primitive type, use the parse method of the wrapper class that corresponds to that type.

Here is an example:

```
int height = Integer.parseInt(
JOptionPane.showInputDialog(
null, "Enter the height:"));
```

The first parameter should be `null` (since we deal only with console applications), and the second is the prompt. The method returns the entry as a string, and we feed the return directly to the parse method of the `Integer` class.

Summary of Key Concepts

1. The **class API** contains everything a client needs to know in order to use the class. The **archive API** is a documentation of all classes in an archive, and it provides links to the individual class APIs within the archive.

2. The class API has four parts: **class section**, **constructor section**, **field section**, and the **method section**.

3. The field and method sections have two parts each: **summary** and **detail**.

4. Parameters in Java are **passed by value**. This means only their values are sent to the invoked method. Other languages provide **pass by reference** in which the address is sent. Passing by value is safer because methods cannot change variables local to the calling program.

5. **Overloaded** methods reside in the same class and have the same name. They must differ in their parameter count or type since signature is unique in a class.

6. When the compiler encounters a method invocation, it must locate the method, and this is called **binding** (or early **binding**). Binding is a three-step process that involves finding the class, finding the method, and selecting the **most specific** method that best suits the invocation.

7. The **development process** has five phases: **analysis** (or **requirements**), **design**, **implementation**, **testing**, and **deployment**.

8. Analysis culminates in identifying **input** (**prompt** and **validation**) and **output** (and its **formatting**).

9. Design culminates in an **algorithm**, a sequence of steps that the main class follows as it delegates to components.

10. Testing may reveal logic errors, in which case we add **debugging statements** to the program in order to print intermediate calculations.

11. Output formatting is done through the `printf` method of the `PrintStream` class. Its first parameter is a string that contains **format specifiers**, codes that specify how the output parameter should be formatted.

12. **Relational operators** compare the values of their two operands and culminate accordingly in a true or false result.

13. Input invalidity is the main source of runtime and logic errors. Programs must **validate** their inputs. If an input is found invalid, the program must print a message and terminate, ask the user to re-enter, or crash.

14. **Assertion** is done in Java through the `assert` keyword. Assertion is meant to express, in an executable manner, the programmer's conviction of the correctness of something. If an assertion fails, then either the programmer made an inconsistent argument or a contract was broken.

15. When a class is compiled, each feature in it picks up an address. The compiler assigns these addresses by assuming (incorrectly) that the class will be loaded beginning at address zero.

16. When an app uses a feature in a utility, the virtual machine determines the actual address of the feature by combining the starting address of the utility, determined at runtime, with the compiler-assigned address of the feature, determined at compile-time.

17. There is a **wrapper** class for every primitive type. Among other benefits, it provides static final fields and static methods.

18. In addition to the console, applications can interact with the user through a **dialog**. Dialogs are not suitable as a replacement for console I/O. The **JOptionPane** class is a utility that provides several dialogs for displaying messages, reading input, or asking the user to make a choice.

Review Questions

1. What is the difference between a class and an archive API?

2. How do you determine the package in which a class resides given the API of its archive (and assuming there is only one such class)?

3. What are the main parts of a class API?

4. How can you determine whether a field in a given class is static?

5. How can you determine whether a field in a given class is final without relying on the letter case and the naming convention?

6. Does the API reveal the value of a final field? Do you consider this a breaking of the encapsulation?

7. Do you need to see the Method Detail to be able to determine the return of a method?

8. Do you need to see the Method Detail to be able to determine the contract of a method?

9. How can you tell whether a method is overloaded?

10. Where do you look to determine whether a method is void?

11. Why is it not possible to have in a class two methods with the same signature but different returns?

12. What are the steps taken during binding? Is the "most specific" rule applicable always or only if overloading is involved?

13. What are the main phases of the development process?

14. Who determines the prompt of each input, the analyst or the customer?

15. Who determines the type of each input, the implementer or the customer?

16. What are the two main deliverables of the analysis phase?

17. Which phase is critically dependent on the fact that the application will be written in Java (as opposed to some other object-oriented language)?

18. Why is output formatting important to the customer?

19. Explain, using an example, how the `printf` method works.

20. What are relational operators? How many such operators are there in Java?

21. Which operator has higher precedence: addition or less than?

22. How should the program react if an input is invalid?

23. Explain how the `crash` method can be used for input validation.

24. Explain how the `assert` method works and how it is different from the `crash` method.

25. Why should input validity not be treated as an assertion?

26. When a class is compiled, how does the compiler know where in memory the class will be loaded?

27. When a method invocation is executed, how does the computer know where in memory a method is located?

28. Why are most classes not utilities?

29. State one class in the Java standard library that is a utility.

30. How do you know whether a class is a utility given its API?

A Development Project

■ L3.1 A Guided Tour of an API

Follow these steps to explore the Java API.

- Launch your browser, and visit the Java API. Maximize the window, and take a close look at the structure of its contents. As we move closer to component-based programming, learning how to read and comprehend APIs will become the key programming skill.

- Notice that the screen is divided into three panes: (1) the upper-left pane lists the packages, (2) the pane below pane (1) lists the classes, and (3) the (large) pane to the right has descriptions. The three panes are "synchronized": if you click on a package in (1), only its classes will be listed in (2), and if you click on a class or a package in (2), only its description will be shown in (3). Spend some time familiarizing yourself with the navigation.

- Descriptions in (3) are available at the class level, package level, or all package levels. To choose, you click a class name, a package name, or the *Overview* link at the top, respectively.

- Click (in the upper-left pane) on the `java.lang` package so that its classes are listed in the lower-left pane. Click on the `Math` class, and examine its description in the right pane. It starts with an unstructured textual description of the class followed by two structures (each identified by a blue banner): *Field Summary* and *Method Summary*. These two blocks reappear afterward as *Field Detail* and *Method Detail*.

- The first field listed in the *Field Summary* is E. The left column describes this field as `static`. This, as we shall see, has a profound effect on how this field is accessed. If you do not see this word in the left column, then the field is not static. The left column also indicates that the type of this field is `double`. The type of data that a field can hold could be primitive or nonprimitive. Nonprimitive types, such as `String`, are in fact class names, and for that reason, their very first character is capitalized and their name is fully qualified, for example, `java.lang.String`.

- What can you say about the second field, PI? Is it `static`? What is its type?

- It is not a coincidence that all fields are `static`. In this lab we are focusing on classes with static features (utilities). Most classes are not like that, and we will turn to nonstatic fields and methods in the next lab.

- Look at the Method Summary. The method `random()`, for example, does not take parameters (because there is nothing between the parentheses), while `rint` (which appears after it) does take a parameter (a `double`).

- The name of a method together with the number, order, and types of its parameters is its *signature*. The signature of `rint` is `rint(double)`.

- It is OK for two or more methods in a class to have the same name as long as their signatures are different. In this case, we say that the method is *overloaded*. For example, the `max` method is heavily overloaded.

- The left column indicates whether the method is `static`. If there is no indication, then the method is not static. All methods in this class are static.
- Unlike fields, methods do *not* store data and, hence, do not have types. Some methods, however, return data and can therefore be indirectly associated with types. The `rint` method, for example, returns a `double`, which is why the API gives it this type in the left column. If a method does not return any data, the API describes it (in the left column) as `void`.

Static fields and methods are the easiest to use: all you need is to precede the name (of the field or method you want to use) by the name of the class and a dot. We say that we invoke them *on* the class. For example, the `E` field of `Math` can be accessed via

```
Math.E
```

Its content can be retrieved and stored in a local variable by writing

```
double x = Math.E;
```

Similarly for methods, to invoke a method such as `pow`, which computes the result of raising a number to another, you would write

```
Math.pow(2, 3);
```

This computes 2^3, or 8. The parameters you pass must be compatible with the types declared in the signature. Note that automatic promotion applies to parameters. The above example is correct even though there is no method with signature:

```
pow(int, int)
```

This is because the compiler will bind the above invocation with

```
pow(double, double)
```

L3.2 A Software Project

We will follow the formal software development process to approach our first project.

Analysis

In this phase, we need to determine *what* the project is all about and specify *exactly* its input and output. After meeting with the customer, our analyst determined that the sought system should be able to convert temperature from Fahrenheit to Celsius. The input must be prompted with the message

```
Enter the temperature in Fahrenheit
```

The entry is made on the next line; it is a whole number that is not less than −250. If the entry is not a whole number, an exception should occur. If the entry is not in range, a runtime error with the message *Value out of range* should occur. The output consists of one line containing, from left to right, the following elements separated by a space: the entered temperature, the letter "F," an equal sign, the corresponding Celsius temperature rounded to one decimal, and the letter "C." Here is a sample run of the proposed system:

```
Enter the temperature in Fahrenheit
55
55 F = 12.8 C
```

Design

In this phase, we make a plan for *how* the system will accomplish its goals by breaking the problem into tasks and identifying the classes and methods responsible for each. The tasks in our project are the following: printing to the screen, reading from the user, converting, and formatting. Before developing a method for each, a good Java designer starts by searching the market to see if a class containing some of the needed methods is already available. Indeed, the ready-made classes `Scanner` and `PrintStream` contain methods for reading input and for writing and formatting output. This leaves the conversion issue, and our physics textbook says that to convert a temperature *f* in Fahrenheit to a corresponding one *c* in Celsius, we use the following formula:

```
c = 5 ( f - 32 ) / 9
```

Hence, all we need to develop ourselves is an app (`Lab3`) that invokes the needed services and performs the conversion.

Implementation

In this phase, we write and compile the `Lab3`. We need a local variable to hold the number entered by the user. Since this is a whole number, we will declare it to be of the `int` type. We must give it a name that describes its content (a temperature in degrees Fahrenheit) and that abides by our style guide. This leads us to the declaration

```
int tempF;
```

We also allocate a second variable to hold the temperature after the conversion. Since the formula yields a real number, we will declare it as `double`:

```
double tempC;
```

The conversion formula also involves the constants 5, 9, and 32. It is possible to incorporate them directly in a Java expression, without allocating variables for them, but that would violate our coding style, which dictates that no magic numbers (except 0, 1, and 2) may appear in expressions. Hence, we declare them like other variables, but we also state that they are constants by using the keyword `final`:

```
final int ZERO_SHIFT = -32;
final double SCALE_FACTOR = 5.0 / 9.0;
```

We gave each a meaningful name and type and used all caps (and an underscore to separate words) as per our coding style for constants. Using these variables, we can perform the conversion using the following assignment statement:

```
tempC = SCALE_FACTOR * (tempF + ZERO_SHIFT);
```

This leaves I/O, validation, and formatting. Complete the development of this application.

Testing

We will use *black box* testing to establish confidence in the correctness of our program. This means we pretend that we do not know how the program is written, only that it takes an input and produces an output. We supply various input cases to it, examine the output for each, and compare it with what we deem to be the correct answer. Here are our findings for valid test cases (ones that abide by the validation rules specified in the analysis):

- Normal cases: 32 and 212
- The program produced the correct answers.
- Extreme & boundary cases: −249 and −250
- The program produced the correct answers.

And here are our findings for test cases involving various invalid inputs:

- Out of range: −251 and −600
- The program produced the specified error message.
- Fractional: 7.5, −12.4, and 0.5
- The program generated a run-time error: `NumberFormatException`
- Non-numeric: testing, +32, and 2020CSE
- The program generated a run-time error: `NumberFormatException`

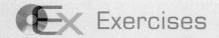 Exercises

Programming exercises are indicated with an asterisk.

3.1 Visit the Java API. (A link to it was added to your browser in Lab 2.) One of the classes is called `Color`. (a) In which package does this class reside? (b) Is this a utility class? (c) One of the fields in this class is called `"blue"`. Is this field final?

3.2 Visit the Java API. (A link to it was added to your browser in Lab 2.) (a) In which package does the `Currency` class reside? (b) Is this a utility class?
Hint: The absence of a constructor section is necessary but not sufficient for the class to be a utility. Check whether all the features are `static`.

3.3 Visit the Java API. (A link to it was added to your browser in Lab 2.) Two of the classes are called `Date`. (a) How can there be two classes with the same name? (b) If such a name were referenced in a program, how would the compiler know which one to bind with? (c) Is the `compareTo` method in `java.util.Date` overloaded?

3.4 Visit the Java API. (A link to it was added to your browser in Lab 2.) One of the classes is called `Double`. (a) In which package does this class reside? (b) Write a short program to output the values of its `MAX_VALUE` and `NaN` fields.

3.5 Visit the Java API. (A link to it was added to your browser in Lab 2.) One of the classes is called `File`. One of the fields in this class is called `separatorChar`. (a) Is it `final`? (b) Is it properly named? (c) What is its significance (what does it hold)? (d) Write a short program that outputs its value.

3.6 Visit the Java API. (A link to it was added to your browser in Lab 2.) One of the classes is called `Math`. (a) In which package does this class reside? (b) Is this a utility class? (c) One of the fields in this class is called "E". Write a short program to output its value.

3.7 The API of `java.lang.Math` lists several methods named `min`. Given that one of them takes two `long` arguments, is there a need for the one that takes two `ints`? In other words, if a program uses the two-`int` method, can we remove this method from the `Math` class without modifying the program?

3.8 Consider the fragment

```
final double LIMIT = 5;
double z = Math.abs(LIMIT);
```

Argue that the fragment might have not compiled successfully had Java allowed parameters to be passed by reference.

3.9 What is the purpose of the `gc` method in `java.lang.system`?

3.10 Bind the invocation `Math.round(2.5)`. Write a short program that proves your binding.

Note: In all the exercises, it is assumed that a `Scanner` instance with reference `input` has been created as explained in Section 2.2.5.

3.11* Consider the fragment

```
byte x = (byte) 5;
byte y = (byte) 7;
output.println(Math.min(x, y));
```

The `min` method is overloaded. With which method will the compiler bind this invocation? How can you prove that your answer is correct? In particular, prove that it will not bind it with `min(long, long)` by compiling and running the fragment. You may modify the fragment in order to construct a proof.

3.12* The `java.lang.Math` class has a method called `round` which rounds a `double` to a `long`. How is this different from simply casting the `double` to `long`? Write a short program that reads a `double` and computes and outputs the `long` both ways.

3.13* Given a `double`, how do you extract its integer part? There seem to be five different ways to do this: cast it to an `int` or pass it to one of four methods in the `Math` class: `ceil`, `floor`, `rint`, `round`. Write an app, and show sample runs that clearly demonstrate the difference between these five approaches.

3.14 Provide a critique of the following fragment:

```
int x = input.nextInt();
ToolBox.crash(x <= 0, "Invalid!");
int y = input.nextInt();
ToolBox.crash(y <= 0, "Invalid!");
boolean z = (x < y);
```

```
boolean t = (x >= y);
assert z != t;
```

In particular, identify the statements that implement input validation and those that implement assertion. Furthermore, explain how any assertion can be made without knowing the values of x and y at program time.

3.15 Consider the fragment

```
int x = 5;
int y = -4;
boolean z = x + y < 0;
```

Is the syntax in the last statement correct? How is its expression evaluated?

3.16 Consider the fragment

```
int x = 5;
int y = x++;
boolean z = x != y;
```

What is the value of z?

3.17 The main class of an application contains the statement

```
output.println(Integer.MAX_VALUE + Math.PI);
```

(a) Show that aside from the I/O classes, three classes will co-exist in memory when this application is launched. (b) Draw a memory diagram that depicts the three classes using arbitrary addresses for their blocks. (c) Show where the MAX_VALUE field resides in memory, and explain how its address is computed.

3.18* Write the Lab3 program in full (with formatting and validation). Make sure your program is free from magic numbers.

3.19* A few months after delivery, the customer of the Lab3 program requested an output modification: both temperatures must now be printed with a thousands separator; for example, 123456 must be printed as 123,456. The Celsius temperature must remain rounded to one decimal. Implement this change.

Note: Do not delete the original program when making modifications because the customer may later revert. Instead, save the original program under a new name, perhaps Lab32, and modify the copy.

3.20* A few months after delivery, the customer of the Lab3 program requested an output modification: the Fahrenheit temperature must be printed right-aligned in a field of 7 characters. For example, if the Fahrenheit temperature is equal to 45, then it appears in the output preceded by 5 blanks. In other words, the letter "F" always appears at column 9 (after the field of 7 and the space).

3.21* Modify the original Lab3 program so that it *tests itself* as follows: after it generates the output line, it takes the computed value of *tempC,* converts it back to Fahrenheit, and prints the result. Does it reproduce the original temperature? Does your answer change if the input is 999999? If the input is 1000000?

3.22* Modify the original Lab3 program so that its I/O is done through dialogs rather than the console.

3.23 The web site for this book contains a collection of tests. You are now in position to take Test A, which covers Chapters 1 to 3. Follow these steps:

- Print and read the outline of the test. It tells you what kind of questions will be on the test, how they are weighted, and what aids are allowed.
- Print the test and take it. Do not use any book or API, and ensure that you do not exceed the allotted time.
- After taking the test, read the answers, and use their marking guidelines to mark your own test.

eCheck

Check03A (TS = 16)

Implement the project described in this lab using the app name Check03A. Here are more sample runs:

```
Enter the temperature in Fahrenheit
76
76 F = 24.4 C
Enter the temperature in Fahrenheit
-5
-5 F = -20.6 C
Enter the temperature in Fahrenheit
112
112 F = 44.4 C
Enter the temperature in Fahrenheit
212
212 F = 100.0 C
```

Once you are comfortable with the app behaviour, run it through eCheck.

Check03B (TS = 21)

Given the altitude of a satellite above Earth's surface, Check03B computes the satellite's orbital period, that is, the time it takes the satellite to make one complete revolution around Earth.

Requirements analysis revealed that your system should prompt for, and input on the same line, the altitude in kilometres (a whole number) without any validation. It should then output, on one line, the computed period in hours (whole number), minutes (whole number), and seconds (one decimal), exactly as shown in these three sample runs:

```
Enter the satellite altitude in km ... 1000
***********************************************
Orbital period = 1 hours, 45 minutes, and 5.7 seconds.
Enter the satellite altitude in km ... 35800
***********************************************
```

```
        Orbital period = 23 hours, 56 minutes, and 29.0 seconds.

        Enter the satellite altitude in km ... 500000
        ************************************************
        Orbital period = 995 hours, 56 minutes, and 21.1 seconds.
```

The design team discovered the following formula, which computes the period *P* (in seconds) in terms of the altitude *A* (in kilometres), where *K* = 0.00995 is the Kepler constant and *R* = 6378 is the radius of Earth (in kilometres):

$$P = K (A + R)^{3/2}$$

Follow the same guidelines as was done for Lab3. You may want to consider the following hints:

- ■ The `pow` and `floor` methods in the `Math` class may be useful.
- ■ The / operator between two integers gives the quotient; % gives the remainder.
- ■ If x is a `double` and k is an `int`, then the cast

  `k = (int) x;`

  stores in k the integer part of x.

Recall that `eCheck` defines correctness relative to specification, not to some subjective measure of goodness. It may consider your app incorrect even if the "important" or "non-cosmetic" part of it is correct.

Check03C (TS = 16)

The `ToolBox` class of the `type.lib` package has a method named `MortgagePayment`. Read its contract and then use it to create the `Check03C` app which behaves as shown in the following sample run:

```
        Mortgage amount: 100000
        Annual interest percent: 3
        Number of years: 5
        Monthly payment = 1,796.87
        Total of all payments = 107,812.14
```

Unlike the app developed in the chapter, `Check03C` should not perform the computation itself; it should instead delegate to the above method. The last line of the output is obtained by multiplying the monthly payment by the total number of months. Note the formatting of the two dollar amounts: rounding to the nearest cent and a thousand separator (the comma). Both can be achieved using `printf`.

Develop your app, test it, and then eCheck it.

Check03D (TS = 16)

The `ToolBox` class of the `type.lib` package has a method named `factorial`. Read its API and use it to create `Check03D` which behaves as shown in the following sample run:

```
Enter an integer ... 18
18! = 6,402,373,705,728,000
Cubic Root of 18 = 3
```

You can assume that the entry is not negative and is below 25. Note that both outputs are rounded to zero decimals and use a thousand separator. Note also that while you can use the `pow` method of the `Math` class to compute the cubic root, It is *not* recommended that you do so because of the round-off involved in expressing 1/3. Instead, look in the API of the `Math` class for a different method that can compute the cubic root.

Develop your app, test it, and then eCheck it.

4

Using Objects

Programming with objects requires a particular point of view: we need to think of objects as autonomous entities. To develop this point of view, we follow an object's lifetime, from beginning to end, and analyze the associated syntax, expose the underlying memory model, and bring into focus the critical difference between an object and a reference. As we become familiar with treating objects as autonomous, we will come to recognize the importance of protecting their privacy. This allows us to understand the rationale behind controlling access to their internal states.

Learning Objectives

1. View objects from an abstraction perspective

2. Learn about the APIs of classes with constructors

3. Gain a thorough understanding of object creation

4. Distinguish objects from their references

5. Become familiar with accessors and mutators

6. Appreciate the importance of attribute privacy

7. Use static features in nonutility classes

Chapter Outline

4.1 What Is an Object?

We first encountered objects in Section 2.1.3 while discussing delegation, and then in Section 3.1.1 in the context of APIs. The coverage in both sections was brief, however, because we wanted to understand the notions of classes and APIs first. Now that we do, we will take an in-depth look at objects in terms of their roles as building blocks and their API features.

4.1.1 An Abstraction View

We arrived at objects in Chapter 2 by evolving the concept of delegation: we delegated methods to a class, then delegated data, and in order to support multiple entities, we envisioned copying the class and called each copy an object.

This reasoning can be reversed, and objects can be thought of as the starting point. Everything can be seen as an object, an entity with some data characteristics, which are the attributes, and some behavioural characteristics, which are the methods. Your car, for example, is an object. Its colour, make, and body type are its attributes; the ability to start, to accelerate, and to turn left and right are its methods. Note that an attribute and the value of an attribute are two different things. If your car is red, then "red" is not an attribute; it is the value of the "colour" attribute. The values of all the attributes of an object are known collectively as the **state** of that object. When we see objects with the same set of attributes and methods, we distinguish them through their states. For example, when we look down the street and see many cars, they all have the same attributes and methods. However, we can easily tell them apart because they probably have different states. But what if two objects have the same attributes, methods, and state? Can we still distinguish them? The answer is yes because we also associate an **identity** with each object and insist that it is unique. Even if two cars are identical, we affix different licence plates on them or find some other way of distinguishing them, in order to preserve the identity of each.

The above discussion can be summarized by saying that the world we live in is made up of objects, and each object has four characteristics: attributes, methods, state, and identity. Confronted with a multitude of such objects, we resort to abstraction to reduce the complexity: we replace each set of objects with the same attributes and methods with just one entity with those attributes and methods. In other words, we treat state and identity as irrelevant details and ignore them. The entity is called a class, and we can now think of the world as made up of classes. The process is depicted in Fig. 4.1, in which nine car objects are replaced with an abstraction of a car, a class.

We will see in Chapter 9 that this abstraction can be layered by replacing classes with nearly similar features with one superclass, which leads to an even simpler view of the world. As suggested in Fig. 4.1, the abstraction process can be reversed through the instantiation: given a class, we can re-create an object that the class abstracts by copying the class and augmenting it with state and identity. We will see in this chapter that the new keyword, the class constructor, and the object reference work together to realize the instantiation mechanism.

Figure 4.1 By ignoring identity and state, abstraction enables us to replace many car objects with one `Car` class. The process can be reversed by instantiation.

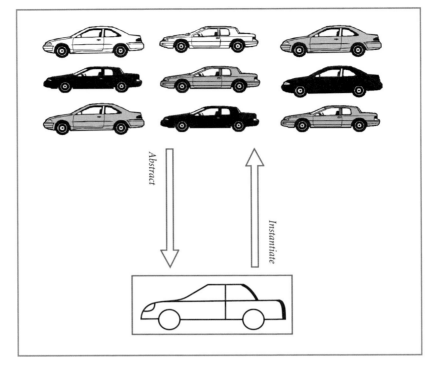

Abstract

Instantiate

4.1.2 An API View

The API of an instantiable class is very similar to the one we studied in Section 3.1 for utilities except that the constructor section is not missing. Just like fields and methods, this section has two subsections: one for a summary and one for the details. Figure 4.2 depicts the **Constructor Summary** of the `Fraction` class, a member of `type.lib`.

As you can see, constructors are similar to methods in that they take parameters; in fact, we use terms such as *parameter list* and *signature* to describe them. They are different from methods, however, in two fundamental respects:

1. There is no column to indicate the return of a constructor; a constructor does not have a return. This implies that we cannot invoke a constructor like we invoke methods because the return is neither void nor nonvoid.

Figure 4.2 The constructor summary section of the `Fraction` class

Constructor Summary

`Fraction()`
    Construct a default fraction with numerator equal to 0 and denominator equal to 1.

`Fraction(long numerator, long denominator)`
    Construct a fraction with the passed numerator and denominator.

2. The name of a constructor is identical to that of the class. This implies that if a class has more than one constructor, all the constructors must be overloaded.

The name of a constructor in the summary is actually a hyperlink that takes us to the **Constructor Detail** subsection in which the constructor's contract is specified. For example, the constructor detail of the `Fraction` class is shown in Fig. 4.3.

As in method detail, the constructor detail repeats and elaborates on the information in the summary and provides a contract. Since a constructor does not have a return, the contract does not have a "Return" clause, but it may have a "Throws" clause.

The `Fraction` class will be used in this chapter to demonstrate several concepts. It encapsulates a fraction, an entity made up of a numerator and a denominator both of which are `long` integers. For example,

$$\frac{3}{5}$$

is a fraction with numerator 3 and denominator 5. This encapsulation allows us to think of fractions as if they were a primitive type in Java; we can declare variables to be of that type, and we can add and multiply these variables and evaluate expressions.

Do not think of this class as merely a container that holds two integers; it is far more than that. And do not think of it as a collection of procedures that operate on fraction parameters and return their sums or products; it is far more than that too. A class allows us to fully

Figure 4.3 The constructor detail section of the `Fraction` class

Constructor Detail

Fraction

```
public Fraction()
```
Construct a default fraction with numerator equal to 0 and denominator equal to 1. The rational value of the constructed fraction is thus zero.

Fraction

```
public Fraction(long numerator,
                long denominator)
```
Construct a fraction with the passed numerator and denominator. If the passed denominator is negative, the sign of the numerator is reversed in order to keep the denominator positive.

Parameters:

numerator - the numerator of the fraction to construct
denominator - the denominator of the fraction to construct

delegate everything related to fractions, both data storage and operations, thanks to its attributes and methods. The class presents a case in point example of why objects are needed because if the class were a utility, we would have been limited to one fraction at a time, and hence, we would never be able to express the addition or the multiplication of two fractions.

4.2 The Life of an Object

The following sections trace the lifetime of an object from birth to death by explaining the applicable Java statements and exposing what happens behind the scenes when these statements are executed.

4.2.1 The Birth of an Object

Classes can be thought of as factories of objects. As an example, suppose the factory makes cars, on demand while you wait. If you want to buy a car, you go to the factory and pick up a blank access card from the basket at the entrance. If you decide to buy a car, the card will be programmed to become an electronic key for your car (it opens the doors and starts the engine); otherwise, you would simply throw away the card when you leave. After you enter the factory, you look for a salesperson. Surprisingly, all salespersons have the same name, being the name of the class, but they differ in the kind of car options that you can pick. One salesperson, for example, may allow you to select the body colour, the GPS feature, and interior finish, while another may not allow any selection whatsoever, that is, the car would come with default options. Once the deal is closed, you are provided with the electronic code of your car, and you store it in your access card.

To purchase a car, you, the customer, must therefore follow four steps:

1. Go to the car factory.
2. Obtain a blank access card.
3. Find a salesperson and select options.
4. Store the car's electronic code in the access card.

Note that obtaining an access card indicates your intention to buy a car from this factory but does not commit you; you can still walk away without buying. Note also that you can make copies of the card using your home PC, but be careful with the copies because whoever finds one can steal your car.

In a similar fashion, we are going to develop a program named `Birth` that creates an instance of the `Fraction` class by following four corresponding steps.

Step 1: Locate the Class

As a car buyer, you must look up the factory's address before leaving home in order to give it to the taxi driver. As a programmer, you must look up the package in which the class resides and provide it to the import statement. The `Fraction` class is in `type.lib` so our program must start with

```
import type.lib.Fraction;
```

Figure 4.4 This memory diagram depicts the main class of an application that is about to create an instance of the `Fraction` class.

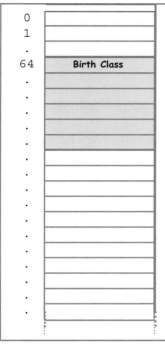

At this stage, we can imagine our main class, `Birth`, residing by itself in memory, as depicted in Fig. 4.4.

Step 2: Declare a Reference

As a car buyer, you must obtain a blank access card. As a programmer, you must declare a variable, called the **object reference**, which will be used later to refer to the object, that is, point at it. Recall that a variable of primitive type `int` and name `number` is declared using

```
int number;
```

When this statement is executed, a memory block big enough to hold an `int` value (4 bytes) is allocated, and its address, shown as 76 in Fig. 4.5, is associated with `number`.

In a similar fashion, a variable of class type `Fraction` and name `f` is declared using

```
Fraction f;
```

(We are keeping the context generic, hence the single-letter identifier.) When this statement is executed, and assuming that this is the first time the class `Fraction` was referenced in this program, the virtual machine searches for the (compiled) `Fraction` class on disk and loads it into memory. Figure 4.5 shows that the class was loaded at address 100. (This step is skipped if the class is already loaded.) Next, a memory block big enough to hold a reference is allocated and its address, shown as 84 in Fig. 4.5, is associated with `f`.

Recall that declaring a primitive variable does not set its content; hence, the value of `number` (the content of block 76) is not set. Similarly, the value of the `f` (the content of block 84) is also not set.

No object has been created yet.

Step 3: Instantiate the Class

As a car buyer, you now look for a salesperson and indicate options. As a programmer, you must look for a constructor in the class API. As we know, all constructors have the same name, the class name,

Figure 4.5 A diagram of memory after the application of Fig. 4.4 has declared an integer variable `number` and a variable `f` of the type `Fraction`

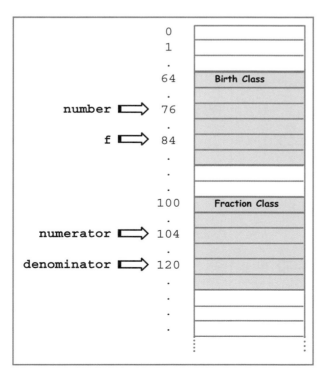

Java Details 4.1

What is "Default" in the Default Constructor?

If an object is created using the default constructor, its attributes will have default values (rather than programmer-selected ones). Furthermore, Java automatically adds a default constructor to any class that does not have a constructor; that is, it adds it by default.

Our program does not want just any fraction; we want to create one with numerator 3 and denominator 5. We therefore use the second constructor and write

```
new Fraction(3, 5)
```

but they differ in signatures. Indeed, `Fraction` has two constructors (see Fig. 4.2): one takes no parameters, and the other takes two. A constructor that does not take any parameter is called the **default constructor** because it does not let you select the object's state. Hence, you end up with an object with default values for the attributes. In our analogy, such a constructor serves customers who are in a hurry to get a car, any car.

Figure 4.6 A diagram of memory after the application of Fig. 4.4 has created a `Fraction` object with numerator 3 and denominator 5

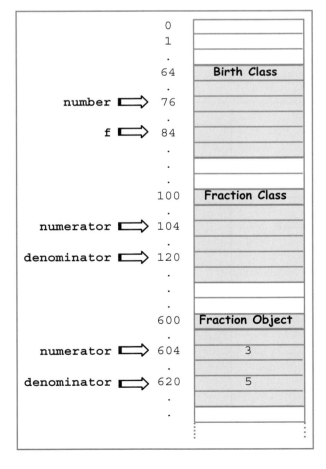

This expression has two pieces, new and `Fraction(3, 5)`. Even though they are inseparable (Java's syntax does not allow writing one without the other), it is important to understand their separate roles. The new keyword performs manufacturing: it makes a copy of the loaded class and stores the copy in a newly allocated block; see Fig. 4.6. The constructor, on the other hand, performs customization: the attributes pick up values based on our preference.

As depicted in Fig. 4.6, the class at block 100 was copied to a block at 600 and was customized. The block at 600 is "the object" (or "the instance"), and the action performed by new is "object creation" (or "class instantiation"). Note that we now have two sets of attributes: one in the class and one in the object. The former is used only as a template (to copy from), while the latter is used to hold the

---

Programming Tip 4.1

Pitfall: Invoking the constructor

Even though the constructor looks like a method, a client cannot invoke it via the dot separator. The only way for a client to use a constructor is through the new keyword.

In More Depth 4.1

The Copying Model

In this model, instantiating a class involves allocating a new block in memory and copying the class into it. This mental model is very useful in that it allows us to visualize the roles played by the new keyword and the constructor; to identify the address of the new block as the object's identity; and to associate the content of the new block with the object's state. It should be noted, however, that this is just a model that allows us to reason about things—a cover story—and may not correspond to how the virtual machine actually implements object creation. In particular, not everything in the class is copied to the object; constructors and static features are examples of things that remain in the class.

---

state of the created object. The numerator of the created object, for example, is stored at address 604.

We saw in Section 4.1.1 that an object has everything that a class has plus identity and state, and we can see this in Fig. 4.6: the block at 600 has everything that the block at 100 has plus the following:

- a unique address, 600, that no other object can have, an identity
- values, 3 and 5, for the numerator and the denominator, a state

Step 4: Assign the Reference

As a car buyer, your last step is to program the access card by storing the electronic code of your new car in it. As a programmer, you must initialize the object reference so that it points at the newly created object. In fact, the Java expression written in step 3 is not a statement but an expression; it gets evaluated and it culminates in a value. That value is the address of the created object, 600 in our case. Hence, what we need to do is to treat this expression as a right-hand side of an assignment statement whose left-hand side is our object reference:

```
f = new Fraction(3, 5);
```

This statement initializes the object reference; that is, it plays the same role that the following plays for primitive types:

```
number = -14;
```

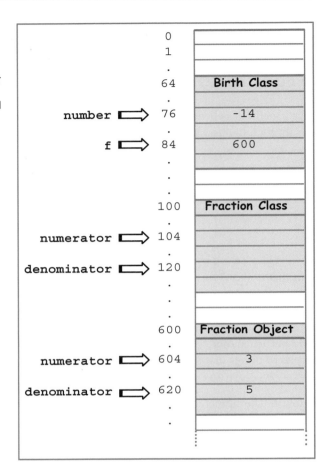

Figure 4.7 The memory diagram after the application of Fig. 4.6 has set `number` to –14 and `f` to the newly created object.

This leads to the final diagram, Fig. 4.7.

We conclude this section with an observation: the object reference behaves like a variable of a primitive type in that it must be declared and initialized before it can be used. The key difference is that we, the programmers, have no control over the value to which it is initialized by the new/constructor process. This value, the address of the block in which the object resides, is set by the memory manager and is therefore beyond the control of any Java program. Because of this, access to the object can only be indirect, through its object reference. In fact, there is nothing in the program that you can point to and say, "this is the object." This point is very important and cannot be overemphasized.

In More Depth   4.2

Skipping Steps 2 and 4

One can create an object (using new) and set its state (using a constructor) without having to associate an object reference with it, that is,

```
new Fraction(3, 5);
```

This statement is odd in that the object ends up with no reference pointing at it, but the syntax is correct. We sometimes pass an object reference to a method (as a parameter), and in that case an expression like the one above becomes meaningful.

Programming Tip	4.2

Fallacy: The object reference can be treated as an integer

While it is true that the content of the object reference is the address of the object it points at, that is, an integer, it cannot be treated as such. You cannot, for example, apply arithmetic operators on object references or compare them with integers.

4.2.2 Objects at Work

Once you have an object reference pointing at an object, you can use it to access/invoke all the features of the object. The syntax is exactly the same as that for utility classes, but the dot separator is preceded by the object reference rather than the class name. In other words, we access fields and invoke methods *on* the reference, not *on* the class. Some of the methods in the API of `Fraction` are shown in Fig. 4.8.

Figure 4.8 The method `Summary` of `type.lib.Fraction` (shown in part)

Method Summary	
double	**add**(Fraction other) Add the passed fraction to the fraction on which it was called.
void	**divide**(Fraction other) Divide the fraction on which the method was called by the passed fraction.
boolean	**equals**(Object other) Determine if this fraction is the same as the passed one.
long	**getDenominator**() An accessor to the denominator of this fraction.
long	**getNumerator**() An accessor to the numerator of this fraction.
void	**multiply**(Fraction other) Multiply the fraction on which the method was called by the passed fraction.
void	**setDenominator**(long denominator) A mutator for the denominator of this fraction.
String	**toProperString**() Return this fraction as a proper fraction.
String	**toString**() Return a string representation of this fraction.

Example 4.1

Write a code fragment that creates a fraction object that corresponds to 8/6 and then outputs the results of invoking `getNumerator` and `toProperString` on it.

Answer:
We create the fraction by writing:

```
Fraction f;
f = new Fraction(8, 6);
```

Just as we can combine declaration and assignment of primitive types, we can combine the above two statements:

```
Fraction f = new Fraction(8, 6);
```

Now that we have a declared and initialized object reference, we invoke methods on it as usual:

```
output.println(f.getNumerator());
output.println(f.toProperString());
```

The output of this example program is

```
4
"1 1/3"
```

This output is consistent with the API of the class.

The object reference allows us to use all the features listed in the API, which is why it is sometimes referred to as the object's **handle**. In addition to invoking methods on it, you can use it to access fields. Some of the fields of `Fraction` are shown in Fig. 4.9.

Example 4.2

Write a code fragment that creates a fraction object that corresponds to 8/6 and then outputs the results of invoking the `toString` method on it, once with the default separator and once with a different separator.

Answer:
The API indicates that the return of this method uses the `separator` field to separate the numerator from the denominator. By default, the separator is `'/'` but since it is a field (a public attribute), we can set it to anything we want. In the following code, we set it to the divide sign `'÷'`:

```
Fraction f = new Fraction(8, 6);
output.println(f.toString());
f.separator = '\u00f7';
output.println(f.toString());
```

The output of this example program is

```
4/3
4÷3
```

The API of `Fraction` has several methods for performing operations such as adding and multiplying (Fig. 4.8). Note that these methods do not return the result of the operation, as you would expect in a procedural paradigm. Instead, they are `void` methods that make the necessary change in the fraction that each encapsulates. For example, if `f` is an object reference that points at a fraction and we want to add 1/2 to that fraction, we write

```
f.add(new Fraction(1, 2));
```

We could have created the 1/2 fraction first and then passed it to the `add` method, but either way, no return is involved. This enforces and enhances full delegation: the class handles fractions and their operations. As client, I do not want to know the outcome of every intermediate result in a calculation.

Example 4.3

Write a code fragment that computes the following expression using fraction arithmetic, that is, without converting to real numbers and risking round-off:

$$\frac{\frac{5}{3} \times \frac{7}{6}}{\frac{31}{45}} + \frac{3}{4}$$

Answer:
The body of the `main` method is shown below:

```
Fraction f = new Fraction(5, 3);
f.multiply(new Fraction(7, 6));
f.divide(new Fraction(31, 45));
f.add(new Fraction(3, 4));
output.println(f.toString());
```

The output of this example program is
```
443/124
```

Figure 4.9 The field API of `type.lib.Fraction` (shown in part)

	Field Summary
static boolean	**isQuoted** A flag that determines whether the return of `toProperString` is surrounded by quotes
char	**separator** A character that separates the numerator denominator pair in the return of the `toString` method

4.2.3 The Object and Its Reference

From a conceptual point of view, there is a similarity between the notion of an object and that of a value: an object to its class is like a value to its type, that is, each being an instance, a special case, of a general category. For example, a fraction object with numerator 3 and denominator 5 is but one instance of the `Fraction` class, and the integer value 4 is but one instance of the `int` type. From a programming point of view, however, these two notions are not treated the same. For a value, we declare a variable to be of its type and store the value in it. For an object, we also declare a variable to be of its type but store the address of the object in it. This added level of indirectness makes it critical that we adopt a different mentality when we write programs involving objects. In the world of primitive types, for example, it is obvious that the fragment

```
int x = 5;
int y = x;
x = 10;
output.println(y);
```

will output 5 because y "holds the value," and since no statement changed y, it will retain its initial value. In the world of objects, however, there is no artifact in the program that "holds the object." All we have is an object reference that holds the address of the object, and because of this, the object counterpart of the above fragment will actually output the equivalent of 10, not 5, as we shall see later in this chapter. The key point is that we need to develop a new mentality that does not confuse an object with an object reference, and this section amplifies this point.

The object reference in our car analogy is merely the access card that allows you to open and start the car. You may find it convenient to make a copy of the card but doing so does not lead to two cars; you still have only one car but now have two keys to it. Similarly, you can have a second reference to the same object. The program `Birth`, for example, contains the following code:

```
Fraction f1;
f1 = new Fraction(3, 5);
Fraction f2;
f2 = f1;
```

As shown in Fig. 4.10, this code creates only one `Fraction` object; indeed, it contains one occurrence only of the new keyword. There are two declared object references of the type `Fraction`. The first, `f1`, was set to the return of the new/constructor process, which is 600 in our figure, and the second was set to the first, that is, also to 600.

The figure makes it clear that while there is only one `Fraction` object (with identity 600), there can be many references pointing at it. It should be evident that it makes no difference which reference is used to access the object. For example, the statement

```
output.println(f1.getNumerator());
```

is fully equivalent to

```
output.println(f2.getNumerator());
```

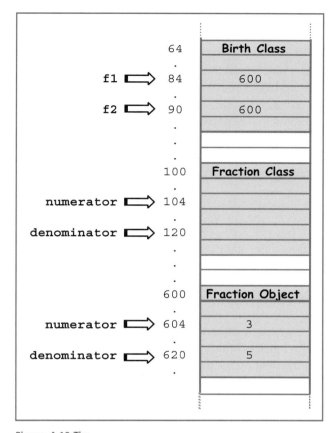

	64	**Birth Class**
	.	
f1 ⇒	84	600
	.	
f2 ⇒	90	600
	.	
	.	
	100	**Fraction Class**
	.	
numerator ⇒	104	
	.	
denominator ⇒	120	
	.	
	.	
	600	**Fraction Object**
	.	
numerator ⇒	604	3
	.	
denominator ⇒	620	5
	.	

Figure 4.10 The memory diagram of an object with two object references pointing to it.

After all, they both fetch the needed data from the same object at block 600. Similarly, it should not be surprising that the output of the following fragment is a pipe '|' even though we changed the field using f1 and printed it using f2:

```
f1.separator = '|';
output.println(f2.separator);
```

The == relational operator accepts operands of any type, including object references, and it returns true when its two operands have the same content. Hence, f1 == f2 is true since each of them contains 600.

An object can have an arbitrary number of references pointing at it, and all of them would be equally valid for accessing its features. If you no longer want a reference to point at an object, you can set it to null:

```
f2 = null;
```

The reserved word null is a special literal in Java whose type is compatible with all class types, that is, you can set a reference of any declared type to it. This statement removes 600 from block 90 and replaces it by the special value null; this action disconnects the reference from the object. This is equivalent, in our car analogy, to wiping out the contents of the access card so that it is blank and can no longer open our car (or any other car). Once a reference is set to null, it can no longer be used to access features. If such an access is attempted, for example, if you now write

```
output.println(f2.getNumerator());
```

then the virtual machine will trigger a runtime error, and your application will crash with the following error message:

```
Null Pointer Exception
```

It is important that you keep at least one reference pointing at an object because the object will otherwise become inaccessible. In fact, we will see in Section 4.2.6 that such an orphaned object will become a candidate for garbage collection.

4.2.4 Objects' Equality

Consider the fragment

```
Fraction f1 = new Fraction(3, 5);
Fraction f2 = f1;
Fraction f3 = new Fraction(2, 7);
Fraction f4 = new Fraction(6, 10);
```

```
Fraction f5 = f4;
output.println(f1 == f2);
output.println(f4 == f5);
```

When these statements are executed, three objects and five references will be present in memory, as depicted in Fig. 4.11 in which the addresses are, of course, just examples.

Do you see things that are equal? When we speak of "equality," we have to distinguish between the equality of object references and that of objects.

Equality of References

The == operator is used to test the equality of object references. The last two statements in the above fragment will output

```
true
true
```

because each involves references that indeed point at the same object. In general, given two references f and g, if f == g is true, then either both are null (in which case no objects are involved) or both point at the same object (in which case only one object is involved). If f == g is false, then either one is null and the other is not (in which case one object is involved) or both are not null and they point at different objects (in which case two objects are involved). We thus conclude that aside from the null issue, the equality of references is a test of identity, *not* of object equality. When confirmed, it means there is really just one object, not two objects that happened to be equal. For example, if we append the following statement to the above fragment,

```
output.println(f4 == f1);
```

then its output would be false, even though the two involved objects (6/10 and 3/5) are equal as fractions. The output is false because the references point at distinct blocks in memory, and it does not matter whether these blocks hold the same state.

Equality of Objects

It is clear that testing object equality cannot be based on simple address comparisons. Only someone with a thorough knowledge of the attributes of the two objects can make a decision about the equality of their states. That someone is the designer of the class, and the decision is implemented in the method equals. Given two references f and g (with f != null), we invoke equals on f and pass g. For example, the statement

```
output.println(f1.equals(f4));
```

outputs true because the objects pointed at by these two references encapsulate the same fraction, and the API indicates that fraction equality is based on the equality of their numerators and denominators in reduced form.

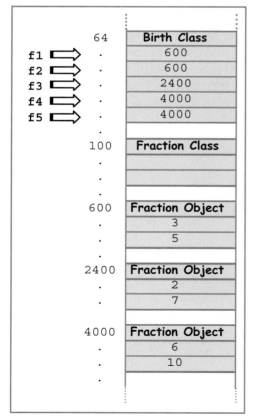

Figure 4.11 The memory diagram of multiple objects and references

Some (poorly designed) classes come without an `equals` method. In this case, Java uses a default method based on `==`; that is, object equality for such classes reduces to reference equality. The equality test in such classes is so strong that it is actually useless because it never considers two objects equal unless they are one and the same, but this is the best Java can do when the designer fails to provide an `equals`. For example, a class by the name of `FractionNS` (Not Standard) is provided in `type.lib`. It is identical to `Fraction` except it does not provide such a method. Hence, the fragment

```
FractionNS x = new FractionNS(4, 5);
FractionNS y = new FractionNS(4, 5);
boolean equalRef = (x == y);
boolean equalObj = x.equals(y);
```

reveals that `equalRef` and `equalObj` are both `false` (only the first would be `false` had we used the `Fraction` class).

4.2.5 Obligatory Methods

You will learn in Chapter 9 that certain methods, called **obligatory methods**, are available in every Java class, whether or not the implementer of the class chose to include them in the API. One example is the `equals` method of the previous section: if a class does not have it, Java will provide it. A Java-added obligatory method is admittedly quite generic, but at least you would not get a syntax error if you invoked such a method on a reference of any type. Properly designed classes provide their own implementations of all obligatory methods.

A second widely used obligatory method is `toString`, and it is meant to return a textual description of the object on which it is invoked. The API of `Fraction` includes such a method; in fact, we have already used it in Example 4.2. The `toString` method is convenient for quickly displaying the key state elements of an object, and for this reason, it is often auto-invoked by output methods: Given *any* object reference x, the statement

```
output.println(x);
```

is interpreted by `println` as

```
output.println(x.toString());
```

As in `equals`, some poorly designed classes come without `toString`, in which case, Java uses a default method that returns the name and a number that is typically the address (in hex) of the object separated by the @ character. (See the API of Object for more details.) You can see this behaviour by outputting any reference to a `FractionNS` instance, a class that does not provide a `toString` method. For example, the fragment

```
FractionNS x = new FractionNS(4, 5);
output.println(x.toString());
```

generates the following output:

```
type.lib.FractionNS@b8df17
```

(You may of course see a different address on your machine.)

4.2.6 The Death of an Object

We saw in Sections 4.2.3 and 4.2.4 that it is important to distinguish between an object (a car) and the reference that points at it (the card that opens it). This distinction is also important when we think about the destruction of objects: do we mean destroying the object itself or only its reference?

Destroying a Reference

We can destroy the access card of a car by wiping out its memory (so it no longer opens the car), by reprogramming it (so it opens a different car), or by throwing it away. The same can be done for an object reference: we can set it to null, make it point elsewhere, or leave its scope. The fragment

```
Fraction x = new Fraction(3, 5);
Fraction y = x;
Fraction z = x;
{
    Fraction t = x;
}
y = null;
z = new Fraction(4, 7);
```

starts by creating one object with four references pointing at it, but at the end of the fragment, only x remains pointing at this object. Reference y was destroyed by making it null; reference z was made to point at a newly created object; and reference t became out of scope.

Destroying an Object

It should be clear from the outset that we cannot destroy an object directly since it does not appear explicitly in our program. We must do something with its references in order to indirectly kill it. In the car analogy, we can imagine destroying each and every access card that we have for the car. Even though this does not damage the car itself, it renders it effectively dead since no one can use it anymore. Similarly, if every reference that points at an object is destroyed, the object becomes inaccessible, and the garbage collector (GC) (one of the managers we met in Section 2.3.4) will reclaim the block occupied by it. The GC keeps a count of the number of references that point at an object, and once this count becomes zero, the object is placed in the deletion queue. An object with no reference pointing at it is called an **orphan**. Consider the following fragment:

```
Fraction x = new Fraction(3, 5);
Fraction y = x;
Fraction y = new Fraction(4, 7);
x = null;
```

The first object (3/5) used to have two references pointing at it but ended up an orphan at the end of the fragment. Hence, the GC will eventually remove it from memory.

4.3 The Object's State

Recall that the power of OOP (object-oriented programming) derives mainly from its ability to support more than one entity at a time, and this translates to the ability to have a separate state per object. Because of this, it is important that we master the ability to access the state of a given object, change it if possible, and determine whether it is shared among all instances of the same class. The following sections explain the concepts behind these tasks, provide a general overview of the most-often-used techniques, and apply these techniques to the `Fraction` class.

4.3.1 Accessors and Mutators

Full delegation requires that we do not keep track of anything related to what has been delegated, neither a behaviour nor a data element. As clients, all we need is the object reference, and through it, we can do whatever we want. In particular, there are two things that a client of an object may want to do:

1. Determine the state of the object
2. Change the state of the object

Recall that the state of an object is represented by the values of its attributes. Hence, the above two goals can be realized by making all the attributes public so that the client can easily look up and change their values. But we found in Section 2.3.3 (and we will elaborate in Section 4.3.2) that it is not a good idea to make attributes public, and this leaves only one means: methods.

Accessors

A method that returns the value of an attribute X is known as an **accessor** (to X), and it typically has the header

```
public typeX getX()
```

where `typeX` is the type of attribute X. For example, the `Fraction` class has the accessors `long getNumerator()` and `long getDenominator()`.

■ `long getNumerator()`

Return the numerator of the fraction.

■ `long getDenominator()`

Return the denominator of the fraction.

You may argue that it is we, the client, who created the fraction and passed its numerator and denominator to the constructor, so why do we need accessors to them? The answer lies in the notion of full delegation: we do not want to keep track of anything other than the object reference. Here is a fragment that emphasizes this point:

```
output.println("Enter the numerator and denominator");
output.println("(press the ENTER key after each):");
Fraction f;
f = new Fraction(input.nextLong(),input.nextLong());
```

As you can see, the values of the numerator and denominator were never stored in the program; they were marshalled from the Scanner class to the Fraction class. At the end of the fragment, the only thing that the client knows about the fraction is its reference f.

The "get" convention for naming accessors has one notable exception: if the return of the accessor is boolean, the *isX* predicate is preferred over *getX*. For example, if one of the attributes of a class is the called visible, and it is a boolean, then its accessor will have the header

```
public boolean isVisible()
```

In this case, you will not find an accessor named getVisible.

Mutators

A method that changes the value of an attribute X is called a **mutator** (for X), and it typically has the header

```
public void setX(typeX value)
```

The Fraction class has several mutators, including the following:

- void setDenominator(long value)

    Change the fraction's denominator to the passed value.

- void setFraction(long numerator, long denominator)

    Change the fraction's numerator and denominator to the passed values.

Example 4.4

Examine the following fragment, and predict its output:

```
Fraction f = new Fraction(5, 3);
f.setDenominator(25);
output.println(f.getNumerator());
```

Answer:

The mutator changed the denominator to 25, leaving the fraction as 5/25, and since this class keeps the fraction in reduced form at all times, it becomes 1/5. Hence, the output of the last statement is

```
1
```

Note that mutators are so named because they mutate attributes, that is, change them. Note also that the change is made in situ; that is, the state of the object changes in place without creating a new object. Example 4.5 amplifies this point.

Example 4.5

Consider the code fragment

```
Fraction f = new Fraction(1, 2);
Fraction g = f;

// Place mystery statement here

output.println(f.getNumerator());
output.println(f == g);
output.println(f.equals(g));
```

Replace the comment with one statement such that
(a) The output of the fragment is

```
3
true
true
```

(b) The output of the fragment is

```
3
false
false
```

(c) The output of the fragment is

```
1
false
true
```

Answer:
(a) Since the two object references are equal, there can be only one object; hence, we must mutate the numerator. The answer is

```
f.setNumerator(3);
```

(b) Since the two object references are different, we must create a second object, and it must have numerator 3. One possible answer is

```
f = new Fraction(3, 2);
```

(c) This is similar to (b), but the new object must be deemed equal to the old one in the eyes of the `equals` method. Thus one possible answer is

```
f = new Fraction(3, 6);
```

Generally speaking, not just any value can be assigned to an attribute of a class. For example, the attribute `age` in a hypothetical `Person` class should not hold a negative value. The context of the class usually dictates a range of values that are meaningful for an attribute, and the contract of its mutator must therefore ensure that parameters passed to it are within the allowed range. The contract can ensure that parameters satisfy a given condition in one of three ways:

1. Make the condition a precondition of the mutator.
2. Make the mutator boolean.
3. Throw an exception if the condition is not met.

The first approach relies on the client to pass legal values; that is, the mutator does not check the passed values. If the values are invalid, the object will end up in an inconsistent state (e.g., a person with a negative age), or the application will either crash or have bugs, and the client will have to deal with the consequences. This approach is ideal for situations in which the client is a responsible programmer.

The second approach sets the precondition to true and leaves checking to the mutator. If the passed values do not meet the condition, the state is not changed, and the mutator returns `false` to inform the client that the request was denied. This approach is more robust than the previous one because the object will never be in an inconsistent state.

The third approach is similar to the second in that it sets the precondition to true and thus leaves checking to the mutator. But if the passed values do not meet the condition, the mutator throws an exception. This approach is even more robust than the previous one because an irresponsible programmer may ignore the return of a mutator (by trashing it), but it is harder to ignore an exception.

One of the attributes of a fraction is the separator inserted between the numerator and denominator in the return of the `toString` method. The class uses a slash '/' by default, but some clients may prefer a division sign '÷', a pipe '|', or some other delimiter. The mutator of this attribute has the header

```
public boolean setSeparator(char newSeparator)
```

You can see from this that the designers of the `Fraction` class chose the second approach to handle the contract of this mutator. Indeed, the API of the class states that the separator must not be a letter or a digit, and that if such a character is passed to the mutator then it will be ignored with a `false` return.

Example 4.6

Examine the following fragment, and predict its output for various inputs:

```
Fraction f = new Fraction(7, 10);
output.print("Enter a separator... ");
boolean ok = f.setSeparator(input.nextLine().charAt(0));
output.println(ok);
output.println(f);
```

Answer:

If the user entered a letter or a digit, the output would be

```
false
7/10
```

On the other hand, if the user entered a symbol such as a comma, the output would be

```
true
7,10
```

The distinction between digits and letters may be obvious in English, but how does the `setSeparator` mutator implement it for any Unicode character? The answer lies in a static method in the `Character` class (in `java.lang`) with the header

```
public static boolean isLetterOrDigit(char)
```

It returns `true` only if its argument is indeed a letter or a digit in the locale in which the application is running.

☐

Our discussion of accessors and mutators is not meant to suggest that every attribute must have such a pair. For example, we shall see in Chapter 6 that the `String` class does not provide a mutator for its key attribute due to performance reasons. The only way to find out what is provided is to look in the API. Luckily, *most* classes adhere to the *getX* / *setX* convention for naming accessors and mutators (with "get" replaced by "is" for booleans), so it is relatively easy to locate them in an API.

4.3.2 Attribute Privacy

One of the most important software engineering guidelines is to make all attributes of a class private because this enhances the encapsulation. We saw in Section 2.3.3 that no contract can be written for a field because Java makes fields available to a client just like local variables. Hence, there is no mechanism for checking, let alone enforcing, any pre- or postconditions. If an attribute is not within the concern of the client, then it obviously should be private because making it public would break the encapsulation. But if the client needs to know the value of an attribute, an accessor to it can be provided. In addition, if it is meaningful for the client to change the value of an attribute, a mutator is provided. Hence, by making all attributes private and providing accessor and mutator methods when needed, we maintain the encapsulation while providing controlled access. The only exceptions to this all-private guideline are final attributes. Since they are constants, an app cannot change them anyway so it does not hurt to make them public.

In general, there are four possibilities for each attribute in the class:

1. Neither an accessor nor a mutator: zero visibility
2. An accessor and no mutator: read-only access
3. A mutator and no accessor: write-only access
4. An accessor and a mutator: read/write access

Case 1 corresponds to an attribute that is beyond the client's concern; that is, the client does not care about the attribute's value or does not even know that it exists. Cases 2 and 3 make attribute privacy manifestly beneficial because they permit either read or write access but not both, which is impossible to achieve through a public attribute. The last case is interesting, for it seems to be, at first glance, equivalent to making the attribute public. Have we come full circle and allowed the very risk we sought to mitigate?

The answer is no. Even if a client can get and set the value of an attribute, there is still a significant degree of separation between the client and the implementer. Specifically, we gain the protection of the mutator's contract and are shielded against name and data structure changes. Let us examine these benefits.

The Contract

A mutator has a contract that can place a condition on the prospective value of an attribute, and as we saw in Section 4.3.1, there are several alternatives for stipulating and handling such a condition. A public attribute provides no similar protection.

As an example, consider the `separator` attribute of `Fraction`. For pedagogical reasons, this attribute was made public so that the negative consequences of doing so could be exposed. The class provides it as a field and also provides an accessor to it and a mutator for it. The following malicious code attempts to make the return of the `toString` method confusing by using a digit as a separator:

```
Fraction f = new Fraction(7, 10);
f.setSeparator('5');
output.println(f);
```

If the code succeeds, the output will be "7510", but it will not succeed, thanks to the contract of the mutator. The following code, however, will succeed:

```
Fraction f = new Fraction(7, 10);
f.separator = '5';
output.println(f);
```

because a public attribute has no means of enforcing a condition.

The Name

Accessors and mutators insulate the client from the particular name that the implementer uses for the attribute's identifier. By the same token, the implementer is free to change the attribute's identifier without affecting any of the clients.

For example, we refer to the numerator of the fraction as "numerator," and we are encouraged to do so by the name of the accessor, `getNumerator`, and mutator, `setNumerator`. The implementer, however, may choose a different identifier for this attribute, perhaps `numer` or even n, but this does not affect us. Contrast this with the separator attribute. It has an accessor `getSeparator` and a mutator `setSeparator`, but since it is a public field, its name "separator" appears in the API, and any change to it may render many client programs inoperable.

The Data Structure

Accessors and mutators insulate the client from the particular data structure that the implementer uses for the attribute. By the same token, the implementer is free to change this data structure without disturbing any of the clients.

The API of `Fraction` states that the numerator's accessor has a `long` return, and its mutator has a `long` parameter, but aside from that, the implementers of the class are free to use any data type for storing the numerator internally. They can, for example, store it as strings of digits, and this will be 100% transparent to us. In the case of `separator`, however, this freedom is no longer available: since it is a field, its type (`char`) is stated in the interface, and neither party can transparently change it.

In More Depth   4.3

It should be noted that not every accessor is necessarily associated with an attribute. The `Fraction` class, for example, may have the accessor

```
public long getLCM()
```

It returns the least common multiplier (LCM) of the numerator and denominator of the encapsulated fraction. The client can gain access to this LCM through the accessor but cannot ascertain whether this is actually an attribute of the class. It is possible that the implementer computes the LCM on demand, when the accessor is invoked, but never stores it. Similarly, not every mutator corresponds necessarily to an attribute.

4.3.3 Objects with `static` Features

Consider the following code fragment:

```
Fraction f = new Fraction(3, 2);
output.println(f.toProperString());
f.isQuoted = false;
output.println(f.toProperString());
```

Its output is

```
"1 1/2"
1 1/2
```

By default, the return of the `toProperString` method is quoted, but we can modify this by changing the value of the `isQuoted` field from `true` (the default) to `false`. This explains the above output, but how about the following fragment:

```
Fraction f = new Fraction(3, 2);
f.isQuoted = true;
Fraction g = new Fraction(5, 2);
g.isQuoted = false;
output.println(f.toProperString());
output.println(g.toProperString());
```

Its output is

```
1 1/2
2 1/2
```

Figure 4.12 The
isQuoted
attribute is static.
Hence, it remains
in the class.
Individual objects
do not have their
own copy of this
attribute.

But we have specifically asked that the return for f be quoted and that for g be unquoted. Why are they both unquoted? A clue to the answer is visible in the Field Summary for isQuoted (Fig. 4.9). It says it is a static field.

The Fraction class is certainly not a utility, but it can have static features. For them, the model developed in Chapter 3 prevails: no copying is involved, and the client accesses the features in the original class. Hence, there is only one copy of isQuoted, and it remains in the class as depicted in Fig. 4.12.

You can see from Fig. 4.12 that when the first object was created, the class (loaded at 100) got copied to a block at 600 and f was made to point at it. The memory blocks set aside to hold the numerator and denominator (and any other non-static feature in the class) were also copied, but the block at address 150 was *not* copied because isQuoted is static. The same thing happened when the process was repeated for the second object, and we can see that even though there are separate copies for the numerator attribute, one per object, there is only one copy of isQuoted. When the statement

```
f.isQuoted = true;
```

was executed, the value true got stored in the block at 150. The fact that access was made on f makes no difference; after all, there is only one such attribute and it stayed with the class. Afterward, when

```
g.isQuoted = false;
```

was executed, the value false was stored in the same location (at 150); that is, the new value over-wrote the previous one. Again, the fact that access was made on g is irrelevant. When the toProperString method was invoked afterward, it used the last stored value of the attribute (false), and that is why both outputs came out unquoted.

Admittedly, there is nothing particularly difficult or confusing about static features except perhaps the syntax. We learned in Chapter 3 that these features are accessed on the class, so we have come to expect a statement like the above to be written as

```
Fraction.isQuoted = false;
```

Indeed, this is the proper syntax, but the compiler is tolerant when it sees a static feature accessed on a reference, and the compiler replaces it automatically by an access on the class. It is recommended that you always access static features using the class name, especially in this early stage. But no matter how you write it, the correct mental model (with or without copying) should come to mind whenever a feature is accessed.

A `static` field can be thought of as a super global variable, because anyone can read it or change it. Furthermore, if one object changed it, the change will be visible to all other objects instantiated from the class.

4.3.4 Objects with `final` Features

We saw in Section 4.3.2 that `final` attributes can be (and are often) made public. Given such a `final` field, do you expect it to be `static`? In almost all classes, `final` fields are made `static` because of the following points:

■ This saves memory since there is only one copy of the variable rather than one per object. It also saves time because, in general, the compiler can optimize better when it translates access or invocation of `static` features.

■ It allows the app to access the value of the final without having to create an instance first. For example, if you want to know the largest `double` that Java can handle, you simply access the field `MAX_VALUE` in the `Double` class. If this field were not static, you would have had to create an instance first.

You do occasionally come across finals that are not static. This is because the values of such blank finals are not assigned by the class but rather by the class constructor. Hence, they are constants within each object, but the constant value is not the same in all objects.

We mention in closing that methods can also be `final`. We will see in Chapter 9 that it is possible for a class to modify a method in another class (modify its logic, not its header) without breaking the encapsulation. Sometimes, the implementer of the original method does not want it to be modified, either for security or for performance purposes, and in that case, the method is declared `final`. In fact, the whole class can be declared `final`, and this makes it optimal performance-wise because none of its methods can be modified. If you look carefully at the API of the `Math` or the `String` classes in `java.lang`, you will see that their headers declare them as `final`.

Summary of Key Concepts

1. Delegation led us to classes and objects, but we could have reached them through an abstraction-based reasoning: The world around us is full of objects. Each object has an identity, attributes, a state, and methods. If we group objects with the same attributes and methods together and ignore their identities and states, we can call the group a class.

2. The API of a nonutility class has a constructor section. Constructors are like methods in that they have signatures and can be overloaded, but they do not have returns. Also, they all have the

same name, which is the class name. As with field and method APIs, the constructor section consists of a **summary** and a **detail** subsections.

3. To create an instance of a class, import the class and then use the new keyword, which takes care of instance creation. The keyword must be used in conjunction with invoking a constructor, which sets the initial state of the created instance.

4. The **default constructor** is one that does not take any parameters. Using it leads to an instance with a default initial state. Nondefault constructors do take parameters; thus, they allow you to customize the initial state of the created instance.

5. The created instance, also called an object, occupies a block in memory reserved for it. The address of that block is the object's identity. To refer to this identity symbolically, we declare a variable, called the object reference, to be of the class type and set it to the object's identity. The object reference is thus a pointer that points at the object. It is sometimes referred to as the object's handle.

6. The reserved literal null is compatible with all nonprimitive types in Java. Setting a reference to null disconnects it from the object.

7. An object can have many object references pointing at it. All these references would be equal in the eyes of the == relational operator because they all have the same content, the object's identity.

8. **Obligatory** methods are present in every class. If the implementer of the class did not provide them, Java would. Two of the most widely used obligatory methods are equals and toString. The equals method is supposed to establish whether two objects are the same (in terms of their state and in the context of the encapsulation). The toString method is supposed to provide a concise textual description of the object on which it is invoked.

9. If an obligatory method is added by Java, an indication of a poorly designed class, it will be quite generic, that is, not aware of the class context.

equals, for example, will base equality on addresses, while toString will typically return the object's address.

10. The object-reference connection can be severed at either end. At the reference end, we can set the reference to null, set it to a different object, or exit its scope altogether. At the object end, the garbage collector automatically deletes any object that becomes an **orphan**, one with no object reference pointing at it.

11. An **accessor** is a method that returns the value of one of the attributes. Most classes use **getX** to name an accessor to a non-boolean attribute X, and **isX** for a boolean attribute.

12. A **mutator** is a method that changes the value of one of the attributes. Most classes use **setX** to name a mutator for attribute X.

13. A mutator ensures that only legal values are assigned to an attribute either through its contract's precondition or by checking the passed parameters to see whether they are legal. In the latter case, and if the parameters are illegal, a mutator will not change the attribute and will inform the client either by returning false or by throwing an exception.

14. Making all attributes private is a key software engineering guideline for class design. Doing so enhances the encapsulation because clients are not dependent on the actual names or data structures that the implementer chose. Furthermore, changing the value of an attribute through a mutator gives us the protection of a contract, whereas doing so through a field does not.

15. Static attributes remain in the class; they do not get copied to the object's block. As such, they are shared by all instances of the class. A static attribute should in principle be accessed on the class, but Java does allow accessing it on an instance. It should be kept in mind, however, that there is only one value per such an attribute, and a change made through one instance would be seen by all other instances.

16. Final attributes are most often made public, that is, fields, because there is no danger in them being changed. In addition, they are often made static to save memory and to make access easier, that is, one can access them without creating an instance.

Review Questions

1. The need to support multiple entities in a delegation has led us from classes to objects (Chapter 2). Explain how the need to simplify leads us from objects to classes.

2. How is the API of a utility class different from that of a nonutility class?

3. Constructors are similar to methods in one respect but different from them in two. State the similarity and the differences.

4. Four steps are involved in creating an instance of a class. Explain the first three steps.

5. Argue that the sentence "Constructors create objects" is inaccurate. Clarify the difference between the role played by the new keyword and that of constructors.

6. What is a default constructor? If we created an object using such a constructor, what would be the initial state of that object?

7. In the "copying model," do all features in the class get copied to the object block?

8. What is involved in the fourth step of object creation? What happens if this step is skipped?

9. Can you point to something in your program and say "This is the object"?

10. Why is the object reference sometimes referred to as a pointer?

11. Why is the object reference sometimes referred to as an address of an address?

12. What is the difference between testing equality using the == operators and the equals method?

13. If two objects were deemed equal using ==, would they be equal using equals?

14. If two objects were deemed equal using equals, would they be equal using ==?

15. Why is the equals method obligatory? Is it possible for a class not to have it?

16. How does the Java-added equals method determine equality?

17. Why is the toString method obligatory? Is it possible for a class not to have it?

18. What is the purpose of the toString method?

19. Give an example of when the toString method is invoked implicitly.

20. What is the return of the Java-added toString method?

21. When does an object become an orphan?

22. How can an object be deleted?

23. Argue that setting an object reference to null does not necessarily lead to the deletion of the object it points at.

24. What is an accessor?

25. Argue that an accessor cannot possibly be void.

26. What is the naming convention for accessors? Make sure you distinguish between boolean and non-boolean accessors.

27. What is a mutator?

28. Most mutators are void but some are boolean. What gets returned from a boolean mutator?

29. How does a mutator ensure that the object is never left in an illegal state?

30. What is the advantage of leaving all attributes private?

31. What is wrong with this statement: "If an attribute has an accessor and a mutator, and if its mutator imposes no validation whatsoever, then this attribute can just as well be made public."

32. A static attribute is accessed on the class. Can it be also accessed on a reference?

33. The value of a static attribute is the same for all objects. How does an object that changes this value inform the other instances of the change?

34. Why are final attributes often static?

Exploring Objects

L4.1   Anatomy of an API: Fields

1. Launch your browser, and visit the TYPE API. Click (in the upper-left pane) on the `type.lib` package in order to list its classes in the lower-left pane.
2. Click on the `Stock` class, and examine its description in the right pane. Note the presence of a *Constructor Summary* section between the *Field Summary* and the *Method Summary*. Its presence indicates that this class is not a utility.
3. The first listed field is `delimiter`. The left column indicates that its type is `char`, and since the keyword `static` is not present, this is a nonstatic field.
4. The third field is `titleCaseName`, and we see that it is `static`. Hence, classes that are not utilities can still have some features that are static. In contrast, the classes we met in Chapter 3 had no constructor section, and all their features were static.

L4.2   Anatomy of an API: Methods

1. The method `getPrice` does not take parameters (because there is nothing within the parentheses), while `setSymbol` does (it takes one parameter, of the type `String`, called `symbol`).
2. How many parameters does the `equals` method take and what are their types? Is it a `static` method? What is the type of its return?
3. Methods are generally classified as *accessors* (allow us to access data), *mutators* (allow us to change data), *obligatory* (like `toString`, `equals`, and `clone`), and *specialized* (differ from one class to another).

L4.3   Anatomy of an API: Constructors

1. The first constructor listed under *Constructor Summary* is called `Stock`! This is not a coincidence: a constructor *must* have the same name (and same capitalization) as the class.
2. Like methods, constructors can have parameters (listed within parentheses) and, thus, a *signature*. A constructor that takes no parameters is called the *default constructor*.
3. Unlike methods, no type is associated with constructors. In fact, the API does not show columns in the *Constructor Summary*, so the notions of *type, return,* and *static* do not exist.
4. The second listed constructor is also called `Stock` (this should not surprise you). It takes one `String` parameter. It is OK for a class to have more than one constructor as long as they have different signatures. Hence, constructor *overloading* is possible.
5. Click on the `Equation` class. Does it have a default constructor? Is it overloaded?

L4.4 Creating Objects

The steps needed to create an instance of the *Stock* class (or any other class) are as follows:

1. The package in which the class resides is written at the very top of its API. Import the class to your program:

```
import type.lib.Stock;
```

2. Pick a name to be used for referring to the instance and declare it. A variable used to refer to an instance is called the *object reference*, and its naming, in our coding style, follows the same rule as that for a variable of a primitive type: lowercase except the first letter of the second word, if any. We will name our reference s. This variable has a non-primitive class type and is declared as follows:

```
Stock s;
```

3. Select a constructor from the class API and invoke it. Since all constructors have the same name, their parameter lists must be different, and hence, each provides a distinct way for customizing the object's state. The Stock class has two constructors, and one of them expects us to pass the stock symbol. Let us use it to create a stock with the symbol ".SX". Unlike methods, constructors cannot be invoked with the dot separators; instead, the new keyword must be used:

```
new Stock(".SX");
```

4. Set the reference to the above expression:

```
s = new Stock(".SX");
```

You can optionally combine reference declaration (Step 2) with reference assignment (Step 4) and write

```
Stock s = new Stock(".SX");
```

Once you have an object reference pointing at an instance, you can use it as you used the class name to access static fields and invoke static methods. For example, to get today's price of this stock, you write

```
double price = s.getPrice();
```

L4.5 What Are Stocks?

A stock is a share in a public company, and a stock exchange is a place where stocks are traded (bought and sold). Companies whose stocks can be traded in a given exchange are known as the *listed companies*. Each company has a *symbol* that uniquely identifies its stock in that exchange. For example, the *JBA Stock Exchange* identifies listed companies by a three-character symbol made up of a dot followed by two letters; hence, it can accommodate $26 \times 26 = 676$ companies (the symbol is case-insensitive). As stocks are traded on the exchange, and according to the principles of supply and demand, the prices of stocks vary continuously as long as the exchange is open for business. Our fictitious JBA exchange is open all the time. Hence, the prices of its stocks are constantly changing. You can find out the price of any stock traded on it by visiting its web site:

```
http://www.cs.yorku.ca/~roumani/jba/se
```

and entering the symbol of the stock. Or you can use the `Stock` class to achieve the same result programmatically. When you create a `Stock` instance with a given symbol, the class looks up the symbol in the exchange and retrieves the company's name and the last-traded price (also known as the market price). Hence, each stock object has three key attributes: symbol, name, and price.

1. Launch your editor, and create this main class:

```java
import java.util.Scanner;
import java.io.PrintStream;
import type.lib.Stock;

public class Lab4
{
   public static void main(String[] args)
   {
      Scanner input =...
      PrintStream output =...
      output.print("Enter stock symbol... ");
      Stock s = new Stock(input.nextLine());
      output.println(s.getName());
      output.printf("%.2f", s.getPrice());
   }
}
```

Notice that since all we want to do with the symbol is pass it on to the `Stock` class, we did not bother to store it in a local variable. Notice also that the format specifier ensures that we see only dollars and cents in the price output.

2. Compile and run this application.
3. When prompted, enter a symbol for a company you know and examine the output. To that end, visit the web site of the exchange, obtain a quote for that symbol, and compare with your output.
4. What happens if you enter a nonexistent symbol such as ".12"?

L4.6 The `toString` Method

1. Add the following statement to Lab4:

```java
output.println(s.toString());
```

Examine the output. Does it agree with the API description of the `toString` method? What if the symbol is not found?

2. Add the following statements (after the one added above):

```
s.delimiter = '-';
output.println(s.toString());
```

Examine the output. Does it agree with the API description of the `toString` method?

3. Add the following statements (after the ones added above):

```
output.print("Enter a second symbol... ");
Stock s2 = new Stock(input.nextLine());
s2.delimiter = ':';
output.println(s2.toString());
```

Run the app, and explain the output.

4. Add the following statements (after the ones added above), and explain the output:

```
Stock s3 = s;
s3.delimiter = '*';
output.println(s3.toString());
output.println(s.toString());
output.print("Enter a third symbol... ");
s.setSymbol(input.nextLine());
output.println(s3.toString());
```

5. Add the following statement (after the ones added above):

```
output.println(s3);
```

Examine the output. The `toString` method is automatically invoked.

6. Add the following statements (after the ones added above):

```
output.print("Enter a 4th symbol... ");
StockNS ns = new StockNS(input.nextLine());
output.println(ns.toString());
output.println(ns);
```

Compilation will lead to a syntax error. Fix it and run. The `StockNS` class does not have a `toString` method so the Java-added one is invoked.

L4.7 The `equals` Method

At this stage, our program contains three references (s, s2, s3) of the type `Stock` and two objects of the type `Stock` (corresponding to the second- and third-entered symbols). Specifically, s2 points at the object with the second-entered symbol, while s and s3 point at the object with the third-entered symbol.

1. Add the following statements (after all the previous additions):

```
boolean test = (s == s3);
output.println("s, s3 via == : " + test);
test = s.equals(s3);
```

```
output.println("s, s3 via equals: " + test);
test = (s == s2);
output.println("s, s2 via == : " + test);
test = s.equals(s2);
output.println("s, s2 via equals: " + test);
```

Compile and run. Provide different symbols for the second and third inputs, and then carefully explain the generated output. Re-run but enter the same symbol for the second and third inputs. Explain the output.

2. Add the following statements (after the ones added above):

```
StockNS ns2 = new StockNS(ns.getSymbol());
test = (ns == ns2);
output.println("ns, ns2 via == : " + test);
test = ns.equals(ns2);
output.println("ns, ns2 via equals: " + test);
```

By construction, the ns2 object has the same symbol as ns. Would you expect the two references to be different and the two objects to be equal? Java recognizes the equality of the objects pointed at by s and s2 when their symbols are the same, but Java does not recognize the equality of the ns2 and ns objects. Why?

L4.8 Static versus Nonstatic Features

1. Create a new class, Lab4S, with the following body:

```
output.print("Enter 1st symbol... ");
Stock s1 = new Stock(input.nextLine());
output.print("Enter 2nd symbol... ");
Stock s2 = new Stock(input.nextLine());

output.println(s1 + " getName: " + s1.getName());
output.println(s2 + " getName: " + s2.getName());
s1.titleCaseName = true;
s1.delimiter = '*';
output.println(s1 + " getName: " + s1.getName());
output.println(s2 + " getName: " + s2.getName());
```

When prompted, enter two different symbols and examine the output. Why does titleCaseName behave differently from delimiter?

2. The API lists titleCaseName as a static attribute yet it was accessed using s1, an object reference, in the above code. Could we have written the following statement instead:

```
Stock.titleCaseName = true;
```

If the two approaches are equivalent, does it matter which instance is used; that is, could we also have written

```
s2.titleCaseName = true;
```

Which approach is better?

3. The API lists `delimiter` as a nonstatic attribute; in fact, the above code accessed it using an object reference. Could we have written the following statement instead:

```
Stock.delimiter = '*';
```

L4.9 String Input Source

1. Launch your editor, and create the program `StringSource` starting with the usual template.

2. Consider the following statement in the template:

```
Scanner input = new Scanner(System.in);
```

It creates an instance of `Scanner` customized to work with `System.in`, which denotes the keyboard. Let us create instead an instance that derives its input data from a string. To do that, replace the above statement with

```
Scanner input = new Scanner("12.75 12 true");
```

3. We should be able to read the contents of the string as if it had been entered from the keyboard. Add the statements

```
double d = input.nextDouble();
int i =...
boolean b =...
```

4. Add statements to output the three variables defined above. Compile and run your program.

5. As you can see, the `Scanner` methods are capable of parsing the tokens in the string based on the spaces that separates them. Explore the dependence of these spaces as follows: replace the string with

```
"12.75 \t 12 \ntrue"
```

Determine whether one can replace one space with two spaces, with a tab, or with a new line character.

6. It looks like when a method like `nextDouble` is invoked, it starts from the current position in the string and moves right skipping encountered whitespace until a `double` is captured. To confirm this, let us use the `nextLine` method whose API states that it returns all characters between the current position and the next new line character. Modify your program by commenting out the integer and boolean inputs and adding

```
String s = input.nextLine();
```

L4.10 File Input Source

1. Launch your editor, and create the program `FileSource` starting with the usual template.

2. Replace the statement

   ```
   Scanner input = new Scanner(System.in);
   ```

   with

   ```
   Scanner input = new Scanner(new File("Lab4.txt"));
   ```

   This creates an instance customized to read input from the named file. The file must be present in the current working directory. If you are not sure which directory that is, write a short Java program containing

   ```
   output.println(System.getProperty("user.dir"));
   ```

3. Use any editor to create the above-mentioned text file in the working directory. Write in it the lines

   ```
   12.75
   12
   true
   ```

4. Add statements to read the three pieces of data and output them as was done when the data source was a string.

5. Whenever a program deals with files, there is a possibility that the file is not present or the disk system is not connected. When this occurs, an I/O exception is thrown, and our app must acknowledge this by modifying the header of `main` as follows:

   ```
   public static void main(String[] args) throws
   java.io.IOException
   ```

6. Another peculiarity of files is that you must close the connection that you established with them once you are done. Add the following statement at the end of the program:

   ```
   input.close();
   ```

7. Compile and run your program.

 Exercises

Programming exercises are indicated with an asterisk.

    4.1 When you visit a supermarket, you see thousands of items, each of which is an object. Name two attributes and two methods of each object.

    4.2 Argue that through abstraction, the thousands of objects described in the previous exercise can be reduced to a single class, `Item`. Explain how the differences between the items and their individualities can be recovered from this class.

4.3 Examine the API of the `Item` class of `type.lib`. (a) Is it a utility? (b) Does it have a default constructor? (c) What attributes can be set through the constructor?

4.4 Does the `type.lib.Item` class provide an accessor to the item number? How about the item name and sale price?

4.5 Does the `type.lib.Item` class provide a mutator for the item number? How about the item name and sale price?

4.6 Examine the sale price mutator in `type.lib.Item`. What approach does it adopt to ensure that the sale price is legal?

4.7 Examine the constructor of `type.lib.Item`. What approach does it adopt to ensure that the sale price is legal? Could it have used another approach, for example, return a `false` or make the legality of the price a precondition?

4.8 Does the `type.lib.Item` class contain obligatory methods? If so, specify what each of them does.

4.9 What are the disadvantages of making the sale price attribute a field (i.e., public) in `type.lib.Item`?

4.10 Does the `type.lib.Item` class contain any `static` features? How about `final` features?

4.11 The `type.lib.Stock` class has a `cloneMe` method that allows you to create a copy of the instance on which it was invoked. Given a `Stock` reference `s`, you create a copy using

```
Stock copy = s.cloneMe();
```

But one can seemingly achieve the same result by a fragment such as

```
Stock copy = new Stock(s.getSymbol());
```

What is the conceptual difference between these two copying approaches? Can you find a tangible (i.e., demonstrable) difference between them?

4.12 The constructor and the `setSymbol` mutator of `type.lib.Stock` update the stock's data by invoking the `refresh` method. Why was that method made public? Can you imagine a scenario where you, the client, may need to invoke it in your app?

4.13* Launch any editor, and create a text file with three records:

```
6.5
12.75
18.25
```

Write a program that reads the above file and outputs the sum of the three values. Will your program compile if `nextInt` is used instead of `nextDouble`? Will it run?

4.14* Create an instance of the `Date` class, a member of the `java.util` package. Read its API and note that it has a default constructor. Afterward, invoke the `toString` method on your reference and output the result.

4.15* Create an instance of the `Random` class, a member of the `java.util` package. Read its API, and note that it has a default constructor. The reference you obtain enables you to generate several kinds of random numbers. (a) Invoke the `nextInt` method two or three times in your app and output the returns. Why was this method overloaded? (b) Modify your program so that it also generates two or three `double` and `boolean` values.

4.16* Consider the `Fraction` class, a member of the `type.lib` package. Read its API and note that it has a constructor that takes a numerator–denominator pair. Create an instance `f1` for the fraction 1/2 and invoke on it the `toString` method. Create a second instance `f2` for the fraction 1/3. Now invoke `add` on `f1` and pass `f2` to it. Output the final state of `f1` by invoking `toString` on it.

4.17* Consider the `Fraction` class, a member of the `type.lib` package. Create an instance `f1` for the fraction 1/2 and another `f2` for the fraction 2/4. `f1` and `f2` are clearly not equal as references (why?), but their objects have identical states (because 1/2 and 2/4 are one and the same as rational numbers). Confirm these two observations by outputting the result of `==` as well as the return of `equals` for these two references.

4.18* Consider the `Equation` class, a member of the `type.lib` package. Read its API and note that it has a constructor that takes the three coefficients of an equation of the second degree. Create an instance `eqn` for the equation:

$$x^2 - 7x + 12 = 0$$

which is known to have two roots: 3 and 4. Invoke the `getRoot` method on `eqn` twice, once passing 1 and once 2 as root numbers, and output the two returns.

4.19* Create an instance `e1` for the `type.lib.Equation` class for the equation:

$$x^2 - 7x + 12 = 0$$

Create another instance `e2` for the equation:

$$3x^2 - 21x + 36 = 0$$

`e1` and `e2` are clearly not equal as references (why?), but their objects have identical states (the second equation is obtained from the first by a multiplication of both sides by 3). Confirm these two observations by outputting the result of `==` as well as the return of `equals` for these two references.

4.20* Create an instance, `soup`, of `type.lib.Item` with the following state:

```
Item Number: "001"
Item Name: "The ABC Chicken Soup"
Sale Price: $9.75 per unit
```

Assume that the store ordered two batches of these soup items. The first is for 100 units and has an overall cost of $500; that is, each unit costs $5. The second order is for 50 units and has an overall cost of $400. Simulate these two orders in your program by using the `purchase` method. Your program must then use the accessors in the class to output the following information for this item: number, name, stock (quantity on hand), and cost price per unit. Justify the generated output by showing how the average cost price, weighted by the quantity of each order, is computed.

4.21* Continue the program of the Exercise 4.20 by processing two more transactions: In the first, the store sells 20 units of soup at the posted sale price, that is, using the `sell(int)` method. In the second transaction, the store sells 10 units for a total of $80, that is, at a discount. Your program must then generate two outputs as follows:

```
output.println(soup.getUnitPrice());
output.println(soup.getSales()/soup.getSoldQty());
```

Run the program and justify the generated output.

4.22* Create two instances, soup and cereal, of type.lib.Item with arbitrary numbers, names, and unit sale prices. Then add the following statements to your program:

```
output.println(cereal == soup);
output.println(cereal.equals(soup));
output.println(cereal.compareTo(soup));
```

Run the program and justify the generated output.

eCheck

Check04A (TS = 26)

Your project involves high-precision computations that deal exclusively with rational numbers, numbers that can be expressed as a ratio (or a fraction) of two integers. Given an expression containing several such fractions, you must evaluate using fraction arithmetic rather than by dividing the numerator by the denominator and putting up with the inevitable round-off of real numbers. To achieve this, you decide to delegate to the Fraction class in type.lib because it provides an abstraction that allows us to treat fractions as if they were primitive types.

Write an application, Check04A, that computes a particular expression A:

$$A = \frac{x+y}{z+t}, \text{ where } x = \frac{83}{100}, y = \frac{5}{9}, z = \frac{667}{1000}, t = \frac{-2}{3}. \quad \text{Answer: } A = \frac{12470}{3}$$

The A expression has the four fractions x, y, z, and t. The above example shows the value of A for the shown values of the four fractions. Here is one sample run of Check04A:

```
For each fraction enter its numerator/denominator,
pressing ENTER after each
Enter x
83
100
Enter y
5
9
Enter z
667
1000
Enter t
-2
3
A = 12470/3 = 4156 2/3 = 4156.666666666667
```

Note that the app outputs the value of *A* as an improper fraction, followed by its proper form, followed by its approximate real value obtained by dividing the numerator by the denominator using `double` accuracy.

Here is a second run:

```
For each fraction enter its numerator/denominator,
pressing ENTER after each
Enter x
112
245
Enter y
-45
87
Enter z
23
7
Enter t
99
100
A = -1220/86797 = -1220/86797 = -0.014055785338202934
```

Notice that the case of a zero denominator is handled internally by `Fraction` so you do not have to worry about it. Nevertheless, you can safely assume that eCheck will not generate test cases with a zero denominator.

Write the `Check04A` app and eCheck it.

Check04B (TS = 21)

The `Check04B` app prompts for a stock symbol and outputs the current date and time, the name of the stock, and its price. Here is a sample run:

```
Enter a stock symbol ... .sx
As of Mon May 17 11:22:26 EDT 2004, the price of a
Compu-SIERRA & X-RAY Corp.
share is: 35.86
```

The first line contains the prompt and the user's input (you can assume that the entered symbol is valid). The second line contains the words "As of" followed by the date and time (and time zone) at which the program was run, followed by ", the price of a". The third line contains the name of the stock as listed on the exchange. The fourth line contains the words "share is:" followed by the price rounded to two decimals.

Write `Check04B` and eCheck it.

Hint:	Use the `Date` class.

Technical Note:
eCheck ignores the seconds in the time stamp when it compares its output with yours.

Check04C (TS = 26)

Use the API of the `Student` class of the `type.lib` package to create the app `Check04C`. The app reads the names and IDs of two students; creates two corresponding student objects; and then outputs the results of invoking `toString`; applying `==`, and invoking `equals` on the two references. Here is a sample run:

```
Student1 name: Adam
Student1 ID: 555396512
Student2 name: Nadia
Student2 ID: 555392512
s1.toString yields ..... CSE student: Adam
s2.toString yields ..... CSE student: Nadia
s1 == s2 yields ....... false
s1.equals(s2) yields ... false
```

Your app needs not perform any input validation. It should just read the input and pass it to the class constructor. Pay attention to output formatting, particularly the alignment.

Develop your app, test it, and then eCheck it.

Check04D (TS = 26)

Create the app `Check04D` as follows:

■ Use the API of the `Item` class of the `type.lib` package to create an item object having the item number 750, the name "Milk carton" and a unit sale price of $3.45.

■ Assume that the store acquired this item through two orders. Prompt the user to enter the number of cartons and the total purchase price in each of the two orders.

■ Output the results of invoking `toString` and `getUnitCost` on the item.

Here is a sample run:

```
First Order:
Quantity purchased ... 100
Cost of purchase ... 275
Second Order:
Quantity purchased ... 20
Cost of purchase ... 65
toString yields ...... Item# 750 Milk carton
getUnitCost yields ... 2.83
```

Note that the final output is formatted by rounding to the nearest cent. Note also that $3.45 is the unit sale price of the item whereas the final output is the unit cost price. The unit cost price derives from the cost of purchasing the item, and when the item is purchases through several orders, the class performs a weighted average to arrive at a cost price per unit.

Develop your app, test it, and then eCheck it.

5 Control Structures

Learning Objectives

1. *Classify alternative flows of control*

2. *Learn about the* `if` *statement*

3. *Use boolean operators*

4. *Become familiar with the versatile* `for` *statement*

5. *Learn about* `do` *and other control structures*

6. *Validate input without a crash*

A program with a sequence flow performs the same action every time it runs. The data it uses can change from one run to the next, depending on user input, but the action it takes does not. In this chapter, you will learn two nonsequential control flows: selection and iteration. Programs that use these flows exhibit "intelligence" because they can adapt their actions as they run depending on the situation at hand.

Chapter Outline

5.1 Selection

All the programs that we have written so far are monotonous in the sense that they always perform the same action. The mortgage payment program, for example, changes its output (the monthly payment) depending on its input (present value, interest, and period), but it always follows a formula that dictates the same sequence of steps. There are many processes in the world around us, however, that do not follow this mode of computing. For example, instructions for cooking a frozen item may be something like "to heat in a conventional oven, do this, but for a microwave oven, do that." The following sections enable us to add selection to our algorithms.

5.1.1 Flow of Control

A program is made up of statements, and when a particular statement is executed, we say that it receives **control**. The phrase **flow of control** refers to the order in which statements are executed. In all programs written so far in this textbook, statements have been executed in **sequence** flow, that is, the order they appear in the program, top to bottom. In Fig. 5.1(a), the program statements $S_1, S_2,..., S_n$ are horizontal line segments, and the time axis is vertical and pointing down. This represents the sequence flow.

Programs with only a sequence control flow may be useful in the sense that a calculator is useful, but such programs lack the ability to adapt or to exhibit change. To enable our programs to exhibit such "intelligence," we seek an additional flow of control, one that resembles the flow in Fig. 5.1(b). This flow, called **selection**, starts like a sequence until a critical statement (depicted in the figure as a disk) is reached. At that point, the flow forks into several possible routes, and a selection needs to be made. If the left route is chosen, statements $A_1, A_2,...$ will be executed, whereas if a different route is chosen, a different set of statements will be executed. No matter which route is taken, statement X will eventually be reached, and sequence flow will resume thereafter.

Figure 5.1 Flow of control.
(a) Sequence;
(b) Selection

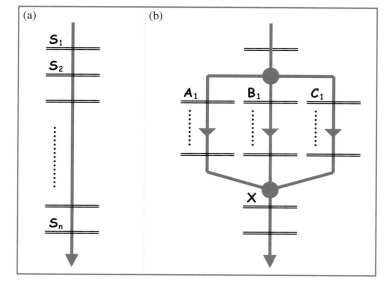

5.1.2 The if Statement

It is a challenge to implement the selection flow in programming languages because the selection diagram is manifestly two-dimensional, whereas statements are typed vertically in a one-dimensional fashion. Java, like all other languages, offers a construct, called **the if statement**, that simulates a two-dimensional flow by skipping over statements. We start with the simplest form whose flow diagram is shown in Fig. 5.2.

Let us assume that the program follows a sequence flow up to statement S.

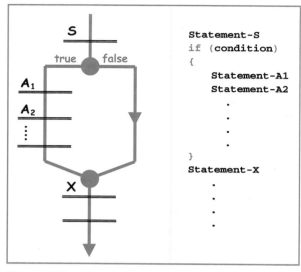

```
                    Statement-S
                    if (condition)
                    {
                        Statement-A1
                        Statement-A2
                            .
                            .
                            .
                            .
                    }
                    Statement-X
                        .
                        .
                        .
                        .
```

Figure 5.2 The flow diagram and the syntax of the simple if statement

Afterward, it reaches a selection point (depicted in the figure as a disk) at which it is confronted with a boolean condition. This is where the if-statement starts, and as you can see from the corresponding right half of Fig. 5.2, its syntax is the keyword if followed by a space (as a matter of style), followed by the boolean condition enclosed in parentheses.

According to the figure, if the condition is true, control will follow the left path and statements A_1, A_2,..., will be executed, and then statement X. Otherwise, X will be executed immediately after evaluating the condition. This is implemented in the syntax by starting a block (opening a brace) after the if statement. All statements written in that block will be executed if and only if the condition is true; this block represents the left path in the flow diagram. If the condition is false, the block is skipped, and X is executed next. This means that even though X and the if statement are physically not consecutive (several statements apart), they can be logically consecutive.

Our style guide requires that the braces of any block be vertically aligned and that all its statements be left justified and indented. This applies, in particular, to the block that follows an if statement, for example,

```
if (count > maximum)
{
    count--;
    output.println("Maximum exceeded.");
}
```

Programming Tip   5.1

Pitfall: Placing a semicolon after keyword if

The fragment

```
if (count > maximum);
{   count--;
    output.println("Maximum exceeded.");
}
```

will compile without errors and will run without runtime errors, but it has a logic error: the block that follows the if will always execute. Keep in mind that the header of any block (whether it is a class, a method, or an if header) is *not* followed by a semicolon.

To save space, the above fragment is sometimes written as follows:

```
if (count > maximum)
{   count--;
    output.println("Maximum exceeded.");
}
```

Note that writing the first statement of the block on the same line as the opening brace does not violate our coding style.

Example 5.1

Write a fragment that prompts for and reads an integer from the user and outputs its absolute value without using Math.abs.

Answer:

```
output.print("Enter an integer... ");
int entry = input.nextInt();
int absValue = entry;
if (entry < 0)
{
    absValue = -entry;
}
output.println(absValue);
```

Programming Tip   5.2

Pitfall: Not using braces after keyword if

The fragment

```
if (count > maximum)
    count--;
    output.println("Maximum exceeded.");
```

will compile without errors and will run without runtime errors but not as its programmer intended. In the absence of braces, Java treats the above fragment as if it were the following:

```
if (count > maximum)
{
    count--;
}
output.println("Maximum exceeded.");
```

Hence, the output statement will be executed in all cases. Make it a habit to always use braces for the block that follows an if, even if it contains only one statement.

In Example 5.1, no action is taken if the condition is `false` (i.e., if `entry >= 0`). This case is handled by setting `absValue` to `entry` before the `if`, which can be thought of as a default action. In general, we recommend that you do not rely on default actions for two reasons:

1. Defaults can hide a missed case and, thus, lead to logic errors.
2. Defaults are executed in all cases and, thus, lead to inefficiencies.

To avoid defaults, we use the `if-else` statement whose flow diagram is shown in Fig. 5.3.

This statement allows true two-way branching by providing two scopes separated by the `else` keyword: one for the `true` action and one for `false`.

Example 5.2

Rewrite the solution of Example 5.1 such that no defaults are used.

Answer:
```
output.print("Enter an integer... ");
int entry = input.nextInt();
int absValue;
if (entry < 0)
{
    absValue = -entry;
}
else
{
    absValue = entry;
}
output.println(absValue);
```

Figure 5.3 The flow diagram and the syntax of the `if-else` statement

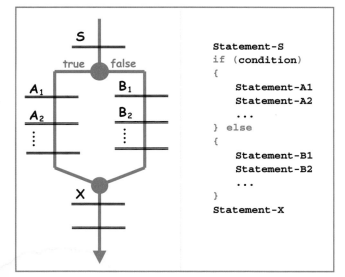

```
Statement-S
if (condition)
{
    Statement-A1
    Statement-A2
    ...
} else
{
    Statement-B1
    Statement-B2
    ...
}
Statement-X
```

It is clear from Example 5.2 that the `if-else` construct makes it easy for the compiler to spot a missed case. If the programmer forgets to assign a value to `absValue` in either scope, the last statement will generate a compile-time error because it attempts to output a variable that may not have been initialized. This is an example of risk mitigation by early exposure (Section 2.3.1) because a potential logic error is turned by this construct to a mere compile-time error. Using a default would have thwarted this.

Our coding style does not dictate a particular placement for the `else` keyword. You can put it on a line by itself or on the same line as the closing brace. Hence, the following (tighter) layout is also acceptable for the answer to Example 5.2:

```
if (entry < 0)
{
    absValue = -entry;
} else
{
    absValue = entry;
}
```

Details   5.1

The if-else Operator

The **?** **ternary operator** (ternary means it has three operands) provides a terse if-else. Instead of writing

```
if (condition)
{
    x = value-1;
} else
{
    x = value-2;
}
```

you can write

```
x = condition ? value-1 : value-2;
```

The keyword else is not indented, but one space is left between it and the preceding closed brace.

5.1.3 Building the Condition

The condition that is inserted between the parentheses in an if statement must be a boolean value, and by definition, the condition is considered met if its value is true. The value can be the result of a relational expression, the content of a boolean variable, the return of a boolean method, or a boolean combination of these. Let us look at each case in more detail.

Relational Expression

A relational expression is the kind of condition that we have been using so far in this chapter. Recall from Section 3.2.4 that Java has seven relational operators, and while they operate on various operand types, their results are always boolean. For example, if x and y are two numeric variables, then the relational expression (x < y) is boolean (being true if x is less than y and false otherwise), and we can use it in an if statement such as the following:

```
if (x < y)
{
    scope-A;
} else
{
    scope-B;
}
```

Programming Tip   5.3

Pitfall: Using == to test the equality of real values

If x and y are two real variables (float or double), you should not test their equality using the == operator because of the inevitable round-off errors. For example, the following fragment will output "Not
Equal!" for almost all inputs:

```
output.print("Enter a real... ");
double x = input.nextDouble();
double y = Math.pow(Math.pow(x, 0.5), 2);
if (x == y)
{
    output.println("Equal!");
} else
{
    output.println("Not Equal!");
}
```

To properly test equality, compare the absolute value of x-y to some number EPSILON (a tolerance) that
is considered infinitesimally small in the application's context:

```
if (Math.abs(x - y) < EPSILON)
{
    output.println("Equal!");
} else
{
    output.println("Not Equal!");
}
```

where scope-A and scope-B represent statements in corresponding blocks.

Note that, as defined above, the mere presence of this boolean in an if statement means
that scope-A would be executed if the boolean were true, and scope-B would be executed if the boolean were false. In other words, you do *not* have to write the condition as

```
        if (x < y == true)
```

Such a style, albeit syntactically correct, is not standard and reflects poor understanding.

Boolean Variable

Perhaps the most natural way to construct a boolean value is simply to assign the condition to
a boolean variable. For example, the above fragment can be rewritten as

```
        boolean less = (x < y);
        if (less)
        {
            scope-A;
        } else
```

Programming Tip   5.4

Pitfall: Using == to test the equality of objects

You should not test the equality of objects using the == operator; doing so would be too strong. Use the equals method instead. For example, if x and y are two non-null references, the test

```
if  (x.equals(y))
```

checks to see if the two objects in question have the same state (as determined by their class). On the other hand, the test

```
if  (x == y)
```

succeeds only if there is in fact one object; that is, x and y are two references pointing at the same object.

```
{
    scope-B;
}
```

Again, make sure you refrain from writing (less == true). Using a variable instead of an expression is generally recommended when the condition is lengthy because this makes the program easier to understand, especially when the boolean is properly named.

Boolean-Returning Method

If a method returns a boolean value, then you can invoke it as part of the condition. For example, if x and y are two non-null object references, then we can write

```
if  (x.equals(y))
```

Programming Tip   5.5

Pitfall: Using = to assign a boolean

Using if-else (as shown below) to assign a boolean is not an error, but it reflects poor style. The code

```
boolean valid;
if (x > a && y <= b)
{
    valid = true;
} else
{
    valid = false;
}
```

should be written as

```
boolean valid = (x > a && y <= b);
```

In this case, `scope-A` will receive control if the objects pointed at by x and y are deemed equal by the class of x.

Boolean Expression

Java has **boolean operators** that take boolean operands and produce boolean results; hence, they satisfy the closure property. These operators, also known as **logical operators**, are listed in Appendix C, but in this textbook, we will be using only the three shown in Fig. 5.4.

You can see from the figure that && (**AND**) and || (**OR**) are binary whereas ! (**NOT**) is unary. Using these operators, we can form **boolean expressions** by combining boolean operands. For example, to express the condition that

$$x \in [a, b)$$

which is equivalent to saying that x belongs to this interval with the left end included and the right one excluded, we can write

```
if (x >= a && x < b)
```

Note that parentheses are not needed because the relational operators (Fig. 3.10) have a higher precedence than &&.

Similarly, we can express the condition that

$$x \in [a, b)$$

Programming Tip   5.6

Pitfall: Using mathlike inequalities

You cannot use mathlike inequalities in conditions. For example, the condition

```
if ((0 < x < 1) || (x && y) > 1)
```

will not compile. It should be expressed instead as

```
if ((x > 0 && x < 1) || (x > 1 && y > 1))
```

Figure 5.4 Some of the boolean operators in Java (the arrow indicates association)

Precedence	Operator	Kind	Syntax	true if
-2 ←	!	prefix	!x	x is false
-12 →	&&	infix	x && y	x and y are both true
-13 →	||	infix	x || y	either x or y or both are true

by writing

```
if (!(x >= a && x < b))
```

Here, parentheses must be used because the so-called **negation operator** (!) has a higher precedence than the other operators in this expression, and we want it to operate last. You can optionally simplify the above expression by using **deMorgan's law**, which states that to negate the so-called **conjunction** A && B, replace && with || and negate the two operands:

```
!(A && B) is equivalent to (!A) || (!B)
```

Hence, we can rewrite the if statement above as

```
if (!(x >= a) || !(x < b))
```

and since the negation of >= is < and that of < is >=, we rewrite the above as

```
if (x < a || x >= b)
```

deMorgan's law has a second form that allows negating a so-called **disjunction** A || B: replace || with && and negate the two operands:

```
!(A || B) is equivalent to (!A) && (!B)
```

The virtual machine evaluates the && and || operators in a manner known as **lazy**, or **short circuit**, and we can see this best through an example. Suppose that we are given the statement

```
if (x.equals(y))
```

and are told to modify it such that it does not lead to a crash if x is null (recall that invoking any method on a null reference leads to the null reference exception). What is your critique of the following modification?

```
if (x != null && x.equals(y))
```

Will it still crash if x is null? Normally, when the virtual machine evaluates an expression, it first evaluates each term in it and then combines their results. But the && operator instructs the virtual machine to evaluate the left operand first, and if it turns out to be false, then the second operand is *not* evaluated (because if you and anything with false you get false). Similarly, the || operator has a short circuit: if its first operand is true, the second is *not* evaluated (because the or of anything with true is true).

Example 5.3

Write a fragment that determines whether a given integer y is a multiple of a given integer x, and outputs a message accordingly. Note that no integer is a multiple of zero.

Answer:

```
if (x == 0 || y % x != 0)
{
    output.println("Not a multiple.");
} else
{
```

```
        output.println("Yes, it is a multiple.");
    }
```

Thanks to the short-circuit behaviour of ||, the condition will not lead to a crash when x is zero.

5.1.4 Multiway Branching

Since the if statement relies on a boolean condition to carry out the selection, its branching is intrinsically two-way; hence, it is incapable of directly implementing the multiway branching envisioned in Fig. 5.1(b). Given a multi-outcome condition, we can break it up into several two-way conditions, each identifying one outcome. The strategy is depicted in Fig. 5.5, where a three-way branch is broken down into two two-way branches.

In general an n-way branch can be expressed using $n-1$ two-way conditions, with the nth outcome being handled by the else clause of the last condition.

Example 5.4

The floor area of a room is divided into six regions as shown in Fig. 5.6. Given the x-y coordinates of a tile, write an app that determines the tile's code.

Answer:
Given the x-y coordinates of a floor tile, we need to determine in which region it resides and then set its code accordingly. Since there are six possible outcomes ($n = 6$), we need five conditions and an else:

```
char code;
if (x <= a && y > d)
```

Figure 5.5 A multiway branch can be broken down into several two-way branches.

```
Statement-S
if (condition-1)
{    Statement-A1
     Statement-A2
     ...
} else if (condition-2)
{    Statement-B1
     Statement-B2
     ...
} else
{    Statement-C1
     Statement-C2
     ...
}
Statement-X
```

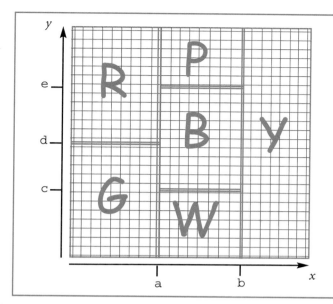

Code	Condition
'R'	x ≤ a, y > d
'G'	x ≤ a, y ≤ d
'P'	x∈(a,b],y > e
'B'	x∈(a,b],y∈(c,e]
'W'	x∈(a,b],y ≤ c
'Y'	x > b

Figure 5.6 Each floor tile in a room is painted red (code R), green (G), purple (P), blue (B), white (W), or yellow (Y) based on its location.

```
{
    code = 'R';
} else if (x <= a && y <= d)
{
    code = 'G';
} else if (x > a && x <= b && y > e)
{
    code = 'P';
} else if (x > a && x <= b && y > c && y <= e)
{
    code = 'B';
} else if (x > a && x <= b && y <= c)
{
    code = 'W';
} else
{
    code = 'Y';
}
```

By elimination, it is clear from Fig. 5.6 that the last `else` corresponds to the right-most region in which x is greater than b. It is therefore a good idea to add an assertion to the `else` block:

```
} else
{
    assert x > b;
    code = 'Y';
}
```

This strategy implements an *n*-way branch by formulating n-1 independent conditions, each of which leads to a unique outcome when met. The conditions are "independent" in the sense that each is self-contained; hence, they can be inspected in any order. If a condition evaluates to true, the outcome is set and we are done; otherwise, we move on to the next condition. As such, the strategy can be thought of as a nesting of if statements on the else (or false) side. This is by no means the only way to nest if statements and may not be the most efficient, but it is systematic. Hence, we are not likely to miss an outcome. Once you master this strategy, you can move on to more efficient strategies where conditions can overlap and nesting can be done on either side.

Example 5.5

Write a program that prompts for and reads a year (an int) from the user. If the entry is not positive, the program must crash. Otherwise, it should output a message that indicates whether the year entered is a leap year.

By definition, a leap year is divisible by 4, but if it is divisible by 100, then it must also be divisible by 400. For example, the year 2004 is a leap year because it is divisible by 4 and not by 100. The year 1900 is not a leap year because it is divisible by 4 and by 100 but is not divisible by 400. The year 2003 is not a leap year because it is not divisible by 4. The year 2000 is a leap year because it is divisible by 4, by 100, and by 400.

Answer:

The input and its validation are straightforward:

```
output.print("Enter the year... ");
int year = input.nextInt();
ToolBox.crash(year <= 0, "Invalid!");
```

The seemingly simple definition of a leap year gives rise to many possibilities. To avoid repeated computations, let us allocate a boolean variable yes4 that remembers if the year is divisible by 4:

```
final int FOUR = 4;
boolean yes4 = (year % FOUR) == 0;
```

Let us do the same thing for the other two divisors:

```
final int CENTURY = 100;
boolean yes100 = (year % CENTURY) == 0;
boolean yes400 = (year % (FOUR * CENTURY)) == 0;
```

The problem is now formulated in terms of three boolean variables; hence, there are 2^3, or 8, cases to consider. Admittedly, since the numbers 4, 100, and 400 are not relatively prime, some of these cases can be merged or eliminated altogether. However, in the spirit of our strategy, let us treat them as eight independent conditions and worry about optimization later. The eight cases are the following:

1. `yes4, yes100, yes400`
   In this case it is a leap year. As an optimization, we can simplify this to `yes400` (because if a number is divisible by 400, it must also be divisible by 100 and 4).
2. `yes4, yes100, !yes400`
   It is not a leap year. We can simplify this to `yes100, !yes400`.
3. `yes4, !yes100, yes400`
   This case is clearly impossible.
4. `yes4, !yes100, !yes400`
   It is a leap year. We can simplify this to `yes4` and `!yes100`.
5. `!yes4, yes100, yes400`
   This case is clearly impossible.
6. `!yes4, yes100, !yes400`
   This case is clearly impossible.
7. `!yes4, !yes100, yes400`
   This case is clearly impossible.

In More Depth   5.1

Nested `if` Statements

As mentioned at the beginning of Section 5.1.4, there are many ways to implement multiway branching. You can **nest** `if` statements any way you like as long as they are either disjoint (one ends before the other begins) or fully nested (one is contained entirely within the other); that is, as long as they do not overlap. For example, the selection in Example 5.4 was implemented using a strategy based on determining the condition that leads to a single outcome. To produce the outcome 'G' (see Fig. 5.6), for example, we imposed the condition

```
if (x <= a && y > d)
```

Using fully nested `if` statements, we can use an alternative strategy in which the conditions derive from the statement of the problem. For example,

```
if (x <= a)
{
    if (y <= d)
    {
        code = 'G';
    } else
    {   code = 'R';
    }
    ...
```

Whether you use fully nested `if` statements or stick to the single-outcome strategy is a matter of personal preference.

8. !yes4, !yes100, !yes400

It is not a leap year. We can simplify this to !yes4.

The program can now perform the selection as follows:

```java
if (yes400)
{
    output.println(year + " is a leap year.");
} else if (yes100 && !yes400)
{
    output.println(year + " is not a leap year.");
```

Java Details   5.2

The switch Statement

Java provides a second statement for implementing selection, but it is extremely limited: it applies only to situations in which the condition to be tested is of the form

```java
integer variable == integer literal
```

For example, instead of writing (gender is a char variable)

```java
if (gender == 'M')
{
    male++;
} else if (gender == 'F')
{
    female++;
} else
{
    other++;
}
```

you can write

```java
switch (gender)
{
    case 'M':
        male++;
        break;
    case 'F':
        female++;
        break;
    default:
        other++;
}
```

The break statement terminates the case and transfers control to the statement that follows the entire switch block. It is a common pitfall to forget this break, in which case the statements of all the following cases will be executed.

```
    } else if (yes4 && !yes100)
    {
        output.println(year + " is a leap year.");
    } else
    {
        output.println(year + " is not a leap year.");
    }
```

We can now combine the same-outcome cases:

```
    if (yes400 || (yes4 && !yes100))
    {
        output.println(year + " is a leap year.");
    } else
    {
        output.println(year + " is not a leap year.");
    }
```

5.2 Iteration

If selection makes computers intelligent, then **iteration** makes them unparalleled hard workers. The ability to execute a chunk of code over and over for an arbitrarily large number of times is a hallmark of computing and a key requirement for almost any algorithm. The following sections show how iteration can be implemented in Java.

Figure 5.7 The iterative flow of control

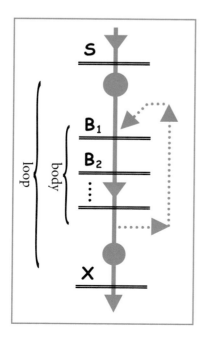

5.2.1 Flow of Control

Figure 5.7 depicts a program that starts off in a sequence flow until it finishes executing statement S. Then it encounters a **loop**, the beginning and end of which are depicted in the figure by two disks. Statements B_1, B_2,..., which are sandwiched between the two disks, are called the **body** of the loop. As indicated by the dotted path, they are executed repeatedly, hence the name "**iteration.**"

After the last iteration of the loop, control is transferred to statement X, the one immediately after the loop, and sequence flow resumes.

To implement an iterative flow, programming languages must incorporate syntax to indicate where the loop starts and ends (the two disks), and to enable the programmer to specify when the loop is exited, for example, after a certain number of iterations or once a particular condition is met. This calls for several syntactical features. Indeed, most programming languages implement iterative flow using three or more different constructs.

5.2.2 The `for` Statement

The `for` statement in Java is an extremely flexible implementation of iterative flow, and it allows you to control iteration either using a counter or a condition. If you have previous exposure to languages such as VB, Turing, or Pascal, then do not let the name similarity fool you. Java's `for` is far more versatile than its namesakes in those languages; in particular, it can be used even when the number of iterations is not known. It is therefore important that you master all its syntactical features. The characteristics of the `for` statement are shown in Fig. 5.8.

We will go over the details of that figure using an example. Consider the following code fragment:

```
final int MAX = 10;
final double SQUARE_ROOT = 0.5;
for (int i = 0; i < MAX; i = i + 1)
{
    double sqrt = Math.pow(i, SQUARE_ROOT);
    output.print(i);
    output.print("\t"); // tab
    output.println(sqrt);
}
```

The loop starts with the keyword `for` followed by a space (as a matter of style) followed by three entities that are separated by semicolons and surrounded by parentheses. The virtual machine executes the loop by following the algorithm shown in Fig. 5.8:

1. We imagine that there is an open brace just before the `for` as if it were { `for`.
2. We execute "initial": a variable `i` is allocated and initialized to 0.

Figure 5.8 The flow diagram, syntax, and algorithm of the `for` statement

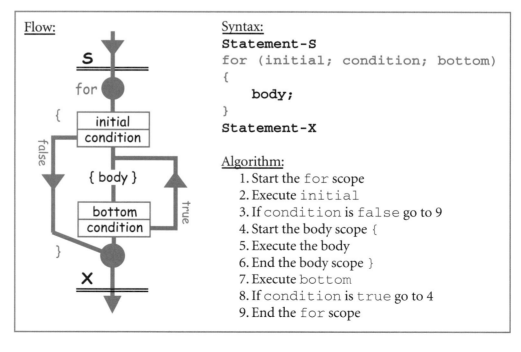

Flow:

Syntax:
```
Statement-S
for (initial; condition; bottom)
{
    body;
}
Statement-X
```

Algorithm:
1. Start the `for` scope
2. Execute `initial`
3. If `condition` is `false` go to 9
4. Start the body scope {
5. Execute the body
6. End the body scope }
7. Execute `bottom`
8. If `condition` is `true` go to 4
9. End the `for` scope

3. We evaluate "condition": the boolean i < MAX is clearly `true`, so we continue.
4. We start the body scope.
5. We execute the four statements in the body, and this leads to the output line: 0 *tab* 0 . 0.
6. The body scope ends; hence, the variable `sqrt` is no longer known.
7. We execute "bottom": the variable i becomes 1.
8. We re-evaluate "condition": i < MAX is still `true`, so we branch to step 4.

Note that two nested scopes are associated with `for`. The variable `sqrt` is in the inner scope, and it becomes allocated and de-allocated in each iteration, whereas the variable i is in the outer scope so it persists across iterations. After 10 iterations, the output becomes

```
0  0.0
1  1.0
2  1.4142135623730951
...
8  2.8284271247461903
9  3.0
```

After executing the body in the 10th iteration, we reach step 7, and this makes i = 10. In step 8, we find the condition i < MAX no longer valid, so we move to step 9. We end the `for` scope, which means variable i is no longer known, and we resume sequence flow.

In general, the `for` syntax is

```
for (initial; condition; bottom)
{
    body
}
```

initial

Any valid Java statement can be used as "initial," including the empty statement. This statement will be executed once (and only once) when the loop is first encountered (and regardless of the state of the condition). If you do not want anything executed, write only the semicolon. For example, you can replace

```
for (int i = 0; i < MAX; i = i + 1)
```

Programming Tip   5.7

Fallacy: The loop's condition is monitored at all times

Aside from the initial check (before the first iteration), the loop's condition is checked only *once* per iteration (after executing the body and "bottom"). Hence, it can become `false` and stay `false` after such a check, and the loop will not exit until the next check. In other words, there is only one spot in which we can confidently put the statement

```
assert condition;
```

namely, as the first statement of the loop's body.

with

```
int i = 0;
for (; i < MAX; i = i + 1)
```

The only difference between the two is that i in the second version is declared outside the for scope; hence, it can be referenced after the loop. A third version, which is equivalent to the second, is to declare before the loop's scope but initialize within it:

```
int i;
for (i = 0; i < MAX; i = i + 1)
```

condition

Any boolean value can be used as a "condition": a boolean literal, variable, or expression. This is the condition for staying in the loop; that is, the loop will keep iterating as long as the condition is met; and it is checked at the end of each iteration, after executing the body and the "bottom" part. Moreover, it is checked before the very first iteration, and if found false at that time, then the entire loop is **skipped**. If you set the condition to the literal true, then the loop becomes an **infinite loop**, one that iterates indefinitely. Note that unlike "initial" and "bottom," you cannot omit "condition" (e.g., by putting only a semicolon) because it must be a value, not a statement.

bottom

Any valid Java statement can be used as "bottom," including the empty statement. This statement will be executed at the end of every iteration as if it appends the body. If you do not want anything executed, write nothing, for example,

```
for (int i = 0; i < 10;)
```

Note, however, that unless the body itself changes i, this will lead to an infinite loop because i starts off at 0 and remains 0, so the condition i<10 is always met.

Example 5.6

Write a fragment that outputs the exponents of all powers of 2 that are smaller than one million. The program needs to keep computing successive powers of 2, that is, $2^0, 2^1, 2^2,...$, as long as each is less than a million.

Answer:

```
final int MILLION = 1000000;
for (int expo = 0; Math.pow(2, expo) < MILLION; expo++)
{
    output.print(expo);
    output.print(" ");
}
output.println();
```

The output of this fragment is

```
0  1  2  3  4  5  6  7  8  9  10  11  12  13  14  15  16  17  18  19
```

Example 5.7

As a variation on Example 5.6, suppose we just needed to output the exponent of the greatest power of 2 that is smaller than one million. The loop needs to keep computing successive powers until one equal to or greater than one million is reached. At that point, the program backtracks one step and outputs the exponent of the previous power. The backtracking step means we need to access `expo` (in order to decrement it) after the loop, and this requires that we declare it before the loop's scope. We also need to inhibit printing in the body. Hence, the answer becomes

```
int expo = 0;
for (; Math.pow(2, expo) < MILLION; expo++)
{
}
output.println(expo - 1);
```

Programming Tip   5.8

Pitfall: Placing a semicolon after a `for`

Instead of writing

```
for (; Math.pow(2, expo) < MILLION; expo++)
{
}
```

we could have written

```
for (; Math.pow(2, expo) < MILLION; expo++);
```

This is because placing a semicolon after a `for` implies an empty body; the loop will iterate, but the statement after it will not. Even though the single-line version works for this particular case, it is not a good idea to get into the habit of placing semicolons after any header (class, method, `if`, or `for`) because it can lead to subtle logic errors.

5.2.3 Building the Loop

The versatility of the `for` loop allows us to use it in any situation involving iteration. We will present two problems and provide a step-by-step discussion of how a loop can be "evolved" to solve each.

Problem 1. Sentinel-Based Input

Write a program that reads integers from the user and then outputs statistics about them. Specifically, the program must keep reading integers until -1 is entered. This entry, called the **sentinel**, is not to be incorporated into the entered data; it is simply a signal that indicates no more input. Once the sentinel is detected, the program must output the average (arithmetic mean) of the entered data.

We need a loop that reads an integer and processes

```
for (?; not sentinel; ?)
{
    read an int
    process the int
}
```

But when the input is the sentinel, this loop will not exit in time because its condition is not tested until the end of the body. By then, the sentinel will have been processed. To remedy this, we move the read statement to the end of the body:

```
for (?; not sentinel; ?)
{
    process the int
    read an int
}
```

The integer being processed at the beginning of any iteration is the one that was entered in the previous iteration. And to take care of the first iteration, we perform one read before the first iteration. When an action must be taken before the loop in order to set it up, we say that the loop needs to be **primed**, and the "initial" part of a for loop is ideal for placing the priming action. This leads to

```
for (read an int; not sentinel; ?)
{
    process the int
    read an int
}
```

Note that since reading the input is the last statement of the body, we can move it to the bottom part of the for loop:

```
for (read an int; not sentinel; read an int)
{
    process the int
}
```

Now to process the data, we need to know the number of integers (excluding the sentinel) as well as their sum. Hence, we need a counter, initialized to zero before the loop, and we must increment it as part of the processing. Similarly, we need an accumulator, sum, that starts at zero and gets incremented by the entered integer in every iteration. This leads to

```
final int SENTINEL = -1;
int count = 0;
int sum = 0;
output.println("Enter the integers pressing ENTER after each");
for (int n = input.nextInt(); n != SENTINEL; n = input.nextInt())
{
    count++;
    sum = sum + n;
```

```
        }
        double average = sum / (double) count;
```

(The cast is needed to avoid truncation.) There is only one remaining problem in this program: what if the user enters -1 as the first entry? The loop will immediately skip and count will end up being 0 (thus leading to division by zero, a runtime error). This is an input validation issue, and we will solve it using a crash; that is, add the following statement after the loop:

```
        ToolBox.crash(count <= 0, "Must have at least one entry!");
```

We will discuss other input validation techniques in Section 5.3.1.

Problem 2. Simple Number Statistics

Write a program that keeps reading integers from the user until the sentinel −1 is entered, and then output the arithmetic mean and the largest of the entries.

This variation on Problem 1 requires finding the largest entry. To that end, we nominate a candidate, max, to be the largest integer entered so far. Whenever an entry is made, we challenge the candidate by comparing the entry with it. If the entry is larger, it becomes max; otherwise max remains unchanged. We therefore append the processing part by

```
        max = Math.max(n, max);
```

If you inspect max at the end of any iteration, you will find it equal to the largest integer entered up to that iteration. Since this property of max is upheld at the end of every iteration, it is known as the **loop invariant**. This leads us the following loop:

```
        for (int n = input.nextInt(); n != SENTINEL; n = input.nextInt())
        {
            count++;
            sum = sum + n;
            max = Math.max(n, max);
        }
```

This works fine except for the first iteration: what initial value should be used for max? You may be tempted to use some magic value, such as 0 or −99, but this would be incorrect because all the entered integers may be smaller than such values. Since any entered integer cannot be smaller than the smallest possible int, we can take

```
        Integer.MIN_VALUE
```

to be the initial value for max, and that would be correct. But in order to keep the approach general, we will select the initial value from the data itself; specifically, let the first entered integer be the initial value of our candidate. To facilitate this, we perform the first read before the loop:

```
        int n = input.nextInt();
        int max = n;
        for (; n != SENTINEL; n = input.nextInt())
        {
            count++;
            sum = sum + n;
            max = Math.max(n, max);
        }
```

Note the flexibility of the `for` statement: since we needed to do something special in the first iteration, we simply pulled the declaration of `n` and its input out of the `for`, leaving its initial statement empty. This is another example of priming.

5.2.4 Nested Loops

You can **nest** `for` statements any way you like as long as they are either disjoint (one ends before the other begins) or fully nested (one is contained entirely within the other); that is, as long as they do not overlap. Two nested loops are shown in Fig. 5.9.

The outer loop iterates five times as its loop counter, `i`, takes on the values 0, 1, 2, 3, 4. In the first iteration, `i` is set to 0 and the body, itself a loop, is executed. When the inner loop receives control, it starts its first iteration by setting its counter `j` to 0. It then executes its body, which consists of output statements. Note that we are still in the body of the outer loop; hence `i` is in scope. The first output, therefore, should be 0 0, and this is indeed what is shown in the first line of the right pane of the figure. At the end of the first iteration of the inner loop, its "bottom" part is executed, `j` is incremented, and the body is re-executed. The process is repeated until all three iterations of the inner loop are completed. At the end of the last iteration, `j` is incremented to 3, which makes the condition (`j < 3`) false so the inner loop exits. Note that `i` is still 0 throughout this process because the outer loop is still in its first iteration. Next, `i` becomes 1, and the inner loop is executed anew.

In general, if a loop that iterates N times is nested within one that iterates M times, then the body of the inner loop will iterate $M \times N$ times.

Figure 5.9 Two nested loops. The output is shown to the right.

```
final int M = 5;
final int N = 3;

for (int i = 0; i < M; i++)
{

    for (int j = 0; j < N; j++)
    {

        output.print(i);
        output.print(" ");
        output.println(j);

    }

}
```

```
0  0
0  1
0  2
1  0
1  1
1  2
2  0
2  1
2  2
3  0
3  1
3  2
4  0
4  1
4  2
```

Java Details 5.3

The while Statement

Java provides a second statement for implementing iteration, but it is less versatile than the for statement; that is, it can always be replaced by a for. It is called the **while statement**, and its characteristics are shown in Fig. 5.10.

As you can see from Fig. 5.10, the while statement does not have an initial part; thus, it has only one scope, the body's scope. Furthermore, it does not have a bottom part. In fact, we can describe the while statement in terms of the for statement as follows: the fragment

```
while (condition)
{
    body
}
```

can be replaced with

```
for (; condition;)
{
    body
}
```

If the loop involves only a condition, no "initial" or "bottom" parts, then it is a matter of personal preference as to which construct to use. However, when all three parts are present, they will be scattered all over the program in the case of while, and this makes the program more susceptible to errors, for example, an infinite or skipped loop, especially when it undergoes modifications.

Figure 5.10 The flow diagram, syntax, and algorithm of the while statement

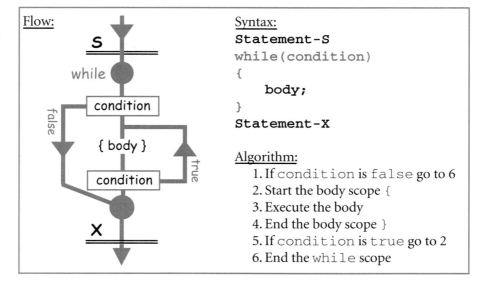

Flow:

Syntax:
```
Statement-S
while(condition)
{
    body;
}
Statement-X
```

Algorithm:
1. If condition is false go to 6
2. Start the body scope {
3. Execute the body
4. End the body scope }
5. If condition is true go to 2
6. End the while scope

Example 5.8

Predict the output of the fragment in Fig. 5.9 if the inner loop header is changed to

```
for (int j = i; j < 3; j++)
```

Answer:

Note that in this case the initial statement of the inner loop depends on the value of the loop counter of the outer loop. During the first iteration of the outer loop, the above change makes no difference because j starts from 0. Hence, the first three output lines remain unchanged:

```
0  0
0  1
0  2
```

In the second iteration of the outer loop, however, j starts from 1, and this means the inner loop iterates twice only. This leads to

```
1  1
1  2
```

In the third iteration of the outer loop, j starts from 2, which allows the inner loop to iterate once:

```
2  2
```

In the remaining iterations of the outer loop, j starts from 3 or above, and this makes the loop's condition (j < 3) false from the outset so it will be skipped. Hence, the six output lines above constitute the whole output.

□

5.3 Applications

The following sections present general applications of the constructs learned in this chapter.

5.3.1 Exception-Free Input Validation

We found in Section 3.2.5 that input validity should *not* be treated as a precondition; instead, it should be validated. Furthermore, we found that there are three different actions that can be taken when the input is found invalid. So far, we have been using the exception-based option:

```
read the input
ToolBox.crash(condition, message);
rest of program
```

We will implement the other two options in this section.

Java Details 5.4

The do Statement

The condition of the for and while loops is checked at the end of each iteration as well as before the first iteration. Java provides a third loop, **do**, in which the condition is checked only at the end of each iteration; that is, it is not checked before the first. Hence, a do loop, also called a **do-while** loop, always iterates at least once. The characteristics of do are shown in Fig. 5.11.

The do-while loop is most appropriate when the loop must iterate at least once. You can simulate the behaviour of the fragment

```
do
{
    body
}
while (condition);
```

by using a for loop primed with a boolean flag:

```
for (boolean test = true; test; test = condition)
{
    body
}
```

Since test was set to true in "initial," the loop's condition will force it to iterate at least once. At the end of the first iteration, "bottom" is executed, and this makes the condition exactly the same as that of the do-while loop.

Note that there is one scenario in which the above replacement will not work: when a variable is declared before the loop, assigned within it, and used after it. In this case, the compiler becomes "overprotective" and issues the following error: "variable may not have been initialized." This point is explored in Exercise 5.18.

Figure 5.11 The flow diagram, syntax, and algorithm of the do statement

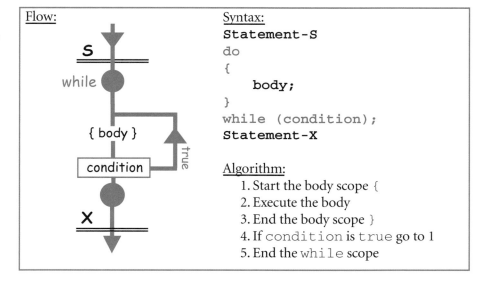

Flow:

Syntax:
```
Statement-S
do
{
    body;
}
while (condition);
Statement-X
```

Algorithm:
1. Start the body scope {
2. Execute the body
3. End the body scope }
4. If condition is true go to 1
5. End the while scope

Message-Based Validation

The message-based validation option calls for displaying a message and ending the program, without throwing an exception, when the input is invalid. It can be easily implemented using the `if-else` construct. The exception-based validation above can be replaced with

```
read the input
if (condition)
{
    output message
}
else
{
    rest of program
}
```

Example 5.9

Write a fragment that prompts for and reads a positive integer from the user and outputs its square root. If the input is not positive, output an error message.

Answer:

```
final double SQUARE_ROOT = 0.5;
output.println("Enter a positive integer... ");
int entry = input.nextInt();
if (entry <= 0)
{
    output.println("Invalid entry - must be positive!");
}
else
{
    double root = Math.pow(entry, SQUARE_ROOT)
    output.println(root);
}
```

Friendly Validation

The friendly validation approach allows the user to retry if the input is invalid. For example, let us write a program that reads an `int` from the user and ensures that it is positive; otherwise, it asks the user to re-enter. Since we must keep retrying as long as the entry is not positive, we set up a `for` loop with negative or zero entry as its condition:

```
int n;
for (?; n <= 0; ?)
{
    output.print("Enter a positive integer... ");
    n = input.nextInt();
    if (n <= 0)
```

```
    {
        output.println("Invalid... please retry");
    }
}
process n
```

Note that n has to be declared before the loop, or else it cannot be used after it. But as written, the loop's condition cannot be evaluated initially since n is not assigned yet. This calls for priming the loop: the very first read must be made before the loop. We therefore pull the prompt outside the loop and place the first read in the "initial" part. And since we need to reread at the end of each iteration, we do this in the "bottom":

```
output.print("Enter a positive integer... ");
int n;
for (n = input.nextInt(); n <= 0; n = input.nextInt())
{
    output.println("Invalid... please retry");
}
process n
```

5.3.2 File I/O

Programs involving file I/O often start by prompting the user to enter the name of the file. You can do this by reading the name as a string, but in order to avoid potential entry errors, you may want to consider using JFileChooser. This class presents the user with a dialog window similar to what you see when you use the "Open" menu in your word processor. The user can navigate through the folders and select a file. Here is a very basic usage of this dialog:

```
JFileChooser chooser = new JFileChooser();
chooser.showOpenDialog(null);
```

This will display the dialog and wait until the user takes an action. The program must then examine the value of the reference:

```
chooser.getSelectedFile()
```

If it is null, then the user must have selected to cancel the dialog. If it is not, invoke toString on it, and you get the name of the file (fully qualified with path):

```
if (chooser.getSelectedFile() != null)
{
    String filename;
    filename = chooser.getSelectedFile().toString();
    ... rest of program
}
```

Note that the user does not have to point at a file; the file name can be typed in.

File Input

Given the file name, we learned in Lab 4 that we could read its content by creating an instance of Scanner that reads from it. Since our application may also want to read from the keyboard, we should create two instances:

```
Scanner input = new Scanner(System.in);
Scanner fileInput = new Scanner(new File(filename));
```

The first statement is part of the standard template that we created in Section 2.2.5. We can invoke on `fileInput` any of the `next` methods that we normally invoke on `input`.

Reading from a file is similar to reading from the keyboard except for two things: no prompt is involved, and sentinels are not customarily used. The latter is because the file has a hidden marker (called **end of file**) after its last record, and it serves as a sentinel. The `Scanner` class has `boolean` methods `hasNext` that determine if you can issue a `next` method without attempting to read past the end of file.

If all the data fields in the file are of the same type, type P, then we can read its contents using a loop such as the following:

```
for (; fileInput.hasNextP();)
{
    x = fileInput.nextP();
}
```

For a file of integers, for example, replace P with `Int` and declare x as `int`. For a file of text (e.g., a document), you can read and process it either line by line or word by word. In the former case, set P=Line and declare x as a `String`. In the latter, remove P (i.e., use the `next()` and `hasNext()` methods) and declare x as a `String`.

If the file contains a mixture of types, we need to adjust the loop in accordance with the file structure. In this case, keep in mind that you may get an unexpected result if you invoke the `nextLine` method immediately after invoking another `next` methods (e.g., `nextInt`). Here is an example: suppose we want to read the data `"15\nText"`. The statements

```
int i = fileInput.nextInt();
String s = fileInput.nextLine();
```

will successfully read the integer but not the text. To fix this, either use `nextLine` twice or read the text using `next()`. The reason for this has to do with how these two methods behave: after `nextInt` reads the integer, it leaves the file cursor pointing at the new line character `\n`. The `nextLine` method, which returns all characters between the current cursor position and the next `\n`, immediately encounters `\n` and thus returns an empty string.

File Output

Output to a file is strikingly similar to output to the screen. Instead of creating an instance of `PrintStream` through `System.out`, we do so through the constructor. This leads to the following two lines:

```
PrintStream output = System.out;
PrintStream fileOutput = new PrintStream(filename);
```

The first statement is part of the standard template that we created in Section 2.2.5. We can invoke on `fileOutput` any of the `print`, `println`, or `printf` methods that we normally invoke on `output`.

Recall from Lab 4 that any program that deals with file I/O must add the following suffix to its `main` method:

```
throws java.io.IOException
```

We will see in Chapter 10 what this means and how it can be avoided. Recall also that once input or output is completed, the connection must be closed:

```
fileInput.close(); or fileOutput.close();
```

In More Depth   5.2

Unconditional Transfer of Control

Java has two constructs that enable unconditional transfer of control:

- `break` provides a transfer out of the enclosing loop

- `continue` provides a transfer out of the current iteration and into the next

Whenever you feel tempted to use either of these, rethink your loop design. These two constructs resemble the dreaded `goto` of older programming languages and often lead to programs that are difficult to understand. A loop should have a single entry and a single exit, and any departure from this makes the loop susceptible to logic errors, especially while being modified by other programmers.
Note that using `break` in a `switch` (see Java Details 5.2) is acceptable.

Summary of Key Concepts

1. A statement in a program receives **control** when it is about to be executed. **Flow of control** refers to the order in which statements are executed.

2. In **sequence flow**, statements are executed in the same order as their physical order in the program, that is, from top to bottom. In **selection flow**, however, the execution order depends on a selection that occurs at a particular statement in the program. The flow branches after that statement.

3. The **if** statement implements selection flow in Java. Its basic form allows taking an action if a condition is met and not taking any action otherwise:

```
S1
if (condition)
{
    B
}
S2
```

After statement S1 is executed, the condition is examined. If it is met, then the statements in block B are executed followed by statement S2. Otherwise, block B is skipped, and statement S2 is executed immediately after S1.

4. If the algorithm calls for taking different actions based on the condition, the `if-else` form is used:

```
S1
if (condition)
{
    B1
}
else
{
    B2
}
S2
```

After statement S1 is executed, the condition is examined. If met, the statements in block B1 are executed followed by statement S2. Otherwise, the statements in block B2 are executed followed by statement S2.

5. The condition can be expressed using relational operators, a boolean variable, a method that returns a boolean, or a **boolean expression**.

6. Java has **boolean operators** (also called **logical**) that take boolean operands and produce boolean results. We will use three of them: `&&` (**conjunction or AND**), `||` (**disjunction or OR**), and `!` (**negation or NOT**).

7. We can negate a boolean expression by interchanging `&&` and `||` and replacing each operand by its negation. This is called **deMorgan's law**.

8. When the virtual machine evaluates boolean expressions involving `&&` and/or `||`, it uses **lazy** (or **short-circuit**) evaluation: `A && B` is deemed `false` if A is `false`; and `A || B` is deemed `true` if A is `true`.

9. Multiway branching can be treated as cascaded two-way branches. A robust strategy for implementing this calls for nesting on the else-side: for each possible outcome of a problem, determine the condition that leads to it, and then place all these conditions in an `if-else-if` statement by putting the first in the `if`, the last in the `else`, and the ones in between in `else-if` statements.

10. `If` statements can be **nested** as long as they are either disjoint or fully nested.

11. **Iteration** is a flow of control that involves repeating the execution of a block of statements called the **loop**.

12. The `for` statement in Java implements iterative flow:

```
for (initial; condition; bot-
tom)
{
    body
}
```

The **initial** statement is executed once before the first iteration. **condition** is a boolean, and the loop keeps iterating as long as it is true. It is

checked before the first iteration and at the end of each one thereafter. The **bottom** statement is executed after the body, in every iteration, but before the condition is checked. Either "initial" or "bottom" can be empty.

13. The `for` statement defines two nested scopes: the outer one includes its header and the body, and the inner one includes the body.

14. A **skipped loop** is one whose condition was `false` before the first iteration. An **infinite loop** is one whose condition is always `true`. These two loops are common pitfalls and should be guarded against.

15. A **sentinel** is used to terminate user input. It should not be treated as part of the input, only as a signal that no more input will be made.

16. **Priming** a loop refers to taking some action to set it up. This involves writing code before it. All or part of the priming action is placed in the "initial." Because "initial" is executed before a `for` loop, it is an ideal location for placing the priming action.

17. A **loop invariant** is a statement that will be `true` at the end of every iteration of the loop. Finding it leads to a well-designed loop that can be proven correct.

18. Loops can be **nested** as long as they are either disjoint or fully nested.

19. We can implement **input validation** without throwing an exception through an `if` statement. And by using a primed `for` statement, we can implement a friendlier validation in which the user is prompted to correct invalid input.

20. We can read data from a disk file by creating a `Scanner` instance and invoking on it the same `next` methods that we normally use for keyboard input. The `hasNext` methods can be used to avoid reading past the end of file. For file output, we create a `PrintStream` instance. In both input and output, the `throws` suffix must be added to the `main` method header, and the `close` method must be invoked at the end.

Review Questions

1. Prescription drugs come with a leaflet that explains how the drugs should be used. Give an example in which the leaflet instructions have a sequence flow and one in which they have a selection flow.

2. The basic form of the `if` statement does not involve an `else` part, yet it is said to implement *two*-way selection. What are the *two* different execution orders?

3. The if-else form of the `if` statement involves two scopes. If a variable is declared in one of them, will it be available in the other?

4. Give an example of a condition (of an `if` statement) expressed using relational operators.

5. Give an example of a condition expressed as a boolean expression.

6. What are the three most commonly used boolean operators?

7. (a) Explain why a programmer who does not know the values of x can write the following statement:

```
assert (x != 3 || x != 5);
```

(b) Use deMorgan's law to express the negation of the condition and then assess the true/false status of the negated condition.

8. Argue that the output of the following fragment is 10, not 0:

```
int x = 4;
int y = 0;
if (x == 3)
x++;
y = 10;
output.println(y);
```

9. Explain the potential runtime error contained in this fragment, and suggest a simple fix (MAX is a `final int`):

```
int x = 4;
int y = input.nextInt();
if (x / y < MAX && y != 0)
{
```

```
    x++;
}
output.println(y);
```

10. Explain the two scopes involved in the `for` statement.

11. What are the roles played by "initial" and "bottom" in the `for` statement? Are these parts optional? Can they be omitted?

12. Give an example of a skipped loop and an infinite loop.

13. How many times will the following loop iterate?

```
for (int i = 0; i < 10; i++)
```

14. How many times will the following loop iterate?

```
for (int i = 0; i <= 10; i++)
```

15. How many times will the following loop iterate?

```
for (int i = 1; i < 10; i++)
```

16. How many times will the following loop iterate?

```
for (int i = 0; i < 10; i++)
{
    i++;
}
```

17. How many times will the following loop iterate?

```
for (int i = 0; i < 10; i++)
{
    i--;
}
```

18. What is the output (if any) of the fragment

```
int sum = 0;
for (int i = 0; i < 10; i++)
{
    sum++;
}
output.println(sum);
```

19. What is the output (if any) of the fragment

```
int sum = 0;
for (int i = 0; i < 10; i++)
{
    sum++;
```

```
    }
    output.println(i);
```

20. What is the output (if any) of the fragment

```
    int sum = 0;
    int i;
    for (i = 0; i < 10; i++)
    {
        sum++;
    }
    output.println(i);
```

21. Explain the concept of a sentinel in user input.

22. There are three ways for handling invalid input. Name them, and give an example of each.

23. Why is it sometimes necessary to prime a loop?

24. What is a loop invariant? Give an example of a loop, and state the invariant.

25. Explain why the compiler will generate errors for this fragment:

```
    int count = 0;
    for (int i = 0; i < 5; i++)
    {
        for (int i = 0; i < 5; i++)
        {
            count++;
        }
    }
```

26. What is an end-of-file, and how is it detected?

◢ L5.1 The == Relational Operator

1. Launch your editor and create the program Lab5 that contains the following:

```
final double THIRD = 1.0 / 3.0;
double x = 1 - THIRD - THIRD - THIRD;
boolean same = (x == 0.);
output.println(same);
```

One would expect the output to be true, but is it? As a rule, the == operator should never be used with real numbers, double, or float. Instead, a very small number—EPSILON—must be declared as final and selected as our round-off tolerance. A test for equality of two real numbers x and y would then be based on whether $|x - y|$ is less than EPSILON. Alternatively, you can look at the relative, instead of the absolute, difference: $|x - y| \ / \ |x + y|$.

2. Add the following lines (after the ones added above):

```
Fraction f1 = new Fraction(1, 2);
Fraction f2 = new Fraction(1, 2);
same = (f1 == f2);
output.println(same);
```

One would expect the output to be true since both fractions represent 1/2, but is it? As a rule, the == operator should never be used to test object equality because it only tests the equality of their references. Use equals instead.

3. Add the following lines (after the ones added above):

```
if (same == true)
{
    output.println("the references are equal");
} else
{
    output.println("the references are not equal");
}
```

The idea here is to print a different message based on whether same is true. Although there is nothing syntactically wrong with this, the == operator is redundant. It is a more proper to write the first statement as

```
if (same)
{    ...
```

Similarly, write !same whenever you are inclined to write (same == false).

L5.2 The Short-Circuit Behaviour

1. Add the following lines to `Lab5` (after the ones added earlier):

    ```
    output.println("Enter two int separated by ENTER");
    int a = input.nextInt();
    int b = input.nextInt();
    boolean multiple = (a % b == 0);
    output.println(multiple);
    ```

    The idea here is to read two integers and determine whether the first is a multiple of the second; that is, if the second is a divisor of the first. The program works correctly if `b` is not zero, but if `b` is zero, we get a runtime error. Try it.

2. To guard against dividing by zero, we modify the boolean so it is false in that case:

    ```
    boolean multiple = (b != 0 && a % b == 0);
    ```

    But would that not lead to the same error? When the machine executes this line, it will have to evaluate the `%`, and this will trigger the error. Try the program in this form, and explain why the problem is avoided.

3. The `||` (or) operator also behaves in a short-circuit fashion. Can you envision a scenario where this is useful?

L5.3 Revisiting the Notion of Scope

1. Add the following lines to `Lab5` (after the ones added above):

    ```
    {
        int hidden = 12;
        output.println(a);
        output.println(hidden);
    }
    {
        int hidden = 15;
        output.println(a);
        output.println(hidden);
    }
    ```

    Note that it is OK to redeclare the name `hidden` because its earlier declaration was in a scope that finished (reached its closing brace). Note also that variables such as `a`, whose scope encompasses an inner scope, are visible in the inner scope (and hence cannot be redeclared).

    In general, two scopes are either disjoint or one is contained in the other; they never overlap.

L5.4 The `if` Statement

1. Add the following lines to `Lab5` (after the ones added above):

    ```
    int value;
    if (1 > 0)
    {
        value = -1;
    }
    output.println(value);
    ```

    Compile and run. Note that since the value 1 is always greater than the value 0, the condition is always met.

2. What if we declared `value` with its assignment, that is,

    ```
    if (1 > 0)
    {
        int value = -1;
    }
    output.println(value);
    ```

    Why is this code suddenly illegal?

3. What if we replaced the (1 > 0) condition by one containing a boolean variable that is set to the same condition; that is, replace the above by

    ```
    int value;
    boolean check = (1 > 0);
    if (check)
    {
        value = -1;
    }
    output.println(value);
    ```

    Why is this code suddenly illegal? What should you do to fix the problem?

4. Add the following lines to `Lab5` (after the ones added above):

    ```
    value = 300;
    int result = 0;
    int c = 12;
    if (value > 500)
        if (c > 5)
            result = 10;
    else
        result = 7;
    output.println(result);
    ```

    Explain the output. As a rule, do not leave any part of an `if` statement without braces. Relying on indentation to identify blocks is misleading.

L5.5 The for Statement

1. Given a positive integer n, how many repeated divisions by 2 does it take before the result becomes 1? For example, if n is 24, then these divisions yield 12, 6, 3, 1, so it takes 4 such divisions. We do this for an arbitrary n by adding the following to our Lab5:

```
output.println ("Enter a value for n");
int n = input.nextInt();
for (int i = 0; n != 1; i++)
{
    n = n / 2;
}
output.println(i);
```

   After reading n, we simply keep dividing it by 2, storing the quotient back in n, until it becomes 1, and we keep track of how many times we iterated. Why is the compiler refusing to compile this? Fix the problem and run. Do you get 4 when the input is 24? What do you get if the input is one million?

2. Note that the last part of the for statement does not have to be of the form i++; any valid Java statement is acceptable. You can write i = i + 1 instead of i++, and you can modify the loop counter in any other way, for example, i = i - 5 or i = 2 * i - 7.

3. Some programming languages use a so-called while loop to perform condition-based loops (as opposed to counter-based ones). Java has such a construct but it is redundant: the for loop can play such a role. Rewrite the above fragment as

```
int n = input.nextInt();
int i = 0;
for (; n != 1;) //equivalent to: while (n != 1)
{
    n = n / 2;
    i++;
}
output.println(i);
```

   Compile and run and convince yourself that the two approaches are equivalent.

4. We want to add the reciprocals of odd numbers; that is, 1, 1/3, 1/5, 1/7,... but with alternating signs; that is, we are interested in computing the algebraic sum

$$\frac{1}{1} - \frac{1}{3} + \frac{1}{5} - \frac{1}{7} + \frac{1}{9} - \frac{1}{11} + \frac{1}{13} - \frac{1}{15} + \cdots$$

   This series is infinite, and the sum converges to $\pi/4$; that is, as we add more and more terms, the sum becomes closer and closer to $\pi/4$.

   Let us write the program Lab5PI to add up all terms in this series until the denominator becomes one million, and then multiply the computed sum by 4:

```
double sum = 0.0;
double sign = 1.0;
for (int i = 1; i < 1000000; ???)
```

```
{
    sum = sum + sign / i;
    ???
}
output.println(4 * sum);
```

Examine the program, and fill in the two missing statements (indicated by ???). Compile and run. Does the output converge to π?

5. We want to examine the role played by the term count, one million, on the output of the above program. Replace the magic number 1 000 000 by a suitable (`int`) variable name, and prompt the user to enter its value. Compile the program and run it. Do you get a good approximation of π if you add only 100 terms? How about one billion terms?

6. When the number of terms to add is large, the execution time of the program becomes noticeable. We like to measure this time exactly (in seconds) using the techniques developed in Lab 2. Add the necessary timing statements.

7. Given an integer n, compute (algebraically in terms of n) the number of times the innermost statement will be executed in the following nested structure. Verify by adding a counter and running.

```
int n = input.nextInt();
for (int i = 0; i < n; i++)
{
    for (int j = i + 1; j < n; j++)
    {
        innermost statement
    }
}
```

Exercises

Programming exercises are indicated with an asterisk.

5.1 Given that x, y, z are declared and initialized boolean variables, whenever the expression

```
(x && z) && (y && z)
```

is `true`, then (`x && y`) must also be `true`. Is this correct?

5.2 Given that x, y, z are declared and initialized boolean variables, whenever the expression

```
(x && z) && (y && z)
```

is `false`, then (`x && y`) must also be `false`. Is this correct?

5.3 Given that x, y are two declared and initialized object references of the same type, whenever (`x == y`) is `false`, then (`x.equals(y)`) must also be `false`. Is this correct?

5.4 Given that x, y are two declared and initialized object references of the same type, whenever (`x != null && x == y`) is `true`, then (`x.equals(y)`) must also be `true`. Is this correct?

5.5 Examine the following fragment:

```
int x = 1;
boolean b1 = (x > 0);
boolean b2 = false;
boolean b3 = b1 && !b2;
if (b3 || x == 1)
{
    x++;
}
```

Create a table (called a **trace table**) with four columns, one per variable, and one row. Fill the row with the values of the variables at the end of the fragment.

5.6 Create a trace table (as in Exercise 5.5) for the following fragment:

```
int x = 1;
int y = -1;
if (x >= y && y > 0)
{
    x++;
    y = x;
}
else if (x == y || y < 1)
{
    x--;
    y = x;
} else
{
    y = 0;
}
```

5.7 Examine the following fragment:

```
final int A = 3;
final int B = 10;
int count = 0;
int sum = 0;
for (int i = A; i < B; i = i + 2)
{
    count++;
    sum = sum + i;
}
```

Create a trace table with three columns corresponding to count, sum, and i. Each row in the table must be filled with the values of these variables at the end of each iteration; specifically, immediately after executing body and before executing the "bottom" part.

5.8 Create a trace table (as in Exercise 5.7) for the following fragment:

```
final int NUMBER = 123;
int n = NUMBER;
int sum = 0;
boolean exit = false;
for (; !exit;)
{
    sum = sum + n % 10;
    n = n / 10;
    exit = (n == 0);
}
```

5.9 Rewrite the fragment of Exercise 5.8 without using the exit variable and with the initialization of sum incorporated as "initial."

5.10 Create a trace table for the following fragment:

```
final int NUMBER = 10;
int count = 0;
for (int i = 0; i < NUMBER; i++)
{   for (int j = 0; j < i; j++)
    {   count++;
    }
}
```

5.11 Create a trace table for the following fragment:

```
final int NUMBER = 10;
int count = 0;
for (int i = 0; i < NUMBER; i++)
{
    for (int j = i + 1; j < NUMBER; j++)
    {   count++;
    }
}
```

5.12 Create a trace table for the following fragment:

```
final int NUMBER = 10;
int count = 0;
for (int i = 0; i < NUMBER; i++)
{
    for (i = 0; i < NUMBER; i++)
    {   count++;
    }
}
```

Note that both loops have the same counter.

5.13 Predict the output of the following fragment:

```
final int NUMBER = 10;
int i;
int j=0;
for (i = 0; i < NUMBER; i++)
{
    for (i = 0; i < NUMBER; i++)
    {
    }
}
output.print(i);
output.print(" ");
output.println(j);
```

5.14★ Write a program that reads an `int` from the user and validates that it is positive using `crash`. It then outputs the same integer rounded up to the next multiple of 7. For example, if the input were 114, then the output would be 119; and if the input were 49, then the output would be 49 (the same). Can you implement this program *without* using selection, just assignment statements?

5.15★ Write a program that reads three integers from the user and outputs the smallest and second smallest among them.

5.16★ Show that the program written in Section 5.2.3 can easily be modified to compute the smallest-entered number instead of the largest.

5.17★ Write a program that reads integers from the user until the user enters the sentinel value 9999. At that point, the program outputs the following:

```
Number of integers: xxxx
Largest integer: xxxx
Smallest integer: xxxx
Arithmetic Mean: xxxx.xx
Standard Deviation: xxxx.xx
```

The *standard deviation* is the square root of the *variance*, which is defined as the mean of the squares of the numbers minus the square of the mean. The output must be formatted exactly as shown. You can assume that the user will make at least one entry but not more than 10 000 entries and that each entry is made up of up to 4 digits plus a sign.

5.18★ The following fragment implements friendly input validation without priming the loop (Section 5.3.1). When compiled, the compiler complains that the variable n may not have been initialized (because the loop may have been skipped). (a) Elaborate on this "overprotective" behaviour by explaining why the compiler "thinks" the way it does. (b) Provide a simple fix.

```
int n;
for (boolean invalid = true; invalid;)
{
```

```
        output.println("Enter a positive integer:");
        n = input.nextInt();
        invalid = (n <= 0);
    }
    output.println(n);
```

5.19* Write a program that reads two integers a and b from the user. If either is not positive or if b is less than a, the program must issue a friendly error message and allow the user to re-enter. Otherwise, the program must output the number of perfect squares in the interval [a, b).

5.20* Write a program that uses friendly input validation to prompt for and read an integer from the user and ensures that it is positive. If it is, the program must output its square root. Otherwise, it allows the user to re-enter up to three times. If the input is still not positive after these four attempts (the original plus three retrials), the program must end with an appropriate error message.

5.21* Write a program that reads an integer and crashes if it is not positive. Otherwise, it outputs "YES" if the entry is a prime number and "NO" otherwise. A number is prime if it is not divisible (evenly) by any positive integer (other than itself or 1).

5.22* Write a program that reads an int n from the user and crashes if the input is not positive. Otherwise it outputs n lines: the first line consists of the numbers 1,2,3,4,... n without any delimiters. The second line is similar but ends at n-1. The third line ends at n-2 and so on. Here is the output for n = 9:

```
123456789
12345678
1234567
123456
12345
1234
123
12
1
```

eCheck

Check05A (TS = 21)

We want to develop the program Check05A that determines the roots of the equation

$$ax^2 + bx + c = 0$$

That is, given the values of the coefficients a, b, c, we seek to find real value(s) for x for which the left-hand-side evaluates to zero. Here are a few sample runs of the sought application:

```
Enter a,b,c pressing ENTER after each...
1
2
3
The equation: 1.0x^2 + 2.0x + 3.0 = 0 has no real
roots.

Enter a,b,c pressing ENTER after each...
1
2
-4

The equation: 1.0x^2 + 2.0x - 4.0 = 0 has the two
roots: -3.23606797749979 and 1.2360679774997898

Enter a,b,c pressing ENTER after each...
1
-6
9
The equation: 1.0x^2 - 6.0x + 9.0 = 0 has the single
root: 3.0

Enter a,b,c pressing ENTER after each...
0
0
0
The equation: 0.0x^2 + 0.0x + 0.0 = 0
is an identity - any value is a root.
```

As you can see, the program reads three doubles and then prints the equation itself followed by a message that depends on the number of roots:

Roots	Message
infinitely many	is an identity – any value is a root.
none	has no real roots.
one root	has the single root: *value*
two roots	has the two roots: *value* and *value*

Note the formatting details: there is a period at the end of the first two messages; there is a space between the colon and the root value in the last two messages; the "and" is surrounded by two spaces (and so is the equal sign in the equation) and so on. Your program must reproduce these details exactly.

Rather than re-inventing the wheel and delving into the various special cases (such as a=0, a=b=0, c ≠ 0, and so on), we want to delegate that work to the class `Equation` in the `type.lib` package. Read its API and note, in particular, that its `toString` method produces the exact string format that we seek, and that its `rootCount` accessor can be used to determine the appropriate message.

Write `Check05A` and eCheck it.

Check05B (TS = 26)

The `Check05B` program prompts for a file name and performs some computations based on the file's content. Here is a sample run:

```
Enter filename ... lab5data.txt
00000 54.05
00002 Symbol mox does not exist!
00004 10.70
00006 Symbol mixe does not exist!
Total value = 896.35
```

The file must be a text file, and it resides in the same directory as your program. It contains data pertaining to a portfolio of stocks and is organized in record pairs:

- The first record in each pair contains a stock symbol.
- The second record contains the number shares bought from that stock.

A sample file is shown below:

```
.ab
15
.ve
16
.fy
8
.xx
34
```

For example, its first pair of records indicates that 15 shares were bought from the stock whose symbol is .ab.

Once the program reads the file name, it should read its records one by one. Whenever a symbol is read, the program should use the services of the `Stock` class to find out if such a symbol exists. If it does, the program should output a line indicating the record number of the symbol (where it was found in the file, beginning with record zero) and the price. Otherwise, the record number is printed along with a message, as shown above.

Note that the record number is zero-filled in a field of width 5. Note also that it is always even because it starts at zero and each symbol record is followed by a number of shares record. The output ends with a line containing the total value of the portfolio (sum of stock price times the number of shares with valid symbols). All amounts are formatted to two decimals as shown.

Write `Check05B` and eCheck it.

- Use `next()` to read symbols and `nextInt()` to read the number of shares
- The file name `"lab5data.txt"` was just an example. Your program shou.ld prompt for and read the name of the file from the user.
- To test your program, create the file using any editor. Make sure you write one piece of data per line.
- You do not have to guard against violations to the above analysis; for example, what if the file does not exist? What if the record after the symbol does not contain a positive integer? You can assume that all entries are as assumed above. The only thing that can be wrong is that the symbol may not exist.
- Your program must close the file once it is done with it.

Check05C (TS = 21)

Take an integer g, raise it to some exponent e, divide by p, and keep the remainder ($1 < g < p$). Is it possible that the result is g? The answer is "yes" if $e=1$ but other possibilities may exist. The question then becomes: Determine the smallest value of e that satisfies:

$$e > 1 \text{ and } g^e \% p = g$$

This computation is known as modular exponentiation and it plays an important role in certain cryptographic algorithms. In particular, the value of e determines the strength of the security of network protocols such as `https`.

Create the app `Check05C` that uses `607` for p, reads g from the end user, and outputs the smallest value of e. Here is a sample run of the sought app:

```
Enter an integer g [1 < g < 607]
7
The smallest e [e > 1 & g^e = g]
102
```

The app must use the `crash` method of `ToolBox` to validate its input, as shown in this run:

```
Enter an integer g [1 < g < 607]
834
Exception in thread "main" java.lang.RuntimeException ...
```

1. In order to compute the smallest e, start with $e=2$ and check the condition. If not met, increment e and check again. Repeat until the condition is met.
2. Do not compute g^e using `Math.pow` because promoting to `double` will introduce round-off errors and these become significant as the exponent increases. Instead, stay with the `int` type by computing the power yourself in a loop keeping only the remainder

after each multiplication. For example, instead of computing $(g\char`\^3)\%p$, you would compute $(g\ast g)\%p$ and then $\{[(g\ast g)\%p]\ast g\}\%p$.

Develop your app, test it, and then eCheck it.

Check05D (TS = 21)

Given a real number a, we want to compute the limit of the sequence:

$$x_{new} = x - (x^3 - a) / (3x^2)$$

where the initial value of x is a. In other words, you start by setting x=a and computing the right-hand side. The result will be the next value of x. Repeat this process until you reach a stage at which the new and the old values of x are the same (within some tolerance). This final value is the limit of the sequence.

For example, if a=15 then we start with x=15, and this leads to 10.02 as the new value of x. Repeating the process yields (approximately): 6.73, 4.60, 3.30, 2.66, 2.48, 2.47, 2.47. As you can see, the values converge toward the 2.47 limit.

Create the app Check05D that uses 0.001 as tolerance, reads a, and outputs the limit. The app stops iterating when the absolute value of the difference between the old and new values of x becomes less than the tolerance. Here is a sample run of the sought app:

```
Enter any real number ... 500
Within 0.0010 the limit is: 7.9370
```

Note that the tolerance and the limit are formatted using 4 decimals.

Develop your app, test it, and then eCheck it.

6

Strings

Learning Objectives

1. *Recognize strings as objects*

2. *Create strings using shortcuts*

3. *Become familiar with the* `String` *class*

4. *Handle string-number conversions*

5. *Experience string processing applications*

6. *Optimize string handling*

7. *Learn about regular expressions*

String applications span several areas, including text processing, encryption, and pattern recognition, making them the second most commonly used data type (after numbers). Realizing this, Java provides an extra special treatment for strings: an optimized class with a host of powerful methods, a second class for in-place mutation, and a special syntax to facilitate usage. In this chapter, you will learn how to create strings and how to benefit from their rich methods. You will also learn general strategies for tackling several categories of string applications.

Chapter Outline

6.1 Language Support

Strings are not treated as "just another object" in the Java language; instead, they receive extraordinary attention: in addition to being supported by two classes in `java.lang`, they are allowed to masquerade as primitive types. This special treatment is explained in the following two sections.

6.1.1 The `String` Class

Recall that a **string literal** is a sequence of characters. We use the word "sequence" rather than "set" to stress the facts that the order in which the characters appear is important, and that the same character may appear more than once. In Java, a string literal is surrounded by double quotes and can contain up to 2G (about two billion) of Unicode characters. Here is an example of a string literal:

```
"Planet Earth"
```

The left-most character in a string literal is said to reside at index zero; that is, positions are numbered left to right starting at zero. In the above example, 'P' resides at index 0 and 'E' at index 7.

Figure 6.1 A memory diagram of four string objects and six references

The **String** class allows us to create a string object that encapsulates a string literal, that is, one whose attribute is the string literal. We do this by following the general four-step procedure from Chapter 4. Note that the String class is in `java.lang` so it is automatically imported. We declare a reference and use a constructor that takes a string literal:

```
String str1;
str1 = new String("Planet Earth");
```

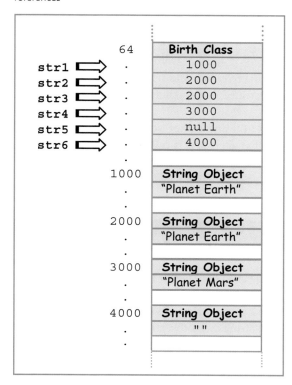

As shown in Fig. 6.1, the new operator creates a copy of the String class and stores it in a new block in memory starting, say, at address `1000`. The class constructor sets the attribute in the new area to the indicated literal. The reference `str1` is set to `1000`; that is, it now points at the string object.

It is important to distinguish between three entities: the **string object** (the allocated block), the **string reference** (a variable that stores the address of the area), and the **string literal** (the state of the string object—the encapsulated sequence of characters). The distinction is important for objects of any type, but it is particularly important for strings because all three entities are referred to by the term *string*. The following fragment will help you understand this point and help you to avoid pitfalls:

```
1 String str1 = new String("Planet Earth");
2 String str2 = new String("Planet Earth");
3 String str3 = str2;
```

```
4 String str4 = new String("Planet Mars");
5 String str5 = null;
6 String str6 = new String("");
```

The first statement creates an object and makes str1 a reference to it. This is depicted in Fig. 6.1 by an allocation of a block at some address, 1000, for the object and the storage of this address at the block allocated for str1. Similarly, the second statement creates an object at address 2000 and makes str2 a reference to it. At this point, we have two objects and two object references. The two objects are different (they start at different addresses), but they have the same state. Hence, comparing them using == yields false, while comparing them using equals should yield true.

Indeed, if you were to add the following two output statements to the fragment, you would see false and true as their respective outputs:

```
output.println(str1 == str2);
output.println(str1.equals(str2));
```

The third statement allocates a third string reference, str3, and sets it to str2. At this point, we have two objects, as before, and three references. If you now add

```
output.println(str2 == str3);
output.println(str2.equals(str3));
```

then both outputs will be true.

The fourth statement creates an object at 3000 and makes str4 a reference to it. Since this object is different in address and state from that at 1000, the following two statements must output false:

```
output.println(str4 == str1);
output.println(str4.equals(str1));
```

The fifth statement declares str5 as a string reference and sets it to null (indicated by the null content in Fig. 6.1). No new object is created in this statement. At this point, we have three objects and five references.

The sixth statement creates an object at 4000 and makes str6 a reference to it. This string object encapsulates a sequence of zero characters and is called the **empty** or the **zero-length** string. Note that the default constructor of the class creates such a string. At this point, there are four objects and six references.

Programming Tip   6.1

Pitfall: Confusing the empty string with the null string

There is a fundamental difference between an empty string and a **null string**. An empty string refers to a string object that encapsulates an empty sequence, while a null string refers to a string reference that is set to null (with no associated string object).

6.1.2 The Masquerade and the + Operator

Strings are so common in programming that the designers of Java went out of their way to make them easy to use and to make their implementation efficient. Specifically, they added shortcuts to the syntax of the language and separated variable and fixed strings into two distinct classes. These string-specific features, albeit quite handy for the experienced programmer, allow strings to masquerade as primitive types, and this can lead to subtle misconceptions in the mind of the beginner. It is therefore important to understand these features so that you can benefit from them without changing the mental model that we have been using to reason about objects in general.

Implicit Object Creation

Whenever a string literal appears, the compiler replaces it by a reference to an implicitly created string object. Hence, instead of writing

```
String str = new String("Planet Earth");
```

you can write

```
String str = "Planet Earth";
```

In other words, you can declare strings and assign them as if they were primitive.

No Mutation

The `String` class does not have a mutator. This means the encapsulated literal that was passed to the constructor is effectively a `final` (albeit not public) attribute of the class. Once a string is created, you cannot change its character sequence, either in content or in length. This was done to make string implementation efficient, but it also enhances the masquerade as demonstrated in Table 6.1.

For primitive types, changing x does not change y, so the output is 5. For nonprimitive types, x and y are pointing at the same object, so changes in it are visible to both; the output is 10/1. Because strings are immutable, x cannot change in place, so the code in the third column leads to creating a new string for x, keeping y's object unchanged; the output is therefore "5." The immutable nature of the `String` class makes its instances behave more like primitives.

Table 6.1

Primitive Types	Nonprimitive Types	Strings
`int x = 5;`	`Fraction x = new`	`String x = "5";`
`int y = x;`	`    Fraction(5,1);`	`String y = x;`
`x = 10;`	`Fraction y = x;`	`x = "10";`
`output.println(y);`	`x.setFraction(10,1);` `output.println(y);`	`output.println(y);`

In More Depth   6.1

Compile-Time String Literals

The compiler can replace statements such as

```
String str1 = "Planet Earth";
String str2 = "Planet Earth";
```

with either

```
String str1 = new String("Planet Earth");
String str2 = new String("Planet Earth");
```

or

```
String str1 = new String("Planet Earth");
String str2 = str1;
```

The two alternatives are not equivalent. The first leads to two objects, each with a reference pointing at it; the second leads to one object pointed at by two references. As client, you can detect which alternative the compiler implemented by a statement such as

```
output.println(str1 == str2);
```

Most compilers choose the second alternative because it saves memory; there is only one copy of each string literal used in the program.

A Concatenation Operator

A new binary operator with symbol + and string operands was added to the language. Since this symbol is already used for addition, it is said to be an **overloaded operator**. The compiler distinguishes between it and the addition operator by detecting the type of its two operands: if at least one of them is a string, it is **concatenation**; otherwise it is addition. For example,

```
String s1 = "Planet";
String s2 = "Earth";
String s3 = s1 + " " + s2;
```

The operator joins its two operands (concatenates them side by side) and forms a new string. In the above example, s3 ends up being "Planet Earth".

The concatenation operator has the same precedence (–5) and association (left to right) as the addition operator. If one of its two operands is not a string, then it is **type-coerced** to a string as follows:

■ If the operand is primitive, it is replaced by the string that appears when it is displayed; for example, the integer 13 is replaced by the string "13" (this is actually done by creating an instance of the corresponding wrapper class).

- If the operand is a class type (an object reference) and is not null, it is replaced by the return of the toString method of its class.
- Finally, if the operand is a null reference, it is replaced with the four-character string "null."

Here is another example:

```
int i = 4;
int j = 5;
String str1 = i + j + " degrees";
String str2 = "" + i + j + " degrees";
```

While evaluating str1, the left-most operator is surrounded by integer operands; hence, it is the addition operator. The final value is therefore "9 degrees." For str2, however, all + operators have at least one string operand and are therefore concatenation operators. The final value is therefore "45 degrees." The empty string (two double quotes next to each other) is often used as a prefix to ensure that concatenation is recognized.

Programming Tip   6.2

Fallacy: The concatenation operator coerces both operands

The + operator is recognized as the concatenation operator if and only if at least one of its operands is a string. In that case, if the other operand is not a string, then it is coerced to a string. But if neither operand is a string, then neither is coerced. For example, consider the last statement in the following fragment:

```
Fraction f1 = new Fraction(1, 2);
Fraction f2 = new Fraction(1, 3);
output.println(f1 + f2);
```

Since neither operand is a string, this statement will lead to a compile-time error. If the intention is to concatenate the two toString returns, then an empty string prefix should be added, that is,

```
output.println("" + f1 + f2);
```

Example 6.1

The following fragment performs the four arithmetic operations on two integers and stores the results in descriptive strings:

```
int i = 8;
int j = 4;
String str1 = "add: " + i + j;
String str2 = "sub: " + i - j;
String str3 = "mul: " + i * j;
String str4 = "div: " + i / j;
```

The compiler refuses to compile the fourth line of the fragment; it says that subtraction is not defined for strings. But neither are multiplication and division. If there is indeed an error in the fourth line, then why is it not also present in lines 5 and 6? Provide a critique of the fragment.

Answer:

It is all about precedence. Recall that * and / have a higher precedence (−4) than + and − (−5); hence, the last two lines reduce upon evaluation to

```
String str3 = "mul: " + 32;
String str4 = "div: " + 2;
```

And this leads to the desired concatenation. The fourth line evaluates to

```
String str2 = "sub: 8" - 4;
```

This is clearly a compile-time error, since the − operator does not take a string operand. Finally, the third line evaluates to

```
String str1 = "add: 8" + 4;
```

which leads to the string "add: 84". While free from compile-time errors, this line has a logic error because it does not create the intended content in `str1`.

To fix the compile-time error in line 4 and the logic error in line 3, and to enhance the readability of lines 5 and 6, the fragment should be within parentheses:

```
String str1 = "add: " + (i + j);
String str2 = "sub: " + (i - j);
String str3 = "mul: " + (i * j);
String str4 = "div: " + (i / j);
```

6.2　String Handling

The API of the `String` class is, of course, the authoritative source of documentation for the multitude of methods provided by this class. The goal of the following sections is to classify the available methods and familiarize you with the most commonly used ones.

6.2.1　Overview of String Methods

The string methods can be grouped in three categories, as shown in Fig. 6.2.

The **accessor** group has methods that return information about the character sequence encapsulated by a string. Methods in the **transformer** group allow us to make changes to certain aspects of a string. This is done by creating a new string, since strings cannot be mutated. The **comparator** group provides methods for comparing two strings and finding features common to both of them.

Sometimes we come across strings that encapsulate numbers. Section 6.2.5 focuses on methods for converting such strings to numbers and vice versa.

Figure 6.2 A classification of commonly used `String` methods

ACCESSORS	
`String` `toString()`	No need to invoke explicitly
`int` `length()`	Returns 0 if the string is empty
`char` `charAt(int index)`	Primitive return—test with ==
`String` `substring(int from, int end)`	The interval is closed-open
`String` `substring(int from)`	Overloaded for convenience
TRANSFORMERS	
`String` `toUpperCase()`	There is a locale-specific version
`String` `toLowerCase()`	There is a locale-specific version
`String` `trim()`	Removes characters with Unicode <= 20 from both ends
`String` `replace(char old, char new)`	Replaces every occurrence
`String` `replaceAll(String e,String s)`	Advanced method—Section 6.4
COMPARATORS	
`boolean` `equals(String other)`	There is an Ignore Case version.
`int` `compareTo(String other)`	Returns the Unicode distance
`int` `indexOf(String s)`	Returns the leftmost index or −1
`int` `indexOf(String s, int from)`	Overloaded for convenience
`boolean` `matches(String regex)`	Advanced method—Section 6.4

6.2.2 Accessors

Here is a list of methods and the return of each when invoked on `"Planet Earth"`:

- **`String toString()`.** This method returns the string literal that the string object encapsulates. You can think of it as an accessor for that attribute. However, the + operator and all `print` methods auto-invoke this method, so you should rarely need to explicitly invoke it in your code. The return for the example string is `"Planet Earth"`.

- **`int length()`.** This method returns the number of characters in the string literal that this string object encapsulates. The return is zero if the method is invoked on an empty string. For the example string, the return is `12`.

- **`char charAt(int index)`.** This method returns the character at the indicated index (the index of the left-most position is 0). Since the return is primitive, you can test it using == and !=. For the example string, the return of `charAt(2)` is `'a'`. This method throws an exception unless `index` is in [0, length).

- **`String substring(int from, int end)`.** This method returns a substring extracted from this string beginning at offset `from` and extending up to but excluding the one at `end`. For the example, the return of `substring(3,8)` is `"net E"`. The extraction interval [from,end) is said to be closed-open because it includes its left end and excludes its right end. This method throws an exception unless `0 <= from <= end <= length`. If `end` is omitted, an overloaded method behaves as if `end` is present and equal to `length`.

6.2.3 Transformers

Here is a list of methods and the return of each when invoked on `"Planet Earth"`:

- **`String toUpperCase()`.** This method returns a new string with the same character sequence as this string but with all characters capitalized. For the example string, the return is `"PLANET EARTH"`. Unicode defines how to capitalize a given character, and while this may be trivial for English, it is not so for other languages, where the number of characters may increase upon capitalization.

- **`String toLowerCase()`.** This method returns a new string with the same character sequence as this string but with all characters in lowercase. For the example string, the return is `"planet earth"`.

- **`String trim()`.** This method returns a new string with the same character sequence as this string but with all leading or trailing whitespace and control characters removed. Such characters have Unicodes between 0 and 32 inclusive (see Appendix A). The return for our example string would be the same as the original string because it does not have such leading or trailing characters.

- **`String replace(char old, char new)`.** This method returns a new string with the same character sequence as this string but with all occurrences of the character `old` in it (if any) replaced by the character `new`. For the example string, the return of `replace('a','*')` is `"Pl*net E*rth"`.

6.2.4 Comparators

Here is a list of methods and the return of each when invoked on `"Planet Earth"`:

- **`boolean equals(String other)`.** This method returns `true` only if the string object on which it was invoked has the same state as the string object passed to it. The case-insensitive version is `equalsIgnoreCase`.

- **`int compareTo(String other)`.** This method scans this string and the passed one character by character, left to right, until a mismatch is found at some index *k*, the end of one string is reached, or the ends of both strings are reached. In the first case, the difference between the Unicode of character *k* in this string and character *k* in the passed string is returned. In the second case, the difference between the length of this string and that of the passed string is returned. In the third case, 0 is returned. The return is therefore negative, zero, or positive if this string is equal to, lexicographically less than, or lexicographically greater than the passed one, respectively. For the example string, the return of `compareTo("Pl")` is +10, and the return of `compareTo("Saturn")` is -3. See Appendix A to learn how characters are ordered within Unicode.

- **`int indexOf(String s)`.** This method determines whether the passed string is a substring of (occurs anywhere in) this string. If it is, it returns the index of the first character of the first occurrence. Otherwise it returns -1. For the example string, the return of `indexOf("net")` is 3 because `"net"` is a substring beginning at index 3. And the return of `indexOf("a")` is 2 because the left-most occurrence of `"a"` is at index 2. Note that only the left-most occurrence is seen by this method. An overloaded version takes a second argument, `int from`, so that you can specify the beginning index from which the search should start.

Example 6.2

Write a program that prompts for and reads a string from the end-user. The string must contain, somewhere within it, the word "the" in uppercase, lowercase, or mixed case followed by a space. If it does, the program must output the remainder of the string (the part that follows the space) exactly as entered. Otherwise, the program must throw an exception.

Answer:

We use the `indexOf` method to check if the indicated word, with the space, is present. To overcome the letter case issue, we look for the word "THE" in a capitalized version of string:

```
final String WORD = "THE ";
output.println("Enter a string:");
String entry = input.nextLine();
int foundAt = entry.toUpperCase().indexOf(WORD);
ToolBox.crash(foundAt < 0, "Invalid entry!");
output.println(entry.substring(foundAt + WORD.length()));
```

Notice that even if the entered string ended after the space, the above fragment would still work without a crash because the `substring` method tolerates an index that is equal to (but not greater than) the length of the string.

As illustrated in Example 6.2, it is quite common in string applications to cascade the invocation of string methods in the same expression, that is,

```
int foundAt = entry.toUpperCase().indexOf(WORD);
```

The compiler treats the dot separator as an operator with precedence −1 (the highest) and left-to-right association. The above statement is evaluated by first computing `entry.toUpperCase()`, which returns a new string, and then invoking `indexOf` on the returned string.

6.2.5 Numeric Strings

Strings that consist of numbers are frequently encountered in applications. For example, you may need to read a numeric input as a string and then process it as a number. To deal with such situations, we should be able to easily convert back and forth between these two types.

Number to String

Converting numbers to strings is trivial thanks to the coercive + operator. By placing the empty string as one of its operands and the number as the other, we can use this operator to convert numbers to their corresponding display strings. For example, the fragment

```
int k = 5;
double x = 25.75;
String kStr = "" + k;
String xStr = "" + x;
output.println(kStr + "\n" + xStr);
```

will output the following:

```
5
25.75
```

Alternatively, you can perform the conversion yourself by first converting the number to an object (using a type wrapper) and then invoking `toString`. Every primitive type in Java has a corresponding **wrapper** class that encapsulates its values. These classes are all in `java.lang`, and their names are paired with primitive types as follows:

```
byte      Byte
short     Short
char      Char
int       Integer
long      Long
float     Float
double    Double
boolean   Boolean
```

Converting a value of a primitive type to an instance of its wrapper class is called **boxing the value** and is done by passing the value to the constructor of the wrapper. For example,

```
int number = 5;
Integer wrapped = new Integer(number);
```

Once the value is boxed, you can convert it to a string by using the `toString` method of the wrapper. This is accomplished in the above example by adding the following line:

```
String str = wrapped.toString();
```

We mention in passing that a boxed value can be converted back to a primitive type, a process called **unboxing**, by invoking a method named `xValue()` in the wrapper, where x is the name of the primitive type. For example,

```
int backToInt = wrapped.intValue();
```

String to Number

Converting strings to numbers is not always possible, since a string may contain characters that are inconsistent with the number. For example, `"-5.3"` cannot be converted to `int` because `'.'` is not valid for `int`. Similarly, `"1,500.75"` cannot be converted to `double` because of the `','`. If we can somehow be assured that the string characters are valid, we can carry out the conversion using one of the static methods in the corresponding wrapper class:

```
output.print("Enter an integer... ");
String entry = input.nextLine();
int number = Integer.parseInt(entry);
```

The method is so named because it involves parsing the string and extracting the number from it. Given a string s that can be converted, we convert it using one of the following static methods:

```
Byte.parseByte(s);
Short.parseShort(s);
Integer.parseInt(s);
Long.parseLong(s);
Float.parseFloat(s);
Double.parseDouble(s);
```

Note that these methods trigger a runtime error (called `NumberFormatException`) if one of the characters in s cannot be converted. Note also that all these methods have an over-loaded version that allows you to specify the radix to be used, for example, 10 for decimal (the default), 16 for hexadecimal, etc.

Java Details   6.1

Automatic Boxing and Unboxing

Beginning with J2SE release 5, boxing and unboxing are done automatically by the compiler.

Programming Tip 6.3

Pitfall: Parsing a number with spaces

The fragment

```
String s = "5 ";
int n = Integer.parseInt(s);
```

will throw an exception even though the string does indeed contain an integer. This is because of the space that follows the digit. Whenever a numeric string is parsed, it is a good idea to remove all leading or trailing spaces first:

```
int n = Integer.parseInt(s.trim());
```

6.3 Applications

The following sections explore applications that are general in scope and help demonstrate the techniques learned in this chapter.

6.3.1 Character Frequency

As a first program, consider the problem of determining how many times a given character occurs in a given string. For example, the character 'a' occurs three times in the following string:

```
"Planet Earth in the Solar System"
```

Let us use generic names for the user-supplied variables: s for the string and c for the character to count.

Approach 1

Visit each and every character in s and see if it is the same as c. If it is, increment a counter that is initialized to zero. To do this, we set up a loop that goes through every possible index (position) in s:

```
int count = 0;
for (int index = 0; index < s.length(); index++)
{
    if the character at index is c then increment count
}
```

At first glance, you may be tempted to write <= instead of <, but the above condition is correct. Since index starts at 0, it never reaches the length; in other words, the length method returns the number of characters in the string, not the index of the very last character.

For a given value of index, we need to extract the character at that position so that it can be tested. There are two ways to do this, and each dictates a different testing method. The first uses charAt; and since its return is primitive (char), we test using ==:

```
char token = s.charAt(index);
if (token == c) count++;
```

Alternatively, we can use the substring method to extract a substring that starts at index and ends at index. Since this method uses a closed-open interval (inclusive from the left, exclusive from the right), we specify the second parameter as index+1. This accessor returns a String, not a char, so we must test using equals. However, equals takes a string, so we coerce the string parameter using the + operator:

```
String token = s.substring(index, index+1);
if (token.equals("" + c)) count++;
```

The two accessors are equally appropriate for this problem, but the second lends itself more naturally to the problem of counting pairs or triplets of characters. The full program is shown in Fig. 6.3.

Figure 6.3 Count the number of occurrences of a given character in a given string.

```java
import java.util.Scanner;
import java.io.PrintStream;

public class CharFreq
{
    public static void main(String[] args)
    {
        Scanner input = new Scanner(System.in);
        PrintStream output = System.out;

        output.print("Enter the string ... ");
        String s = input.nextLine();
        output.print("Enter the character to count ... ");
        char c = input.nextLine().charAt(0);
        int count = 0;
        for (int index = 0; index < s.length(); index++)
        {
            String token = s.substring(index, index+1);
            if (token.equals("" + c))
            {
                count++;
            }
        }
        output.println(count);
    }
}
```

Approach 2

Instead of visiting the characters of s one by one, we can use the `indexOf` method:

```
int at = s.indexOf(c);
```

The above statement sets `at` to the index at which `c` first occurs in `s`, or to `-1` if it never occurs (note that the method is overloaded to accept `char` in addition to `String`). If `at` is not `-1`, we count this occurrence (i.e., increment `count` as in Fig. 6.3) and then look for additional occurrences. To bypass the first occurrence, we re-invoke the method but start the search beyond `at`, that is, from `at+1`:

```
at = s.indexOf(c, at + 1);
```

By repeating this invocation and counting until `-1` is returned, we can account for every occurrence of `c` in `s`. The resulting program is identical to that of Fig. 6.3 except for the loop: rather than "creeping" one character at a time, the new loop "hops" from one occurrence to the next. The new loop is shown in Fig. 6.4.

Note that this approach scales smoothly to cases where we seek to compute the frequency of a given substring (not just one character); in fact, the loop can be left unchanged.

6.3.2 Character Substitution

Character substitution refers to a class of problems in which certain characters in a given string are to be replaced, on a one-to-one basis, by other characters as indicated in a given substitution table. Such problems arise in encryption and data coding apps. Let us tackle a problem in this class that is simple enough to allow a variety of approaches. This allows us to determine the strength and weakness of each approach and to select the one that can scale to more complicated cases.

We seek a program that prompts for and reads a single character from the user. The character can be assumed (without the need for verification) to be a capital letter between 'A' and 'F', inclusive. The program must convert the input to a digit in accordance with the substitution table in Fig. 6.5.

This problem is simple because its input is a single character rather than a string and because the mapping is highly regular: consecutive letters are mapped to consecutive digits. Note that the program must culminate in a digit, that is, a `char`, not an `int` and not a `String`.

The program has the following structure:

```
char old, nu;
output.print("Enter the character to convert...");
old = input.nextLine().charAt(0);
// map old to nu
```

Figure 6.4 The loop of Fig. 6.3 is rewritten using the `indexOf` method.

```
for (int at=s.indexOf(c); at != -1; at = s.indexOf(c,at+1))
{   count++;
}
```

Figure 6.5
Substitution table

Old	New
A	5
B	4
C	3
D	2
E	1
F	0

Approach 1

Recall that `char` variables are nothing but integer codes and that consecutive letters and digits have consecutive codes. Hence, the expression

```
'F' - old;
```

leads to subtracting the code of `'F'` from that of the input, which yields 0 if old were `'F'`, 1 if it were `'E'`,... and 5 if it were `'A'`. These are the exact values we seek except we want them as characters, not integers; that is, we seek `'0'` rather than 0. This latter conversion can also be obtained by simple code shifting: by adding the code of `'0'` to the obtained integer value, we convert it to its corresponding digit character. The mapping can therefore be done in the single line:

```
nu = (char) ('F' - old + '0');
```

The cast is needed because of the automatic promotion to `int`.

Approach 2

The Unicode distance can be obtained via `compareTo`:

```
nu = (char) ("F".compareTo("" + old) + '0' );
```

Note that we expressed F as a string to invoke `compareTo` on it, and we had to convert the input to a string in order to pass it as a parameter.

Approach 3

We can use an `if` statement to go through all the possibilities:

```
if (old == 'A')
{   nu = '5';
}   else if (old == 'B')
{   nu = '4';
    . . .
```

Unlike the first two approaches, this does not rely on the regularity of the mapping; hence, it does generalize to any mapping. This approach, however, is not scalable: if the number of substitutions is large, it will be cumbersome to write all these `if` statements.

Approach 4

We start by defining two **parallel strings**, one containing all the possible old values and one containing the corresponding new values. The strings are called parallel because their characters correspond: A with 5, B with 4, and so on:

```
final String GRADES = "ABCDEF";
final String POINTS = "543210";
```

The algorithm of this approach is to locate the position of the entered character in the first string and then look up that position in the second string:

```
int position = GRADES.indexOf(old);
nu = POINTS.charAt(position);
```

The strength of this approach is that it relies on neither a special pattern in the mapping nor the number of substitutions. It is therefore versatile and scalable. It is also easy to maintain because the two strings that control the substitution can be read from a file. This means the mapping can be changed without recompiling the program. Figure 6.6 shows a program that uses this approach to map a string of A-F letters. The program can be easily modified so that if other characters are found in the input string, they are left unchanged.

6.3.3 Fixed-Size Codes

We deal with **fixed-size codes** all the time: `"2"` for "Feb," `"Feb"` for "February," `"kg"` for kilogram, `"M"` for "mega," and so on. Therefore, we are constantly confronted with the problems of encoding (turning "Feb" to `"2"`) and decoding (turning `"2"` into "Feb"). It may happen that the code or the data to be encoded is numeric, but we will focus on the more general case in which both are strings. Furthermore, we will assume that all codes are of equal length, and all the corresponding pieces of data are of equal length too. An example of a fixed-size code is character substitution (Section 6.3.2) in which all codes are one character each and all data pieces are also one character each. Another example is the day-of-the-week coding that uses `"0"` for "Sun," `"1"` for "Mon," `"6"` for "Sat," and so on. In this code, all codes have the same size (one), and all data items have the same size (three). Note that the code that uses "2" for "Feb" is *not* a fixed-size code (because months 10, 11, and 12 have two-digit codes). This will be dealt with in Section 6.3.4.

Figure 6.6 Given a string of [A-F] letters, replace them by digits as per Fig. 6.5.

```java
import java.util.Scanner;
import java.io.PrintStream;

public class Substitute
{
    public static void main(String[] args)
    {
        Scanner input = new Scanner(System.in);
        PrintStream output = System.out;

        final String GRADES = "ABCDEF";
        final String POINTS = "543210";
        output.println("Enter the string to map:");
        String s = input.nextLine();
        for (int index = 0; index < s.length(); index++)
        {
            int position = GRADES.indexOf(s.charAt(index));
            char nu = POINTS.charAt(position);
            s = s.substring(0, index) + nu + s.substring(index + 1);
        }
        output.println(s);
    }
}
```

For definiteness, let us write a program that reads a string from the user containing exactly one digit between `"0"` and `"6"`, inclusive, and outputs the corresponding day name with `"0"` being "Sun" and `"6"` being "Sat." The program starts with input

```
output.print("Enter the day code [0-6]... ");
String code = input.nextLine();
```

We adopt the parallel-strings approach that was explored in the previous section. We use two strings, one for the codes and one for the data pieces they represent:

```
final String DAY_CODE = "0  1  2  3  4  5  6  ";
final String DAY_NAME = "SunMonTueWedThuFriSat";
```

As you can see, spaces have to be added to ensure the strings are parallel. The algorithm is to locate the position of the entered code in the upper string and then look up that position in the lower string:

```
int position = DAY_CODE.indexOf(code);
ToolBox.crash(position < 0 || position % SIZE != 0, "invalid!");
String name = DAY_NAME.substring(position, position + SIZE);
```

where we used a final to hold the size of each day name:

```
final int SIZE = 3;
```

The validation ensures that the entered code must be present and that it must be present at certain locations only, and this precludes inputs such as "7" or " ". Hence, this elegant solution not only accomplishes the encoding, but it also validates the input.

Note that since the codes are consecutive digits, we could have replaced the `indexOf` search by an arithmetic computation of `position`, but we opted for a solution that generalizes to non-numeric, nonconsecutive codes. The only critical requirement for this algorithm is that the two strings are made parallel: depending on whichever is longer, we must add spaces to either the codes or the data items to ensure their positions correspond.

The inverse problem, decoding a given name, can be handled using the same approach:

```
output.print("Enter the day name... ");
String name = input.nextLine();
int position = DAY_NAME.indexOf(name);
ToolBox.crash(position < 0 || position % SIZE != 0, "invalid");
String code = DAY_CODE.substring(position, position + SIZE);
code = code.trim();
```

The validation allows us to detect such invalid inputs as "nTu," which spans the two names "MonTue" and whose `indexOf` return is 5, not a multiple of 3. Note that we had to trim the obtained code to get rid of spaces that were added to make the two strings parallel, that is, ones that are not actually part of the code. In general, you must trim any code or data item obtained by this algorithm lest it includes such trailing spaces.

The algorithm as implemented is case-sensitive. It should be straightforward to modify it so that it can recognize the day name even if entered with a different capitalization.

It is possible to avoid the addition of spaces by keeping *two* sizes, one for the codes and one for the data items. The position obtained in one string can be mapped to a different position in the other by multiplying it by the ratio of the two sizes. Such a technique, while economical in terms of memory usage, ends up with two strings that are not parallel and, hence, difficult to maintain visually. Any savings in memory usage is more than offset by the increased vulnerability to human error.

6.3.4 Variable-Size Codes

When either the codes, their corresponding data pieces, or both are of variable size, that is, they are **variable-size codes**, we can continue to use the algorithm from the previous section provided we force the strings to have a common length. We do this by padding them with spaces. The number of spaces we append depends on the length of the longest string.

As an example, consider the same day-of-the-week code as in the previous section but with the full day name. Since the longest day name is "Wednesday," with 9 characters, we append enough spaces to the other names to make them all 9 characters in length:

```
final String CODE1 = "0        1        2        3         ";
final String NAME1 = "Sunday   Monday   Tuesday Wednesday";

final String CODE2 = "4        5        6       "   ;
final String NAME2 = "Thursday Friday   Saturday";

final String CODES = CODE1 + CODE2;
final String NAMES = NAME1 + NAME2;
final int SIZE = 9;
```

With this setup, all the techniques of the previous sections can be applied without change.

6.4 Advanced String Handling

While the capabilities of the `String` class enable us to solve any string problem, there are two areas that can be improved. The first is purely a performance issue and concerns the immutability of strings and the resulting frequent creation and destruction of string objects. The second area concerns the formalization of how string patterns can be specified and has wide-ranging applications. These areas are explored in the following two sections.

6.4.1 The `StringBuffer` Class

We mentioned in Section 6.1.2 that in order to optimize the implementation of strings, the designers of Java provided two distinct classes: `String`, which we have been dealing with thus far in this chapter, and `StringBuffer`. The `String` class encapsulates immutable strings, strings that cannot change in content or length once created, while the `StringBuffer` class encapsulates **mutable strings**.

To create a string buffer object, you can either create an empty one and then add characters to it, or create one with some initial character sequence:

```
StringBuffer empty = new StringBuffer();
StringBuffer sb = new StringBuffer("Test");
```

The class provides a variety of methods, but the key methods are mutators, methods that modify the encapsulated sequence without creating a new object. We will present three and describe how each modifies an example sequence containing `"Sware"`:

- **StringBuffer append(*anything*)**
  This method appends the sequence of this string buffer by the string representation of the passed parameter. If the parameter is primitive, its display string is used. If it is a non-null reference, its `toString` return is used. If it is `null`, the string "null" is used. For the example, `append("s")` changes the sequence to `"Swares"`.
  Note that this mutator (as well as all others) modifies the string buffer on which it was invoked; that is, this is an in-place change and does not involve creating a new instance. Hence, the mutator could have been made `void`, but as a convenience, it was decided to return a reference to the same string buffer to make chained invocations easier to write.

- **StringBuffer insert(int index, *anything*)**
  This method inserts the string representation of the passed parameter into this sequence of this buffer starting at the passed index. For the example, `insert(1, "oft")` changes the sequence to "Software".

- **StringBuffer delete(int start, int end)**
  This method removes characters from the sequence of this buffer from the one at index start up to that at index `end-1`. For the example, `delete(0, 2)` changes the sequence to `"are"`.

An application that uses extensive string mutations may start by reading its inputs, from the user or from a file, as strings, convert the strings into string buffers to benefit from the optimized mutators, and then convert the buffers back to strings. To that end, the following lines of code demonstrate how we can convert back and forth between these two classes:

```
StringBuffer sb1 = new StringBuffer("Test");
String s1 = sb1.toString();
String s2 = "Earth";
StringBuffer sb2 = new StringBuffer(s2);
```

As mentioned in Section 6.1.2, the concatenation operator + was added to make the handling of strings as easy as that of primitive types. In fact, + is not a genuine language construct but an illusion created by the compiler as follows: whenever we write

```
String s = x + y;
```

where x and y are previously declared and initialized strings, the compiler replaces it by

```
String s = new
StringBuffer().append(x).append(y).toString();
```

In other words, the compiler starts by creating an empty buffer and then appends to it the listed string operands one by one. This chained invocation is possible because the append mutator returns a reference to the buffer. Finally, the obtained buffer is converted back to a string using the `toString` method.

Example 6.3

Write a program to demonstrate that StringBuffer does indeed have a performance advantage over String. To that end, and also to quantify the advantage, let the program create a string containing 10 000 repetitions of the word "TEST " using both classes and provide timing for each.

Answer:

We start by defining the needed constants:

```
final String WORD = "TEST ";
final int COUNT = 10000;
```

The String approach starts with an empty string and repeatedly applies the + operator:

```
long start = System.currentTimeMillis();
String str = "";
for (int i = 0; i < COUNT; i++)
{
    str = str + WORD;
}
output.println(System.currentTimeMillis() - start);
```

The StringBuffer approach also starts with an empty string sequence, but it then invokes the append method repeatedly:

```
start = System.currentTimeMillis();
StringBuffer sb = new StringBuffer("");
for (int i = 0; i < COUNT; i++)
{
    sb = sb.append(WORD);
}
output.println(System.currentTimeMillis() - start);
```

And to ensure that the two approaches are equivalent (aside from performance), we should add a statement that asserts our conviction that their results are the same:

```
assert sb.toString().equals(str);
```

The output generated by the program depends, of course, on the system on which the virtual machine is running. Nevertheless, the difference between the two displayed times is enormous. On one system, the String approach took a hundred times longer. This is because the str object of the first approach has to be created and garbage-collected in every iteration, that is, 10 000 times. On the other hand, the sb object of the second approach is created once (before the loop) and is mutated in situ.

□

6.4.2 Pattern Matching and Regular Expressions

All the applications we have seen so far have involved straightforward string searches. We have determined whether a given string contains a given substring somewhere inside it. We were able to count how many occurrences of a certain letter are present and to make the search case-sensitive or case-insensitive, but the search criterion was always the same: find an exact match. Because of this, the algorithms that we developed will become cumbersome if we change the criterion to something less exact; for example, determine whether a given string is made up of two words, or if it contains an integer surrounded by letters and separated from them by whitespace. In these examples, we seek to determine whether the content of the given string matches a given pattern, hence the term **pattern matching**.

A **regular expression**, or **regex**, is a string that describes a pattern in a formal, unambiguous fashion. These expressions originated in Unix but are now used in almost all programming languages and in many text-processing applications under all platforms. In this section, we cover only the basics of regexes and two methods in the `String` class (`matches` and `replaceAll`) that allow **regex-based processing**.

We start with a simple pattern: suppose our program needs to read a time from the user. To be valid, the entered time has to be 3, 6, or 9 am or pm. Specifically, the entered string must start with a digit, which is 3, 6, or 9, followed by one space, followed by the letters am or pm (case-sensitive). Such a pattern is matched by all the following strings: `"3 am"`, `"6 am"`, `"9 am"`, `"3 pm"`, `"6 pm"`, and `"9 pm"`. It is not matched, however, by any of the following strings: `"8 am"`, `"6pm"`, `"6  PM"`, and `"  3 AM"`.

To express this pattern as a regex, we start by specifying its first character as `"[369]"`. This setlike notation indicates that the character has to be 3, 6, or 9. The next character must be a space, so we simply append a space, and the regex becomes `"[369] "`. The next character can be either a or p, so we append `"[ap]"`. Finally, the last character has to be m so we append m. Thus the final regex for our pattern is `"[369] [ap]m"`.

To get a feel for this regex, let us invoke the `matches` method of the `String` class. As shown in Fig. 6.2, this method takes a regex and returns `true` if the string on which it is invoked matches this regex. A code fragment that uses this regex may look like this:

```
output.println("Enter the time...");
String s = input.nextLine();
if (! s.matches("[369] [ap]m"))
{
    output.println("Invalid entry!");
}
```

Figure 6.7 lists some of the basic regex constructs.

To see how a quantifier works, let us relax the input condition and allow the user to enter any number of spaces between the hour digit and the am/pm indicator.

The regex `"[369] +[ap]m"` specifies that the initial digit can be followed by one or more spaces. Had we used * instead of +, the user would have been able to either leave no space at all (e.g., `"3pm"`) or insert an arbitrary number of spaces.

CHARACTER SPECIFICATIONS

[a-m]	Range. A character between a and m, inclusive
[a-m[A-M]]	Union. a through m or A through M
[abc]	Set. The character a, b, or c
[^abc]	Negation. Any character except a, b, or c
[a-m&&[^ck]]	Intersection. a through m but neither c nor k

PREDEFINED SPECIFICATIONS

.	Any character
\d	A digit, [0-9]
\s	A whitespace character, [\t\n\x0B\f\r]
\w	A word character, [a-zA-Z_0-9]
\p{Punct}	A punctuation character, [!"#$%&'()*+,-./:;<=>?@[\]^_`{|}~]

QUANTIFIERS

x?	x, once or not at all
x*	x, zero or more times
x+	x, one or more times
x{n,m}	x, at least *n* but no more than *m* times

Figure 6.7 The basic constructs for regular expressions

As a second example, suppose we want to filter out a string that contains an integer that is surrounded by nondigit characters. The pattern starts with zero or more nondigits, which can be specified as "[^0-9]*" (the ^ specifies negation and the * is for 0 or more). Next, we may have the integer sign, which can be +, -, or nothing at all. This is expressed using "[+-]?". The integer itself is made up of one or more digits, and hence, is specified using "[0-9]+". The terminal pattern is similar to the leading one, so the full regex is

"[^0-9]*[+-]?[0-9]+[^0-9]*"

The String class has additional methods that use regular expressions, for example, String **replaceAll**.

■ String **replaceAll**(String regex, String replacement)

String **replaceAll** replaces each substring of this string that matches the passed regex with the passed replacement string. In other words, each matching substring is first removed from this string, then the replacement string is inserted. The substring and the replacement can be different in length.

For example, consider the following fragment:

```
String regex = "[^0-9]*[+-]?[0-9]+[^0-9]*";
output.print("Enter string: ");
String s = input.nextLine();
if (s.matches(regex))
{
    output.println(s.replaceAll("-?[0-9]+", ""));
}
```

If the input matches our pattern (an integer surrounded by nondigits), we replace the integer and its sign (if any) with the empty string. Here are two sample runs:

```
Enter string: ABC-56XYZ
ABCXYZ
Enter string: QWE/?201**P
QWE/?**P
```

Java Details   6.2

The regex Package

The String class acts as a front end when it gets to regular expressions. Behind the scenes, it delegates to the Pattern class in order to encapsulate the regex and to the Matcher class in order to perform the matching. These two classes are in the java.util.regex package.

6.4.3 Command-Line Arguments

We have been using the Scanner class to supply input to our apps. This, so-called *standard input* approach, is how end users typically interact with console apps. In this section we look at a second approach based on *command-line arguments*. It provides a lightweight alternative which can be very attractive, even if less versatile, in certain applications.

Consider, for example, the app CharFreq which reads a string and a character from the user and outputs the number of times the character occurs in the string (see Fig. 6.3). In the standard approach, the app must make two prompts and two reads:

```
output.print("Enter the string ... ");
String s = input.nextLine();
output.print("Enter the character ... ");
char c = input.nextLine().charAt(0);
```

The user launches the app and then supplies each input upon seeing its prompt:

```
java CharFreq
Enter the string ... university
Enter the character ... i
```

Using command-line arguments, the app does not make any prompts or reads. Instead, the end user supplies the needed input on the same line in which the app is launched:

```
java CharFreq university i
```

The VM makes these values available to the app through the variable args that appears in the header of the main method. The app can access the first value using the syntax args[0] and the second using args[1]. Using these variables, the app can proceed as follows:

```
String s = args[0];
char c = args[1].charAt(0);
```

The line that launches the app is known as the command-line and the values listed on it can be thought of as arguments to be passed to the main method, hence the name of this approach. The operating system parses the command line into separate strings, using spaces and tabs as delimiters, and then passes these strings to the launched app. This parsing process has three important implications:

1.   In order to pass a string that contains spaces as a single input, the string must be quoted (surrounded by single or double quotes). For example, if we want to count the frequency of the letter i in the string *Java By Abstraction*, then we would launch the app as follows:

```
java CharFreq "Java By Abstraction" i
```

   Note that the quote characters themselves are not passed. Had we not quoted the string, the operating system would have passed four arguments and populated the four variables: args[0], args[1] , args[2] , args[3].

2.   Some characters have special meanings to the operating system's shell. In order to pass a string that contains such characters, the string must be quoted. For example, a string containing '>', '<', or '|' must be quoted.

3.   The parsing process treats all values as strings. If an input is intended to be something else (int or double for example) then the app must use one of the methods of Section 6.2.5 to convert the received string to a number.

The variable args that receives the arguments is declared in the header of the main method:

```
public static void main(String[] args)
```

The type String[] is known as a *string array*, a non-primitive type. One can think of args as a collection, or an aggregate, of string variables sharing a common base name. Each one of these variables is known as an *array element*. In order to access a particular array element, we suffix the base name with a bracketed, zero-based index that identifies that element. We can think of args as an object reference that points at an instance of String[]. The instance has one public final attribute length that holds the number of elements in the array. This attribute helps us validate the number of arguments that the user passed.

Example 6.4

Write the app Power that takes a base and an exponent as command-line arguments and outputs the power. Treat the two inputs as int and output the power without decimals. If the user does not supply two arguments then an error message is displayed.

Answer:

Here is the body of the main method of the Power class:

```
if (args.length != 2)
{
    output.println("Usage: java Power <base> <exponent>");
```

```
    } else
    {
        int base = Integer.parseInt(args[0]);
        int expo = Integer.parseInt(args[1]);
        output.printf("%.0f\n", Math.pow(base, expo));

    }
```

The `split` Method

One of the most powerful methods in the `String` class is `split`. We delayed its discussion until now because it relies on string arrays. It takes a regular expression and splits the string on which it was invoked using the matches of the regular expression as delimiters. The split pieces are returned in a string array.

In its simplest form, the regular expression contains only delimiters, as shown below:

```
String s = "Toronto, Ontario";
String[] pieces = s.split("o");
```

This fragment splits the string into a separate piece whenever the letter 'o' appears in it. We can visit these pieces one by one using a loop like this:

```
for (int i = 0; i < pieces.length; i++)
{
    output.println("Piece #" + i + " " + pieces[i]);
}
```

In this particular example, the loop's output is:

```
Piece #0 T
Piece #1 r
Piece #2 nt
Piece #3 , Ontari
```

More sophisticated splits can be achieved using the various constructs shown in Fig. 6.7. For example, the regex `[oa\s*]` splits the above string to the 6 pieces:

```
Piece #0 T
Piece #1 r
Piece #2 nt
Piece #3 ,
Piece #4 Ont
Piece #5 ri
```

Notice that if no matches are found then the returned array has only one piece and that piece contains the entire string. Note also that if two consecutive delimiters are encountered then the method behaves as if there is an empty string between them. Hence, the regex `[ar]` leads to four pieces rather than three:

```
Piece #0 To
Piece #1 onto, Ont
Piece #2
Piece #3 io
```

To familiarize yourself with this method and with regex in general, it is recommended that you write an app that takes a string and a regex as command-line arguments and outputs the result of invoking `matches` and `split` on the string. You can conduct experiments quickly and easily this way by using the up-arrow to repeat the command. This is a case in point for choosing command-line arguments to supply input.

Summary of Key Concepts

1. Strings are created like all other objects: you need a **string reference** that points at a **string object**, which holds the **string literal** being encapsulated as its state. All three entities (reference, object, and literal) are referred to as strings.

2. In a string literal, characters are indexed using a zero-based number, and their count is called the **length** of the string.

3. An **empty string** is a string object whose state is a literal containing no characters at all. You can express such a literal by two consecutive double quotes. Such a string has a **zero length**. A **null string** is a string reference set to `null`; that is, it does not point to a string object.

4. Strings can also be created using shortcut syntax similar to that used for primitive types.

5. When the compiler encounters a + operator with at least one of its operands being a string, it interprets it as the **concatenation operator**, which joins the two operands. The other operand, if not already a string, is **type-coerced** to a string. This is an **overloaded operator** because it shares the same symbol with the addition operators of primitive types.

6. The `String` class encapsulates **immutable strings**. Any method in it that returns a string actually returns a new string.

7. The methods of the `String` class can be classified as **accessors** (`charAt`, `length`, `substring`, `toString`), **transformers** (`toUpperCase`, `toLowerCase`, `trim`, `replace`), and **comparators** (`equals`, `compareTo`, `indexOf`).

8. Each primitive type has a corresponding **wrapper class** that encapsulates its values. Converting a value to its corresponding wrapper instance is called **boxing**, and the inverse operation is called **unboxing**.

9. To convert a numeric string to a number, we use a **parse** method in the appropriate wrapper class. To convert a number to a string, we either concatenate it with an empty string or box it and invoke `toString`.

10. Two common operations in string processing are **character frequency** and **character substitution**.

11. Creating two **parallel strings** and using `indexOf` on one to substring from the other is an efficient technique for encoding and decoding.

12. The `StringBuffer` class encapsulates **mutable strings**. It offers significant performance advantage over the `String` class.

13. The most commonly used methods in `StringBuffer` are `append`, `insert`, and `delete`.

14. **Regular expressions**, or **regex**, are used to formally describe a pattern in a string. They are used in pattern-matching applications (as well as applications beyond strings).

15. Some methods in the `String` class allow **regex-based** processing, such as `matches` and `replaceAll`.

16. Command-line arguments allow us to supply input to an app on the same line that launches it. They appear in the app as elements of a string array. The app can use the `length` attribute of the array to determine the number of arguments.

Review Questions

1. Give an example that clearly explains the difference between a string object, a string reference, and a string literal.

2. What is the length of a string literal that contains 10 characters? What is the index of the last character in it?

3. (a) What is the difference between an empty and a null string? (b) What is wrong with the statement "A null string has a zero length"?

4. Show how strings can be created without using the `new` operator. Provide a critique on whether you like or dislike this abnormal creation process.

5. Why is the + operator called overloaded? Explain why this operator would still be overloaded even if it were not used for strings.

6. There are four possibilities for the two operands of the + operator: each can either be a string or not. Explain how the operator operates in each of the four cases.

7. How does type coercion work? Is it always successful; that is, can anything be coerced into a string?

8. Instances of `String` are said to be immutable. Explain what this means, and give an example of a method that would be available if the instances were mutable.

9. Give an example that shows how the `charAt` method works. Does it return a string?

10. What exactly is returned by the `toString` method of `String`?

11. Give an example that shows how the `substring` method works. What exactly is returned by this method if the index `from` were equal to the string length?

12. Does the `trim` method remove the space between the words in the string "The Book"?

13. Does the `replace` method replace the first or every occurrence of the character indicated in its first argument?

14. What is the significance of the integer returned by `compareTo`?

15. Give an example that shows how the `indexOf` method works.

16. What does it mean if the return of `indexOf` is 0?

17. What is a wrapper class, and why is it needed?

18. What do boxing and unboxing mean?

19. How do you convert a string that contains an amount to a `double`?

20. Give an example of parallel strings and how they are used in encoding and decoding.

21. Why do we need the `StringBuffer` class?

22. Explain how the `append` method of `StringBuffer` works. Could this method have been made `void`?

23. How can a `String` instance be converted to a `StringBuffer` instance?

24. How can a `StringBuffer` instance be converted to a `String` instance?

25. What is a regular expression?

26. Give an example of a regular expression that uses the "?" quantifier.

27. Give an example that shows how the `matches` method works.

28. Give an example that shows how the `replaceAll` method works.

29. How is the `replaceAll` method different from the `replace` method?

30. Can the `replaceAll` method be used without knowing anything about regular expressions?

31. Compare and contrast command-line arguments and input via `Scanner`.

32. Your operating system has a console command that copies files. Do you see a similarity between the syntax of that command and command-line arguments?

33. Argue that the name of the string array that is populated by command-line arguments does not have to be `args` and show how to change it.

34. How can command-line arguments be used to read a `long` value?

35. How can command-line arguments be used to read a `boolean` value?

36. Give an example that shows how `split` can be used to identify the words in a sentence.

Lab 6

L6.1 The Masquerade

1. Examine the two fragments below. The left-hand fragment deals with integers, while the right-hand fragment deals with strings. The striking similarity between the two, in terms of declaration, assignment, computation, and output, makes strings look like primitives.

```
int s1;                          String s1;
int s2;                          String s2;
int s3;                          String s3;
s1 = 5;                          s1 = "Uni";
s2 = 3;                          s2 = "Con";
s3 = s1 + s2;                    s3 = s1 + s2;
output.println(s3);             output.println(s3);
```

    Predict the output of each fragment, then verify.

2. Consider the following fragment:

```
String s;
s = new String("Planet Earth");
int len = s.length();
output.print("s.length yields: ");
output.println(len);
```

    Here, strings behave more like objects. There seems to be a class, called `String`, whose constructor creates a string containing the characters passed in the parameter. Moreover, the class seems to have an instance (nonstatic) method, `length`, because it is invoked on the reference `s` using the dot operator. If you put the above fragment in a program, what output will be generated?

3. Predict the output of the following fragment and then verify by running it. Was your prediction correct?

```
String s1;
String s2;
s1 = new String("earth");
s2 = s1;
s1 = s1.toUpperCase();
output.println(s1);
output.println(s2);
```

4. Launch your editor and create a program, Lab6, containing the following:

```
String s1 = "Test";
String s2 = "Test";
output.println(s1 == s2);
```

Predict the output of Lab6, then verify by running it.

5. Add the following lines to Lab6 (after the ones added above):

```
String s3 = "Testing";
String s4 = s1 + "ing";
output.println(s3 == s4);
```

Predict the output, then verify by running it.

6. Add the following lines to Lab6 (after the ones added above):

```
s3.toUpperCase();
output.println(s3);
```

Predict the output, then verify by running it.

L6.2 Exploring the String Class

1. Add the following lines to Lab6 (after the ones added above):

```
String phrase = "this is the planet earth";
output.println("Enter any string...");
String pattern = input.nextLine();
output.println("length: " + phrase.length());
```

When prompted, enter the string "net." Predict the output.

2. Add the following lines to Lab6 (after the ones added above):

```
final int FROM = 3;
final int UNTIL = 6;
output.println("substring: " + phrase.substring(FROM,
UNTIL));
```

Try to predict the output before you run the program.

3. What happens if you change the value of UNTIL from 6 to 24 in the above substring?

4. Add the following line to Lab6 (after the ones added above):

```
output.println("index: " + phrase.indexOf(pattern));
```

Try to predict the output before running the program.

5. Add the following line to Lab6 (after the ones added above):

```
output.println("compareTo: " + phrase.compareTo(pattern));
```

Try to predict the output before running the program.

6. Add the following line to `Lab6` (after the ones added above):

```
output.println("upper: " + phrase.toUpperCase());
```

Try to predict the output before running the program.

L6.3 Symmetric-Key Cryptography

We want to develop a program that encrypts a message using a user-defined password or key. The receiver of the encrypted message should be able to decrypt it using the same key (symmetric-key cryptography). To keep things simple, we will restrict the alphabet of the characters in the message to uppercase letters and a space:

```
final String ALPHABET = " ABCDEFGHIJKLMNOPQRSTUVWXYZ";
```

Given a message, we first capitalize its letters and then treat any character in it that is not in the above alphabet as a space. For example, the message

```
A Client-View Approach
```

becomes

```
A CLIENT VIEW APPROACH
```

The encryption process relies on a key that is generated as follows: create a user-defined personal identification number (PIN), then concatenate the PIN with itself as many times as necessary until a string of the same length as the message or greater is obtained. For example, if the PIN is "1956," then the key would be

19561956**19561**956**1956**19

To encrypt the message, imagine placing the key physically under it:

```
A CLIENT VIEW APPROACH
```

19561956**19561**956**1956**19

Next, encrypt each character in the message by shifting it to the right, within the alphabet, by the amount indicated beneath it. For example, the first letter in the message, A, must be shifted right by one, and this makes it B. The next character in the message is a space, and it must be shifted right in the alphabet by nine positions. Looking at the `ALPHABET` string above, this makes it I. The next character in the message is C and shifting it by five positions makes it H. Continuing along these lines leads to the cipher

```
A CLIENT VIEW APPROACH
```

19561956**19561**956**1956**19

```
BIHRJNSZADNKXIFVQ TGDQ
```

Note that when the letter V was to be right-shifted by nine positions, it reached beyond the right edge of the alphabet. In such a case, we wrap around the alphabet as if it is written on a circle; that is, we treat space as if it occurs after Z. Hence, the letter that occurs circularly nine positions after V is D.

The receiver of the message can decrypt it using the key by shifting left instead of right (also circularly).

1. Launch your editor and create the program Encrypt. We will fix the PIN but you can change it later:

```
final String ALPHABET =...
final String PIN = "1956";
output.println("Enter the message to encrypt:");
String message = input.nextLine();
```

Capitalize all letters in the message.

2. Create the key:

```
String key;
for (key = PIN;...
```

The length of the key string must be not less than that of the message.

3. Set up the encryption loop so that it examines the message character by character:

```
String cipher = "";
for (int i = 0; i < message.length(); i++)
{
    int position = ALPHABET.indexOf(message.charAt(i));
```

The position variable holds the position in the alphabet of the current character of the message. Add logic to ensure that if the current character is not in the alphabet, it is treated as if it is a space.

4. Determine the shift amount:

```
int shift =...
```

The shift amount can obtained either from key.charAt(i) or by using substring, but either way, it must somehow be converted to an integer.

5. Circular shifting can be implemented as follows:

```
position = position + shift;
if (position >= ALPHABET.length())
{
    position >= position - ALPHABET.length();
}
```

It is far more natural, however, to do so using the % operator. Replace the above logic by a single line that accomplishes the same result.

6. Store the encrypted character in the result string:

```
cipher = cipher + ALPHABET.charAt(position);
```

It is more efficient to use a StringBuffer, but performance is not our primary concern. For testing purposes, it is a good idea to output the generated key and the cipher immediately below the message. Compile and run the program and then conduct a few tests. Convince yourself that the program works as expected.

7. Save the program under a new name, Decrypt. Modify it so that it decrypts a given ciphered message. Only one statement needs to be changed.

Compile and run the decryption program and then conduct a few tests. Convince yourself that it works as expected.

8. The two programs written earlier can easily be combined into one, Crypt. Write this program so that it starts by prompting the user to enter a command. Here is a sample run:

```
Enter Command: e A Client-View Approach
A CLIENT-VIEW APPROACH
19561956195619561956
BIHRJNSZADNKXIFVQ TGDQ
```

The first letter in the command is either e (for encryption) or d (for decryption). It can be in lower- or uppercase. Next is a space followed by the message to be processed. The output consists of an empty line, the capitalized message, the key, and the result. Here is a second sample run:

```
Enter Command: d KJ GAKCFBKXZSJHZJXS
KJ GAKCFBKXZSJHZJXS
1956195619561956
JAVA BY ABSTRACTION
```

 ## Exercises

Programming exercises are indicated with an asterisk.

6.1 If a string literal is defined as a *set* (rather than a sequence) of characters, what will the equals method return when invoked on "ONLY" with argument "LOONY"?

6.2 How can a program determine whether a string is empty or a null string?

6.3 Consider the following fragment:

```
String s = "YORK";
s = s.toLowerCase();
```

It starts with a string s with a certain state, and it ends up with the same string s with a different state. This seems to contradict the fact that strings are immutable. Explain this mystery by exposing the difference between an object and an object reference.

6.4 Predict the output of the statement (or indicate that it will lead to an error)

```
output.println(x);
```

for each of the following possibilities for x:

```
(a) "planet" + 15
(b) 7.54 + "planet"
(c) 15 + 4.6 + "Earth"
(d) "Earth" + 15 + 4.6
(e) "planet" + (1 > 0)
(f) new Fraction(1, 2)
(g) "planet" + new Fraction(1, 2)
```

(h) new Fraction(1, 2) + "planet"

(i) new Fraction(1, 2) + new Fraction(1, 2)

6.5 Provide a critique of the following fragment:

```
char x = "Java".charAt(2);
String s = "Java".substring(2, 3);
assert x == s;
```

In particular, what does the last statement mean? Show that it is semantically correct but syntactically incorrect, and provide a fix by using the empty string.

6.6 Predict the output of the statement (or indicate that it will lead to an error)

```
output.println(x);
```

for each of the following possibilities for x:

(a) "Java".substring(2, 4);

(b) "Java".substring(1);

(c) "Java".substring(3, 3);

(d) "Java".substring(3, 4);

(e) "Java".substring(4, 4);

(f) "Java".substring(3, 4);

6.7 Predict the output of the statement (or indicate that it will lead to an error)

```
output.println(x);
```

for each of the following possibilities for x:

(a) "University".compareTo("Universe");

(b) "University".compareTo("Universe".toLowerCase());

(c) "University".indexOf("Universe");

(d) "University".equals("Universe");

6.8 Provide a critique of the following fragment:

```
int x = input.nextInt();
assert (new Integer(x)).toString().equals("" + x);
```

In particular, what does the last statement mean? Show that the assertion is correct.

6.9 Provide a critique of the following fragment:

```
String s = input.nextLine();
long x = Long.parseLong(s);
assert s.equals("" + x);
```

6.10 The following fragment uses parallel strings to map a user-entered character to another:

```
final String PLAIN = "1234";
final String CODED = " WTHA";
char inp = input.nextLine().charAt(0);
char out = CODED.charAt(PLAIN.indexOf(inp) + 1);
```

Specify the mapping of each of the following inputs:

    (a)   1
    (b)   3
    (c)   5

6.11 Predict the output of the following fragment, or indicate that it will lead to an error:>

```
final int A = 7;
final int B = 4;
StringBuffer sb = new StringBuffer("University");
sb.delete(A, sb.length()).insert(A, sb.charAt(B));
output.println(sb);
```

6.12 Predict the output of the fragment

```
final String REGEX = "[a-d]?[xyz]+[R]";
String s = input.nextLine();
output.println(s.matches(REGEX));
```

for each of the following inputs:

    (a) xxx
    (b) xxxR
    (c) dyR
    (d) abR
    (e) axR

6.13* The following fragment is meant to read a string from the user and then replace each occurrence of an integer followed by a colon by the letter "x."

```
final String REGEX = ?
String ss = input.nextLine();
output.println(ss.replaceAll(REGEX, "x"));
```

For example, if the user entered

```
2456 24567: 23546:42356
```

then the output would be

```
2456 x x42356
```

What should the regular expression be to accomplish this?

6.14* Write a program that reads a string containing two space-delimited integers from the user and outputs their sum. For example, if the input is "12 8", then the output would be 20. You can assume without validation that the input conforms to the stated pattern.

6.15* Write a program that reads a string from the user and outputs its length exclusive of any trailing asterisks. For example, if the user entered "java**", the output should be 4; if the user entered "**", the output should be 0.

6.16* Write a program that reads a string from the user and outputs it after the following changes: every occurrence of A becomes B, of B becomes C, and of C becomes A (case-sensitive).

All other characters remain unchanged. For example, if the input is <IPGM>"jaBAA Cb", then the output would be "jaCBB Ab".

6.17* Write a program that reads a credit card number (a string of digits) and *says* its digits as output. For example, if the input is "123", then the output would be "OneTwoThree". Note that each digit name starts in uppercase and that there is no delimiter between names. Such a program is typically used to echo back important entries made through a telephone.

6.18* Write a program that reads a string and corrects one aspect of its spelling as follows: whenever the letter pair "ei" is found, it should be replaced by "ie" unless it is preceded by the letter c. The search must be case-insensitive but the replacement must be case-sensitive, that is, lower (upper) case letters must be replaced by lower (upper) case letters. For example, "BELEIVE, seive, conceive" becomes "BELIEVE, sieve, conceive".

6.19* Write a program that reads the age of the user as an int. If the entered age is less than 13, the output is "You cannot be this young!", and if it is more than 99, then the output is "Too old for me!". Otherwise, the output is the string "You are in your " followed by "teens", "twenties", "thirties", etc. depending on the entered age.

6.20* Write a program that reads a string made up of the capital letters R, B, and W and outputs a string with the same letters except that the Rs appear first, followed by Bs, and followed by Ws. For example, if the input is "BRRBWBBR", the output would be "RRRBBBBW"; and if the input is "WBB", the output would be "BBW". If the entered string is empty or is not made up exclusively of these three letters, an error message should be generated.

6.21* Write a program that reads a string and outputs the most frequent character in it. If two or more characters occur most frequently, then output any one of them. For example, if the input is "abc123aB", then the output would be "a" because it occurs twice while all other characters occur once each. If the input is "abc123ab", the output would be either "a" or "b" (both occur a maximal number of times).

6.22* Write a program that reads a DNA sequence from the user (a string) and determines whether it is valid. To be valid, the sequence must be made up exclusively of the capital letters

    A, C, G, T

Furthermore, it must start with "ATG" and its character count must be a multiple of 3.

6.23* Write a program that reads a valid DNA sequence from the user (defined in Exercise 6.22) and outputs the code of the most frequent amino acid in it. Any sequence of three letters (e.g., ACG, CTA, TTT) is an amino acid. If two or more amino acids occur equally most frequently, output any one of them. For example, if the input is

    "ATGTTTAAAGCTAAAGCTGATAAACCG"

then the output would be "AAA".

6.24 The web site for this book contains a collection of tests. You are now in the position to take Test B, which covers Chapters 1 to 6. Follow these steps:

■ Print and read the outline of the test. It tells you what kinds of questions will be on the test, how they are weighted, and what aids are allowed.

■ Print the test and take it. Do not use any book or API, and ensure that you do not exceed the allotted time.

■ After taking the test, read the answers and use their marking guidelines to mark your own test.

eCheck

Check06A (TS = 21)

You need to build (and *eCheck*) the program Check06A, which prompts for and reads a string from the user and processes it as follows: Locate the first pair of slashes in the string and convert the digits between them into a number. Interpret this number as a month and output the name of its quarter (months 1, 2, 3 are in the first quarter, and so on).

The output layout should be *exactly* as shown in these three sample runs:

```
Enter a slashed month embedded in any string
the results of /11/ were /6/ in number
********************************************
This is the fourth quarter.
Enter a slashed month embedded in any string
/3/ of the results matched /5/
********************************************
This is the first quarter.
Enter a slashed month embedded in any string
Even if /11/ of them were over /20/
********************************************
This is the fourth quarter.
```

No validation is needed: you can safely assume that the entered string does indeed have the expected content; that is, an integer between 1 and 12 surrounded by two slashes with the left one being the first slash in the string.

Notice that the rest of the string may contain additional slashes, but we are to extract from the first to the second-encountered ones. Note also that your output must be as shown above; in particular, one space only between the last two words.

> **Hint:** Although you can solve this problem by using if, for, or other Java constructs, it would be most instructive, and indeed optimal, if you did not use any.

Spend some time trying to use indexOf and substring to locate the two slashes and extract the digits between them. Turn these digits into a number and use mathematics to map the month number to a quarter number. Finally, use substring again to turn the quarter number into quarter name (a variable-size code).

Check06B (TS = 21)

Documents requiring fast, automated processing, such as cheques, envelopes, and supermarket items, are often encoded to make key data fields machine-readable. The U.S. Postal Service, for

Figure 6.8
(a) The POSTNET bar code for zip code 61181. (b) Colon and pipe characters represent the bars.

example, uses the POSTNET (POSTal Numeric Encoding Technique) bar code to encode zip codes on letters. The zip code is made up of 5 to 9 digits. Each digit is represented by a set of 5 bars: three short bars and two long ones. For example, the POSTNET bar code for zip code 61181 is shown in Fig. 6.8(a). For convenience, we will use colon and pipe characters to represent short and long bars, so the POSTNET code in Fig. 6.8(a) can be written as shown in Fig. 6.8(b).

The code is constructed as follows: two long bars, called the *frame bars*, surround the code and are used to align the code reader with the code. The 5 bars corresponding to each digit are shown in Fig. 6.9. The encoded digits are followed by a correction digit, called the *check digit* (also called the CRC digit), and it is used to detect reading errors. Its value is chosen so that the sum of all digits in the code, including the check digit, is divisible by 10 (the MOD 10 rule). In the above example, the check digit is 3.

Write and eCheck the program Check06B. It prompts for and reads an arbitrary string of digits (of any length) and outputs its POSTNET code. Here are four sample runs:

```
Enter a string of digits: 61181
POSTNET Code: |:||:::::||:::|||::|::::||::||:|
Enter a string of digits: 61820
POSTNET Code: |:||:::::|||::|:::|:|||:::::||:|
Enter a string of digits: 321456
POSTNET Code: |::||:::|:|:::||:|::|:|:||::|:|::|
Enter a string of digits: 1001
POSTNET Code: |:::||||:::||::::::|||::|:|
```

Figure 6.9 The POSTNET code table

After reading the string, the program goes through its digits, converting each to an integer and using the integer as an index to look up its corresponding code. At the same time, a running total is kept to compute the check digit. The codes are concatenated, surrounded by frame bars, and displayed. You can assume that the entered string is indeed made up of digits.

0	|	|	:	:	:
1	:	:	:	|	|
2	:	:	|	:	|
3	:	:	|	|	:
4	:	|	:	:	|
5	:	|	:	|	:
6	:	|	|	:	:
7	|	:	:	:	|
8	|	:	:	|	:
9	|	:	|	:	:

Check06C (TS = 16)

Run-length encoding is a method used to compress images, but we will examine it here in terms of strings of letters. The idea is to replace a run of a repeated character with a repetition count. For example, the string:

```
aaaaaaaaPPPrrrr
```

is replaced with:

```
8a3P4r
```

Create the app Check06C that takes a string of letters as a command-line argument and outputs its run-length encoding. Here are three sample runs:

```
java Check06C
Usage: java Check06C <string>

java Check06C AAABB@I5P
The string must consist of letters!

java Check06C AAAAAAAwwwwwwwwwwTTT
7A11w3T
```

Note that if no command-line argument was supplied then the app ends with an error message that explains its usage. Note also that when the argument contains a non-letter, a message is displayed. You may want to use the matches method to detect this case.

Develop your app, test it, and then eCheck it.

Note that run-length encoding is not useful for text because it is not common to have repeated characters in typical text. It is very useful for images, however, and many image file formats rely on it.

Check06D (TS = 16)

When a form is submitted to a web application, the http protocol requires that the browser packs all its data in one string, known as the query string. The string consists of several *variable=value* substrings delimited by the '&' character, as shown in this example:

```
id=575&country=Canada&name=Adam
```

At the server, the web app must parse this string in order to determine the values. We simulate that here by creating the app Check06D that takes aquery string and a variable name as command-line arguments and outputs the value of the indicated variable or a message if the variable is not in the string. Here are three sample runs:

```
java Check06D
Usage: java Check06D <query_string> <variable>

java Check06D "id=575&country=Canada&name=Adam" country
Canada

java Check06D "id=575&country=Canada&name=Adam" age
No such variable "age"!
```

Note that if no command-line arguments were supplied, or only one was, then the app ends with an error message that explains its usage. Note also that when a variable is not found, the error message echoes back its name quoted.

Notes:

1. If the shell of your operating systems interprets the '&' character then double-quote the first command-line argument, as was done in the sample run above.

2. We will assume that the values are made up of letters and digits exclusively. In real life, if a value contains a space or any reserved character then the browser replaces that character with %n, where n is the character's code in hex. For example, a space is replaced with %20.

3. You can assume that the supplied query string is valid.

4. Make sure your app handles boundary cases in which the sought variable is the very first or the very last. You may want to prepend the query string with '&' so you can handle all cases in a uniform way.

5. You may want to use the split method.

Develop your app, test it, and then eCheck it.

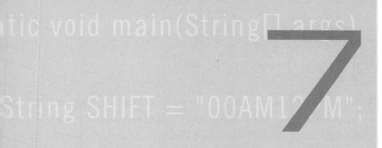

7

Software Development

Learning Objectives

1. *Identify the five key phases of software development*

2. *Understand the drawbacks of the waterfall model*

3. *Learn about architectural, requirement, and assumption risks*

4. *Experience the iterative methodology*

5. *Become familiar with UML diagrams*

6. *Learn about test harnesses and oracles*

7. *Construct test vectors for black-box and white-box testing*

8. *Learn how to tokenize a string*

arly software development relied heavily on an ad hoc process and the person developing the software. Now, we follow a methodology that is similar to an industrial process—we have come a long way! In this chapter, you will learn an iterative process that integrates analysis, design, unit testing, and coding into one seamless process that allows the software to evolve iteratively and in increments. You will also learn about testing and how it can be designed and automated. A case study at the end of the chapter applies these ideas.

Chapter Outline

7.1 The Development Process

We saw in Section 3.2.1 that software development can be viewed as a five-phase process in which each phase involves certain activities and culminates in clearly defined deliverables. The following sections cover this process in more detail and expose the dynamics that govern the sequencing of the phases. It should be noted that our coverage continues to adopt the client view; that is, we are concerned with developing an app (a main class) that drives an application using ready-made components.

7.1.1 The Waterfall Model

The classical view of software development depicts a predominantly linear process in which the five phases are executed in sequence. The deliverables of each phase form the basis on which the next phase is built. This view is called the **waterfall model** because one can think of the phases as containers and of the sequencing as a flow of water. Water starts at the top, and when it fills the top container, it overflows to the lower one, and so on, as shown in Fig. 7.1.

The flow is not top-down at all times because a problem uncovered in one phase may necessitate revisiting an earlier phase. Such upward moves, however, are thought to be rare and are handled on an exceptional basis. The bulk of the flow remains downstream. We now take a closer look at each phase.

Figure 7.1 The waterfall model: five phases and a predominantly sequential flow

Requirements

The **requirements** phase is sometimes called **definition and analysis**. In this phase, the analysts work closely with the customer to determine *what* the system is supposed to do, regardless of *how* it will do it. For applications involving just one service, this means determining what input the user will provide, along with its validation rules, and what output the system should produce in return, along with its formatting details. For more complicated applications, such as applications with menus of several services, analysis needs to identify each possible interaction between the end-user and the system. Such an interaction is called a **use case**, and analysis must specify how the system should handle it; that is, if the user did this, the system should do that, and so on.

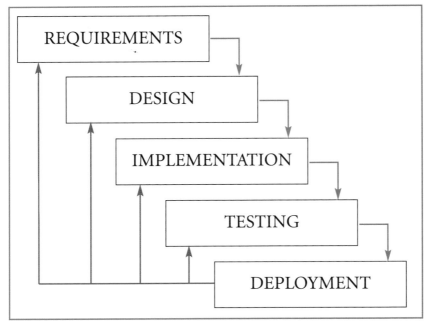

Design

The **design** phase determines *how* the system will handle each use case; that is, it finds the algorithm that generates the desired output. For a trivial application, the algorithm is simply a formula that derives the output from the input. In that case, design reduces to finding that formula. In the general case, however, delegation is a must and design becomes involved with identifying the needed classes and orchestrating the exchange of data among them. It does not matter whether or not these classes exist; the designers can envision any class they want, with any fields and methods that they need.

Implementation

In the **implementation** phase, sometimes called **coding and unit testing**, every class that was dreamt up by the designers must be realized. Sometimes, the required features can all be found in ready-made classes, and in that case, no implementation is needed. This case will become more likely as more and more ready-made components become available. If a certain requirement is not provided by any known ready-made class, implementers can build the needed class either from scratch or by modifying a ready-made one. Regardless of how the class was acquired, this phase must test it by writing a fictitious main class that uses it. This testing is called **unit testing** because it is done at the class level (i.e., each class is tested by itself). We will revisit unit testing later in this chapter.

Testing

In the **testing** phase, which is sometimes called **integration testing**, we must validate the entire system. In the implementation phase, unit testing ensured that each class conforms to its specification. However, in the testing phase we put all the components together and test their integration. The customer must be involved in this phase because **signoff**—an acknowledgment by the customer that the system does indeed behave as specified for all use cases—is based on witnessing that the system does pass integration testing.

Deployment

In the **deployment** phase, which is sometimes called **operation and maintenance**, we must package the system, install it on the customer's machines or arrange for a web installation, assist the customer in migrating to the new system, and provide maintenance.

7.1.2 The Iterative Methodology

In a perfect world, requirements do not change, specifications are never misunderstood, and programmers produce error-free code. In that world, the waterfall model is perfect. In the real world, however, the waterfall model has a serious drawback: it postpones detection and handling of risks to the last phase rather than mitigating or confronting them early as advocated in Section 2.3.1. If any of the risks are manifested, and some almost always are, the project will inevitably be over-budget and late, and its quality will undoubtedly suffer. The risks include the following:

■ **Architectural risks** An example of an **architectural risk** is an interoperability problem among classes or an inconsistency among use cases. Such problems will not show up until the integration testing phase, that is, after the entire system is built.

■ **Requirement-change risks** Changes to use cases are considered the norm in business applications. These **requirement changes** are extremely difficult to accommodate, especially in the later phases, and will lead to extensive delays, frustrated developers, and unsatisfied customers.

■ **Assumptions risks** Each of the parties involved in the development of the software (customer, analyst, designer, implementer, tester) may make implicit assumptions, leading to **assumptions risks**, and not convey them to the others (perhaps because they are deemed obvious). The ensuing misunderstandings remain undetected until the very end.

The **iterative methodology** mitigates all these risks by exposing them early, but it does not abandon the waterfall model. It does follow the waterfall from beginning to end but for only a very small subset of the requirements. During the so-called first **iteration**, we consider only one aspect of the system (e.g., one use case or a simplified requirement) and then proceed to the remaining phases until we culminate in a first **release**.

The first release will not support many of the required features of the system, and may not even have the final user interface, but it will be produced very quickly. This means all parties, including the customer, will have a chance to see it very early in the development. This will undoubtedly expose any misunderstanding or integration risks. After a short evaluation period, a second iteration is started, and all documents and programs are updated to benefit from the lessons learned from the first iteration. We keep iterating this way until a release that meets the requirement subset is produced. Then, and only then, we incorporate a bigger subset of the requirements and start a new iteration cycle.

The project is said to evolve **iteratively** when an iteration corrects the mistakes exposed by its predecessor. And it is said to evolve **incrementally** when an iteration incorporates more use cases than its predecessor. This cycle is repeated until a final release is produced and deployed, as shown in Fig. 7.2.

Going through all phases in every iteration exposes risks early. And by repeatedly modifying documentation, design, and code, this approach embraces change in an inherent way; hence, it can naturally accommodate requirement changes.

It should be mentioned that managing iteratively developed projects is far more complex than managing projects using the waterfall process. Progress across iterations is tracked by keeping track of the remaining risks, whereas progress across increments is based on identifying milestones that measure the convergence toward the final release. This is a far cry from the tracking measures used for the waterfall model where, for example, the requirements and design documents are expected to be complete and more or less "frozen" by the time the implementation phase starts.

The iterative methodology is widely accepted in the software engineering community, but there are differing points of view as to how it should be implemented. These views are beyond the scope of this book, but we will note the names of two prominent viewpoints: the Rational Unified Process (RUP), invented by Booch, Jacobson, and Rumbaugh (see www.rational.com), and Extreme Programming (XP), invented by Kent Beck (see www.xprogramming.com). These implementations use the same iterative idea from Section 7.1.2 but differ in such details

Figure 7.2 The iterative methodology: each iteration churns out an executable release, and these releases converge toward the sought system.

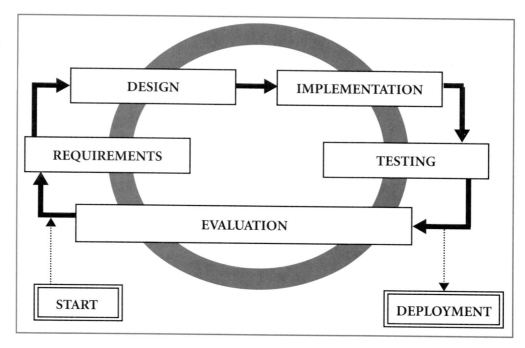

as monitoring of progress, allocation of resources, guiding principles, and the best practices to achieve the principles.

Example 7.1

Recall the mortgage application that was developed in Section 3.2.2. Provide a critique of the process in which it was developed.

Answer:

The mortgage application project was developed using the iterative methodology. Only one use case was considered (compute the monthly payment given the interest rate, the present value, and the period), and in the first iteration, input validation and output formatting were ignored. When a release was produced and it passed the tests, output formatting was incorporated and the process was repeated. Similarly, input validation was not included until after all other features were implemented and tested.

☐

7.1.3 Elements of UML

We used **UML (Unified Modelling Language)** diagrams in Chapter 2 to depict classes and objects and to denote relationships among them. UML is a visual specification language that allows its users to visualize and document software-related elements (such as classes) and the processes that use these elements (such as use cases). It is a formal language in the sense that there are rules for its syntax and semantics, but its graphical nature and flexibility make it easy to learn and adapt. Indeed, it is used today by all development methodologies, including XP and RUP, despite their differences.

UML was invented by Booch, Jacobson, and Rumbaugh, the same group that invented RUP, and is now adopted as a standard by the **Object Management Group** (**OMG**), an industry body in charge of maintaining specification, ongoing maintenance, and future revision of several object-based technologies (www.omg.org). We will focus on only a small subset of UML, specifically, diagrams to represent classes and relationships.

Classes

There are several class diagrams in UML depending on the level of displayed details. It is such flexibility that makes UML useful throughout the development process because the amount of known details about a class increases iteratively. We discuss a few representative possibilities for the displayed details in a class diagram (see Fig. 7.3):

■ **Class Name** If all you know about a class (or all you want to expose) is its name, use a rectangle and place the name inside it (Fig. 7.3(a)). The name can be fully qualified but with a double colon instead of a dot as the delimiter, and can be optionally preceded by a stereotype between two guillemets, for example, «utility».

■ **Class Name and Fields** If all you know about a class (or all you want to expose) are its name and fields, use a two-compartment rectangle, and place the name in the top compartment and list the fields in the lower one. For each listed field, you specify the name and, optionally, the type (Fig. 7.3(b)).

■ **Class Name, Fields, and Public Methods** If all you know about a class (or all you want to expose) are its name, fields, and public methods, use a three-compartment rectangle to specify the class name and list all its features. For each method, specify the name, return type, and signature (Fig. 7.3(c)).

Figure 7.3 Class diagrams: (a) Name. (b) Name and fields. (c) Name, fields, and methods.

If a feature is preceded by + then it is public. Since we adopt the client view in this book, all features will be prefixed by + because we cannot see private features.

What typically happens is that during requirement analysis, we may be able to identify that a particular class, say, Fraction, is needed, but that is all we know at that stage. We therefore use a diagram like that in Fig. 7.3(a). Once we elaborate on use cases that demonstrate how the user interacts with this class, we may identify the need for certain attributes, which leads to a diagram like that in Fig. 7.3(b). Once the class reaches implementation, more details need be gathered about its features, and a diagram like that in Fig. 7.3(c) will emerge. Note that UML does not specify the order in which the features are listed. You can sort them alphabetically or group them according to functionality.

(a)
```
type::lib::Fraction
```

(b)
```
type::lib::Fraction

+ isQuoted: boolean
+ separator: char
```

(c)
```
type::lib::Fraction

+ isQuoted: boolean
+ separator: char

+ getNumerator(): long
+ setFraction(Fraction)
+ toString(): String
```

Relationships

A typical software system consists of several classes, one of which is the app, and we may need to depict certain relationships that exist among them. We will focus on three relationships: dependency, aggregation, and inheritance (see Fig. 7.4).

- ■ **Dependency** Class A is said to **depend** on, or **use**, class B if A uses at least one feature of B, for example, it accesses one of B's fields or invokes one of its methods. UML depicts this by drawing a dashed line connecting the rectangles of the two classes with an arrowhead at the B end.

- ■ **Aggregation** Class A is said to **aggregate** class B if A has an attribute (public or private) of type B (or class A **has-a** class B). We will study aggregation in Chapter 8. UML depicts this by drawing a solid line connecting the rectangles of the two classes with a diamond at the A end.

- ■ **Inheritance** Class A is said to **inherit** from class B if A is a specialization of B (or class A **is-a** class B). We will study the meaning and implication of inheritance in Chapter 9. UML depicts this by drawing a solid line connecting the rectangles of the two classes with a triangle at the B end.

Now we look at an example of relationships. Consider an application that involves four classes:

```
App
GlobalCredit
CreditCard
RewardCard
```

The first class is the app, and the remaining three are components in `type.lib`. The application handles the credit card operations of a fictitious bank called Global Credit. The `GlobalCredit` class encapsulates the bank, and the `CreditCard` class encapsulates a credit card. The bank class can thus be viewed as a collection of credit cards, that is, as an aggregate. As shown in Fig. 7.5, this aggregation is depicted by a solid line with a diamond next to the class that encapsulates the bank.

Suppose also that the bank issues a special kind of credit card (`RewardCard`), one that gives reward points with every purchase charged. The new card *is* a credit card but not just any kind of credit card; it is a special kind. This implies inheritance and is depicted in the figure by a solid line and a triangle next to the credit card class.

Figure 7.5 also shows the main class (`App`) that uses these three classes, as evidenced by the dashed lines and the arrowheads.

Figure 7.4 UML relationship diagrams

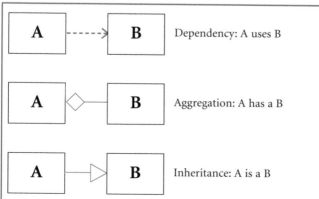

Figure 7.5
Relationship dia-
grams:
`RewardCard`
is a special kind
of (inherits from)
`CreditCard`,
`GlobalCred`
`it` is an aggre-
gate containing
many credit card
instances, and
`App` is an appli-
cation that uses
all three classes.

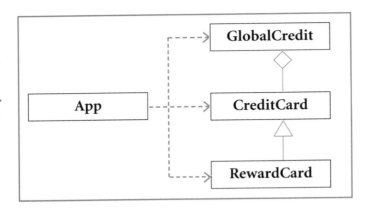

Programming Tip   7.1

Pitfall: Reversing the aggregation direction

The diamond in the UML aggregation diagram must be at the aggregate class, the one whose attributes are instances of another class.

7.2 Software Testing

Software developed by humans will probably continue to contain errors even when all the software engineering guidelines are followed. Testing is our last line of defence against errors and is thus an integral part of software development. The following sections explore the meaning of testing and how it can be conducted, as well as debugging, an activity that is closely associated with testing.

7.2.1 The Essence of Testing

Each piece of software, be it a method or an app, should have a contract that specifies what it does. Using mathematics or English text, the contract states what the output should be for every valid input. In the case of a method, the words *input* and *output* refer to the parameters we pass to the method and the return we receive from it, respectively. For example, here is a contract of a method:

```
isPrime(int n)
```

Parameters:
   n - an argument.

Precondition:
   n > 1

Returns:
```
true if n is prime, false otherwise.
```

Given a piece of code that purports to implement such a contract, how do you know that it is correct? There are two approaches to determine correctness.

A Formal Proof

The precondition is guaranteed by the contract to be true, so make the precondition your circle of knowledge, the start. You then construct a logical proof that uses the semantics of the first executable statement in the code in order to expand the circle of knowledge. Repeat this process by considering every statement in the code, in the order of the statement execution, until the circle of knowledge encompasses the postcondition. Such a **formal proof** is beyond the scope of this textbook.

Testing

Testing is a direct **verification** that every input that satisfies the precondition leads to the postcondition. Such a brute force approach would constitute a proof if one could indeed enumerate every possible valid input, but this is impractical, even impossible in most cases. Imagine, for example, enumerating every possible string of any length and any content. To make testing practical, we resort to sampling: we select a sample of all the possible valid inputs and verify the correctness only for the sample. Each element in this sample is called a **test case**, and the sample as a whole is called the **test suite**, or the **test vector**. If the sample is fairly representative, and the code passes the test, then we would have confidence (in a statistical sense) in the correctness of the software. It should be kept in mind, however, that this is only a statistical tool, not a formal proof, and that such testing can only show the presence of errors, not their absence. (This was first pointed out by E.W. Dijkstra in "Notes on Structured Programming," 1970.)

Given a unit (a method or an app), we automate its testing by writing a program, called the **harness**, that operates as shown schematically in Fig. 7.6.

The harness fetches the test cases one by one from the test suite, sends each to the unit being tested, and captures the unit's response. Communication between the harness and the unit is done using parameter passing if the unit is a method and using I/O redirection and capture if the unit is an app. (I/O capture for app testing is explored in Lab 7.) The suite can create the test cases in one of four ways: input, loop, random, and file.

- **Input** Entering test cases manually is sometimes done for quickly testing one or two cases, but is otherwise not recommended because it is prone to error and is not reproducible.
- **Loop** Regularly spaced test cases (e.g., even integers between 1 and 100) can be generated by one or more nested loops. This is often used for semi-exhaustive tests.
- **Random** Randomly generated test cases are useful when we have an idea about the distribution of inputs, for example, normally distributed with a known average and standard deviation.
- **File** The test cases are stored in a file, often a delimited text file.

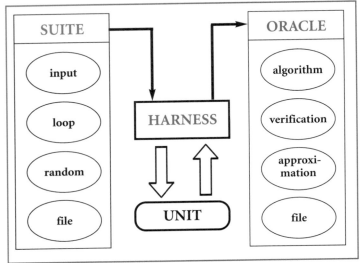

Figure 7.6 The testing process: a harness reads a test case from a suite, sends it to the unit to be tested, and captures the unit's response. The response is then sent to an oracle to establish its correctness. (See below for explanation of an oracle.)

After a test case is sent and the response is received, the harness must establish correctness. For example, if the test case `"11235371"` was passed to `isPrime` and the return came back as `true`, the harness must determine whether this integer is indeed a prime number. To that end, each harness must be equipped with an **oracle**, an independent mechanism that can establish correctness in an authoritative way. There are four candidates for an oracle: algorithm, verification, approximation, and file.

■ **Algorithm** The oracle executes an algorithm that is different from the one used by the unit. This algorithm must be known to be correct, and we must trust its implementation.

■ **Verification** It is sometimes straightforward to verify whether an answer is correct even though obtaining the answer is quite complex, for example, if a number is a root of a nonlinear equation.

■ **Approximation** The oracle may rely on a trusted but approximate algorithm, or one that works only for ranges of certain test cases. This is used when all else fails.

■ **File** If the test cases were created using a file, the oracle may also use a file to hold their corresponding correct answers. The answers may have been generated by a different program or may have been obtained empirically.

Example 7.2

Describe an appropriate oracle for each of the following scenarios:
(a) A program that sorts a list of numbers in nondescending order
(b) A program that determines whether a given positive integer is a prime number
(c) A program that finds the median of a set of an odd number of numbers

Answer:
(a) **Verification** The oracle goes through the elements of the sorted list and verifies that every element after the first is less than or equal to its predecessor.
(b) **Approximation** The oracle creates an instance of the `BigInteger` class and invokes on it the method `isProbablePrime`.
(c) **Verification** The oracle verifies that the computed median is indeed an element of the set. It then verifies that the number of elements in the set that are not greater than the median is the same as the number of elements in the set that are not less than it.

□

7.2.2 The Test Vector

It should be evident that the success of testing rests fully on the appropriate selection of cases in the test vector. The vector should be constructed with a view of forcing the software to fail; after all, testing is considered successful only if this happens. Any input that is consistent with the code's precondition can be included in the vector, but to make the sample representative, the guidelines outlined below should be considered.

■ **Domain Coverage** Test cases must be selected from a set that covers the entire input domain. Most cases should be in the **likely range**, the input range considered normal within the application context, but there should also be a few **boundary** cases, cases at the edge of the input domain. For example, the domain of interest rates (entered as a percent) for a hypothetical app is [0, 100]. Most test cases should be in [1, 20] because these are the rates that are likely to be used in practice. Nevertheless, there should be a few test cases outside this range, for example, 50% and 85%, as well as boundary cases: 0% and 100%. Note that making such a selection requires an understanding of the requirements, not the code, and it therefore leads to **black box testing**, which is testing the code without seeing it. These test cases are ideally chosen by the customer and the analyst, not the developer; this can be done before implementation begins.

■ **Execution-Path Coverage** The test vector must also include cases to ensure that every statement and every path in the code will execute. Such cases, which lead to so-called **white box testing**, can only be selected by the developer after implementation.

■ **Regression** Whenever a test case is added to the vector, whether for domain or path coverage, it should not be removed. Sometimes a test case detects a bug in the software and the developers correct it. Further tests reveal that the bug is no longer present, and this prompts the tester to remove the case from the vector since "it has played its role." But what often happens afterward, when a new feature is added, is that the same bug is reintroduced and we no longer have a test case that detects it. To prevent such a bug cycling, we always perform **regression testing** by keeping all cases in the vector.

7.2.3 Debugging

When a test detects an error, the developers must examine the code, perhaps working backward from the statement that produced the wrong result, until they find the cause of the problem and correct it. This process is called **debugging**; it is time-consuming and requires experience. During debugging, the developer works like a detective, gathering clues and establishing the "innocence" of statements and methods, one by one, until the culprit is found. We now look at an example. The following program fragment takes a string `str` and determines whether the string contains digits:

```
boolean containsDigits = false;
for (int i = 0; i < str.length(); i++)
{
    containsDigits = Character.isDigit(str.charAt(i));
}
output.println(containsDigits);
```

The program compiled without any problem, but its testing produced erratic results:

```
Test Case       Output
"1234"      true
"F304"      true
"TEST"      false
"99MM"      false
```

The first three outputs are correct but the fourth is not. You can look at the code and ponder, and this may lead you to discover the error, but what if you remain convinced that the program is correct? This is when debugging is called for, and to that end, we explore four general techniques: print statements, error messages, internal assertions, and debuggers.

■ **Print Statements** Despite all the advances in debugging technologies, "print" is still the single most powerful, most versatile tool for locating errors in a program. When code does not behave as expected or fails to show output altogether, a few `output.print` statements inserted at key locations within your code to display the values of key variables allow you to quickly track the source of the problem. For the above fragment, a print statement should be placed just before the loop to establish that the test case is indeed what we think it is; that is, that it was not changed after the input. In addition, we add a print statement within the loop body to trace the values of the loop counter and the boolean. These statements change the fragment as follows:

```
boolean containsDigits = false;
output.println("Test case: " + str);
for (int i = 0; i < str.length(); i++)
{
    containsDigits = Character.isDigit(str.charAt(i));
    output.println(i + " " + containsDigits);
}
output.println(containsDigits);
```

Running the fourth test case with these debugging statements produces the following output:

```
99MM
0 true
1 true
2 false
3 false
false
```

This output makes the error quite clear: our final output reflects only the test of the *last character* of the string. The solution is either to terminate the loop once a digit is found, that is,

```
for (...; i < str.length() && !containsDigits;...)
```

or to update the boolean accumulatively:

```
containsDigits = containsDigits || Character...
```

In general, do not worry about using as many print statements as needed. And when you do locate and correct the error, do not delete these prints; just comment them out. Chances are you will need them later.

- ■ **Error Messages** When a runtime error is encountered, most beginning developers say: "This code didn't work; let's try something else." This is unfortunate because the error message that gets displayed, while not verbose, contains vital information that allows us to not only locate the problem but solve it. Make it a habit to actually read the message and invest some time in understanding what the message is trying to tell you. We will analyze the structure of error messages in Chapter 11.
- ■ **Internal Assertions** We introduced assertions in Section 3.2.6 as a tool for expressing our conviction that a certain condition must hold at a certain location in our program. Assertions are very helpful to the person debugging a code because, while every statement is a suspect, that is, could be the culprit that caused the error, assertions are always innocent and can, in fact, be relied on.
- ■ **Using Debuggers** A debugger is a ready-made program that allows you to monitor the execution of your Java application. If an error occurred while running your program, you can inspect, through the debugger, the value of any variable at the instant the error occurred, and you can sometimes change that value manually and resume the execution. The debugger can be a separate program, or it can be integrated with the development environment. An example of a separate program is `jdb` (free from Sun Microsystems, included with the JDK), and an example of an integrated program is `Eclipse`, also free (see Lab 2).

Once the error is identified, the code can be corrected, but this often introduces new errors. This is because when you develop software, you are aware of all its aspects and have the correct state of mind, but when you debug, you tend to focus on the bug and ignore other issues. This may lead to correcting one bug and introducing another. Because of this, modifying code should be done with more care than writing fresh code, and regression testing is extremely helpful in this regard.

7.3 CASE STUDY

Trajectories

The following sections apply the concepts and techniques introduced in this chapter to a hypothetical development project.

7.3.1 Iterative Development

Let us walk through the iterative methodology for our project.

The First Iteration

First, we play the role of the analyst: we meet with the customer team and analyze the requirements. The members of the team seem knowledgeable, but since we are not familiar with their business and its terminology, we do not fully understand what they need. It seems that they need to study several trajectories, each of which is a parabola (described by a quadratic function), and select the one with the *largest intercept* (LI) with a given target. They used Fig. 7.7 to clarify their needs.

Figure 7.7 Given a trajectory, the app must determine its LI, defined as the *x*-coordinate of the farthest point at which the trajectory intersects with the target (the thick horizontal line). For the top trajectory, the LI is approximately 1.35.

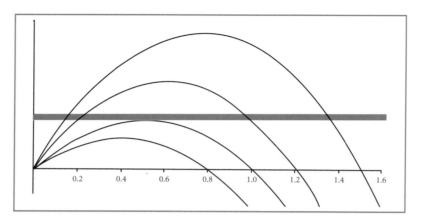

The figure clarifies the statement about the LI but leaves many questions unanswered. We therefore turned to use cases and asked: "Once the system is built, how do you envision using it"? Their answer: "The user supplies trajectories, and the system identifies the right one." The use case has established a framework that focuses on two issues:

- How is a trajectory "supplied to the system"?
- How do you determine the "right trajectory"?

Once the questions were posed like this, we gained more understanding. It seems they have developed a model that describes each trajectory by three real numbers a, b, c. In this model, the LI of a given trajectory is the larger of the two roots of the equation

$$ax^2 + bx + c = 0$$

For example, the trajectory given by $(a, b, c) = (1, -12, 20)$ has an LI of 10 because the equation $x^2 - 12x + 20 = 0$ has two roots, 2 and 10, and the larger is 10.

At this point, we have a reasonable understanding of input, the needed computation, and the output. We still do not know the user interface, how the three numbers will be entered, how the output is formatted, what should be done if the equation does not have two real roots, and how multiple trajectories will be processed. However, rather than dwelling on all this now, as in the old waterfall model, we proceed with what we know so far and build our first release. Once it is built, we can obtain confirmation from the customer that our understanding is correct, and we can

then solicit answers to remaining questions.

We now play the role of designer and search for classes that provide the needed services. We clearly need an encapsulation that can hold three real numbers as attributes (so it can be thought of as a trajectory) and provide the root functionality. The class `Equation` in `type.lib` provides such an encapsulation, and we will use it. Note that when a ready-made class is used, no unit testing is performed on it—its developer is assumed to have done that—but we do perform integration testing.

Finally, we play the role of developer and write the app. Since the input structure has not been specified, we select the easiest: three real numbers each entered on a separate line. We then create an `Equation` instance by passing the entered coefficients to the class constructor. Note that we do not need to declare variables to hold these numbers. The point of encapsulation is to delegate everything—not only root computation functionality but also the storage of data. The class API states that the two roots are ordered, within the class, so that the first root is smaller than the second, and hence, `getRoot(2)` returns the larger of the two roots. The app is shown in Fig. 7.8.

We use the `toString` method to echo the equation in its output. Here is a sample run of this app corresponding to the test case that the customer used:

```
Coefficients (ENTER-delimited):
1
-12
20
1.0x^2 - 12.0x + 20.0 = 0 > 10.0
```

Figure 7.8
Release 1.0 of the Trajectory App: one ENTER-delimited input and a crude output of the largest root

```
import java.util.Scanner;
import java.io.PrintStream;
import type.lib.Equation;


public class Trajectory
{

    public static void main(String[] args)
    {

        Scanner input = new Scanner(System.in);
        PrintStream output = System.out;

        Equation eqn;
        output.println("Coefficients (ENTER-delimited):");
        eqn = new Equation(input.nextDouble(),
                           input.nextDouble(),
                           input.nextDouble());
        output.println(eqn + "\t>> " + eqn.getRoot(2));
    }
}
```

The Second Iteration

The customer team was happy to see the first release so quickly, but they pointed out the following:

- **Input must be on one line only.** There should be three real comma-delimited numbers on one line (instead of one number per line).
- **Runtime exceptions are seen in some test cases.** Testing quickly revealed that exceptions are sometimes thrown by the class in response to getRoot(2). Indeed, the class API warns that the passed number must be valid in the context of the root count returned by getRootCount, which can be 2 (indicating two roots), 1 (one root), 0 (no roots), or -1 (infinitely many roots). When confronted with this, the customer indicated that the equation must have either two roots, in which case LI is the larger of the two, or exactly one root, in which case LI is that root. Any other case should be rejected with the message "miss".

In terms of design, the input change calls for a new class, one that can parse a comma-delimited string and extract the three numbers from it. The class StringTokenizer in java.util performs parsing based on any one or more delimiters that we specify in its constructor. Note that if you do not specify delimiters, the class uses whitespace (defined as all characters in the string "\t\n\r\f") as default delimiters. As an example of using this class, consider the following fragment:

```
StringTokenizer st = new
    StringTokenizer("A,BC,D", ",")
for (; st.hasMoreTokens();)
{
    String token = st.nextToken()
    output.println(token);
}
```

The output would consist of three lines:

```
A
BC
D
```

Keep this class in mind whenever you need to parse a string based on some delimiter. It will **tokenize** the string and deliver its tokens to you on demand one by one.

In our case, the substrings are numbers, so we must convert them to `double` by using the static `parseDouble` method in the `Double` class. It will look something like this:

```
double number =
    Double.parseDouble(token);
```

Regarding the computational change, we first determine the number of roots by examining the return of `getRootCount`. If it is 0 or -1, that is, not positive, we declare this a `"miss"` and output a message. Otherwise, we determine the root by using `getRoot` and pass to it either 1 or 2, depending on whether the equation has 1 or 2 roots. This can be done without an `if` statement by simply passing the return of `getRootCount`.

Our second release, which incorporates these two changes, is shown in Fig. 7.9.

As in the earlier release, we output the return of the `toString` method to identify the trajectory in question and then output a tab character followed by `">"`. If the trajectory is valid, we follow this by its LI; otherwise, we output the `"miss"` message.

Here is a sample run of this app corresponding to the test case that the customer used:

```
Coefficients (comma-delimited):
1,-12,20
1.0x^2 - 12.0x + 20.0 = 0 > 10.0
```

Figure 7.9
Release 2.0 of the Trajectory App: one comma-delimited input and an output based on the largest root or target miss.

```java
import java.util.*;
import java.io.PrintStream;
import type.lib.Equation;

public class Trajectory
{
    public static void main(String[] args)
    {
        Scanner input = new Scanner(System.in);
        PrintStream output = System.out;

        Equation eqn;
        output.println("Coefficients (comma-delimited):");
        String str = input.nextLine();
        StringTokenizer st = new StringTokenizer(str, ",");
        eqn = new Equation(
                    Double.parseDouble(st.nextToken()),
                    Double.parseDouble(st.nextToken()),
                    Double.parseDouble(st.nextToken()));
        output.print(eqn + "\t>> ");
        int count = eqn.getRootCount();
        if (count > 0)
        {
            output.println(eqn.getRoot(count));
        }
        else
        {
            output.println("miss");
        }
    }
}
```

And here is a sample run for a case in which the trajectory misses the target:

```
Coefficients (comma-delimited):
1,3,4
1.0x^2 + 3.0x + 4.0 = 0 > miss
```

The Third Iteration

Evaluation of release 2.0 identified two additional requirements:

- **Handling multiple trajectories** The user enters one comma-delimited trajectory per line, as before, but there can be an arbitrary number of such lines, each representing a trajectory. The app must keep reading lines until an empty line (a sentinel) is entered.
- **Determination of the hit rate** The app must compute and output the hit rate, defined as the number of trajectories that intersect the target divided by the total number of trajectories entered, expressed as a percentage with two decimals.

In terms of design, we clearly need to set up a loop that reads one line per iteration and exits when the user presses ENTER on an empty line, that is, when the entered string has a zero length. The following `for` loop accomplishes this:

```
for (String s=input.nextLine();
    s.length() != 0;
    s=input.nextLine())
```

The computation of the hit rate is done as follows: we need a counter, `total`, to count the total number of entered trajectories, and another, `hit`, to count the number of times the equation had 1 or 2 roots:

```
int total = 0;
int hit = 0;
```

These declarations and initializations are done at the beginning of the program. `total` is incremented in every iteration of the loop, whereas `hit` is incremented only in the iterations in which the equation being examined has 1 or 2 roots. Note that since input and sentinel detection are handled in the loop header, we can rest assured that the body of the loop will execute

only if the sentinel is not reached, that is, `total` will not over-count.

Once the loop exits, we can compute the ratio as follows:

```
hit / (double) total
```

The cast is needed to avoid integer division. Without it, the answer will likely be zero. (Why?) Finally, we turn this into a percentage by multiplying it by 100, and output it with rounding to two decimals:

```
output.printf("%.2f", 100 * hit /
    (double) total);
output.println("%");
```

Our third release, which incorporates these two changes, is shown in Fig. 7.10.

Here is a sample run of this release:

```
Comma-delimited (ENTER=sentinel):
1,-12,20
1.0x^2 - 12.0x + 20.0 = 0 > 10.0
1,3,4
1.0x^2 + 3.0x + 4.0 = 0 > miss
1,4,3
1.0x^2 + 4.0x + 3.0 = 0 > -1.0
```

The hit rate is: 66.67%.

The Fourth Iteration

Evaluation of release 3.0 identified two additional requirements:

- **File input** Trajectory data is captured into a text file; hence, the user wants the app to read its input from the file. The user supplies the file name at runtime, and we can assume that each record in the file contains one comma-delimited trajectory and no sentinel.
- **Determination of the optimal trajectory** The app must determine and output the trajectory that has the largest LI.

In terms of design, reading input from a file is not very different from reading from the keyboard except for end of file detection: rather than detecting a sentinel like an empty line, we rely on the `eof` method, as shown in Fig. 7.11.

Figure 7.10
Release 3.0 of the
Trajectory App:
multiple comma-
delimited inputs
and an output
based on the
largest root or tar-
get miss. The hit
rate is computed.

```java
import java.util.*;
import java.io.PrintStream;
import type.lib.Equation;

public class Trajectory
{
    public static void main(String[] args)
    {
        Scanner input = new Scanner(System.in);
        PrintStream output = System.out;

        final int PERCENT = 100;
        int total = 0;
        int hit = 0;
        output.println("Comma-delimited (ENTER=sentinel):");
        for (String str = input.nextLine();
                    str.length() != 0;
                    str = input.nextLine())
        {
            total++;
            StringTokenizer st = new StringTokenizer(str,",");
            Equation eqn;
            eqn = new Equation(
                    Double.parseDouble(st.nextToken()),
                    Double.parseDouble(st.nextToken()),
                    Double.parseDouble(st.nextToken()));
            output.print(eqn + "\t>> ");
            int count = eqn.getRootCount();
            if (count > 0)
            {
                output.println(eqn.getRoot(count));
                hit++;
            }
            else
            {
                output.println("miss");
            }
        }
        output.print("The hit rate is: ");
        output.printf("%.2f", PERCENT * hit / (double) total);
        output.println("%");
    }
}
```

```
import java.util.*;
import java.io.*;
import type.lib.Equation;

public class Trajectory
{
    public static void main(String[] args) throws IOException
    {
        Scanner input = new Scanner(System.in);
        PrintStream output = System.out;

        final int PERCENT = 100;
        Equation max = null;
        int total = 0;
        int hit = 0;
        output.println("Filename:");
        Scanner fileIn = new Scanner(new File(input.nextLine()));
        for (; fileIn.hasNextLine();)
        {
            String str = fileIn.nextLine();
            total++;
            StringTokenizer st = new StringTokenizer(str,",");
            Equation eqn;
            eqn = new Equation(
                        Double.parseDouble(st.nextToken()),
                        Double.parseDouble(st.nextToken()),
                        Double.parseDouble(st.nextToken()));
            output.print(eqn + "\t>> ");
            int count = eqn.getRootCount();
            if (count > 0)
            {   double root = eqn.getRoot(count);
                output.println(root);
                hit++;
                if (max == null || root > max.getRoot(max.getRootCount()))
                {   max = eqn;
                }
            }
            else
            {   output.println("miss");
            }
        }
        fileIn.close();
        output.print("The hit rate is: ");
        output.printf("%.2f", PERCENT * hit / (double) total);
        output.println("%");
        output.print("The optimal trajectory is: (");
        output.print(max.getCoefficient(2) + ",");
        output.print(max.getCoefficient(1) + ",");
        output.println(max.getCoefficient(0) + ")");
    }
}
```

Figure 7.11 Release 4.0 of the Trajectory App: read trajectory data from a user-named file and output the hit/miss state, the hit rate, and the optimal trajectory.

To determine the optimal trajectory, the one with the largest LI, we need to nominate a candidate for it, say max. Whenever we compute the LI of a new trajectory, we challenge the candidate, possibly replacing it with the new trajectory if it has a larger LI. As the loop iterates, max would change, but one thing remains invariant: max is the trajectory with the largest LI seen so far. But how is the candidate chosen initially? We initialize max by setting it equal to the very first trajectory we read. This is done in the shown code by first setting it to null (so that we can identify the first iteration) and then initializing it to the first trajectory in the first iteration. Note that the candidate is an object reference, not a number. This allows us to encapsulate the entire optimal trajectory in it as opposed to keeping several variables for its coefficients and roots. Once the loop exits, we can output any desired property of the optimal trajectory by invoking its accessors. A sample run of this release is shown in Fig. 7.12, along with the data file it uses.

We note in closing that the final release does not handle the case of an empty data file. You can see from Fig. 7.11 that such a file would lead to total being zero and max being null. The former causes a division by zero (not a runtime error for double), and the latter causes a null pointer exception, a runtime error. Our analyst should go back to the customer and ask how this case should be handled. This falls under the category of input validation, and as we saw in Section 3.2.5, it can be handled in one of three ways:

displaying a message, reprompting, or throwing an exception. We leave it to the reader to amend Release 4.0 accordingly.

7.3.2 Unit Testing

We mentioned in the previous section that when an app is built using ready-made classes, unit testing is typically not performed because each such class must have been already thoroughly tested as part of its development process. It is possible, however, that the source of a used class is not trusted, in which case we would perform unit testing on it. For example, the app of the case study uses three classes: Scanner, PrintStream, and Equation. Assuming we do not trust Equation, we must conduct unit testing of all its features. To demonstrate this, we will build a harness that tests some of the features of Equation for the cases in which the equation has at least one root. We leave it to the reader to extend the coverage to other features and cases.

To come up with test cases for which we have an oracle, we start from the roots. If we know that the roots are r_1 and r_2, we can write

$$(x - r_1)(x - r_2) = 0$$

Upon expansion this becomes

$$x^2 - (r_1 + r_2)x + r_1 r_2 = 0$$

Multiplying both sides by an arbitrary factor f, we obtain:

Figure 7.12 A sample run of release 4.0. The data file is shown to the right.

Filename:		Data File
trajectory.data		
1.0x^2 + 3.0x + 4.0 = 0	>> miss	1,3,4
1.0x^2 + 4.0x + 3.0 = 0	>> -1.0	1,4,3
4.0x^2 + 13.0x - 35.0 = 0	>> 1.75	4,13,-35
1.0x^2 + 4.0x + 89.0 = 0	>> miss	1,4,89
0.0x^2 + 4.0x + 8.0 = 0	>> -2.0	0,4,8
0.0x^2 + 0.0x + 0.0 = 0	>> miss	0,0,0
1.0x^2 + 3.0x + 0.0 = 0	>> 0.0	1,3,0
1.0x^2 + 0.0x + 4.0 = 0	>> miss	1,0,4
-8.0x^2 + 6.0x + 35.0 = 0	>> 2.5	-8,6,35
2.0x^2 + 4.0x + 8.0 = 0	>> miss	2,4,8
The hit rate is: 50.00%		
The optimal trajectory is: (-8.0,6.0,35.0)		

$$fx^2 - f(r_1 + r_2)x + fr_1r_2 = 0$$

This allows us to identify the coefficients of the general form of the equation:

$$ax^2 + bx + c = 0,$$
$$a = f, \ b = -f(r_1 + r_2),$$
$$c = fr_1r_2$$

Using the services of the Random class, we generate two real random numbers as roots. They will be in the range [0,1), but we can map them to any range appropriate for the problem at hand as determined by the user. The harness therefore starts with

```
output.print("Root Range: min = ");
double min = input.nextDouble();
output.print("Root Range: max = ");
double max = input.nextDouble();
Random random = new Random();
```

To generate a root in the desired range, we write

```
double root1 = min + (max - min)
    * random.nextDouble();
```

If the randomly generated number is zero, the computed root will be min; while if the random number is very close to 1, the computed root will be very close to max. Hence, this yields a root in the interval [min, max). The same technique can be used to generate a second root and the factor f.

The test harness generates as many test cases as indicated and outputs any discrepancy it detects between the class returns and the oracle. It consists of a loop:

```
output.print
    ("Number of test cases?");
int count = input.nextInt();
output.println
    ("Conducting test...");
for (int test = 0; test < count;
    test++)
{
    output.print(test + ", ");
    double root1 = min + (max -
        min) * random.nextDouble();
    double root2 = min + (max -
        min) * random.nextDouble();
```

```
    double factor = min + (max -
        min) * random.nextDouble();
    double a = factor;
    double b = -(root1 + root2) *
        factor;
    double c = (root1 * root2) *
        factor;
    Equation eqn =
        new Equation(a, b, c);
    // For each feature, compare
    // return with oracle
}
```

For each feature to be tested, we add a comparison and a message. For example, we can test the coefficient accessor by writing

```
double coef =
    eqn.get Coefficient(2);
if (Math.abs(a - coef) <
    Equation.EPSILON)
{
    output.println
        ("Coefficient Test Failure");
    output.println
        (coef + " instead of " + a);
}
```

In this fragment, we needed to test the equality of two real numbers, but since this is unachievable for any finite-size representation, we resort to the interval test: if the distance between the two numbers is small, we consider them equal. The definition of "small" is context-dependent, and in our case, the class itself defines a measure of smallness through its EPSILON field.

Similarly, the root count accessor can be tested as follows:

```
if (Math.abs(factor) <
    Equation.EPSILON)
{
    ToolBox.crash(eqn.getRootCount()
        != -1, "Root count should be -1");
} else if (Math.abs(root1 -
    root2) < Equation.EPSILON)
{
    ToolBox.crash(eqn.getRootCount()
        != 1, "Root count should be 1");
} else
{
```

```
ToolBox.crash(eqn.getRootCount()
    != 2 "Root count should be 2");
}
```

The case of factor = 0 (or very close to zero) leads to an identity, that is, any value of x is a root since all three coefficients are practically zero. This case is signalled in the class by a return of -1 from the root count accessor.

A test of the computed values of the roots, along with appropriate messages, can be easily embedded in the above count test.

7.3.3 Integration Testing

Even if all the pieces behave as specified, the system as a whole may not be correct. This may be due to incorrect invocations, invocations that violate preconditions, or to computations done within the app itself. Even if we assume that all classes used by the app of our case study have passed unit testing, our app's output may still be incorrect. Some of the possible sources that an integration test should detect are listed below.

- **Hit rate computation** Even if the roots are correctly captured, the two counters, hit and total, may not have been initialized or incremented correctly.
- **Identification of the optimal trajectory** Even if the roots are correctly captured, it is possible that max does not point to the trajectory with the highest LI. A common pitfall is the initialization of this reference.
- **Formatting** Even if all computations are correct, the output may not be formatted as specified by the customer. This is more than an aesthetic issue. The app's output may be redirected to another program that uses it as input for further computation or storage. If the other program misread a piece of data because of a formatting issue, its output would be wrong, not just "wrong looking."

Since our app takes its input from a file, the harness can be set up as a script that starts by creating test cases and storing them in a file, launching the app with its output redirected to a file, and then running a harness that reads the app's output and verifies it.

Summary of Key Concepts

1. The development process consists of five phases: **requirements** (also called **definition and analysis**), **design**, **implementation** (also called **coding and unit testing**), **testing** (also called **integration testing**), and **deployment** (also called **operation and maintenance**).

2. In the **requirement** phases, analysts must identify every possible **use case**, a scenario in which the user interacts with the system, and document how the system should respond in each.

3. In the **design** phase, the needed classes are identified and specified.

4. Every class identified by the design must be turned into a concrete Java class during **implementation**. This can be quick if the class is already available as a ready-made component. Otherwise, implementers build it either from scratch or by modifying an existing class. In all cases, the class must undergo **unit testing** to validate its behaviour.

5. During **integration testing**, the classes that make up the application are put together, then tests are conducted to validate the overall behaviour of the application. When the application passes these tests, the customer will provide a **signoff**, an assertion that the application behaves as specified.

6. The deployment phase consists of delivering the system to the customer, installing it, and providing support.

7. The classical model for sequencing the five phases is called the **waterfall model**, in which the phases are represented as steps. Hence, requirement takes place in the early stages of the project, and testing is conducted toward the end.

8. The waterfall model works well only when nothing changes, and this is rarely the case. Typically, requirements change frequently during development because of a change in the business logic or because of a misunderstanding. This is called a **requirement-change risk**.

9. Even if nothing changes, the waterfall model will still not work if any problem occurs in an early stage because such a problem would not be detected until the end. **Architectural risks**, such as an incompatibility between two classes, or **assumption risks**, such as a misunderstanding, are examples of problems that cannot be detected until integration testing at the earliest.

10. In the **iterative methodology**, the project is developed in releases. For each **release**, a small subset of the requirement is considered, and the waterfall model is then applied without the deployment phase. Afterward, all parties, including the customer, evaluate the release and determine how to proceed accordingly.

11. If the release uncovers problems, they are corrected in the next release. This leads to an **iterative** refinement of the project. If a release is successful, a bigger subset of the requirement is incorporated in the next release. This leads to an **incremental** evolution of the project.

12. The **Unified Modelling Language (UML)** is a visual language that allows us to describe software in a flexible way. We can use simple UML diagrams in the early stages of project development, but as we gain more understanding of the project, we can expand these diagrams by adding more details.

13. UML **class diagrams**, introduced in Chapter 2, can be drawn in three different ways depending on the level of detail that we want to expose.

14. Interclass relationships can also be depicted in UML diagrams. We use a dashed line and an arrow for **dependency** (a class that **uses** another), a diamond and a solid line for **aggregation** (a class that **has an** instance of another), and a solid line ending with a triangle for **inheritance** (a class that **is a** kind of another).

15. Code correctness is relative to its contract. Correctness can be established either by a **formal**

proof (a logical proof) or by **verification** (an exhaustive test of every valid input). In this textbook we consider testing, a subset of verification.

16. **Testing** means verifying the correctness for only a subset of **test cases**, called the **test suite** or **vector**.

17. Testing is automated by having a **harness** fetch the test cases from the test suite and feed them to the unit being tested. The result of each test case is compared with that of an **oracle**. The oracle can be based on an algorithm, an approximate algorithm, direct verification, or a file of known answers.

18. The test vector for a **black-box test** should ensure **domain coverage**: **likely** cases as well as **boundary** cases should be present. The test vector for a **white-box test** should ensure **execution-path coverage**: every possible execution path should be exercised. In both cases, **regression testing** should be performed to prevent **cycling**.

19. **Debugging** refers to examining code with a view of locating an error uncovered by testing. The print statement, inserted at key locations in the code, is the simplest and most powerful debugging tool. Reading error messages thoroughly, adding assertions for key assumptions, and using debuggers are also helpful. Debugging should be done with care because it is common to introduce a bug while removing another.

20. Whenever you need to parse a string that is based on some delimiters, delegate to the `StringTokenizer` class in `java.util`.

Review Questions

1. In your own words, briefly describe the five phases of the development process.
2. Which phase is particularly sensitive to the delegation paradigm (none or object-oriented)? Which phase is particularly sensitive to the choice of programming language?
3. Is there a phase in which the customer does not need to participate?

4. Why is it a good idea to ask the customer to provide and supervise integration testing?
5. The term *software architect* is sometimes used to describe a professional working in the design phase. Argue that this title is consistent with the activities involved in this task.
6. How is unit testing different from integration testing?
7. What is wrong with the waterfall model? Describe a scenario that shows one of its drawbacks.
8. Argue that unit testing does not mitigate architectural risks.
9. Explain through an example the difference between an iterative and an incremental iteration.
10. What does UML stand for?
11. The success of UML is often attributed to its flexibility. Explain this.
12. Draw a class diagram of `type.lib.Stock` so that only its name is shown.
13. Draw a class diagram of `type.lib.Stock` so that only its name and fields are shown.
14. Given two class diagrams connected by a dashed line with an arrow, what do you conclude about these classes?
15. Given two class diagrams connected by a solid line with a triangle, what do you conclude about these classes?
16. Given two class diagrams connected by a solid line with a diamond, what do you conclude about these classes?
17. Explain why testing cannot prove the absence of bugs.
18. Explain the difference between a proof and a test.
19. How can an oracle determine whether a result computed by a program is indeed correct?
20. What is a test harness?
21. How does the test suite create the test cases?
22. What is the difference between black-box testing and white-box testing?
23. Why cannot the customer be involved in white-box testing?
24. How do we ensure domain coverage when we construct a test vector?
25. What is bug cycling, and how can it be avoided?

26. What is the simplest and most powerful debugging tool?

27. What is a tokenizer? When do you use it? Give an example.

28. What role does the Random class play in testing?

29. How do you test a class made up of several methods?

30. Why is output formatting critical for testing purposes?

Testing and HTML Parsing

◼ L7.I   Newton's Square Root Method

1. How do you compute the square root of 50 while stranded on an island without the Math class? Newton suggests we start by dividing 50 in half, which leads to 25 as a first approximation. To obtain a better approximation, Newton suggests we then compute the average of "our guess" and "50 divided by our guess," that is,

   ```
   (25 + 50 / 25) / 2
   ```

   This works out to be 13.5, definitely much better than 25. Let us apply Newton's idea again using 13.5 as the starting point:

   ```
   (13.5 + 50 / 13.5) / 2
   ```

   This leads to about 8.6. Continue this process until you reach a number whose square is 50.000. How many times did it take?

2. Newton's method works for any positive integer num. Starting with an initial guess g_0 (like num/2), Newton's method leads to a better guess, g_1, given by

   $$g_1 = (g_0 + num / g_0) / 2$$

   Verify this for the case of a perfect square like 25. Starting with 12.5, how quickly does the sequence of guesses converge to 5?

3. Launch your editor, and create the program Lab7, which starts by reading a positive number (a double) from the user. If the entry is not positive, crash.

4. Declare a double variable guess that will hold the guess and initialize it to half the entered number.

5. Write the rest of Lab7 so that it implements Newton's method 10 times and then outputs the final approximation. It should not take more than five terminated statements (TS=5) to accomplish this.

6. The problem with the above implementation is that we have no way of telling whether the magic number 10 is too high or too low. It is possible that 5 iterations are sufficient to reach our desired accuracy, but it is also possible that 20 iterations are needed. Save your app under a new name, Sqrt.java, and rewrite its loop so that it keeps iterating until two successive values of guess become equal within a tolerance of three decimals. To that end, define

   ```
   final double EPSILON = 1.E-3;
   ```

   and change the loop so that it stops when

   ```
   Math.abs(guess - oldGuess) < EPSILON
   ```

The variable oldGuess stores the value that guess had at the end of the previous iteration. The value of EPSILON is usually derived from the accuracy of other numbers used in the application or from the output-formatting requirement.

L7.2 Testing Using I/O Capture

We want to test the square root application by an automated process. Since the harness does not require prompting, we start by removing the prompt.

1. Comment out the prompt in Sqrt.java (there is only one prompt in it). Save the modified program and compile it.

2. Launch your editor, and create a new program, MyHarness, as follows:

```
public class MyHarness
{
    public static void main(String args[])
    {   PrintStream output = System.out;
        double testCase = 50;
        String inp = testCase + "\n";
        String out = ToolBox.launch("Sqrt", inp);
        double unit = Double.parseDouble(out);
        output.println(unit);
    }
}
```

The key method here is launch: it takes the name of the app to launch, as a first parameter, and the input to be supplied to the app, as a second parameter. inp must be the exact same string that a human would have supplied had the app been launched on its own. A human user would typically enter a number like 50 and then press ENTER. We simulate this by defining a string containing 50 and "\n". The return of launch is the output of the app, as it would have appeared had the app been launched on its own. Hence, if the app made one output using println, the return would be a string containing that output and a "\n". On the other hand, if the app made an output using print, the return would be a string containing that output without a "\n". Run the harness and compare its output to that of Sqrt.

3. We want to generate the test cases randomly. Let us assume that the range of interest (conveyed to us by the analyst) is all the positive integers less than 100. Add the following declarations to MyHarness:

```
final int SUITE_SIZE = 25;
final int MAX = 99;
```

We want to generate 25 random integers uniformly distributed in [1,99], send them to our app, and capture the outputs. Note that the Random class does have a method that returns random integers in [0,n) so you will have to map its closed-open interval to our closed-closed interval. Modify MyHarness accordingly.

4. We will use the `sqrt` method of the `Math` class as an oracle. Whenever our app returns a square root, we will compare it with the return of the oracle. If the two are close enough within some tolerance, we say that the app has passed this test case. Otherwise, we say it failed the test case and output the difference between the unit's roots and the oracle's roots. Add the following declaration to `MyHarness`:

```
final double SMALL = 1.E-8;
```

We will use this number as tolerance. It is not fair to use such a small number to test an app whose tolerance is set by us to `1.e-3`. We do this here only to demonstrate pass and fail cases. Incorporate the oracle functionality in `MyHarness`.

5. Complete the development of the harness. It should generate 25 lines of output similar to the following:

```
. . .
9   5       pass
10  57      pass
11  26      pass
12  47      fail    6.108670103088798E-8
13  71      pass
. . .
```

Each line shows the test number, the randomly generated test case, and the result of the test. If the absolute value of the difference between the app's result and that of the oracle is less than `SMALL`, the harness displays "pass"; otherwise, it displays "fail" and shows the difference. Make all fields in the output line tab-delimited.

The fact that the app failed in some cases is merely an artifact of our choice of tolerance. Had we used the same tolerance in both the app and the harness, or if that of the app were the lesser of the two, no failures would have been reported. Indeed, the app failed when the difference was around 1.e-8, which is less than the app's own tolerance.

Technical Note: Newton's method is used in numerical analysis to solve the equation $f(x) = 0$, where f is an arbitrary function of x. In this general framework, the method states that starting from an initial guess g_0 for the value of x, one can obtain a better one, g_1, by using

```
g₁ = g₀ - f(g₀) / f'(g₀)
```

where f' is the derivative of f. What we have done in the Lab is simply apply this to the function $f(x) = x^2 - num$ because the value of x for which $f(x) = 0$ is clearly the square root of num. Applying the above to this particular function yields

```
g₁ = g₀ - (g₀² - num) / (2g₀)
   = g₀ - g₀ / 2 + num / (2g₀)
   = (g₀ + num / g₀) / 2
```

which is the recurrence we started the Lab with.

L7.3 Parsing an HTML Document

1. Launch your browser and visit your favourite web site. The URL that you type in the address of the browser has the following structure:

```
http://server_address/document_name
```

The prefix "http://" specifies the protocol used for the communication between your browser and the server. This is followed by the server's address, expressed as a name or an IP number, which is optionally followed by the name of the document that you wish to visit. If you do not supply a document name, a default document will be sent.

2. Upon receiving the document, the browser renders it on the screen. This means it interprets its content, which is typically in HTML, and displays it on the screen accordingly. Take a look at the actual document that was received (rather than its rendering) by using the View Source facility of your browser (typically under the View menu).

3. We would like to automate the above two steps by writing a Java program that visits a web site and retrieves a particular piece of information from it. Reading a document on a remote computer is pretty much like reading a file on the local disk. All you need to do is supply a URL instead of a file name.

4. Launch your editor, and create a new program, Web, that prompts for and reads a URL from the user and establishes a connection with it. Since users are not accustomed to including the "http://" prefix, we add it in the program:

```
output.println("Enter the web site:");
URL url = new URL("http://" + input.nextLine());
Scanner reader = new Scanner(url.openStream());
```

Set up a loop that reads the document line by line and prints each. Your output should match the "document source" obtained earlier from the browser.

5. Examine the document as rendered in the browser, and select a particular feature in it, a number or a word that appears in its text. Locate this feature in the document source and come up with a strategy for locating this feature in a program. One strategy you can use is determine the line number in which the feature resides, but this makes your program very sensitive to any change in the document; for example, if a line is added or deleted, your program will no longer be able to find the feature. There is no foolproof strategy, but some strategies are more robust than others.

6. Web documents are not all static; some are generated on demand. Visit the web site

```
http://www.cs.yorku.ca/~roumani/jba/se
```

Enter a stock symbol, for example, .AB, and click the button to obtain the current price of its stock. Notice that the address field in your browser shows the above URL followed by a question mark and a string that contains the symbol you selected. This means we could have visited this page directly (without having to manually enter a symbol and click a button) had we known this amended URL.

7. Write a Java program that prompts for and reads a stock symbol from the user and outputs its price by connecting to the above site. Note that your app must handle the case of the nonexistent symbol.

Technical Note: When XML completely replaces HTML, it will be much easier to automate the parsing of documents. This is so because features will be identified by tags, and a parser can locate these regardless of their positions within the document; for example, they can still be found even if more lines are added to the document.

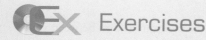 # Exercises

Programming exercises are indicated with an asterisk.

7.1 Of the five phases that make up the development process, determine the one in which the following activities are most likely to occur:

(a) Writing a manual for the application
(b) Determining whether a certain quantity is an integer or a real number
(c) Determining the classes to delegate to
(d) Removing compile-time errors
(e) Determining whether the application works as specified
(f) Detecting whether a class behaves as specified
(g) Deciding on how the output should be laid out

7.2 Argue that the waterfall model can be thought of as a single iteration of the iterative methodology. What subset of the requirement should be used in that single iteration?

7.3 Of the five phases involved in the development process, determine the one in which the following skill is needed the most:

(a) Understanding the business of the customer
(b) Understanding syntax error messages
(c) Drawing UML relationship diagrams
(d) Performing statistical analysis
(e) Drawing UML class diagrams
(f) Debugging

Note that certain skills are equally needed in more than one activity.

7.4 Some historians claim that after Roman engineers built a bridge, they were forced to stand under it as the heaviest carriage was pulled across. The rationale behind the Roman's test vector is that if the bridge can withstand the heaviest carriage, then it can withstand anything lighter. Compare and contrast this approach with integration testing. Do we have a corresponding test case in software construction?

7.5 A and B are two unrelated classes except that A invokes one of the methods of B. Is there a UML relationship between these two classes? If yes, depict it using UML.

7.6 You are asked to perform black-box testing on a method that takes two integer parameters and returns a string. The method's precondition states that the two integers must be positive and less than 50. Of the following test vectors (each containing a set of x, y pairs), which one would you select, and why:

(a) $(-5,5)$, $(-1,0)$, $(1,-5)$, $(3,0)$
(b) $(5,3)$, $(3,5)$, $(5,5)$, $(3,3)$

(c) (1,3), (3,5), (10,49), (1,49), (49,1), (49,15)

(d) (71,12), (50,5), (12,75), (51,7)

7.7 You are asked to test an application that reads two integers, x and y, and outputs a string. The key part of the code is shown below:

```java
final int MIN = 5;
final int MAX = 10;
final int LIMIT = 5;
if (x < MIN)
{
    output.println("Left");
} else if (x < MAX && y < LIMIT)
{
    output.println("Middle");
} else if (x < MAX)
{
    output.println("Top");
} else
{
    output.println("Right");
}
```

Propose a test vector (made up of x, y pairs) that is appropriate for white-box testing.

7.8 The following runtime error occurred:

```
java.lang.NullPointerException
        at Exercise_7.main(Exercise_7.java:9)
Exception in thread "main"
```

(a) Determine the name of the class in which the problem occurred. (b) Determine the line number at which the problem occurred. (c) What could the source of the problem be? (d) Write a fragment that leads to the same kind of problem.

7.9 The following runtime error occurred:

```
java.lang.StringIndexOutOfBoundsException:
String index out of range: -1
        at java.lang.String.substring(String.java:1438)
        at java.lang.String.substring(String.java:1411)
        at Exercise_7.main(Exercise_7.java:15)
Exception in thread "main"
```

(a) Determine the name of the class in which the problem occurred. (b) Determine the line number at which the problem occurred. (c) What could the source of the problem be? (d) Write a fragment that leads to the same kind of problem.

7.10 Predict the output of the following fragment:

```java
String test = "this is a test";
String delimiter = " ";
```

```
StringTokenizer parse;
parse = new StringTokenizer(test, delimiter);
output.println(parse.countTokens());
```

7.11 Predict the output of the following fragment:

```
String test = "this is a test";
String delimiter = "abcdefghijklmnopqrstuvwxyz";
StringTokenizer parse;
parse = new StringTokenizer(test, delimiter);
output.println(parse.countTokens());
```

7.12* Write an app that reads a `double` x from the user, ensures that it is in $[0,1]$ or else crashes, and then computes and outputs the following sum:

$$x - \frac{x^2}{2} + \frac{x^3}{3} - \frac{x^4}{4} + \frac{x^5}{5} - \frac{x^6}{6} + \cdots$$

This is an infinite sum, but the terms of the series drop in absolute value. After adding a certain number of them, most digits in the sum will stop changing. Your app should stop adding when the absolute value of the term to be added is less than EPSILON = `1.e-3`. Test your app at the following three test cases: $x = 0$, $x = 0.5$, and $x = 1$. The correct sums for these cases are approximately $0, 0.41$, and 0.69, respectively.

7.13* Write a harness to automate the testing of the app in Exercise 7.12. It should have the same structure as the harness developed in the Lab but with the following characteristics:

- It generates 50 test cases.
- It generates random real numbers in $[0,1)$.
- It uses `Math.log(1+x)` as an oracle.
- It use `1.e-3` as a tolerance for the unit/oracle deviation.

Remember to comment out the prompt for x as was done in the Lab.

7.14* Write an app that reads a `double` x from the user, ensures that it is in $[0,1]$ or else crashes, and then computes and outputs the following sum:

$$x - \frac{x^3}{3} + \frac{x^5}{5} - \frac{x^7}{7} + \frac{x^9}{9} - \frac{x^{11}}{11} + \cdots$$

This is an infinite sum, but the terms of the series drop in absolute value. After adding a certain number of them, most digits in the sum will stop changing. Your app should stop adding when the absolute value of the term to be added is less than EPSILON = `1.e-3`. Test your app at the following three test cases: $x = 0$, $x = 0.5$, and $x = 1$. The correct sums for these cases are approximately $0, 0.46$, and 0.79, respectively.

7.15* Write a harness to automate the testing of the app in Exercise 7.14. It should have the same structure as the harness developed in the Lab but with the following characteristics:

- It generates 20 test cases.
- It generates random real numbers in $[0,1)$.
- It uses `Math.atan(x)` as an oracle.
- It uses `1.e-4` as a tolerance for the unit/oracle deviation.

Remember to comment out the prompt for x as was done in the Lab.

7.16* Write an app that reads two `int` values a and b from the user, ensures that they are positive (or else crashes), and then swaps them, if need be, to ensure a >= b. Next, the app computes their greatest common divisor (gcd) by using the *Euclid* algorithm:

```
precondition: a >= b > 0
for (int c = a % b; c != 0; c = a % b)
{
    a = b;
    b = c;
}
postcondition: gcd = b
```

The app should then output the computed gcd.

7.17* Write a harness to automate the testing of the app in Exercise 7.16. It should have the same structure as the harness developed in the Lab but with the following characteristics:

■ It generates 20 test cases.
■ It generates random integers in [1,100).
■ It uses direct verification as an oracle.
■ It uses zero tolerance for the unit/oracle deviation (since these are integers).

Remember to comment out the prompt for a and b as was done in the Lab. Note that since the app requires two inputs, each must be suffixed by a new line character before passing the input to the `launch` method:

```
generate the random int a
generate the random int b
interchange a and b if a < b
String input = a + "\n" + b + "\n";
```

7.18* In Chapter 5 (Exercise 5.21) you wrote an app that determined whether a given positive integer is a prime number. Write a harness to automate its testing with the following characteristics:

■ It generates 10 test cases.
■ It generates random integers in [1,100).
■ It uses zero tolerance for the unit/oracle deviation (since this is a binary outcome).
■ It uses `java.Math.BigInteger` as an oracle.

The oracle class was designed to handle huge integers, beyond the range of `long`, but we are using it because it has a method that determines whether a big integer is a prime number. The oracle can be used as follows:

```
generate the random integer
convert the integer to a string
pass the string to the constructor of BigInteger
invoke the isProbablePrime method
```

```
The population of Canada is about 30.50 million. Ontar-
io is one of the provinces in Canada, the most populous.
I live in Toronto; do you? Do you like it?
```

Figure 7.13 A
sample essay

Since prime numbers are sparse, you cannot rely on the usual statistical sampling in order to populate the test vector. To ensure domain coverage, we chose to generate a large number of cases in a small range. In general, random test-case generation is inadequate for apps whose binary (yes/no) outcome is mostly yes (or no).

7.19* The file "essay.txt" contains an English essay, one line per record. Write an application that reads this file and outputs the average number of words per sentence in the essay. A word is defined as any sequence of non-whitespace characters, and a sentence is defined as any sequence of words whose last word ends with one of the following characters:

. ; : ? !

Note, however, that if the last word in a line ends with a hyphen, it means it is continued on the next line, and hence, should not be counted more than once. For example, consider the essay shown in Fig. 7.13.

Your app should output

```
Average number of words per sentence = 5.8
```

In this example, the essay contains 29 words and 5 sentences; and 29/5 = 5.8. Note that 30.50 is a word because it contains non-whitespace characters. Note also that the decimal point in 30.5 did not end the sentence because it did not occur at the end of its word. Note also that "Ontar" and "io" were not counted as two words.

7.20* The file "maturity.txt" contains information about financial papers, one paper per record, as shown below:

```
SKMG:20/2/2047:47.56
CH:14/9/2043:3047.56
UBS:5/9/2013:47.56
CS:29/10/2011:56847.56
. . .
. . .
. . .
```

For each paper, the record stores three fields delimited by colons: a code, a maturity date, and an amount. You can assume, without validation, that each record is formatted exactly as specified. Note, however, that all three fields are variable-length; in particular, the month in the date field can have one or two digits.

Write an app that uses Scanner to read these records one by one as strings. For each, create a StringTokenizer instance so that the three fields can be parsed. When you extract the date field, create a separate StringTokenizer instance for it (using / instead of : as the delimiter) so that you can extract the date's fields.

The app must output the paper with the latest date and format the output as follows:

```
Latest maturity date is: 14/9/2043
         Code="CH", Amount=3,047.65
```

As you can see, the code is double-quoted, and the amount has a thousands separator.

7.21* Write an app that starts off with the following fragment, which creates an instance of the CreditCard class of the type.lib package:

```
CreditCard cc;
cc = new CreditCard(1020, "Java By Abstraction");
output.println(cc);
output.println(cc.charge(500));
cc.pay(200);
```

The fragment issues a new card, charges a $500 purchase on it, and then makes a payment of $200. Add lines to the app to perform the following tasks in the order shown:

- Output the card's number on a line by itself.
- Output the card's balance rounded to two decimals and with a thousands separator.
- Output the card's issue and expiry dates.
- Attempt to charge an $800 purchase on the card, then output the result of the attempt (did it succeed?), and the card's balance.
- Attempt to decrease the credit limit of the card to $250, then output the result of the attempt (did it succeed?).

7.22* Write an application that determines and outputs the current price of gold. Look for a local web site that displays this price, and use the techniques you learned in the Lab to automate connecting to the site and parsing its HTML content.

7.23* Write an application that determines and outputs the current temperature in a user-defined city. Look for a web site that displays these temperatures, and determine how cities are identified in it, for example, by name or number. Use the techniques you learned in the Lab to connect to the site and request a document about a specific city.

eCheck

Check07A (TS = 41)

This project uses the type.lib.CreditCard class. Keep its API in your browser and familiarize yourself with its features. The app Check07A posts transactions stored in a file to one credit card. Let us start by looking at Fig. 7.14, which depicts a particular transaction file and the corresponding output.

The app reads the input line from the user as one string entry, and breaks it into three pieces. The input contains three comma-delimited fields and can easily be parsed using a StringTokenizer instance. Note that indexOf / substring can also be used for parsing, but a tokenizer is more scalable, as you will see shortly.

```
Enter name, limit, and trx filename
(comma-delimited):
Adam,7500,lab7data.txt
00000  C          500.00  done.
00001  C         2100.00  done.
00002  P          550.00  done.
00003  C         5950.00  rejected.
00004  C         3000.00  done.
00005  invalid record.
00006  L         4000.00  rejected.
00007  P         4050.00  done.
00008  L         2500.00  done.
00009  C         2750.00  rejected.
00010  P          500.00  done.
00011  C          200.00  done.
00012  P         1000.00  done.
Card Balance =      -300.00
Credit Limit =      2500.00
```

```
C           500
C          2100
p    550
       C    5950
C  3000

1  4000
p  4050
                L  2500
C  2750
   P  500
C  200
   p  1000
```

The three input fields are the name of the credit card holder, its credit limit, and the name of the transaction file. The first two fields allow you to create a CreditCard instance (use any number you like for the card number).

The file contains transactions, one per record, to be posted against the created card. Each record in it (see the above sample) contains a transaction code and an amount. The code can be C = Charge, P = Pay, or L = set Limit. The first record in the above sample has a transaction that charges $500 on the card. The two fields

Figure 7.14 This sample run of Check07A uses the data file shown in the inset.

are delimited by whitespace, and the code may be preceded by whitespace, too, so a tokenizer is the ideal parser.

The only deviation from the above specs is that the transaction code may be in lowercase, and some records may not contain two tokens (e.g., may be blank, may contain only one token, or may contain three or more tokens). When such a record is encountered, it should simply be skipped (ignored), but it should nevertheless be counted (for record numbering purposes).

The app must start by creating a CreditCard instance using any credit card number. It then reads the records one by one. If two tokens are present in a record, then the first (the code) should be treated in a case-insensitive manner, and based on it, the app invokes (on the instance created before the loop) the appropriate method. The app outputs one line per record containing the record number (generated serially starting from zero and formatted as 5Z), the code in upper-case, the amount (formatted 10.2), and whether it was approved (done.) or not (rejected.). If the record is empty, its number is displayed followed by the message "invalid record." This log is followed by two lines showing the card's balance and limit (each formatted as 10.2).

Trace the above run record by record using a calculator, and make sure you understand why a record was accepted or rejected and why the final balance and limit have the shown values.

Develop and eCheck Check07A.

Check07B (TS = 36)

A file contains English words, one per record, as shown in the following sample:

```
        realize
        book
        realtor
        Souvenir
        the
        callee
        . . .
```

Write the program Check07B, which prompts for and reads the name of this file, then outputs the number of syllables in each word in the file. Here is a sample run:

```
Enter filename:
words.txt
        0       2       realize
        1       1       book
        2       2       realtor
        3       3       Souvenir
        4       1       the
        5       2       callee
Average syllables per word = 1.8
```

The output consists of as many lines as there are records in the file. Each output line has three tab-delimited fields: the first is the record number (a serial number that starts at 0), the second is the number of syllables that the word in that record has, and the third field is the word itself. The listing is followed by a line that gives the average number of syllables per word, rounded to one decimal.

The number of syllables in a word is computed using the following three rules:

- A syllable is a sequence of vowels.
- An "e" by itself at the end of a word does not count as a syllable.
- Each word must have at least one syllable.

There are six vowels in English: a, e, i, o, u, y. Note, however, that the app must be case-insensitive when counting syllables.

For example, the words "book", "Ant", and "meal" all have one syllable each. "java" has two syllables and "souvenir" has three. All these are direct applications of the first rule. The word "realize", however, has only two syllables because, according to the second rule, the last "e" does not count. The second rule applies only to an "e" by itself, without other vowels immediately before it; hence, the word "callee" has two syllables (the last "ee" does count).

If applying the first two rules on a given word leads to a zero count (no syllables), then the third rule tells us to assign one syllable to the word. Hence, the word "the" is considered to have one syllable.

Note that even though syllable recognition is case-insensitive, the case of the words in the output must be exactly as in the file. Note also that you can safely assume that each record in the file contains only one word, that is, only letters, no punctuation, whitespace, or any other character.

Develop and eCheck Check07B.

Check07C (TS = 26)

We want to compute the following infinite sum:

$$1 + 2^2 \ast x + 3^2 \ast x^3 + 4^2 \ast x^3 + \ldots$$

As you can see, each term in this series is made up of a coefficient multiplying a power of x. The coefficients are the squares of successive integers, starting with 1, and the powers uses successive exponents starting at 0. The sum converges when $|x|$ is less than 1.

Write the app Check07C that reads x, verifies that $|x| < 1$ or else crashes, and then computes and outputs the sum together with the oracle's answer. The oracle is:

$$(1 + x) \ / \ (1 - x)^3$$

To compute the sum, keep adding terms until you reach a term whose value is less than 0.0001 in absolute value. Here are two sample runs:

```
Enter the value of x ... 2.4
Exception in thread "main" java.lang.RuntimeException: |x| must be < 1.
...

Enter the value of x ... 0.001254
The sum of the series = 1.005016
The Oracle's answer is: 1.005030184256893
```

Do not format the numbers.
Develop your app, test it, and then eCheck it.

Check07D (TS = 26)

Write the app Check07D that reads an integer from the user and determines if the integer is prime or not. The integer must be greater than 1 or the app will crash with an error message.

Primality can be established by trying each and every possible divisor of the integer, starting with 2 and ending with one less than the integer (in fact, you can stop at its square root). If no divisor can be found in this range then the number is deemed prime. This is what we will call the "direct algorithm".

For an oracle, we will use the randomized algorithm employed by the BigInteger class (Exercise 7.18) with a certainty of 10; i.e. if the isProbablePrime returned true then the probability that our integer is indeed prime is greater than $(1 - 2^{\wedge}10)$ which is ~ 99.9%.

Here are three sample runs:

```
Enter an integer greater than 1 ... -67
Exception in thread "main" java.lang.RuntimeException: Integer must
be greater than 1!
...

Enter an integer greater than 1 ... 51599
The primality of your entry is:
- Using the direct algorithm: true
- Using the BigInteger class: true
```

```
Enter an integer greater than 1 ... 234573
The primality of your entry is:
- Using the direct algorithm: false
- Using the BigInteger class: false
```

Develop your app, test it, and then eCheck it.

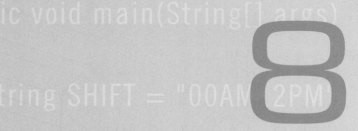

Aggregation

8

Learning Objectives

1. Create, copy, and delegate to aggregates

2. Recognize aggregates from their APIs

3. Learn about I/O streams and graphics

4. Work with collections and their APIs

5. Learn about traversal and search techniques

6. Experience algorithm complexity

C lasses used by your application may have attributes that are themselves instances of other classes. Such arrangements of "objects within objects" are called aggregations, and their presence makes the features of both the aggregate and the aggregated, directly or indirectly, available to the program. Our journey into the object world started with "Layered Abstractions," where a user delegates to a manager, who in turn delegates to another. Aggregation is the most general framework for implementing layering. In this chapter, you will learn how to recognize aggregates, what to expect to see in their APIs, and how to distinguish ordinary aggregates from compositions and collections.

Chapter Outline

8.1 What Is Aggregation?

The world we live in is full of objects, most of which are not simple; rather, they are compound, made up of other objects. For example, your car is an object, but it contains a radio, a separate object manufactured at a factory other than the one that made the car. Your CD player is an object, and it can hold one CD, itself an object. Your wallet is an object, too, and the whole purpose of a wallet is to store other objects, for example, money. We clearly need a context to determine whether an object is compound; nevertheless, it is a fact that everyday objects exhibit this **whole-part relationship**. For example, the radio is related to the car because it is a part of it; the car in this example is the whole. The following sections show how such a relationship manifests itself in the software world.

8.1.1 Definition and Terminology

A class C is said to be an **aggregate** if one of its attributes is an object reference. And if we denote the type of that object reference by T, then C and T are said to have a "**has-a**" relationship, in which C (the whole) *has a* T (the part). This relationship is also called an **aggregation**. No standard term exists for T, the aggregated part, in the nomenclature. It is sometimes referred to as the "part" or the "component," but neither of these terms is standard.

To see how aggregation models the whole-part relationship, we look at an example. Imagine instantiating C. This involves assigning values to all the attributes of C including, in particular, the object reference of the type T. The only way to assign a value to this object reference (aside from setting it to `null`) is to create an instance of T and have the reference point at it. Hence, aside from the null case, every instance of C has an instance of T held within it, an object in an object, and this is exactly what the notion of "whole-part" implies.

Note that if all the attributes of a class are primitive, then it is *not* an aggregate. Strings are not primitive, but they masquerade as primitive (Section 6.1.2). Hence, it would trivialize aggregation if we were to treat them as aggregated parts. We therefore adopt the following revised definition in this textbook: to be an aggregate, a class has to have at least one attribute whose type is neither primitive nor `String`.

Example 8.1

For each of the following pairs of objects, determine whether the first can ordinarily be considered an aggregate of the second.
(a) Camera, Film
(b) Vehicle, Car
(c) Library, Book
(d) Animal, Dog
(e) Car, Tree

Answer:
(a) Yes, this is an aggregation. A camera *has a* film.

(b) No, this is not an aggregation; a vehicle does *not* have a car. In fact, a car *is a* vehicle. We will pursue this kind of generalization relation in Chapter 9.

(c) Yes, this is an aggregation; a library *has* books.

(d) No, this is not an aggregation; an animal does *not* have a dog. In fact, a dog *is an* animal. We will pursue this kind of generalization relation in Chapter 9.

(e) No, this is not an aggregation, at least not ordinarily. We can contrive a scenario in which a car has a tree attribute, but it would not be a customary relation.

□

We saw in Chapter 7 that aggregation is depicted in UML diagrams by connecting the two classes by a solid line and placing a diamond next to the aggregate. Figure 8.1 shows the UML diagrams of three examples of aggregation.

Each of the examples in Fig. 8.1 illustrates a different aspect of aggregation. The UML diagram in Fig. 8.1(a) depicts the fact that there is an aggregation between the `CDPlayer` class and the CD class. Furthermore, it indicates that the former has exactly one attribute of the latter type, which means that this CD player can hold one CD at a time. In general, the number of attributes in the aggregate that are of the aggregated type is called the **multiplicity** and is written next to the aggregated part.

Figure 8.1(b) indicates that the `Wallet` class has attributes of the type `Bill` but it uses * for the multiplicity. This means the number of bills that the wallet can hold is not fixed; it can vary from time to time. In general, if the multiplicity can change as the application runs, then it is referred to as **variable multiplicity**. In that case, the aggregate class becomes known as the **collection**, and each instance of the aggregated class becomes known as an **element** of the collection. Collections (also called **containers**) are widely used in programming and are examined in depth in Section 8.2.

Figure 8.1(c) indicates that the `Car` class has four attributes of the type `Wheel` and one of the type `Radio`. A class may thus aggregate several classes each with a different multiplicity. Similarly, a class may be aggregated by more than one class; for example, `Radio` could be aggregated with multiplicity 1 by `Car` and with multiplicity * by `House`. Note that the diamond in Fig. 8.1(c) is filled. This means that the car comes with four wheels and a radio; that is, you do not need to purchase these parts and take them to the car factory to have them installed. In general, if creating an instance of the aggregate automatically leads to creating an instance of the aggregated part, then the aggregation becomes known as a **composition**. In a composition, the aggregate and the aggregated objects have a shared lifetime: they are born together, and they die together.

It should be noted that whether or not an aggregation is a composition is not something that we, the client, can predict based on common sense. The implementer implements the aggregate one way or the other depending on the nature of the application.

Figure 8.1
Aggregation UML diagrams. (a) A CD player has one CD. (b) A wallet has several bills (paper money). (c) A car has one radio and four wheels.

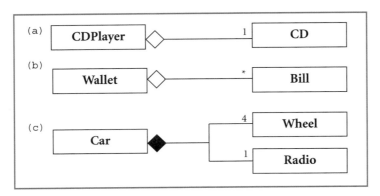

Example 8.2

Assume that a `Camera` class has an attribute of the type `Film`. Describe a hypothetical scenario in which this aggregation is (a) a composition and (b) not a composition.
Answer:

(a) Some cameras are of the disposable, one-time-use type. When you buy such a camera, it comes with the film already in it; hence, creating an instance of the camera auto-creates an instance of the film. This aggregation is thus a composition.

(b) Non-disposable cameras are normally sold without film. The store that sells the camera may, as a promotion, give a free roll of film with it, but this is still not a composition because the film instance is created separately from the camera instance; their birth dates are not coincident.

The `CreditCard` class in `type.lib` is an example of an aggregate. It encapsulates a credit card and has the following attributes: card number, cardholder's name, credit limit, balance, and issue/expiry dates. This class is an aggregate because of the last two attributes, which are of the type `Date` (the `Date` class is in `java.util`). As the UML diagram in Fig. 8.2 shows, this aggregation is in fact a composition: the two date objects are auto-created when the card is instantiated, and they are automatically deleted when the card is deleted.

The `Investment` class in `type.lib` is another example of an aggregate. It is meant to encapsulate an investment in the stock market, and it has three attributes: the stock itself (an instance of `Stock`), the number of shares bought (an `int`), and the purchase price (also called the book value) per share (a `double`). The UML diagram is shown in Fig. 8.3(a).

When you purchase several stocks and create an investment instance for each, you will want to hold all these instances in some container. The `Portfolio` class plays the role of such a container, and, as shown in Fig. 8.3(b), it is a collection.

8.1.2 The Aggregate's Constructor

When we, the client, create an instance of an aggregate C, we use its constructor to initialize its attributes. And since one of the attributes is an object reference, it is initialized by making it point at an instance of the aggregated part T. Hence, the instantiation of C has led us, as it should, to thinking about the instantiation of T. This, in turns, leads us to ask: who instantiates T? There are two possible answers:

1. The aggregate's constructor
2. The client

Figure 8.2 A credit card has an issue and an expiry date.

In the first scenario, we do not do anything with T. We merely create C, and this will automatically create T. This case corresponds to a composition because the part is created together with the whole by the whole, and since we have no direct reference to it, it will die (i.e., be garbage-collected) when the whole dies. In the second scenario, we create the part instance and pass its reference to the constructor of the aggregate. In this case, the part is created before the whole.

| Credit card | 2 | Date |

Figure 8.3 An investment has one stock, while a portfolio has several investments.

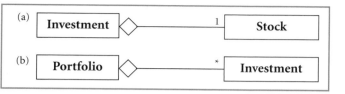

Furthermore, since we hold a reference to the part, it can remain alive even if the whole died. This therefore is not a composition.

For example, the constructor of `Investment` (whose API is in the top part of Fig. 8.4) must receive the `Stock` reference from the caller, which means that the client must first create a stock instance and then an investment instance.

The following fragment demonstrates creating an investment to represent the purchase of 15 shares of a stock with the symbol ".AB" at a price of $12.25 per share:

```
int number = 15;
double cost = 12.25;
Stock stock = new Stock(".AB");
Investment inv = new Investment(stock, number, cost);
```

It is clear from this fragment that `stock` and `inv` do not have a common lifetime. Moreover, we can delete `inv` without deleting `stock`:

```
Stock stock = new Stock(".AB");
{
    Investment inv = new Investment(stock, number, cost);
}
output.println(stock);
```

At the end of the fragment, the "whole" is deleted (because we exited its scope) while the "part" remains.

As a second example, consider the constructor of `CreditCard` whose API is shown in the lower part of Fig. 8.4. The following fragment demonstrates creating a credit card with number 123 and cardholder name "Adam":

```
int number = 123;
String name = "Adam";
CreditCard card = new CreditCard(number, name);
```

Figure 8.4 The constructor of a non-composition aggregate such as `Investment` expects the part (a `Stock`) to be passed; it therefore expects the caller to create it. For a composition such as `CreditCard`, however, the constructor does not refer to the part (a `Date`); it creates it internally as part of its implementation.

Constructor Summary — Investment

`Investment(Stock stock, int quantity, double bookValue)`
    Construct an investment with the passed fields.

Constructor Summary — CreditCard

`CreditCard(int no, String aName)`
    Construct a credit card with the passed number and holder's name.

Programming Tip 8.1

Fallacy: Passing objects to the constructor rules out composition

While it is true that an aggregate constructor that does not take any object parameters is indicative of a composition, the inverse is not necessarily true. The `CreditCard` class, which we know is a composition, has an overloaded constructor that allows the client to specify the issue date of the card. This does not violate the coincident lifetime definition because the constructor does *not* set the issue date attribute to the passed parameter but rather to a copy of it. Hence, the client does not create the "real" attribute and does not even have a reference to it.

In More Depth 8.1

Composition versus Aggregation in Java

The notion of composition as a strong form of aggregation is rooted in UML, not in Java. The general idea is that the aggregate in a composition is an entity that is the sum of its parts; without the wheels, the engine, and the body, a car is simply not a car. The aggregate in an aggregation, however, is an entity on its own. It is capable of holding components, but can exist without them. For example, a CD player exists even if there is no CD in it. This reasoning leads naturally to requiring coincidental lifetimes for the whole and the part in a composition: when you buy a car, the radio comes with it, and when you sell the car, you are expected to leave the radio in it.

Java treats composition like any other aggregation; it does not have any special language construct for it. To counter that, implementers simulate composition by insisting that the part instance be created by the constructor of the aggregate, and that any part instance received from or sent to the client is copied before being processed. The former condition guarantees that the whole and the part have the same birth date. The latter condition ensures that the client does not have a reference to the part, and hence, the part will die upon the death of the whole.

The signature of the constructor completely hides the aggregation. The API of the class indicates that the created card would have an issue date of today and an expiry date two years from today. Both date objects are auto-created by the constructor; we are not involved in their creation.

8.1.3 Accessors and Mutators

Whether the relation is one of aggregation or composition, the aggregate must provide some means for accessing each aggregated part. Failing that, the part would be purely internal, and the outside world would never know it existed. As a minimum, an accessor must be provided for each aggregated part. Such an accessor will have the signature

```
getX()
```

(where X is the name of the aggregated part) and the return T. For example, the aggregate Investment provides the accessor

```
public Stock getStock()
```

We can use it, given an investment reference inv, as follows:

```
Stock stock = inv.getStock();
```

The reference returned by the accessor can point either at the aggregated part or at a copy of it. The latter approach is used in compositions to prevent the client from having access to the part.

To determine the approach that the Investment class adopts, we mutate the instance returned by the accessor and see if the aggregated part was mutated. An easy way to do this is to negate the boolean titleCaseName field of the Stock class:

```
Stock stock = inv.getStock();
char old = stock.delimiter;
stock.delimiter = '-';
boolean isCopy = inv.getStock().delimiter == old;
```

If we execute this fragment, we find that isCopy is false. This means that the accessor returned a reference to the actual aggregated stock, not to a copy of it.

Example 8.3

Determine whether the getIssueDate accessor of the CreditCard class returns a reference to the actual date embedded in the credit card or to a copy of it.

Answer:
We use the same technique, mutate the instance returned by the accessor and check to see whether the aggregated part changed:

```
int number = 123;
String name = "Adam";
CreditCard card = new CreditCard(number, name);
Date issue = card.getIssueDate();
issue.setTime(0);
output.println(card.getIssueDate());
```

The fragment creates a credit card, retrieves a reference to the auto-created issue date, and changes it to January 1, 1970 GMT. Finally, it re-retrieves and outputs the issue date. If we execute this fragment, we find that it outputs today's date. This means the accessor returned a reference to a copy of the aggregated date, not to the actual attribute. ∎

In addition to an accessor, an aggregate may provide a mutator to allow the client to replace an aggregated part. If present, such a mutator would have the following signature:

```
        setX(T newInstance)
```

where X is the name of the aggregated part. For example, the `CreditCard` aggregate provides the mutator

```
    public boolean setExpiryDate(Date expiry)
```

It is meant to renew the credit card by changing its expiry date to the passed date. If the passed reference is null or if it points to a date that occurs prior to the issue date, nothing is mutated and the return is false. Otherwise the expiry date is mutated.

An operation that is closely related to aggregate creation is **aggregate cloning**. Given an instance x of an aggregate, make a copy of it and call it y (x and y are object references). The initial situation is depicted in Fig. 8.5(a), with x pointing at an aggregate at block 100 and with the aggregate pointing at a part at block 600.

There are three ways to do the copying depending on the intended level of copying: aliasing, shallow copying, and deep copying.

- **Aliasing Set y Equal to x.** This amounts to simply having a second reference; the instance itself is not copied. Any mutation made through x will be reflected through y. The resulting memory diagram is shown in Fig. 8.5(b). As you can see, no new objects were created; the only change is that y now points at 100.

- **Shallow Copying** Make a new instance of the aggregate with the same state as the given one, that is, its attributes have the same values, and let y point at it. This is shallow because non-primitive attributes are simply aliased; a mutation of them made through x will be reflected through y. The resulting memory diagram is shown in Fig. 8.5(c). As you can see, a new aggregate was created at block 2400, and y was made to point at it, but the new aggregate still points at block 600; that is, it shares the same part with x.

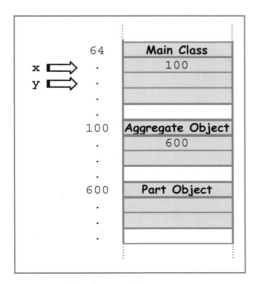

Figure 8.5(a) Before copying

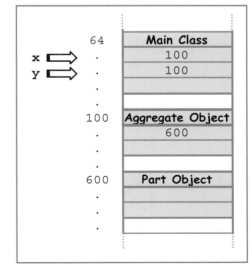

Figure 8.5(b) After aliasing

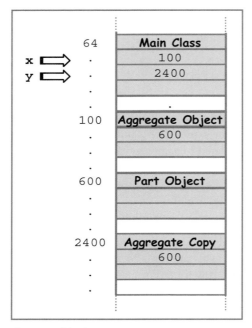

Figure 8.5(c) After shallow copying

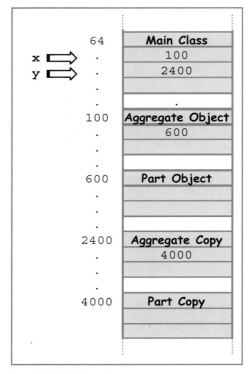

Figure 8.5(d) After deep copying

■ **Deep Copying** Let y point to a new instance in which each non-primitive attribute is itself deep-copied. Any mutation made through x will *not* be reflected through y. The resulting memory diagram is shown in Fig. 8.5(d). Now we have a new aggregate at block 2400 as well as a new part at block 4000.

Note that if the aggregation is a composition, then a client cannot shallow-copy it because it has no direct access to the aggregated parts.

Example 8.4

Given that `card` is a reference to a credit card, clone it using deep copying. You can assume as a precondition that it is not `null`.

Answer:
We retrieve the state of the given aggregate using its accessors and create a new instance with the same state. Since the card number accessor returns a formatted number, we need to extract its left-most part. And since there is no constructor that allows us to specify the expiry date, we create an instance using the default expiry and then mutate it to set its expiry date:

```
assert card != null;
CreditCard copy;
final int SIZE = CreditCard.SEQUENCE_NUMBER_LENGTH;
String cardNumber = card.getNumber().substring(0, SIZE);
copy = new CreditCard(Integer.parseInt(cardNumber),
      card.getName(),
      card.getLimit(),
      card.getIssueDate());
copy.setExpiryDate(card.getExpiryDate());
```

8.1.4 The Client's Perspective

We saw in Section 2.2 that when confronted with complexity, a client delegates work to helper classes. This does not mean that those who implement helper classes must do so from scratch; they can, and often do, delegate. This second layer of delegation occurs when the implementer uses a feature of another class. One way to do that is to create an instance of that other class and store it as an attribute. We thus conclude that aggregation is a signal of layered delegation.

The above observation seems to imply that aggregation is an implementer's concern, not ours. Why should we, the client, care if the implementer performed the task from scratch or sought the help of some other class? Would it not break the encapsulation if we knew how the implementation was done?

The answer has to do with flexibility. At one extreme, implementers can create components that are so basic that the client will find it pretty complex to build an application out of them. At the other extreme, implementers can create components that are so elaborate that the client is not likely to find components that fit the requirement of the application. Aggregation provides a solution that combines the benefits of both extremes: components that are basic in what they do, yet are capable of interfacing with other components. This gives the client flexibility in choosing components without the complexity of assembling them.

To better relate to this flexibility, let us imagine that it is available in the material world, not just in the world of software. Suppose that we were asked to build a car with a rather peculiar combination of features, for example, a certain body type, engine, entertainment system, etc. At one extreme, we can shop around for basic components, but this approach is fraught with problems because components do not always fit snugly with each other, for example, the engine's gasoline intake may require a higher pressure than the fuel pump can provide, or the screws in the seat frame may not fit the holes in the chassis. Solving these problems adds enormous complexity to our job. At the other extreme, we can shop around for ready-made cars. Car manufacturers do offer minor customizations (i.e., they have constructors other than the default constructor), but the choices are extremely limited, and it is usually not possible to find a peculiar mix of specifications. The ideal solution is to find components that can be simply "plugged" with each other. The chassis component, for example, is still just a chassis but it "knows" how to attach seat frames to it. It is an aggregate in the sense that it contains the "know-how" of attaching frames to it.

By providing aggregates instead of basic components, implementers maximize the likelihood for the client to find ready-made building blocks and, hence, help fulfill the dream of component/service-oriented software architecture.

8.1.5 CASE STUDY

I/O Streams

We have been using the `Scanner/PrintStream` classes for both console and file I/O. In this section, we will remove this delegation layer and use lower-level classes in the Java standard library. Doing so has two advantages: First, we will gain first-hand experience in how delegation hides complexity. Second, we will learn about classes whose capability and flexibility go beyond the text-only scope of the `Scanner` and `PrintStream` classes. Text I/O is one in which all input and output is done exclusively in terms of strings of characters: when a program needs to output an integer, it first converts it to a string and then outputs it. Similarly, if the user enters a number, the program reads it as a string and then parses it.

The Java standard library has approximately 100 classes dedicated to I/O. They are in the `java.io` and `java.nio` packages, and their services allow clients to delegate all I/O-related operations. In the following, we will use the services of classes in the first package, so we will assume the following statement:

```
import java.io.*;
```

Keyboard Input

Figure 8.6 The `System` class is a composition. The two instances are auto-created when the virtual machine is first started.

Aggregation allows us to read input from the keyboard, also called **standard input**. In order to read from the keyboard, we must establish a data conduit that starts at the keyboard and ends within our pro-

gram. Such a conduit is called a **stream**; in it, the keyboard plays the role of the **data source**, and our program plays the role of the **data sink**. From the program's point of view, this is an **input stream** because data moves in it toward the program.

As we know, Java comes with an object of the type `java.io.InputStream` that is already connected to the keyboard end and is ready to be used. The virtual machine creates this object when it starts and leaves a reference to it in the field `"in"` of the `System` class, as depicted in Fig. 8.6.

Hence, if we write

```
InputStream keyboard = System.in;
```

then we can invoke methods on `keyboard` in order to read input:

```
int input = keyboard.read();
```

The API of the `read` method indicates that it will wait until the user makes an input. We say that the method **blocks** until an input is made. A user input is considered done when the user presses the ENTER key. At that point, the above method returns the codes of the characters entered by the user byte by byte; that is, each invocation returns the next byte. And after returning the very last byte, the next invocation would return `-1` to indicate that no more bytes are present; that is, the end of the stream has been reached.

It would be a nightmare if we were to read input like this in our applications. First, we do not represent each character in a byte; we use `char`. Hence, we would need to somehow convert bytes to `chars`.

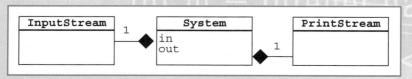

Second, we do not normally like to receive input one character at a time. If the user entered 75, then we like to see the input as the integer 75 or the string 75, but not 7 then 5. Hence, we would need to set up a loop that keeps reading characters and concatenating them until -1 is reached. At that point, the resulting string can be used as is or parsed into a number.

This work is too distracting for an application so let us delegate. We hire one person to take care of turning a byte stream into a character stream. Then we hire a second to collect the characters generated by the first person until a full line of input is accumulated; then the second person delivers this line to us when we ask for it. In the context of streams, these two persons are commonly referred to as the **reader** and the **buffer**. Through these two helpers, a conduit is created between the keyboard and our program, as depicted in Fig. 8.7.

The situation is obviously much better after the delegation, but whenever you delegate work involving the exchange of data to two (or more) helpers, the exchange has to be done through you. Rather than having to manage this exchange, it would be even better if we ask the reader to report to the buffer. This way, we need to deal only with the buffer. Aggregation is how this management hierarchy is realized in the object world. The UML diagrams of the involved classes are shown in Fig. 8.8.

We create the needed instances bottom up and pass them to the constructor of the next aggregate in the chain:

```
InputStream keyboard =
    System.in;
```

Figure 8.7 The byte input stream coming from the keyboard is widened to a character stream in the reader. It is then buffered so the program can read it line by line.

```
InputStreamReader reader =
    new InputStreamReader(keyboard);
BufferedReader buffer =
    new BufferedReader(reader);
```

Since we will not invoke methods on `keyboard` or `reader`, only on `buffer`, we do not need to have object references for them; that is, the instances can be created on the fly, and the above statements can be reduced to one:

```
BufferedReader buffer =
    new BufferedReader(
    new InputStreamReader(
    System.in));
```

Given this reference, we can now read inputs easily one line at a time. The statement

```
String input = input.nextLine();
```

can be replaced with

```
String input = buffer.readLine();
```

Similarly, the statement

```
int number = input.nextInt();
```

can be replaced with

```
int number =
    Integer.parseInt(buffer.readLine());
```

It should be kept in mind, however, that whenever the Java stream classes are used, the header of the main method of our app should be modified to become as follows:

```
public static void main(String[]
    args) throws Exception
```

Input Stream   Reader

ONE WAY

Buffered Reader

Figure 8.8 The underlying aggregations of Fig. 8.7

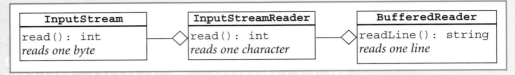

The significance of the "throws" suffix will be clarified in Chapter 11.

File Input

Reading characters from a text file one line at a time is not much different from keyboard input. We still need to convert bytes to characters and to buffer the data. The only difference is the initial stream that connects to the file. The FileInputStream class plays this role. Its constructor takes a file name and creates the stream instance, which can then be connected to a reader and a buffer as before. The chain is shown in Fig. 8.9, along with that of keyboard input to emphasize the similarity.

As before, we can instantiate the entire chain in one statement:

```
BufferedReader filer =
    new BufferedReader
    new InputStreamReader(
    new FileInputStream(
    filename)));
```

As in the Scanner class, we must close the stream once we are done in order to free any resources:

```
filer.close();
```

Unlike the Scanner class, however, there are no hasNext methods to detect end-of-file. Instead, the readLine method returns null when end-of-file is encountered. Hence, you would use a loop like this to read the entire file line by line:

```
for (String line = filer.readLine;
        line != null;
        line = filer.readLine)
{

}
filer.close();
```

Alternatively, you can use techniques shown in Chapter 11 in order to monitor the exception that is generated when attempting to read past the end of the file.

Screen Output

The basic operation of any console application is writing output on the screen, called **standard output**. To create standard output, we must establish a data conduit that starts within our program and ends at the screen. From the program's point of view, this is an **output stream** because data in it moves away from the program.

As we know, Java comes with an object of the type java.io.PrintStream that is already connected to the screen end and is ready to be used. The virtual machine creates this object when it starts, and it leaves a reference to it in the field "out" of the System class, as depicted in Fig. 8.6. We have been using this object throughout for console output.

Figure 8.9 Aggregations for reading characters one line at a time from the keyboard or a file

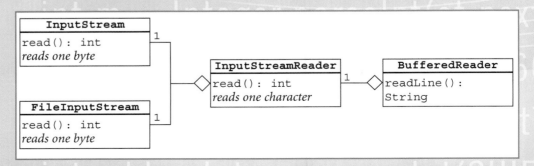

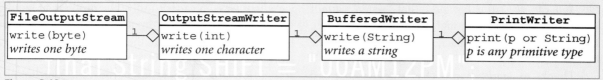

FileOutputStream	OutputStreamWriter	BufferedWriter	PrintWriter
write(byte)	write(int)	write(String)	print(p or String)
writes one byte	*writes one character*	*writes a string*	*p is any primitive type*

Figure 8.10
Aggregations for
writing data to a
text file

File Output

To write data to a text file, we delegate to the aggregation chain shown in Fig. 8.10.

An output operation begins at the program end of the conduit and involves writing data (primitive types and strings). The PrintWriter class has methods that accept such data and convert it to a character stream. Hence, a double such as 3.75 is converted from its internal 8-byte representation to the following 4-character sequence: "3.75". The character stream must be converted to a byte stream because all I/O devices expect bytes. Hence, we need a character-to-byte bridge that plays the opposite role of a reader. Such a class is called, in the context of streams, a **writer**. Finally, we need a stream that takes bytes from the writer and delivers them to the file, and that is the role of the FileOutputStream class.

Delegation to the above aggregation chain works, but it is inefficient because the overhead incurred by the writer is expended per character. For example, the writer program may start by loading a Unicode table,

determining the encoding based on the computer's locale (country and language) and similar preparatory tasks. These tasks take time, and it would be better to amortize this time by asking the writer to convert a whole string of characters at a time rather than one character at a time. That is why Fig. 8.10 introduces a buffer before the writer. The entire chain can be instantiated in one statement:

```
PrintWriter filer = new PrintWriter(
    new BufferedWriter(
        new OutputStreamWriter(
            new FileOutputStream(
                filename))));
```

The overall conduit is depicted with a plumbing analogy in Fig. 8.11.

All streams are auto-closed when a program ends gracefully (i.e., without a runtime error), but since I/O devices are prone to errors, it is a good habit to always close a stream once we are done with it. Closing an output stream will not only free resources, but will also **flush** the buffer; that is, write any data still in it to the

Figure 8.11 Data
of any type is
converted to a
character stream
by the print
writer and fed to
the buffer. A
writer converts it
to bytes and
feeds the byte
stream connected
to the file.

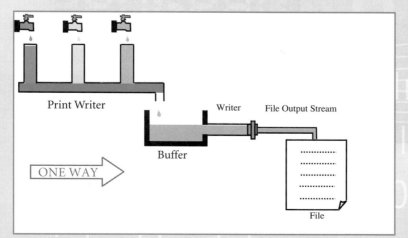

file. You can see from Fig. 8.11 that "water" cannot reach the writer until enough of it is in the buffer. Flushing the buffer acts like a pump that empties the buffer.

Thanks to aggregation, I/O in the Java standard library is remarkably flexible. The involved classes behave as building blocks that can be arranged in a variety of ways in order to solve the problem at hand. Our discussion focused on text I/O, but once you become comfortable with the notion of building a conduit by attaching I/O classes, you will find it straightforward to handle other types of I/O, including binary I/O (covered in the exercises of this chapter) and object I/O (covered in Chapter 9).

Java Details   8.1

The `FileReader` Class

As a matter of convenience, Java provides a class that hides the creation of a reader that aggregates a file input stream. Instead of creating

```
InputStreamReader reader = new InputStreamReader(
    new FileInputStream(filename));
```

you can create

```
FileReader fReader = new FileReader(filename);
```

You still need to wrap a buffer around this because like all readers, the file reader cannot read lines, only character by character.

In More Depth   8.2

Why Are Streams Not Compositions?

Since we like to wrap the byte stream in a reader and wrap the reader in a buffer, the Java standard library could have been designed to do this wrapping behind the scenes by using compositions. If it did, all we would have needed to do is instantiate the buffer, and it would internally create whatever parts it needs.

The reason streams are not compositions is flexibility. The fact that we are aware of the individual layers, and have references to each, means that we can communicate with any layer, not just the top one. If we want to read raw bytes from a file, perhaps because it contains a picture, then we do so by invoking methods directly on the stream. Similarly, we may want to communicate directly with the reader in applications that process the data one character at a time.

8.1.6 CASE STUDY

Graphics

All the applications that we have developed so far are console applications in which the output is character-based; that is, the smallest element in it is the character. To draw graphics (lines, rectangles, shapes, etc.), we need to work at a lower level, one whose smallest element is the so-called **picture element**, or **pixel**. To put things in perspective, keep in mind that in a typical resolution, a line on the screen contains less than 100 characters but over 1000 pixels.

Non-console applications, also called **GUI apps**, use a window on the screen to interact with their users. That window is called the **frame** and is implemented in a class called JFrame in the javax.swing package. This class represents the pinnacle of delegation because it is the root of many aggregation chains. One of these chains is shown in Fig. 8.12.

One of the parts aggregated in a frame is a container called the **content pane**. The aggregation is a composition: the pane is automatically created by the frame. The frame provides an accessor for the aggregated content pane. Hence we can write

```
JFrame frame = new JFrame("My
    Frame");
Container content =
    frame.getContentPane();
```

The obtained part is itself an aggregate of parts; in fact, it is a collection. Its add method allows us to add a part of the type Component. As we will see in Chapter 9, this is a rather generic type that can be substituted for by a number of types. As shown in the figure, the type we are interested in is UniPanel (from type.lib), so we create an instance of it and add it as follows:

```
UniPanel panel = new UniPanel();
content.add(panel);
```

As shown in the figure, the panel is itself a composition; creating it auto-creates within it an instance of Graphics2D. This is, finally, what we set out to find so that we can draw graphics: each instance of this class can be thought of as a canvas on which we can draw. In summary, we draw graphics on a canvas that is attached to a panel that is affixed to the content pane of a frame. Given a canvas, we can draw geometrical shapes, display images, and even write text. The three parts aggregated within Graphics2D allow you to control the colour, stroke (thickness of the brush), and font. The details are covered in the Labs starting with Lab 8.

In More Depth 8.3

Why Are the Read/Write Buffers Not Symmetric?

At first glance, buffering in input and output streams is symmetric because both streams involve a buffer between the byte stream and the program. If you take into account the direction of data movement, however, you will see that the two buffers do not correspond. The input buffer, for example, does not amortize the overhead of converting bytes to characters because it is placed after the reader.

The reason for this difference is that a buffer is needed between a fast stream and a slow stream. The rates at which programs can generate output or read input is much higher than the rate at which files can write or read. By placing the buffer next to the program, we ensure it will not be slowed down because of a slow operation in the chain.

Java Details   8.2

The `FileWriter` Class

As a matter of convenience, Java provides a class that hides the creation of a writer that aggregates a file output stream. Instead of creating

```
OutputStreamWriter writer = new OutputStreamWriter(
    new FileOutputStream(filename));
```

you can create

```
FileWriter fWriter = new FileWriter(filename);
```

You still need to wrap a buffer around the writer to facilitate line output and wrap a printwriter around the buffer to facilitate the output of non-character data.

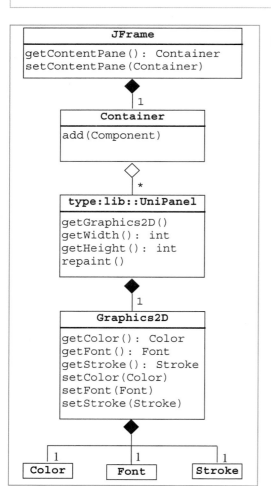

Figure 8.12 Aggregations for drawing graphics

◾ 8.2 Working with Collections

We saw in Section 8.1.1 that a collection is an aggregate in which the multiplicity is variable and in which the aggregated parts are called elements. The fact that the number of elements is variable requires a special API to enable clients to add or remove elements on demand, browse through all the elements, or search for particular elements. These operations are explored in the following sections.

8.2.1 Creating the Collection

The constructor of a collection cannot expect the caller to pass the elements in one shot as parameters because their number can change after the collection is created. This leaves the API with only one option: provide a constructor that creates an empty collection, and provide a method that enables adding elements after the collection is created.

Note that a collection may also provide constructors that allow the caller to specify the initial content of the collection by passing a reference to another collection. Such overloaded constructors are for convenience only and do not change our general observation that the constructor of a collection creates an empty one.

The fact that the multiplicity is variable places a challenge on the implementer of the collection class: should a large block of memory be reserved ahead of time for all the elements, or should memory be allocated when needed? A tradeoff between convenience and efficiency exists here: if a collection allocates memory all at once, the app must estimate the needed capacity and pass it to the constructor. This is called **static allocation** ("static" here means unchanging and is not related to `static` features). On the other hand, if memory is allocated as needed, which is called **dynamic allocation**, the app does not have to pass the capacity because the collection can grow and shrink as the application runs. Figure 8.13 shows the constructors of two collections.

The first constructor is for `Portfolio`, and we can see that it is a statically allocated collection. Recall that this class is a collection of investments and that each investment represents a stock investment, an aggregation of a stock, a quantity, and a cost.

The second constructor is for `GlobalCredit`, a dynamically allocated collection of `CreditCard` objects. You can think of this collection as an encapsulation of a bank, the Global Credit Bank, which issues credit cards. Whenever a credit card instance is created, the instance is added to the collection so that the bank can keep track of it.

Understanding the role of the constructor enables you to see the rationale behind the API design of aggregates. For example, you can see that `StringBuffer` is simply a collection of characters whose default constructor creates an empty collection but whose `append` / `insert` methods allow adding elements after creation. The `String` class is also a collection of characters, but one that cannot change after creation. Its constructor reflects this by expecting a collection (`String` or `StringBuffer`) to be passed.

8.2.2 Adding/Removing Elements

A collection must provide a method for inserting elements; this method is often called `add`. When a component is to be added, two issues can arise:

- **The collection is full** A full collection applies only to statically allocated collections that cannot grow automatically. In this case, the `add` method must indicate to the caller that it failed. This is usually done by making it a `boolean` method and returning `false`.

Figure 8.13 The constructor of a collection neither refers to components nor creates them internally. They are added on demand using a method.

Constructor Summary — Portfolio
`Portfolio(java.lang.String title, int capacity)`
Construct an empty portfolio with the passed name, capable of holding the specified number of investments.

Constructor Summary — GlobalCredit
`GlobalCredit()`
Construct a GC processing centre with the name "NoName".

■ **The element is already present** This occurs when the same element is inserted a second time. By "same," we mean the `equals` method would return `true` for these two elements. In some contexts, known abstractly as **list collections**, it is permissible to have duplicates so the repeated element is added as usual. In others, known abstractly as **set collections**, the elements must be distinct so `add` must not insert and must return `false`.

We therefore conclude that `add` is `void` for list-based, dynamically allocated collections and is `boolean` for set-based or statically allocated ones.

Figure 8.14 shows a partial API for the two collections of the previous section.

In both, the `add` method is a `boolean` method but for two different reasons. The first reason is that `Portfolio` has a fixed capacity, so its `add` must return `false` if there is no room to add more investments. The return is `true` otherwise; in particular, the class does not mind if the same investment is added repeatedly.

The second reason is that `GlobalCredit` does not have a capacity problem, but it cannot tolerate duplicates, so its `add` must return `false` if a credit card with the same number as the passed one already exists in the collection. The return is `true` otherwise.

As an example, let us write code to read several investments from the user and add them to a portfolio object. As shown in Fig. 8.15, the fragment starts by asking the user how many investments are involved. This is important since `Portfolio` allocates memory statically. It then asks the user to enter the three attributes of each investment. Once the investment object is created, it is added to the portfolio.

Note that since all investment-related variables are declared in the loop body, their lifetimes are limited to one loop iteration. A stock instance created in any particular iteration will have no reference (in the app) pointing at it after the iteration is over. This instance will not be lost to the garbage collector, however, because the `add` method will force an attribute in the collection to point at it. In general, even though the app is responsible for creating elements, it is the collection that keeps them alive. The fragment is rewritten in an equivalent way in Fig. 8.16 to better expose the fact that the app does not need to keep track of the elements it creates and that the collection is their ultimate owner.

Figure 8.14 The `add` method in `Portfolio`, a static, list-based collection, and in `GlobalCredit`, a dynamic, set-based collection

Method Summary - Portfolio	
boolean	**add**(Investment inv) Attempt to add the passed investment to this portfolio.

Method Summary - GlobalCredit	
boolean	**add**(CreditCard card) Attempt to add the passed credit card to this GCC.

```
output.print("How many investments? ");
int count = input.nextInt();
Portfolio pf = new Portfolio("MySavingPlan", count);
for (int i = 0; i < count; i++)
{
    output.println("Enter stock symbol, number of shares, ");
    output.println("and purchase price per share [press ");
    output.println("ENTER after each]:");
    String symbol = input.next();
    Stock stock = new Stock(symbol);
    int qty = input.nextInt();
    double cost = input.nextDouble();
    Investment inv = new Investment(stock, qty, cost);
    pf.add(inv);
}
output.println("Portfolio created.");
```

Figure 8.15 This fragment creates a portfolio and populates it by several investments.

As a final example of element addition, let us create a GlobalCredit collection. This is a dynamically allocated collection; hence, we can create and add elements without worrying about capacity. The fragment in Fig. 8.17 performs this by creating a collection instance and then entering a loop.

In each iteration, and after ensuring the entered card number is not the sentinel, the fragment creates a credit card object with the entered number and the cardholder name "Eve." The created object is passed on the fly to the add method of the collection as done in Fig. 8.16 for the Portfolio class.

The fragment ends with a message that confirms the exit from the loop. It also displays the number of cards added to the collection as returned by a method, size, which will be explained in the next section.

Figure 8.16 The code of Fig. 8.15 is rewritten to better expose ownership.

```
output.print("How many investments? ");
int count = input.nextInt();
Portfolio pf = new Portfolio("MySavingPlan", count);
for (int i = 0; i < count; i++)
{
    output.println("Enter stock symbol, number of shares, ");
    output.println("and purchase price per share pressing ");
    output.println("ENTER after each.");
    pf.add
    (   new Investment(new Stock(input.next()),
                        input.nextInt(),
                        input.nextDouble())
    );
}
output.println("Portfolio created.");
```

8.2.3 Indexed Traversals

Given a reference to a collection, how do you traverse its elements? A **traversal** can be thought of as a trip that visits each element once and only once; that is, no element is missed and no element is visited twice or more. We cannot expect the collection to provide an accessor per element, as is done for a non-collection aggregate, because the elements have no names and their number changes. Instead, collections support traversals through one of two approaches: indexed traversal and iterator-based traversal. We look at indexed traversal below and iterator-based traversal in Section 8.2.4.

Indexed traversal allows you to think of the elements as if they are numbered. The element number is called its **index**, and the index is zero-based. These numbers do not necessarily reflect the adding order (i.e., element 0 may not be the one first added); all that we require here is a one-to-one mapping between the elements and a set of consecutive integers starting with 0. Using this approach, access is made easier using two methods.

- **public int size()** This method, an accessor, returns the number of elements in the collection. If the return is zero, then the collection is empty. The index of any element in the collection is always in [0, size()). Notice that the interval is closed-open.
- **public _type_ get(int index)** This method, an accessor, returns a reference to the element with the passed index. The return has the same type, type, as the element. The passed index must of course be in the above closed-open interval. Some collections treat this as a precondition; others check it and throw an exception or return null if it is not met.

Using these two methods, we can traverse a collection bag by a loop like this:

```
for (int i = 0; i < bag.size(); i++)
{
    e = bag.get(i)
    // visit element e
}
```

The loop is based on the number of elements, as returned by the size method. If the collection is empty, the return is zero and the loop will be skipped. Otherwise, the loop will iterate as many times as there are elements.

As an example, let us use this approach to generate a report listing the contents of a given portfolio. We can use the fragment of Fig. 8.16 to create the portfolio and populate it, but to allow faster testing, we use the getRandom method as a test suite. A code fragment that implements these ideas is depicted in Fig. 8.18.

Figure 8.17 This fragment creates a gcc and populates it by several credit cards.

```
GlobalCredit gcc = new GlobalCredit();
output.print("Credit card number [0 to quit]: ");
for (int cardNo = input.nextInt(); cardNo != 0;
            cardNo = input.nextInt())
{
    gcc.add(new CreditCard(cardNo, "Eve"));
    output.print("Credit card number [0 to quit]: ");
}
output.println("GCC created. Size = " + gcc.size());
```

```
Portfolio pf = Portfolio.getRandom();

for (int i = 0; i < pf.size(); i++)
{
    output.print(pf.get(i).getStock().getSymbol() + "\t");
    output.print(pf.get(i).getQty() + "\t");
    output.printf("%.2f%n", pf.get(i).getBookValue());
}
```

Figure 8.18 A fragment that uses indexed traversal to browse a collection

8.2.4 Iterator-Based Traversal

This traversal provides a higher level of abstraction than indexed traversal. You don't have to associate an integer with each element or worry about the index becoming out of range. You don't even think about element order or which element comes first or last. The only thing you require is that the traversal must visit all elements without missing one and without visiting the same element more than once.

To support this abstract traversal, an enhanced `for` loop is used. Using it, we can traverse the `bag` collection of the previous section as follows (`E` is the type of the elements):

```
for (E e : bag)
{
    // visit element e
}
```

Note that the `Portfolio` class provides both types of access, indexed and iterator-based. Figure 8.19 uses this approach to generate a report similar to the one in Fig. 8.18. We will see in Chapter 10 that collections that represent lists (duplicate elements allowed) generally provide both types of access, and the retrieval order is the same in both (being the order in which elements are added). On the other hand, collections that represent sets (no duplicates) provide only iterator-based access with an indeterminate retrieval order.

Figure 8.19 A fragment that uses iterator-based traversal to browse a collection

```
Portfolio pf = Portfolio.getRandom();

for(Investment inv : pf)
{
    output.print(inv.getStock().getSymbol() + "\t");
    output.print(inv.getQty() + "\t");
    output.printf("%.2f\n", inv.getBookValue());
}
```

To determine if a class supports iterator-based traversal, look at the top of its API and see if it implements the `Iterable` interface.

8.2.5 Searching

Consider the problem of determining whether a given collection contains an element with a given property. For example, determine whether a portfolio contains an investment with a given stock symbol or whether a Global Credit instance contains a credit card with a given number. This problem is called **search**. A search either fails, if the sought element is not found, or succeeds, in which case it culminates in a reference to the sought element. Note that it is possible for more than one element to satisfy the search condition.

Search can be implemented by adapting either of the traversals of the previous two sections. Whenever we visit an element, we check to see if it is the one we are looking for. Here is a first attempt to search for the instance `"given"` using iterator-based traversal:

```
found = false;
for (E e : bag)
{
    found = e.equals(given);
}
```

The problem with this loop is that if it ends with `found` being `true`, then the search will have succeeded, but if it ends with it being `false`, then we cannot draw any conclusion. This is because the final value of `found` is determined by the last iteration, not by the cumulative findings of all iterations. In other words, this loop is wrong because it does not have a loop invariant (Section 5.2.3) that involves `found`. What we want is for the value of `"found"` to match the true/false value of the sentence

```
"given is one of the elements visited thus far"
```

at the end of *every* iteration. To that end, we rewrite the statement in the body so that the findings of earlier iterations are not forgotten:

```
found = found || e.equals(given);
```

This way, if `found` became `true` at any iteration, it will remain true in all future iterations.

The advantage of designing loops with an invariant is that not only can you see that the loop is correct, you can also prove that it is. (For the mathematically minded, the proof is based on mathematical induction on the number of iterations in the loop.)

Based on the above, the correct iterator-based search becomes:

```
found = false;
for (E e : bag)
{
    found = found || e.equals(given);
}
```

Iterator-based search can be modified to also obtain a reference to an element in the collection that matches the given instance (if any). This is pursued in Example 8.5 using the enhanced for loop and also in Chapter 10 using the iterator object.

Search can also be implemented via an indexed traversal. Since this traversal relies on the ordinary for loop (which allows us to set the exit condition), we can construct the loop so that it exits when the traversal ends or upon encountering a match, whichever occurs first (note that the enhanced for loop, alas, does not provide this flexibility):

```
found = false;
E lastVisited = null;
for (int i = 0; i < bag.size() && !found; i++)
```

```
        {
            lastVisited = bag.get(i);
            found = lastVisited.equals(given);
        }
```

The search culminates in a boolean, as before, and a reference to the last visited element in the collection before the loop exited.

Example 8.5

Write a program that uses the getRandom method of the GlobalCredit class to generate a collection of randomly created credit cards. It should then prompt the user to enter a card number and determine whether the card is in the collection. If it is, its balance must be displayed; otherwise a message must be printed.

To verify the correctness of the search, it would be helpful if the program started by displaying a list of all cards in the collection, one card per line. Display the number and the balance of the card separated by a tab.

Answer:

The program is shown in Fig. 8.20.

Since this listing is for debugging purposes only, we surround it by braces so that it has a scope of its own. This way, it can be later commented out or deleted without affecting subsequent declarations.

8.2.6 Search Complexity

Traversal-based search is an **exhaustive** search because you test each and every element until you find what you are looking for, in other words, you exhaust all the elements. The complexity of a search is defined as the number of tests it must perform in the worst case before it can reach a conclusion. If the collection has N elements, then the complexity of exhaustive search is clearly N because if the element you are looking for is not in the collection, or it happens to be the last in retrieval order, then you need to make N tests before you can reach any conclusion. Using the so-called **big-O** notion, the complexity of exhaustive search is said to be O(N). And since the complexity of exhaustive search is a linear function of the number of elements, it is sometimes referred to as **linear** search.

Complexity does not measure the actual execution time of a program, but it tells us how the execution time depends on N, the size of the problem at hand. Hence, we can say that the execution time of an O(N) program doubles if N doubles. Some algorithms do not depend on the size of the problem, and these are said to have a complexity of O(1). Others have complexities that grow sublinearly, like O(logN), or faster than linear, like $O(N^2)$, $O(N^3)$, or even O(N!). For large values of N, it can be shown that the execution time T of a program with complexity O(f(N)) is given by

```
GlobalCredit gcc = GlobalCredit.getRandom();
//------------------------------------------List all:
{
    for (CreditCard c : gcc)
    {
        output.print(c.getNumber() + "\t");
        output.printf("%.2f%n", c.getBalance());
    }
}
//----------------------------------------Search:
output.println("Enter the card number to look for: ");
String cardNo = input.nextLine();
CreditCard lastVisited = null;
boolean found = false;
for (CreditCard cc : gcc)
{
    found = found || cc.getNumber().equals(cardNo);
    if (cc.getNumber().equals(cardNo)) lastVisited = cc;
}
if (!found)
{
    output.println("No such card!");
}
else
{
    output.print("Card found. Its balance is: ");
    output.printf("%.2f%n", lastVisited.getBalance());
}
```

Figure 8.20 After generating a listing of the contents of a randomly generated collection of credit cards, this fragment uses iterator-based traversal to search for a user-entered card number.

$$T \approx \alpha\ f(N)$$

where α is a proportionality constant. This allows us to predict the execution time at N_1, given its value at N_2 (both must be large). For example, if an $O(N^2)$ program runs in 5 s when N is 1000, then we can compute how long it will take to run when N is 2000 as follows: since the complexity is quadratic, we can write (for large N)

$$T(N) \approx \alpha\ N^2$$

Applying this to $N = 1000$ and $N = 2000$ and taking the ratio yields

$$T(2000)\ /\ T(1000) \approx (2000)^2\ /\ (1000)^2 \approx 4$$

Hence, this program will take approximately 20 s to run if N is 2000.

It is not surprising that the complexity of exhaustive search is linear. Imagine that you were given a bag of N credit cards and were asked to look for a particular one. Can you do so without looking at each and every one of them in the worst case? The answer is no. Can you imagine a special setup that allows you to perform the search faster than O(N) in the worst case? Here are two ideas:

1. If the cards are stacked such that their numbers are ordered, for example, cards with smaller numbers are on top, then we do not need to look at all the cards, even in the worst case.
2. If the cards are placed, say, on the floor, such that those whose numbers end with 0, 1, or 2 are next to the east wall, those whose numbers end with 3, 4, or 5 are next to the north wall, and so on, then, given a number to look for, you no longer need to look through all the cards.

These observations imply that if a collection organized its elements in some sophisticated way, then it is possible to search it with a sublinear complexity if the search benefited from the organization of the elements. We, the client, cannot benefit from this because such an organization is internal, and it would break the encapsulation if the implementer told us about it. Hence, such collections must provide a search method in their APIs, one that is aware of how the elements are arranged internally.

The `GlobalCredit` class is one such collection, and we will see many more in Chapter 10. It provides the method

```
public CreditCard get(String number)
```

This method determines whether a credit card with the passed number is present in the collection. If so, it returns a reference to it; otherwise it returns `null`. Do not confuse this `get(String)` method with the earlier `getFirst()` and `getNext()` methods. This is a search method that looks for an element with a given attribute; the earlier methods are simply accessors.

Example 8.6

Rewrite the search program in Example 8.5 so that it benefits from the search method provided in the API of the `GlobalCredit` class.

Answer:
The needed modifications are shown in Fig. 8.21.

Figure 8.21 The search part of Fig. 8.20 is rewritten to benefit from the built-in search method.

```
//------------------------------------------------Search:
output.println("Enter the card number to look for: ");
CreditCard card = gcc.get(input.nextLine());
if (card == null)
{
        output.println("No such card!");
}
else
{
    output.print("Card found. Its balance is: ");
    output.printf("%.2f%n", card.getBalance());
}
```

Summary of Key Concepts

1. An **aggregate** is a class that has at least one attribute whose type is neither primitive nor `String`. The type of that attribute is called the aggregated part.

2. The aggregate and the aggregated part are said to have an **aggregation**, or a **has-a** relationship. It resembles the **whole-part relationship** between real objects.

3. The **multiplicity** of an aggregation is the number of attributes in the aggregate that have the aggregated type. It is written next to the aggregated part in UML.

4. If the aggregate and the aggregated part have coincident lifetimes, the aggregation becomes known as a **composition**. This is implemented by having the aggregate's constructor create the part rather than having the client create it and pass it.

5. An aggregate must provide an **accessor** for each aggregated part. It returns a reference to the part itself or a copy of it, depending on whether this is a general aggregation or a composition. The aggregate may provide a **mutator** to enable changing the part.

6. **Aggregate cloning** refers to making a copy of a given aggregate reference. It can be done by **aliasing, shallow copying**, or **deep copying**.

7. During I/O operations, data travels either in an **input stream** from a **data source** (e.g., the keyboard or a disk file) to the program or in an **output stream** from the program to a **data sink** (e.g., the screen or a disk file).

8. An input stream connected to the keyboard is called **standard input**. An output stream connected to the screen is called **standard output**.

9. A **reader** is a stream that translates bytes to characters. A **writer** is one that translates characters to bytes. Both work by using a character-set mapping (user-defined or the platform's default).

10. A **buffer** is a stream that can hold data; hence, it can connect streams of different widths. On input, a buffer is used to enable programs to read line by line. On output, a buffer is used to amortize the overhead incurred by the writer.

11. At the end of any stream operation, the input or output stream must be closed to free resources and to **flush** buffers.

12. In a **GUI (graphical user interface)** program, the program interacts with its user through a screen window rather than through a text console. Graphics requires GUI because it works with **pixels (picture elements)** rather than characters.

13. We draw graphics on a canvas that is attached to a panel, and the panel is affixed on the content pane of a frame. The classes form an aggregation chain.

14. If the multiplicity can change as the program runs, that is, parts can be added or removed dynamically, then it is denoted by an **asterisk** in UML. In that case, the aggregate is called a **collection** (or a **container**), and the part is called an **element**.

15. Collections use either **dynamic** or **static allocation**. In the case of dynamic allocation, they can grow without bounds, while in the case of static allocation, the client has to specify a capacity (maximum number of parts) when the collection is created.

16. **List** collections allow duplicates; **set** collections do not.

17. **Traversal** means visiting each element in a collection once and only once. An API that supports an **indexed traversal** provides two methods (`size` and `get`) to enable traversal as if the elements are numbered (the index is zero-based).

18. A class that implements the `Iterable` interface supports **iterator-based** traversals. You can use the enhanced for loop to visit each element aggregated by the class.

19. **Search** refers to establishing whether a given instance is present in a collection. **Exhaustive** search examines all the elements of the collection in the worst case.

20. The **complexity** of a search refers to the number of comparisons that it makes (e.g., invocations of `equals`) in the worst case as it searches a collection of N elements. It is expressed using **big-O** notation. Exhaustive search is **linear**; its complexity is O(N). Some collections come with a sublinear search method.

21. If the number of elements in a collection N is large, then the ratio of the execution times of a search program for two values of N is approximately equal to the ratio of the complexities at these values of N.

Review Questions

1. Every instance of the `Fraction` class has a `long` numerator. Yet we do not call the relation between `Fraction` and the `long` type an aggregation. Why not?

2. A UML diagram shows two classes, A and B, and a solid line connecting them with an unfilled diamond at the A end and the number 3 at the B end. Which class is the aggregate? Is it a collection? What can be said about the number/type of attributes in the aggregate? Is this a composition?

3. Who creates instances of the aggregated parts in a composition? Justify your answer.

4. It is said that the accessor to a part in a composition should not return a reference to the actual part instance but to a copy of it. Explain why not by showing that if it did, then it would violate the coincident death condition of compositions.

5. What is the role of a mutator in an aggregate?

6. Explain the meaning of "aliasing an object."

7. Given an instance of an aggregate, suppose that someone copied the block it occupies in memory, bit by bit, to a new block. Argue that the new block would be a shallow copy of the aggregate, not a deep one.

8. Given two instances of a class whose attributes are all public, how can you determine whether one instance is a shallow copy of the other?

9. What is the name of the class that represents a stream connected to the keyboard? How do you obtain an instance of it?

10. A software engineering guideline recommends that all attributes be private unless they are final. Are the `"in"` and `"out"` fields of the `System` class final? Do not rely on the letter case; check the detailed API.

11. Is it possible for a program to read keyboard input directly from the input stream?

12. Is it possible for a program to read keyboard input directly from a reader?

13. Why is it important to close an input stream after reading from it?

14. Closing an output stream will auto-flush. What does that mean?

15. The API of a method indicates that it blocks if no characters are available. What does that mean?

16. What is the job of a writer in an output operation?

17. How is screen resolution related to pixels?

18. An instance of a particular class acts like a canvas on which we can draw. What is the name of that class?

19. What does variable multiplicity mean, and how is it depicted in UML?

20. If a collection is statically allocated, then what should be passed to its constructor?

21. Can you add an element to a collection even if it is already in it?

22. What happens if you attempt to add an element to a full, statically allocated collection?

23. What is a traversal?

24. How do you determine the number of elements in a collection if it supports indexed traversals?

25. How do you determine the number of elements in a collection if it supports iterator-based traversals?

26. (a) Explain how a traversal can be used to perform a search. (b) Why are traversal-based searches called exhaustive?

27. Explain the statement, "For complexity purposes, an unsuccessful search represents the worst case."

28. A linear search takes 5 s in the worst case on a collection of 5000 elements. How long will it take in the worst case on a collection of 20 000 elements?

29. Repeat question 28 but for a search algorithm with $O(\sqrt{N})$ complexity.

30. Repeat question 29 but for a search algorithm with $O(\lg N)$ complexity. In computing, the symbol "lg" refers to the base 2 logarithm.

L8.1 Date-Calendar Composition

The `Date` class in `java.util` is a simple class that encapsulates an instant of time. It defines this instant as the number of milliseconds that have elapsed since midnight January 1, 1970 GMT (called the **epoch**). As such, it has a simple API consisting mainly of the following:

- `Date()` This default constructor creates an instance corresponding to the instant at which the constructor was invoked.

- `long getTime()` and `void setTime(long ms)` These two methods allow you to access or mutate the encapsulated number of milliseconds (stored as a `long`). Note that if you pass `ms` as negative, the time will be before the epoch.

- `toString` This method returns the following textual representation of the encapsulated number:

      dow mon dd hh:mm:ss zzz yyyy

  where `dow` is the day name (3 letters), `mon` is the month name (3 letters), `dd` is the date (ranges between 1 and 31), `hh:mm:ss` is the time, `zzz` is the time zone, and `yyyy` is the year.

1. Launch your editor, and write the program `Lab8` that creates a `Date` instance `dt` using the default constructor and outputs the return of its `toString` method. (Depending on the local time zone, the shown time zone may indicate daylight-saving time.)
2. Mutate `dt` so that it represents an instant that is 5 min ago. This requires that you first retrieve the current millisecond count since the epoch and then subtract from it 5 min (expressed in milliseconds). Print the `toString` return to confirm.
3. Mutate `dt` one more time, and set it to 5 min before the epoch. Note that this does not require fetching the current millisecond count. Print the `toString` return. Note that the epoch is defined relative to GMT, not necessarily to your local zone.

The `Date` class does a very good job maintaining the date (and time) as a millisecond count, but as you must have noticed above, its mutator is not very useful because we, humans, do not think in terms of milliseconds. We think in terms of calendar and time. Instead of specifying a `long`, we would rather specify a date and a time.

Converting a millisecond count to a calendar, however, is calendar-dependent. Different cultures adopt different calendars, and the time zone may differ from one place to another in the same country. Hence, incorporating calendars is not something simple that can be added to the `Date` class; it requires a class of its own. The `Calendar` class represents a higher-level abstraction that "speaks" with us in the language of date and time, but behind the scene, it speaks to Date in the language of milliseconds. As shown in Fig. 8.22, it implements this layered abstraction through an aggregation: one of the attributes of Calendar is a Date object. And since a calendar is meaningless without a date, the aggregation is a composition, and the date attribute is auto-created when the calendar is created.

Calendar provides an accessor and a mutator for the aggregated Date attribute (do not confuse them with the similarly named ones in the Date class):

■ Date getTime() This method returns a copy of the aggregated instance.

■ void setTime(Date time) This method mutates the aggregated instance.

To create a Calendar class instance, the class provides static methods (in lieu of a constructor):

■ static Calendar getInstance() This method returns a calendar instance for the computer's locale and time zone.

■ static Calendar getInstance(TimeZone t, Locale l) This method returns a calendar instance customized for the passed locale and time zone.

The first is typically used unless you want to create a calendar that is different from your machine's default.

The main methods in the Calendar API allow us to express and manipulate date/time values. They include the following:

■ void add(int field, int amount) This method increases the indicated field by the indicated amount.

■ int get(int field) This method returns the value of the indicated field.

■ void set(int field, int value) This method mutates the indicated field, making it equal to the indicated value.

These methods refer to an integer field code, and these codes are listed as final fields in the class API. The most commonly used codes are listed in Fig. 8.23. Note that while the month number is zero-based, the day number is one-based.

4. Add the following lines to your Lab8 (after the ones created earlier):

Figure 8.22 The Calendar-Date composition

```
Calendar cal = Calendar.getInstance();
dt = cal.getTime();
output.println(dt);
dt.setTime(0);
output.println(cal.getTime());
```

After retrieving the aggregated attribute, we mutated it back to the epoch. Nevertheless, the attribute inside the calendar did not change. Why?

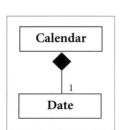

Figure 8.23
Some of the commonly used constants (final fields) in Calendar

DAY_OF_MONTH *(1=first)*	HOUR_OF_DAY	MILLISECONDS
DAY_OF_WEEK *(1=Sunday)*	MINUTE	MONTH *(0=Jan)*
ZONE_OFFSET *(from GMT)*	SECOND	YEAR

5. Add the following lines to your Lab8 (after the ones added earlier):

```
cal.add(Calendar.MONTH, 1);
output.println(cal.getTime());
```

Explain the output.

6. Add the following lines to your Lab8 (after the ones added earlier):

```
cal.add(Calendar.DAY_OF_MONTH, 60);
output.println(cal.getTime());
```

Explain the output.

7. Add the following lines to your Lab8 (after the ones added earlier):

```
cal.set(Calendar.YEAR, 1956);
cal.set(Calendar.MONTH, 8);
cal.set(Calendar.DAY_OF_MONTH, 14);
output.println(cal.getTime());
output.println(cal.get(Calendar.HOUR_OF_DAY));
```

Note that 8 means September, not August. Note also that if you do not set a field, it retains its old value (the time fields were not set above).

8. Add the following lines to your Lab8 (after the ones added earlier):

```
TimeZone tz;
tz = TimeZone.getTimeZone("Japanese Standard Time");
Calendar calOther = Calendar.getInstance(tz,
    Locale.JAPAN);
output.println(calOther.getTime());
output.println(calOther.get(Calendar.HOUR_OF_DAY));
```

Note how the aggregated date attribute is incapable of recognizing other time zones, whereas the calendar (the last output) expressed the hour in Japan's local time.

L8.2 The Graphics Aggregations

Graphics represents perhaps the ultimate in layered abstraction. Drawing requires a brush, and someone must take care of the brush's stroke (thickness) and colour. Drawing can be freeform, but it often involves regular geometrical shapes, such as lines and rectangles. Hence, someone must take care of these basic shapes. Sometimes, drawing involves text, and this raises issues such as font and style, so we need someone to take care of that. When a program draws something, it draws it on a virtual screen, not on the real one, because there is no guarantee that the screen size and resolution are the same for every user. Hence, we need someone to manage the transformation from the virtual to the actual device coordinates when the program runs. Finally, the drawing must appear in some window on the screen, and someone must manage the appearance, movement, and state of that window. We will see that aggregation plays a central role in implementing these delegations.

Let us create the aggregate shown in Fig. 8.12 step by step:

1. Launch your editor, and create the program `Paint` that creates a frame:

```
JFrame frame = new JFrame("My Frame");
frame.setDefaultCloseOperation(JFrame.DISPOSE_ON_CLOSE);
frame.setVisible(true);
frame.pack();
```

Make sure you import the needed package. The second statement mutates the frame so that it closes (and is deleted) when the user clicks on its close button. By default, the constructor creates the frame as invisible, which is why we used another mutator in the third statement. The last statement determines the appropriate initial size of the frame (based on its contents) and displays it.

Run the program, and verify that it creates a frame. Notice that since our frame is currently empty, it is rendered in a very compact size. Use the mouse to stretch it and experiment with minimizing and maximizing it. If you prefer the initial displayed frame to be not so compact, replace the last statement above with the following:

```
frame.setSize(400, 300);
```

This sets the initial size to 400 pixels across by 300 down.

2. The created frame is in fact a composition. Creating it auto-created a container in it, one to which we can get a reference to through a mutator:

```
Container content = frame.getContentPane();
```

This aggregated attribute represents the back of the frame and is itself a collection. In other words, you can affix many things on the back of a frame. We are interested in affixing a panel, so we create one and add it to the above collection:

```
UniPanel panel = new UniPanel();
content.add(panel);
```

3. You can think of the panel as a piece of cardboard affixed to a frame. We can use two of its accessors (see Fig. 8.12) to display the resolution on the console:
```
output.println(panel.getWidth() + "x" +
panel.getHeight());
```

In fact, we should allow the user to adjust the size of the frame before we proceed so that we know exactly the size of the drawing area. Add the following lines:

```
output.println("Resize the frame then press ENTER");
input.nextLine();
int width = panel.getWidth();
int height = panel.getHeight();
output.println(width + "x" + height);
```

4. We do not draw directly on the panel; instead, we draw on a piece of canvas attached to it using a composition. Obtain a reference to this canvas:

```
Graphics2D canvas = panel.getGraphics2D();
```

This canvas instance is auto-created by the panel, and its size is the same as that of the panel.

5. Add the following lines to `Paint`:

```
output.print("Enter any text to draw... ");
String str = input.nextLine();
canvas.drawString(str, width / 3, height / 3);
panel.repaint();
```

The `drawString` method "draws" the string on the canvas at the specified position (the second and third parameters are the *x-y* coordinates). The coordinate system is such that the origin is in the upper-left corner of the canvas, the *x*-axis extends to the right, and the *y*-axis extends downward. The `repaint` method must be invoked to force the panel to redisplay its canvas.

The `Graphics2D` instance is itself an aggregate. It is made up of a `Color` instance that controls the colour of the brush, a `Font` instance that controls the font, style, and point size of written text, and a `BasicStroke` instance that controls the width of the brush. All three classes reside in `java.awt`. `Graphics2D` gives us full read/write access to these three elements using three accessor/mutator pairs:

- Colour `getColor()`, `setColor(Color c)`
- Font `getFont()`, `void setFont(Font f)`
- Stroke `getStroke()`, `void setStroke(Stroke s)`

6. Change the colour of the displayed string. You can use any of the ready-made colour objects in the `Color` class (see the fields in its API) or create your own colour.

7. The `Font` constructor takes three parameters: the font name, style, and point size. For example,

```
Font font = new Font("Serif", Font.ITALIC, 45);
```

Use this instance to change the font of the displayed string.

8. Add the following line to your program:

```
canvas.rotate(Math.PI * 30 / 180);
```

The `Graphics2D` class has many methods for transforming coordinates, for example, rotate, translate, and scale. These transformations do not affect existing drawings on the canvas, only future drawings. Hence, we must first invoke `rotate`, then draw the string, and then repaint the panel. Run the fragment and observe.

After the above steps, your frame will resemble the one shown in Fig. 8.24. We will revisit the graphics aggregates in Lab 9 and see how we can use them not only to draw text, but to draw shapes as well.

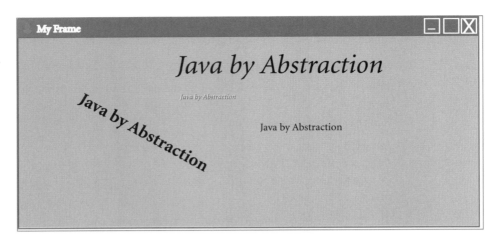

Figure 8.24 A snapshot of the canvas after performing the operations in the Lab

Exercises

Programming exercises are indicated with an asterisk.

8.1 Write a program that creates a credit card, then determine and output its expiry date. According to the API of the `CreditCard` class, the date should be two years from today.

8.2 Consider the following fragment:

```
CreditCard card = new CreditCard(1020, "Java");
Calendar cal = Calendar.getInstance();
cal.set(Calendar.YEAR, 2002);
output.println(card.setExpiryDate(cal.getTime()));
```

Predict the output and justify your answer.

8.3 Consider the following fragment:

```
CreditCard card = new CreditCard(1020, "Java");
Calendar cal = Calendar.getInstance();
cal.add(Calendar.SECOND, 2);
card.setExpiryDate(cal.getTime());
output.print("Press ENTER...");
input.nextLine();
output.println(card.charge(10));
```

The output of the fragment depends on how quickly the user presses ENTER when prompted. Explain.

8.4 Write a code fragment that takes two `Date` instances, `dt1` and `dt2`, and outputs the number of days between them rounded to the nearest day. Note that the output is negative if `dt1` occurs later than `dt2`. To test your program, create a `CreditCard` instance using any name and number, and compute the number of days between its issue and expiry dates.

8.5* Write a program that prompts for and reads the user's birth date and outputs the day name on which the user was born. The input is slash-delimited and is in the year/month/day format (day and month can be one or two digits). The output should be as shown in this sample run:

```
Enter your birth date [yyyy/mm/dd] 1985/10/29
You were born on a Tue
```

8.6* Write a program that outputs the date 1000 hours ago and the date 1000 hours from now. This should be a simple, five-line program.

8.7* Write a program that determines whether or not the `type.lib.Fresh` aggregate is a composition vis-à-vis the `Date` class.

8.8* Write a program that generates two random investments using the `getRandom` method of the `Investment` class. If the stocks aggregated in these two investments are different, then output the market and book values of each investment. Otherwise, amalgamate the two investments, and output the total market and book values. Note that the book (market) value of an investment is obtained by multiplying the book (market) value of its aggregated stock by the number of shares held in it.

8.9* Write a program that generates a random portfolio of investments using the `getRandom` method of the `Portfolio` class. Use indexed access to traverse the portfolio (visit all its elements), and output its total market value.

8.10* Write a program that generates a random portfolio of investments using the `getRandom` method of the `Portfolio` class. Use iterator-based access to traverse the portfolio, and determine which investment has the highest market value.

8.11* Write a program that generates a random portfolio of investments using the `getRandom` method of the `Portfolio` class. Use indexed traversal to output a table showing how much each investment contributes to the total market value of the portfolio. An example portfolio is shown in Fig. 8.25.

Let us assume that the current market prices of the stocks are $10 for A, $112 for B, and $26 for C. We thus conclude that the total market value of the three investments is $200, $1680, and $260, which means that $2140 is the total portfolio market value. In this case, the program's output must look like this:

```
A.....9%
B....79%
C....12%
```

Note that the percentages are without decimals, are followed by the percent sign, %, and are separated from the symbols by dots. Notice also that the percent signs are vertically aligned.

8.12* Write a program that generates a random portfolio of investments using the `getRandom` method of the `Portfolio` class. Use indexed traversal to output the

Figure 8.25 An example portfolio

Stock Symbol	Quantity	Book Value
A	20	12.5
B	15	100.00
C	10	25.00

investment whose stock has the highest *yield*. We define the yield of a stock as the percentage difference between its market and book values. For example, the yield of stock C in Exercise 8.7 is computed as follows:

```
Yield of C = (26 - 25) / 25 is 4%
```

The yields of the other two investments are −20% and +12%; hence, your program must output the second investment (with symbol B).

8.13* Write a program that generates a random collection of credit cards using the getRandom method of the GlobalCredit class and then uses its sublinear method, the get method, to search for a credit card with a user-entered number. Test your program entering the card number 123456-6. Your program should find it in the collection.

8.14* Write a program that reads input from the keyboard character by character in order to determine the character(s) used to represent the ENTER key. Note that you must not buffer the input.

8.15* Write a program that reads its own source file line by line and displays it on the screen.

8.16* Write a program that uses JFileChooser to prompt the user to select an existing file and display its contents 10 lines at a time.

8.17* Consider the fragment shown in the upper and middle panes of Fig. 8.26.
The upper pane connects a byte stream to the file, and the middle pane connects three additional streams culminating in a print writer.

(a) Argue that the size of the created file should be 7 bytes. Run the fragment, and verify the size using your operating system.

(b) Recall from Chapter 1 that a short variable occupies 2 bytes in memory and a byte variable occupies 1 byte. This implies an overall size of 3 bytes for our data. Explain the discrepancy between this size and the size mentioned in (a) (3 versus 7).

(c) The DataOutputStream class provides a stream that accepts primitive type data at one end and provides a byte stream at the other end. The bytes correspond to the internal binary representation of the data, not to its character representation. Write a program that uses this stream to generate the file (i.e., by removing the middle pane in Fig. 8.26), and verify that the size of the generated file is indeed 3 bytes.

Figure 8.26
This fragment contrasts text output with binary output.

```
short s = 1450;
byte b = 100;
FileOutputStream fos = new
FileOutputStream("test.txt");


OutputStreamWriter osw = new OutputStreamWriter(fos);
BufferedWriter bw = new BufferedWriter(osw);
PrintWriter pw = new PrintWriter(bw);
pw.print(s);
pw.print(b);
pw.close();


DataOutputStream dos = new DataOutputStream(fos);
dos.writeShort(s);
dos.writeByte(b);
dos.close();
```

8.18* Write a program that reads the contents of the binary file created in Exercise 8.17.

Hint: Use the DataInputStream class.

8.19* Suppose that the programmer who wrote the program for Exercise 8.18 made the following mistake: instead of reading a `short` and then a `byte`, the program invoked `readByte` twice. Argue that this will *not* lead to a runtime error. This implies that binary files can be read in many ways and that there is nothing in the file that allows us to identify the correct way of reading it.

8.20* Write a program that draws your name in a graphics panel using a monospaced font (e.g., Courier) in bold. The name must be displayed twice, once in magenta and once in dark magenta, and the program must output (on the text console) the RGB (red, green, blue) decompositions of these two colours.

   Hint: Use the `darker`, `getRed`, and similar methods in `Color`.

8.21* Consider the aggregation chain shown in Fig. 8.27.
   Use this chain to create a frame that has a menu bar with two drop-down menus: File and View. The file menu should contain two items: Open and Exit; and the view menu should contain one item: Arrange. These menus will of course be inactive; that is, nothing should happen if you click any of the items.

8.22* This is the same as Exercise 8.21, but add a solid line to separate the two items in the File menu.

Figure 8.27 The menu aggregation chain of JFrame

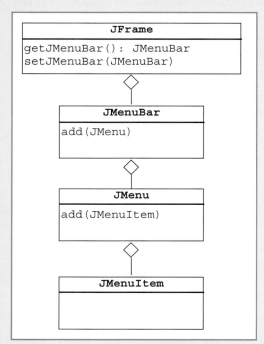

eCheck

Check08A (TS = 26)

Write the app `Check08A` that generates a random collection of credit cards using the `getRandom` method of the `GlobalCredit` class. It then outputs the number and expiry date of each card in the collection and flags the ones that will expire within a given number of years from today. Here is a sample run:

```
Enter report range in years ... 3
Cards expiring before 3 years from now:
639865-8    20/11/2015
046865-7    22/02/2017
123456-6    16/04/2013    *
044076-6    19/08/2016

Flagged-card count = 1
```

You can assume, as a pre, that the user will enter a non-negative integer for the number of years. The above report was generated on May 31, 2010 and that is why only the card expiring on April 16, 2010 was flagged. The fields in each line are delimited by a tab character. If a card is not flagged then neither a tab nor an asterisk should appear after its expiry date. The listing ends with an empty line followed by a count of the flagged cards. The dates are formatted such that the day and month are zero-filled to two digits.

Develop your app, test it, and then eCheck it.

Check08B (TS = 31)

Write the app `Check08B` that generates a random portfolio using the `getRandom` method of the `Portfolio` class. It then outputs some portfolio data followed by a listing of all stocks in this portfolio whose market price is below a given cutoff. Here is a sample run:

```
Cutoff Price........ 500
Portfolio Name...... The Random Portfolio BHRM
Portfolio Capacity.. 14
Investment Count.... 4

3095    59.94 TANGO-UNIFORM Inc.
3041    9.62  GOLF-Tech and CHARLIE Co.
2817    51.26 Compu-CHARLIE & TANGO Corp.
130     31.11 ROMEO X-RAY Ltd.

Value of portfolio below cutoff is: 363,212.44
```

The listing displays the quantity, price, and name of each stock separated by a tab character. The stock price (which must be below the supplied input) is formatted with two decimals. The listing ends with the total value of the listed stocks (sum of quantity times price) formatted with two decimals and a thousand separator. Note that there is an empty line before the listing and one after it.

If the portfolio contains no stock below cutoff, a message is displayed, as shown here:

```
Cutoff Price........ 5
Portfolio Name...... The Random Portfolio ZYGE
Portfolio Capacity.. 24
Investment Count.... 14

There are no stocks below your cutoff!
```

In this example, the generated portfolio had no stock with a price below $5. Note that the two empty lines that used to surround the listing are still there.

Develop your app, test it, and then eCheck it.

Check08C (TS = 31)

Write the app `Check08C` that starts by obtaining a random `type.lib.Student` instance using the `getRandom` method of that class. It then outputs some student data followed by a listing of all courses of a given year that this student has taken. Here is a sample run:

```
Enter the year ... 3
Student Name: FSLL
Student ID:   396578338
Student GPA:   2.3
-----------------------
3640  C
3914  D
GPA in year 3 is: 2.5
-----------------------
```

In this run, the user is interested in third-year courses, i.e. ones whose numbers begin with '3'. Note that the student GPA is formatted with one decimal. Note also that the listing is surrounded by two dashed lines (23 hyphens each). Each line in the listing contains a course number and the obtained grade in that course separated by a tab character. The listing is followed by the GPA of the student in the listed courses. You can assume, as a pre, that the user's input is an integer between 1 and 4, inclusive. If the student has not taken any course in the specified year, a message is displayed:

```
Enter the year ... 4
Student Name: QRPF
Student ID:   357633975
Student GPA:   2.3
-----------------------
No courses taken in year 4!
-----------------------
```

Develop your app, test it, and then eCheck it.

Check08D (TS = 31)

Write the app `Check08D` that behaves as shown in the following sample run:

```
Enter trigger level [1-100] ... 10
142687-8    5000   59.97
123456-6*   1000   104.46          <
672410-7    1000   19.24

Number of cards = 3
Average balance = 61.22
```

The app starts by prompting for and reading a trigger level, which is interpreted as a percent. You can assume as a pre that the input is an integer between 1 and 100. Next, the app generates a random `GlobalCredit` instance using its `getRandom` method. It then traverses the cards; determines their average balance; and produces the listing shown above. Each line starts with the card number suffixed with an asterisk if this card's balance is above average, i.e. exceed the average balance of all cards. This is followed by a tab character and the cards credit limit formatted without decimals. The next, tab-delimited, entry is the card's balance formatted with two decimals. If the card's balance divided by the credit limit is less than the indicated trigger, i.e. less than 10% in the above example, then the line ends. Otherwise, the balance is followed by a tab and the "<" character. The listing ends with an empty line followed by the shown stats. The average balance is formatted with two decimals.

As you can see, this report flags cards in two different ways. A card whose balance is greater than average is flagged by '*' and a card whose balance is greater than a given percentage of its credit limit is flagged by '<'.

Develop your app, test it, and then eCheck it.

9

Inheritance

Learning Objectives

1. *Think of classes as hierarchies*

2. *Recognize subclasses from their APIs*

3. *Learn about early and late bindings*

4. *Work with abstract classes and interfaces*

5. *Meet the Object class*

6. *Appreciate the rationale and role of generics*

Inheritance is a second technique for implementing layered abstractions. However, rather than aggregating types under one roof, inheritance "fuses" them into one. In this chapter, you will learn how to recognize subclasses, how to interpret their extended APIs, and how to develop programs that benefit from polymorphism. You will also learn that the disparate types encountered so far are, in fact, all related through one omnipresent hierarchy of types.

Chapter Outline

◢ 9.1 What Is Inheritance?

We saw in Section 4.1.1 that abstraction allows us to reduce a world of many objects to one of a few classes. Doing so proved extremely successful and laid the foundation for the object-oriented paradigm. Recall that reducing objects to classes involves grouping objects based on their attributes and methods and then replacing each group by a class. In other words, we strip away what sets objects apart (identity and state) and focus only on what is common among them (attributes and methods).

In this chapter, we explore the possibility of layering this abstraction; that is, we apply it to a world of classes. Given a group of classes that have some attributes and methods in common, we can focus on these common features and ignore the ones that are not common. This could lead us to an entity with a higher level of abstraction than a class. The following sections pursue this idea.

9.1.1 Definition and Terminology

The API of a class C may indicate that it **extends** some other class, say, P. This means that the two classes are linked in such a way that every field and public method present in P is also present in C. The link is called an **inheritance** relation between the **child** and the **parent** P, and we say that C **inherits** from P. A second set of terms comes from set theory, and in it, P is called the **superclass** and C is its **subclass**.

Note that the definition of inheritance does not break the encapsulation because it is expressed in terms of public features, ones that the client can see. As far as the client is concerned, C has everything that P has; hence, it is reasonable to say that C *is a* P. Because of this, inheritance is also called an **is-a** relation between two classes. It is possible of course that C has more public features than P because, in addition to the features it inherits from P, it can also have its own public features. Since C is a P plus possibly more, we can say that C is a **specialization** of P and that P is a **generalization** of C.

Example 9.1

For each of the following pairs of objects, determine whether the first can ordinarily be considered a superclass of the second.
- **(a)** Camera, Film
- **(b)** Vehicle, Car
- **(c)** Library, Book
- **(d)** Animal, Dog
- **(e)** Car, Tree

Answer:
- **(a)** No inheritance is involved here; a film is *not* a camera. This is in fact an aggregation because a camera *has a* film.
- **(b)** Yes, this is inheritance; a car *is a* vehicle.

(c) No inheritance is involved here. A book is *not* a library. This is in fact an aggregation because a library *has a* book.

(d) Yes, this is inheritance; a dog *is an* animal.

(e) This is neither an inheritance nor an aggregation, at least not ordinarily.

We saw in Chapter 7 that inheritance is depicted in UML diagrams by connecting the two classes with a solid line and placing an arrowhead next to the superclass. Figure 9.1 shows the UML diagrams of three examples of inheritance.

The figure shows that in addition to the child-parent relation depicted in Fig. 9.1(a), it is possible that class P is itself a child of some other class G (Fig. 9.1(b)). Such a linear structure is called an **inheritance chain**, and in it, class C would have every public feature of its direct superclass P and of its superclass G. A different structure appears in Fig. 9.1(c), in which a parent has several children. Such a tree structure is called an **inheritance hierarchy**. In it, the grandparent R is called the **root**, and all the other classes are called the **descendants**.

Note that no inheritance relation exists between siblings such as A and B of Fig. 9.1(c). The only statement we can make about them is that they both have the features of their parent R. Note also that while a parent can have many children, a child can have only one parent because Java does *not* allow **multiple-inheritance**. The UML diagram in Fig. 9.2 is therefore illegal in Java.

You can easily spot inheritance in the API of a subclass. It is indicated by the presence of the word **extends** in the header of the API. Note that "extends" is a keyword in Java (keywords are defined in Section 1.1.2). This word appears in the API followed by the name of the superclass. For example, the API of the RewardCard class has the following header:

```
public class RewardCard
extends CreditCard
```

If you examine the APIs of classes you know, you will find examples of this keyword in their APIs. Curiously, you will find that *all* of them extend some other class, mostly the

Figure 9.1
Inheritance UML diagrams. (a) C inherits from P. (b) An inheritance chain. (c) An inheritance hierarchy rooted at R.

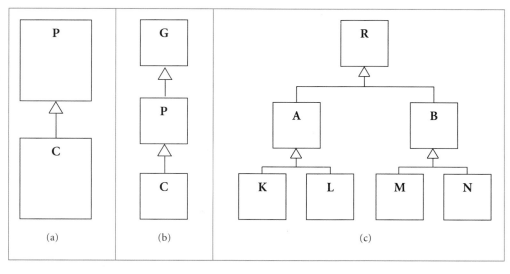

(a)   (b)   (c)

b j m :AM or PM >

Figure 9.2
Multiple-inheritance is not allowed in Java. A class cannot have more than one direct superclass.

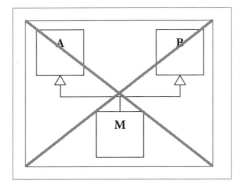

Object class. This special superclass will be discussed in Section 9.3. For now, we will focus on subclasses whose parent is not Object.

9.1.2 The Subclass API

Consider the two classes C and P whose UML diagrams are shown on the left-hand side of Fig. 9.3.

As you can see from the figure, each class contains five public features, two fields and three public methods. When no inheritance is involved, the features shown in the UML diagram of a class are exactly those listed in its API. But when a class extends another, its API amalgamates its features with *some* of its parent's features. Hence, while inheritance does not affect UML diagrams (aside from adding a line with an arrowhead), it does change the API of the subclass. We now examine these changes.

Figure 9.3 The API of a subclass lists all its features and some of the features of its parent.

The Constructor Section

The constructor section of a subclass is not affected by the inheritance. This is because inheritance applies to features, and constructors are not features. In other words, they are *not* inherited. (When you use a subclass constructor, Java invokes the constructor of its superclass, but this is part of the implementation and is of no concern to the client.)

The Method Section

The method section in the API of a subclass has two tables: the upper one is the familiar table that lists all the methods that this class provides. The lower table lists methods that were inherited from the superclass. The new structure is depicted in Fig. 9.4.

All these methods, whether in the upper or the lower table, are effectively present in the subclass. If M denotes the total number of methods listed in both tables, then a client of the C class can use the subclass as if it had M methods of its own. At first glance, you may conclude that

$$M = M_{\text{C-UML}} + M_{\text{P-UML}}$$

```
            P
+ a: int
+ b: double

+ k(int): void
+ l(): long
+ m(double): void
```

```
            C
+ a: double
+ c: char

+ k(double): void
+ l(): long
+ n(long): int
```

The API of C

```
a: double
c: char
b: double

k(double): void
l(): long
n(long): int
k(int): void
m(double): void
```

⟶ Upper API Table
⋯⋯▶ Lower API Table

Figure 9.4 The method section in the API of a subclass has two tables. The upper one lists the child's own methods; the lower one lists methods inherited from the parent.

Method Summary	
return	*method name and signature*
...	...
Methods inherited from class `parent`	
comma-delimited list of method names	

where M_{X-UML} is the number of methods listed in the UML diagram of class X. But what if one of the methods in the parent had the same signature as a method in the subclass? Including such a method in the lower table would effectively leave C with two methods with the same signature, which is illegal. We must therefore refuse to inherit the parent's method in this case. A method in a subclass is said to **override** a method in the superclass if the two methods have the same signature. Hence, the sum in the right-hand side of the above formula must be reduced by the number of overriding methods in the subclass.

Note that nothing stops a method in the parent from having the same name but a different signature from a method in the child. In this case, the parent's method will be inherited, and the child will end up effectively with two overloaded methods.

The above discussion can be generalized to an inheritance chain in which the subclass has n superclasses. The upper table will show the subclass methods as before, and it will be followed by n tables, one per superclass, showing the methods inherited from each.

The Field Section

The field section in the API of a subclass has two tables: the upper one is the familiar table that lists all the fields that this class provides. The lower table lists fields that were inherited from the superclass. The new structure is depicted in Fig. 9.5.

All these fields, whether in the upper or the lower table, are effectively present in the subclass. If F denotes the total number of fields listed in both tables, then a client of C can use it as if it had F fields of its own. At first glance, you may conclude that

$$F = F_{C-UML} + F_{P-UML}$$

Figure 9.5 The field section in the API of a subclass has two tables. The upper table lists the child's own fields; the lower table lists fields inherited from the parent.

Field Summary	
type	*field name*
...	...
Fields inherited from class `parent`	
comma-delimited list of field names	

where $F_{X\text{-}UML}$ is the number of fields listed in the UML diagram of class X. But what if one of the fields in the parent had the same name as a field in the subclass? Including such a field in the lower table would effectively leave C with two fields with the same name, which is illegal. We must therefore refuse to inherit the parent's field in this case. A field in a subclass is said to **shadow** a field in the superclass if the two fields have the same name (regardless of type). Hence, the sum in the right-hand side of the above formula must be reduced by the number of shadowing fields in the subclass.

The above discussion can be generalized to an inheritance chain in which the subclass has n superclasses. The upper table will show the subclass fields as before, and it will be followed by n tables, one per superclass, showing the fields inherited from each.

Example 9.2

Justify the API depicted in Fig. 9.3.

Answer:
In terms of fields, the API listed the fields of C plus the field b that was inherited from P. The other field in the parent, the integer a, was not inherited because it was shadowed. Hence, C has effectively three fields.

In terms of methods, the API lists the methods of C plus two methods, k and m, that were inherited from P. The other method in the parent, method l, was not inherited because it was overridden. Hence, C effectively has five methods (two of which are overloaded). ☐

Java Details   9.1

An Illegal Method Combination

Our discussion did not cover the case of a parent's method that has the same signature as a method in the child but with a different return. This is because it cannot occur. The Java compiler will not compile a subclass if it contains a method that has the same signature as a parent's method but a different return.

9.1.3 Case Study: Credit Cards

Let us review the main characteristics of the following class:

    type.lib.CreditCard

You create a credit card instance by writing

    CreditCard card = new
    CreditCard(9, "Adam");

The credit card will have the number 9 and will be assigned to a cardholder named "Adam." Given this reference, consider the following fragment:

```
card.charge(500.0);
card.pay(300.0);
double owing = card.getBalance();
```

The first statement indicates that Adam made a $500 purchase on his credit card. This will increase the balance of the card by that amount. The next statement indicates that Adam made a $300 payment, thereby reducing the balance. The last statement uses an accessor to determine the balance, which should be $200.

Let us now assume that the bank that issues the credit card decides to launch a second one, a reward card. The new card behaves exactly like the old one; indeed, it *is a* credit card, but it offers reward points. Whenever a purchase is charged on the card, a certain number of points are rewarded. Hence, in addition to the dollar balance, this card keeps track of a point balance. The cardholder can redeem the points in the point balance for some free merchandise.

Since a reward card is a credit card but with some peculiarities, the bank's developers decide to implement it as a subclass. The subclass name is

```
type.lib.RewardCard
```

Most of the features in the parent class apply as is to a reward card and, hence, must be inherited. Some features, however, should not be inherited. The charge method, for example, is not aware of the reward aspect and will therefore not work for a reward card. Hence, the new class must come with its own charge method, and its signature must be the same as in the parent. This way, the parent's method will be overridden. We can now write a fragment similar to the above but for a reward card:

```
RewardCard card = new
    RewardCard(9, "Adam");
card.charge(500.0);
card.pay(300.0);
double owing = card.getBalance();
```

If you examine the API of the RewardCard class, you will find that the pay and getBalance methods are in the lower table, whereas the charge method is in the upper. Since there is nothing special about making a payment on a reward card, the developers did not override the pay method in the parent, and similarly for the balance accessor. The subclass must have a method, of course, for accessing the point balance. The API shows such a method in the upper table, and it can be used by adding the following statement to the above fragment:

```
int points =
    card.getPointBalance();
```

For example, if the reward rate is one point for each $20 charged on the card, then there should be 25 reward points available at this stage ($500 / $20).

Example 9.3

Examine the API of the reward card subclass and its superclass in Fig. 9.6, and identify the methods that were (a) overridden and (b) added by the subclass. Based on the context of these classes, provide a rationale to justify why these methods were overridden or added.

Answer:

(a) Here is a list of methods present in the CreditCard class but overridden in the RewardCard class for the reason indicated:

- ■ `boolean charge(double)` This method is used when a purchase is charged on the card, thereby increasing its dollar balance. It is overridden because it must also increase the point balance.
- ■ `void credit(double)` This method is used when goods charged on the card are returned for refund, thereby decreasing the dollar balance. It is overridden because it must also decrease the point balance.
- ■ `boolean equals(Object)` This method tests equality. It considers two instances equal if they are credit cards and have the same number. It is overridden to ensure the two instances are reward cards with the same number.

Method Summary

boolean	charge(double amount) Attempt to charge this card.
void	credit(double amount) Credit the credit card (decrease its dollar balance) by the passed amount.
boolean	equals(java.lang.Object other) Test the equality of reward cards.
int	getPointBalance() Return the number of reward points accumulated on this reward card.
boolean	isSimilar(RewardCard other) Test the similarity of two reward cards.
void	redeem(int point) Redeem the passed number of points and reduce the point balance accordingly.
String	toString() Return a string representation of this card.

Methods inherited from class `type.lib.CreditCard`

getBalance, getExpiryDate, getIssueDate, getLimit, get-Name, getNumber, isSimilar, pay, getExpiryDate, setLimit

- **String toString()** This method returns the string "CARD" followed by the card's number and dollar balance. It is overridden so that it returns instead the string "RWRD" followed by the card's number, dollar balance, and point balance.

(b) Here is a list of methods added by the RewardCard class for the reason indicated:

- **int getPointBalance()** This method returns the point balance. It was added because no reward-aware method exists in the superclass.
- **void redeem(int)** This method allows the cardholder to redeem some of the reward points, thereby decreasing the point balance. It was added because no reward-aware method exists in the superclass.
- **boolean isSimilar(RewardCard)** This method tests similarity. Two reward cards are considered similar if they carry the same dollar balance (to the nearest cent) and the same point balance. It was added because the parent's similarity test is based on the dollar balance only, and we did not want to override the parent method in this case.

9.2 Working with Inheritance Hierarchies

As long as the client deals with one, and only one, subclass at a time, no special consideration needs to be given to inheritance. The only difference that the client will notice is the presence of two (or more) tables in the API of the subclass, which is a minor issue. Indeed, we found in Section 9.1.3 that the fragment that charges and then makes a payment on a reward card is almost identical to the one that deals with an ordinary credit card. The situation becomes dramatically different, however, when the client deals with several subclasses on an inheritance chain at the same time. In fact, such multi-subclass applications are the very essence of inheritance, and the following sections explain how these applications are supported in Java.

9.2.1 The Substitutability Principle

In applications involving a class C that extends a class P, it is often the case that we do not know at the time of programming which of the two classes is involved. For example, suppose you need to write a fragment that prompts the user to choose the class to be instantiated (C or P) and then instantiates the chosen class using its default constructor. Your fragment must culminate in an object reference x pointing at the created instance. Here is a first attempt:

```
output.println("Enter C or P");
char choice = input.nextChar();
if (choice == 'P')
{
    P x = new P();
}
else
{
    C x = new C();
}
```

There is nothing wrong with this fragment (i.e., it will compile), but it is useless. Any code written after it cannot benefit from x because it will be out of scope. The root of the problem is that there are actually two different classes here, yet we are attempting to use only one object reference. How can an object reference declared to be of one type point at instances of another type? To address this problem, Java provides the **substitutability principle**, which states that

When a parent is expected, a child is accepted.

This principle applies in any context in which we normally insist on type matching. In an assignment statement, for example, we normally insist that the right-hand side has the same type as the left-hand side. This principle allows us to tolerate a difference in type: if the left-hand-side is of the type P, then it is acceptable for the right-hand side to be of the type C. Similarly, if a method takes a parameter of the type P, then you can pass it a value of the type C.

The principle is not restricted to the immediate superclass of a class; it applies to any two classes on an inheritance chain. Hence, if an instance of a particular class is expected, then an instance of any descendant of that class is accepted. In an inheritance hierarchy such as the one shown in Fig. 9.1(c), the principle allows us to substitute an instance of K for an instance of R. In other words, you can move up the hierarchy tree, not down and not sideways.

Using this principle, we can solve the question posed at the beginning of this section as follows: we declare the reference to be of the type P before the `if` statement. This allows us to assign to it either instance, and it allows us to use it after the `if` statement blocks:

```
output.println("Enter C or P");
char choice = input.nextChar();
P x;
if (choice == 'P')
{
    x = new P();
}
else
{
    x = new C();
}
```

The last assignment will compile without errors thanks to the substitutability principle.

It may be seem odd at first that we are using the same reference to point at objects of different types, but we do so in everyday language. Consider, for example, the following sentence:

```
The fare is $5 per person.
```

If a man read it, he would realize that he should pay $5 because "a man *is a* person." Hence, we subconsciously subscribe to the substitutability of a class for its superclass because we accept substituting "man" for "person." Similarly, if a woman read the sentence, then she, too, would realize that she must pay $5 because "a woman *is a* person." The same applies if a child or any other "subclass of person" reads the sentence.

Example 9.4

Write a fragment that asks the user whether an ordinary or a reward card is wanted, then create the appropriate card with card number 9 and cardholder name "Adam." The fragment must culminate in a reference `card` to be used afterward.

Answer:

```
CreditCard card;
output.println("Ordinary or Reward [O/R]?");
String type = input.nextLine().toUpperCase();
if (type.equals("O"))
{
    card = new CreditCard(9, "Adam");
}
else
{
    card = new RewardCard(9, "Adam");
}
```

It should be noted that the client would not have reaped the benefits of inheritance had it not been for the substitutability principle. Without it, we would have to write a separate fragment to handle each subclass, which means many if statement blocks containing more or less the same code.

9.2.2 Early and Late Binding

Recall from Section 3.1.3 that binding refers to the ability of the compiler to resolve an expression such as the following:

```
r.m(...)
```

where r is an object reference and m is a method. We saw in Section 3.1.3 that binding is a three-step process: we first find the target class based on the *declared* type of r, then we find the target method based on the invocation signature, and finally we select the most specific method if more than one target is found. If any of these steps fail, a compile-time error is generated. Otherwise, we bind with the found target.

When no inheritance is involved, the process described above determines the binding, which is why we have been using it so far in this textbook. But when inheritance is involved, the above process represents only half the full binding process, the so-called **early binding** half. The other half is called **late binding**. Here is a description of the full process:

1. The compiler performs early binding as before. Assuming no errors, it culminates in a target, that is, a method with a particular signature S residing in the *declared* class of the reference r.

2. The virtual machine performs late binding as follows: it first determines the class of the object that r points at. If no such class exists (because r is null), then a "Null Pointer Exception" is thrown. Otherwise, the virtual machine searches for S in that class and binds with it. It *will* find the exact S in the target class.

Note that the two parts of the process are performed at different times. Early binding occurs when the program is compiled. Late binding occurs every time a program is run. The two parts communicate with each other through S, the signature determined by early binding. Note, also, that late binding upholds S and looks for an exact match of it, but it does so in the class of the object, not that of the reference. These two classes are normally the same unless we are dealing with a multi-subclass application and substitutability.

The binding process described above does *not* apply to fields or to static methods. For these two, early binding is the final binding.

Example 9.5

Bind the following statement:

```
card.charge(500);
```

It uses the card reference that was constructed in Example 9.4.

Answer:

To perform early binding, the compiler searches the program for a statement in which the reference `card` is declared. It finds the following statement:

```
CreditCard card;
```

The target class of any invocation that involves `card` is thus `CreditCard`. Next, the compiler searches the target class for the signature

```
charge(int)
```

During this search, widening conversion of primitive types and substitutability of non-primitive types are automatically performed if needed. The search culminates in the signature S being

```
charge(double)
```

When the program is run and the virtual machine encounters this statement in the compiled class, it starts by determining the target class of late binding, that is, the type of object at which `card` points. This type depends on the input made by the user. If the user indicates an ordinary card, the virtual machine will look for the signature S in `CreditCard`; otherwise, it will look in `RewardCard`. The search will be successful either way. ◻

It should be noted that while the signature search is tolerant during early binding, it is very strict during late binding; it looks for an exact match. The following fragment brings this point to focus:

```
CreditCard card1 = new RewardCard(9, "Adam");
CreditCard card2 = new RewardCard(9, "Eve");
card1.charge(500);
card1.pay(500);
output.println(card1.isSimilar(card2));
```

The two created cards are reward cards, and both have the same card number, 9, and the same dollar balance, 0. They differ, however, in their point balance. The output of the fragment depends on how you bind the `isSimilar` method. If you bind it with the superclass, then the output will be `true`; otherwise it will be `false`.

Let us perform a careful, step-by-step binding of `isSimilar`: during early binding, the compiler determines that the target class is `CreditCard`. It searches in it for

```
isSimilar(CreditCard)
```

and it finds it. The above is thus the signature S that gets passed to the virtual machine within the compiled class file. During late binding, the virtual machine determines that the target class is `RewardCard`. It searches in it for the above S. Notice that the target class contains two effectively overloaded versions of this method:

```
isSimilar(CreditCard)
isSimilar(RewardCard)
```

The first one will be selected because the virtual machine does not "think"; it looks for an exact match to the signature determined during early binding. Hence, the method in `CreditCard` will be selected, and the fragment output will therefore be `true`.

Example 9.6

Bind the invocation in the following fragment:

```
CreditCard card = new RewardCard(9, "Adam");
card.redeem();
```

Answer:

During early binding, the compiler determines that the target class (the declared type of card) is CreditCard, and it searches in it for

```
redeem()
```

The search will fail, and the compiler will generate a compile-time error. Note that it does *not* matter that the actual object is a reward card, which does have a redeem method.

9.2.3 Polymorphism

Consider the following fragment:

```
CreditCard card;
...
card.charge(500.0);
```

The invocation in the last statement will either bind to the superclass or to the subclass, depending on the type of the actual object that card points at. In one case, only the dollar balance will be affected; in the other, both the dollar and the point balances will change. The charge method is said to be **polymorphic**, that is, capable of having multiple forms, because it actually represents two methods (one in the subclass and one in the superclass), and it switches between the two depending on the type of the object (not reference) on which it is invoked.

In general, **polymorphism** refers to the ability of the same entity to have multiple forms. It occurs in an inheritance chain when two or more classes on the chain provide a method with the same signature. When such a method is invoked on a reference whose type is the root of the chain, early binding binds the invocation with the root. But when the virtual machine late-binds the invocation, it can resolve it in a number of ways based on the type of the object that the reference points at.

Polymorphic programs are elegant because they self-adapt without the need for if statements. There are situations, however, when one must use non-polymorphic methods. For example, how would you determine the point balance given the above reference card? The first thing you need to do is determine whether the actual object is indeed a reward card (otherwise, the question is meaningless). To do that, Java provides a relational operator (Section 3.2.4) with precedence -7 and left-to-right association. The expression

reference **instanceof** *class*

returns a boolean that is equal to true if *reference* is not null and if it points to an instance of *class* or one of its subclasses. The return is false otherwise. Hence, our first attempt would be to write

```
if (card instanceof RewardCard)
{
    int points = card.getPointBalance();
    ...
}
```

But this fragment will not compile because the compiler will fail to find the invoked method in the early-binding target class. What we need to do is ask the compiler to treat the reference as if it were declared to be of the type RewardCard. We do this through a **cast**:

```
if (card instanceof RewardCard)
{
    RewardCard rc = (RewardCard) card;
    int points = rc.getPointBalance();
    ...
}
```

In general, you can cast an object reference of any type to any other type as long as the two are on the same inheritance chain. You can cast down (as was done above) or cast up, but casting up is needless, since it is done automatically (casting up is simply the substitutability principle). If the compiler accepts a cast, the virtual machine might still reject it at runtime. The virtual machine bases its decision on the type of the object involved and accepts a cast only if it is the exact type of the object or up the inheritance chain. Otherwise, it rejects it and generates a runtime error.

Generally speaking, you should avoid casting. However, if you must cast, then make sure you first use instanceof (as done above) to ensure no runtime errors.

Example 9.7

Predict the output of the following fragment:

```
1  CreditCard card1 = new RewardCard(9, "Adam");
2  CreditCard card2 = new RewardCard(9, "Adam");
3  card1.charge(100);
4  card1.pay(100);
5  output.print(card1.isSimilar(card2));
6  output.print(card1.isSimilar((RewardCard) card2));
7  output.print(((RewardCard) card1).isSimilar(card2));
8  output.print(((RewardCard)
     card1).isSimilar((RewardCard) card2));
```

Answer:
Statement 5
Early binding binds with isSimilar(CreditCard) in CreditCard. Late binding finds this very signature in RewardCard and binds with it. Hence, the method inherited from the superclass will end up being invoked. Since that method tests only the dollar balance, the output is true.

Statement 6

Early binding also binds with `isSimilar(CreditCard)` in `CreditCard` (thanks to substitutability). Late binding finds this very signature in `RewardCard` and binds with it. Hence, the method inherited from the superclass will end up being invoked. Since that method tests only the dollar balance, the output is `true`.

Statement 7

Early binding binds with isSimilar(CreditCard) in RewardCard. Late binding lands on the same method in the same class. Hence, the method inherited from the superclass will end up being invoked. Since that method tests only the dollar balance, the output is `true`.

Statement 8

Early binding binds with `isSimilar(RewardCard)` in `RewardCard`. Late binding lands on the same method in the same class. Hence, the method of the subclass will end up being invoked. Since that method tests both the dollar and the point balances, the output is `false`.

9.2.4 Abstract Classes and Interfaces

Inheritance is the second most important hallmark of the object-oriented paradigm (after encapsulation), and it has enormous benefits to both implementers and clients. Because of this, designers endeavour to create classes in inheritance chains or hierarchies whenever applicable. When two classes are being designed, and one of them is to contain a subset of the features of the other, then it is quite natural to design them as a superclass and a subclass in an inheritance chain. In many situations, however, designers are confronted with a pair of classes that share some features, yet each must have features not present in the other. Hence, neither class can be designated as the superclass. To cater to such situations, Java provides two constructs: the abstract class and the interface. The abstract class is stronger than the interface but is restrictive; the interface is weaker but is flexible. Let us take a closer look at each one from the client's perspective.

Abstract Classes

Given two classes with some features in common, create an artificial third class to hold the common features and make it the superclass of each of the original two classes. The artificial class is called the **abstract class** because it does not encapsulate an actual object. The three classes become an inheritance hierarchy with the abstract class at its root. For example, suppose that we need to design two classes to encapsulate a chequing account and a savings account. There are obviously many common features in these two classes, for example, accessors for the account number and the balance and a method for depositing money. The chequing account class must keep track of withdrawal fees, whereas the savings account class must be able to compute interest. These differences lead us to design an abstract class called `Account`. Similarly, we can place a `Car` class and a `Bus` class in an inheritance hierarchy by having both of them extend an abstract `Vehicle` class, as shown in Fig. 9.7.

Figure 9.7 This UML diagram depicts two classes extending an abstract class.

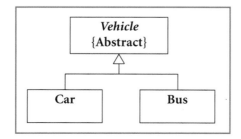

You can easily recognize an abstract class in the API header because the word *abstract* is added, for example,

```
public abstract class Vehicle
```

In UML, you can recognize an abstract class by noting that its class diagram has its name italicized and followed by the word *abstract* within braces.

Keep in mind that the abstract class was introduced as an artifact to hold common features; it was *not* obtained by ignoring the identities and states of a group of objects. It is essential therefore that no one instantiate an abstract class. Doing so would be as meaningless as going to a factory that makes cars and buses and asking for a "vehicle." Instantiating an abstract class is illegal in Java, and the compiler will issue a compile-time error if a program attempts to do that.

To use an abstract class in any program, we must somehow obtain an instance of one of its subclasses. Thanks to substitutability, that instance would have the abstract class as its type. Once this instance is obtained, we can use the features of the abstract class as we use any other class, but how do we find such an instance? There are usually two ways: the factory method and a subclass constructor.

■ **Factory Method** Find a method that gives you the instance. Such a method is called a **factory method** because it creates the instance for you. For example, our hypothetical abstract `Vehicle` class may have the factory method

```
public static Car createCar()
```

In this case, our program obtains the instance as follows:

```
Vehicle myCar = Vehicle.createCar();
```

■ **Subclass Constructor** Find a subclass and use its constructor. To that end, look under "Direct Known Subclasses" in the header of the API of the abstract classes. For example,

```
Vehicle myCar = new Car();
```

We used several abstract classes in Chapter 7, for example, the `Graphics2D` class, the `Calendar` class, and the `InputStream` class. We could not, of course, have instantiated them; instead, we were given instances of their subclasses as follows:

```
UniPanel.getGraphics2D()
Calendar.getInstance()
System.in
```

Example 9.8

Create an instance of the type `Calendar` without using the `getInstance` factory method.

Answer:
Since this is an abstract class, we search for subclasses. The API header lists the `GregorianCalendar` subclass. Hence, we create the instance as follows:

```
Calendar cal = new GregorianCalendar();
```

Interfaces

Creating an abstract class for the common features and making classes extend it will not work if any of the classes already extend some other class. Since a class cannot extend more than one class (no multiple inheritance), the applicability of this approach is rather limited in scope. For example, in an application dealing with transportation in a city, the Bus class may need to be a subclass of the PublicTransitFees class in order to inherit features related to fees and fee collection. This application requirement makes our earlier approach (of making Bus a subclass of the abstract class Vehicle) not possible.

Java solves this problem with the type **interface**, a new nonprimitive type. You can easily recognize an interface in the API header because the word *interface* replaces the word *class*, for example,

```
public interface Comparable
```

Furthermore, when the API is presented as a three-pane HTML document, interfaces are italicized in the lower left list. In UML, interfaces are depicted using class diagrams but with an «interface» stereotype in the name compartment or a small circle.

Like a class, an interface is an abstraction, but it is obtained by layering the abstraction twice. Given a group of objects, you start by ignoring their identities and states to obtain classes, and then ignore features that are not common to obtain superclasses. The final layer is obtained by ignoring all the attributes and the implementations of all methods, and this yields the interface. In other words, the interface retains only the contracts of the shared methods. A class that contains an implementation of these methods is said to **implement the interface**. Implementing an interface is similar to extending a superclass in that they both imply an is-a relationship and, hence, the substitutability principle. But since a class that implements an interface does not inherit the methods in full from the interface, only the headers, it can implement more than one interface.

The fact that a class can implement more than one interface makes this approach far more flexible than an approach based on abstract classes. You place the headers of all common methods in an interface and require that classes implement it. This allows you to reap the benefits of substitutability and polymorphism without imposing inheritance requirements.

For example, if you observed rectangles, circles, and cylinders and started this abstraction process, you might end up with the interface HasArea that has only one method:

```
public double getArea()
```

The interface retains only the above header, not the actual implementation because the area is computed differently based on the shape. Given this interface, we can require that the Rectangle, Circle, and Cylinder classes implement it. The obtained hierarchy is depicted in Fig. 9.8. Note that a dashed line with an arrowhead represents that a class implements an interface.

Since the interface is obtained by abstracting twice, two steps are needed for a client to use it: first, the client must find a class that implements

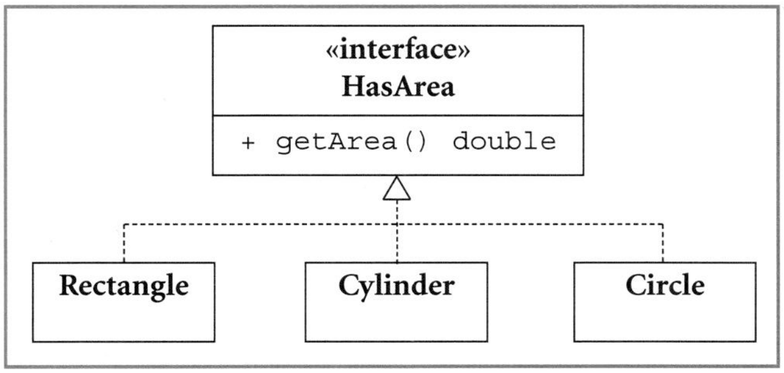

Figure 9.8 This UML diagram depicts three classes implementing an interface. A dashed line with an arrowhead denotes an "implements" relationship.

the interface; second, it must create an instance of that class. The instance will have the interface as its type and can be substituted wherever the interface type is expected. For example, the statement

```
HasArea shape = new Rectangle(3, 4);
```

creates a 3 × 4 rectangle object and declares the instance using the interface. The object reference, shape, has HasArea as its type and can be used wherever the interface can.

9.2.5 Case Study: Revisiting Streams

We saw in Section 8.1.5 that aggregation provides the client with flexibility in selecting streams that are appropriate to the problem at hand. For example, instead of delegating to a single component FileReader that connects to a file and delivers its contents as characters, the client can use FileInputStream, which connects to a file and delivers its contents as bytes, and then select an appropriate stream to convert the bytes either to characters (InputStreamReader) or to other primitive types (DataInputStream). Thanks to aggregation, all the streams between the data source and the program communicate seamlessly. The added flexibility can be appreciated by comparing Fig. 9.9(a) to Fig. 9.9(b).

Inheritance provides its own flexibility to streams but in a different dimension. Thanks to the substitutability principle, a client can work with the same object reference and invoke methods on it, even though the actual instance it points at may change from one run to the next. For example, the fragment

```
InputStream input;
... // assign input
int oneByte = input.read();
```

uses the object reference input to read data one byte at a time. The statements denoted by the ellipsis (...) in the fragment must create an instance of the type InputStream and let the object reference point at it.

For example, the missing statement can create a stream connected to the keyboard:

```
input = System.in;
```

Or the missing statements can create a stream connected to a file:

```
input = new FileInputStream
    (filename);
```

Or the missing statements can create a stream connected to a file on a remote computer:

```
input =
    (new URL(someURL)).openStream();
```

The point here is that thanks to inheritance, no matter which subclass is used, the rest of the program will not be affected. A client can therefore use the same code for handling the read bytes regardless of their source. This can be seen by comparing Fig. 9.9(b) to Fig. 9.9(c).

The above two flexibilities, one provided by aggregation and the other by inheritance, can be combined, and this is how the I/O classes in Java's standard library were designed. This provides the ultimate flexibility for the client in mixing and matching components. This is depicted in Fig. 9.9(d), where the various possibilities for combining data source streams and data conversion streams are shown.

Figure 9.9 Input streams as examples of delegation levels.
(a) One class handles file input and delivers characters.
(b) Aggregation allows the client to read either text or binary data from a file.
(c) Inheritance allows the client to read bytes from three different sources using the same method.
(d) Components based on aggregation and inheritance provide the client with flexibility in choosing the data source and the data type.

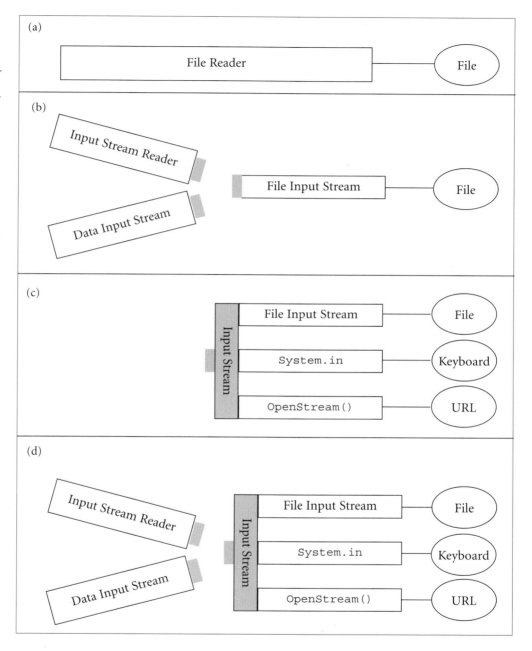

9.3 Obligatory Inheritance

We saw in Section 9.1 that the API of any class we know shows it as a subclass, even though we do not believe it is part of an inheritance hierarchy. We also noticed that the superclass in these cases is one called Object. These observations seem to imply that inheritance is obligatory;

every class must inherit from some other class. The following sections explore this notion and explain its rationale and implication.

9.3.1 The `Object` Class

The inheritance mechanism enables classes to form hierarchies in which members of the same hierarchy are linked, whereas members in different hierarchies are completely decoupled. When a new class is developed, either it becomes a subclass in an existing hierarchy, or it stands on its own. As classes are added, the set of all classes written by all developers will form disparate hierarchies, each of which contains one or more classes, as depicted in Fig. 9.10.

All classes in the set are subclasses except for the ones at the top level; those are "orphan" classes, since they do not inherit from a parent.

The designers of Java prefer to see a world in which the set of all classes looks instead like Fig. 9.11.

The built-in **Object** class was provided to adopt all the orphan classes in Fig. 9.10. In other words, if a class extends some other class, then it is a subclass of the class it extends; otherwise, it is automatically a subclass of `Object`. This implies that, except for the `Object` class itself, every class is a subclass whose superclass is ultimately the `Object` class.

One benefit of having the `Object` class as a universal root is that every class inherits whatever the `Object` class has in its API. If we look at that API, we see no fields and a variety of highly generic methods. These methods are often overridden by subclasses to make them more specific, and thus more useful for client programs. It is instructive to look at some of these methods because they shed some light on certain default behaviours in Java, behaviours that we have been using without understanding them.

boolean equals(Object other) This method tests equalities of objects and therefore must be overridden by subclasses so that an equality test that is meaningful in the context of the subclass can be defined and implemented. The contract of this method in the `Object` class specifies that it returns `false` if `other` is `null` or if the two objects occupy different blocks in memory. It returns `true` otherwise, that is, when the two references are actually pointing to the same memory block. This behaviour is identical to the `==` operator.

String toString() This method is meant to return a concise but informative textual representation of the object; it therefore must be overridden by subclasses. The return of this method in the `Object` class is the name of the class to which the reference is pointing, followed by the @ symbol, followed by the hexadecimal number which typically is the address of the block in memory where the object is stored. Notice that the + concatenation operator

Figure 9.10 Left to evolve on their own, classes end up in disparate hierarchies.

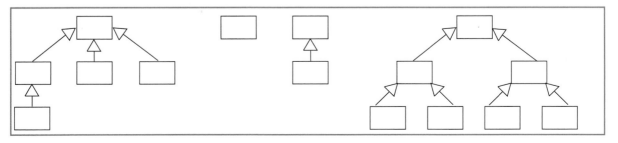

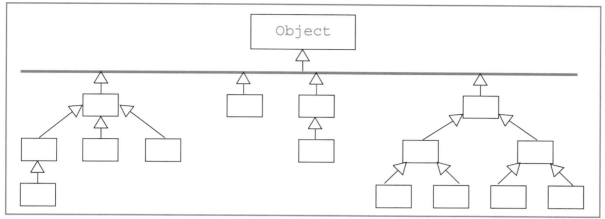

owes its existence to the presence of this method in the `Object` class. If either operand of this operator is a string and the other is an object, it coerces the nonstring object to a string too by invoking this method. If the `Object` class did not contain it, the + operator would have no guarantee that every reference has it.

Class getClass() This method returns the class of the reference on which it is invoked. The return is an instance of `Class`, which has an accessor called `getName()`, which returns the name (and package) of the class. For example,

```
CreditCard rc = new RewardCard(9, "Adam");
output.println(rc.getClass().getName());
```

The output is `type.lib.RewardCard`. Contrast this with `instanceof`, which is only a test and does not distinguish between "class of" and "subclass of."

9.3.2 Case Study: Object Serialization

In all the applications seen so far, all objects were created and used as the program was running. But there are situations in which objects may need to be created in one run and used in another. Here are some scenarios:

- After creating a collection and adding elements to it, the user may want to quit the program for the day and come back the next day to resume working. The user expects that all elements will remain available on the next day, and in the same state.
- After creating an object through a program, the user may want to be able to launch another program to process the object created in the first; that is, the second app must be able to access objects created by the first.

- After creating an object through a program, the user may want to be able to share it with someone else; that is, make the created object accessible to a remote location.

All these scenarios can be realized if we can somehow "save" objects in some persistent storage, one that does not disappear when our program ends. This means we need to write code that writes all the attributes of the object to a disk file. Primitive attributes can easily be written, but non-primitive attributes need to be handled recursively. This is because an object attribute of a class refers to another class and that class may itself have object attributes, and so on. This recursion will ultimately yield primitive or string data. This complex process is called **serializing** the object, and it culminates in a set of binary data that captures the state of the object. Given this data, and the classes of which the object and its attributes are instances, we should be able to reconstitute the object. This reverse process is called deserialization.

Java comes with ready-made components that implement both processes. The class

```
java.io.ObjectOutputStream
```

is responsible for serialization. Its constructor takes an OutputStream as a sink (a place to which the data should be written). Hence, if we want to serialize an object to a disk file, we provide a file as a sink:

```
FileOutputStream fos = new
    FileOutputStream(filename);
ObjectOutputStream oos = new
    ObjectOutputStream(fos);
```

The key method in the class is

```
void writeObject(Object obj)
```

Thanks to the object hierarchy and the substitutability principle, this method accepts *any* object type parameter. As an example, given an instance gc of GlobalCredit, a collection of CreditCard objects, we can serialize it as follows:

```
oos.writeObject(gc);
oos.close();
```

Note that gc may contain thousands of credit cards and that each credit card aggregates two dates and a host of attributes, yet this simple invocation will store everything in the file. The process can be reversed with the help of the class:

```
java.io.ObjectInputStream
```

Here is a fragment that deserializes the collection:

```
FileInputStream fis = new
    FileInputStream(filename);
ObjectInputStream ois = new
    ObjectInputStream(fis);
gc = (GlobalCredit)
    ois.readObject();
ois.close();
```

Note that the readObject method returns an Object; hence, the return must be cast to the proper type before the application can use the deserialized object. This is a weak point in the process because the cast may lead to a runtime error when the actual type of the serialized object is different from, and not a subclass of, the cast type. It is therefore prudent to check the type before casting:

```
if (ois.readObject() instanceof
    GlobalCredit)
```

The object stream methods throw several types of exceptions, and until we learn how to handle them (Chapter 11), we must add a suffix to our main method:

```
public static void main(String[]
    args) throws Exception
```

We conclude this section by observing that all methods that are based on the Object class are quite useful, in terms of generality and reusability; however, they invariably lead to casts and, thus, possible runtime errors. For methods that deal with serialized objects, this means we should exercise care and check types before casting. For other methods, we will learn in Section 9.3.3 that there is a way to transfer the burden of these errors to the compiler.

9.3.3 Generics

We saw from the outset (Section 1.1.1) that Java is a strongly typed language and that its compiler checks for type mismatches at compile-time. Type mismatch makes every assignment statement and every method invocation a potential runtime error, but as long as you do not cast, the compiler can detect these errors and turn them into harmless compile-time errors.

Exposing errors at compile-time falls under the guideline of Section 2.3.1, "Risk Mitigation by Early Exposure," and is becoming increasingly relevant today as more and more developers rely on ready-made components in their applications. If you use a ready-made component, you certainly want any potential runtime error in it to have been exposed when it was compiled. Otherwise, your application could crash, and you would not be able to fix it. Compile-time type checking has served us well; since casting thwarts it, we have made it a point not to cast except in limited and controlled situations.

We found in this chapter that compile-time type checking is not rigid but rather flexible. For example, consider the method m whose signature is

```
m(type p)
```

When a client that invokes this method is compiled, the compiler must verify that the passed value is indeed of the type *type*, but this is not as strict as you might think. For example,

- If *type* is double, then the client can pass any numeric value.
- If *type* is some class, then the client can pass an instance of any subclass of it.
- If *type* is an interface, then the client can pass an instance of any class that implements it.

This flexibility means we can write applications that deal with a family of related classes and still reap the benefits of type checking. For example, the GlobalCredit collection (Section 8.2.1) is a collection of credit cards. One of its methods is

```
boolean add(CreditCard card)
```

Since RewardCard is a subclass of CreditCard, we can use this collection to store reward cards. This extremely useful flexibility does not come at the expense of losing type checking: if a client invoked the above method and passed a String, a compile-time error would be generated.

The introduction of the universal superclass Object, however, makes type checking so loose that it can be rendered useless. For example, suppose that the GlobalCredit collection were designed to accept elements of any type, not just CreditCard:

```
boolean add(Object element)
```

Admittedly, the prospect of having such a collection is quite attractive: rather than using a different collection for each problem, the client would learn and use just one. And since many clients would be using this one collection repeatedly, its runtime and logic errors would likely be exposed and fixed over time. But this ultimate flexibility annihilates all the benefits of type checking. When the compiler checks an invocation of the above add method, for example, it ensures that the passed reference is of the type Object, but *any* reference is, which means the client can pass anything. The problem resurfaces when elements are retrieved from the collection. The get method returns an instance of the type Object, and the client must cast it back to its original type before working with it. All these casts escape the thorough checking of the compiler, and safety is again sacrificed.

The above discussion seems to imply that developing one component to cater for all types is inconsistent with type checking. This was indeed the case until **generics**, also called **parameterized types**, were introduced. The generics idea allows an implementer to write a component that can handle only one type T but without specifying T. It is the client who specifies T.

In other words, the component is non-specific—hence the adjective "generic"—until it is used. As an example, assume that the collection Bag is generic, and we want to use it to store credit cards. We do so along the following lines:

```
Bag<CreditCard> bag = new Bag<CreditCard>();
```

The addition of a class name between angle brackets after the name of the collection class allows the client to specify the type T. From now on, the bag instance accepts only credit cards as elements. For example, the statement

```
bag.add("Java");
```

which attempts to add a string, will produce a compile-time error, *not* a runtime error.

In summary, generics allow developers to write components that work with a type that is determined by the client. This combines the benefits of generic reusable components with type checking. Generics were added to Java in J2SE 1.5. We will see concrete examples of generics in Chapter 10.

Summary of Key Concepts

1. A class C is said to be a **subclass** of class P if its API indicates that it **extends** P. In that case, P is said to be the **parent** or the immediate **superclass** of the **child** C.

2. If C is a subclass of P, then every public feature in P is also in C. This is why the two classes are said to have an **inheritance** or an **is-a** relationship. Specifically, C is said to **inherit** (some of its features) from P. You can say that C is a **specialization** of P or that P is a generalization of C.

3. A group of classes related by is-a relations can form an **inheritance hierarchy**: a treelike structure in which the **root** is the superclass or the great grandparent of all classes, and the remaining classes are its **descendants** (children and grand children). In the special case in which each parent has one child, the structure reduces to a linear one called an **inheritance chain**.

4. Java does not allow a class to extend more than one superclass. **Multiple-inheritance** is therefore *not* allowed in Java.

5. The API of a subclass amalgamates its features with those of its parent. It splits the field and method tables into two: the upper table lists the features added by the child, and the lower table lists the features inherited from the parent.

6. If a child-added method has the same signature as one present in the parent, it is said to **override** it. The parent's method in this case will not appear in the lower table. It becomes inaccessible to the client.

7. If a child-added field has the same type as one present in the parent, it is said to **shadow** it. The parent's field in this case will not appear in the lower table. It becomes inaccessible to the client.

8. The CreditCard class in type.lib encapsulates a credit card that can be used to charge purchases. The card keeps track of, among other things, the dollar balance that the cardholder owes. The RewardCard class (also in type.lib) is a subclass of CreditCard. It encapsulates a card, which is a credit card, but offers reward points with every purchase. It therefore also keeps track of a point balance.

9. The **substitutability principle** states that whenever a reference of the type X is expected in a Java program, you can substitute a reference of the type Y if Y is a subclass of X.

10. The compiler performs **early binding** of methods at compile-time. It searches for the method's

signature in the class of the reference on which the invocation is made. This class is determined based on the declaration statement of the reference, *not* on the actual object that the reference points at.

11. The signature search of early binding is tolerant: it performs widening conversions for primitive types and subclass-superclass substitutions for references. The search culminates either in a compile-time error (if the signature was not found) or in a signature. In the latter case, the signature is stored in the class file.

12. The virtual machine performs **late binding** of methods at runtime. It searches for the exact signature determined by early binding in the class of the object that the reference points at. If the reference is not `null`, the signature *will* be found.

13. No late binding is done for static methods and fields. For them, early binding is the final binding.

14. When a method is invoked on a reference whose type is a root of some hierarchy, then the invocation is said to be **polymorphic** because the method that will actually be invoked is determined at runtime and can be one of several.

15. The `instanceof` relational operator enables us to test whether a given reference points to an instance of a given class or to of one of its subclasses.

16. It is possible to manually **cast** a reference. The syntax, similar to the cast of primitive types, asks that we place the name of the class to cast to between parentheses. We should design our programs to avoid casting as much as possible. If a cast is necessary, then it should be preceded by a test using the `instanceof` operator.

17. The compiler examines a cast based on the declared type of the reference and allows it only if it is up or down an inheritance hierarchy. The virtual machine examines a cast based on the type of the object that the reference points at and allows it only if it is the type of the object or up an inheritance hierarchy.

18. An **abstract class** is a class that cannot be instantiated. It is used as a superclass to hold features common to a number of classes. To use such a class, you must obtain an instance to a subclass of it. This is typically done through a **factory method** or a subclass constructor.

19. An **interface** is a (non-primitive) type that cannot be instantiated. To use it, you must find a class that **implements** it and then instantiate that class. Since a class can implement multiple interfaces, the interface is often used like an abstract class but in situations where a sub/superrelation is already used up. Technically, an interface is like a class, but it has only the headers of methods, not their bodies. As for attributes, it can have only `static final` attributes.

20. All Java classes form a giant hierarchy with the `Object` class at its root. As such, all classes inherit, and often override, the methods in `Object`. These methods include `equals`, `toString`, and `getClass`.

21. Components that handle `Object` elements are general, in that they can handle *any* type, but their generality thwarts the powerful type-checking mechanism that makes Java a safe programming language. **Generics**, also called **parameterized types**, allow us to have general components yet retain type checking.

22. A generic component can handle a specific type `T` determined by the client, not the implementer. Using `<T>` after the component's name (i.e., the desired class between two angle brackets), the client informs the compiler that only elements of the type `T` (or its subclasses) can be used with this component.

Review Questions

1. How do you determine whether a class extends another given its API? What if you were given the UML class diagram?
2. Given that a class extends another, what can you say about the features of the two classes?
3. If a class extends another, why is it thought of as a specialization?

4. Argue that an inheritance hierarchy can be thought of as several inheritance chains with a class in common.

5. Is it possible for a class to have two children? How about two parents?

6. If a subclass has a method with the same name as a parent's method but with a different parameter list, which method will appear in the subclass API and in which table? Will your answer change if the child's method has the same parameter list as that of the parent?

7. If a subclass has a field with the same name as a parent's field, which of the two will appear in the subclass API and in which table? Will your answer change if the child's field has the same type as that of the parent?

8. Why is the `charge` method in `CreditCard` boolean?

9. Why is the `pay` method of the `CreditCard` class not overridden in `RewardCard`?

10. What is the substitutability principle?

11. Substitutability applies in assignment statements. Name another location within a program where it also applies.

12. Give an example of substitutability in everyday (not software) objects.

13. It is said that early and late bindings differ in the class in which the signature search is conducted. Explain this difference.

14. It is said that early and late bindings differ in the strictness of their signature searches. Explain this difference.

15. Is late binding applicable to static fields? How about nonstatic fields?

16. (a) Is late binding applicable to static methods?
    (b) Argue that invoking such methods on a refer-ence (rather than a class name) is therefore misleading.

17. Explain the meaning of polymorphism.

18. A repair shop has a sign that says, "We Repair Home Appliances." Argue that this is a polymor-phic statement.

19. Argue that static methods are not polymorphic.

20. Give an example of a cast that triggers a compile-time error.

21. Give an example of a cast that triggers a runtime error.

22. Why is it a good idea to avoid casts?

23. Can the `instanceof` operator lessen the risks of casts?

24. Why do we need abstract classes? Can they have attributes?

25. How do you obtain an instance whose type is an abstract class?

26. What is a factory method?

27. What is an interface, and how is it different from a class?

28. Argue that if an interface is allowed to have non-static attributes, the attributes would be inaccessible to any class.

29. If class C extends class P, is C a descendant of the `Object` class?

30. Explain the benefits of compile-time type check-ing in Java.

31. Explain the advantages and disadvantages of hav-ing collections that accept elements of the type `Object`.

32. How can a generic collection be generic (i.e., gen-eral) yet enable type checking?

The Fraction and Shape Hierarchies

L9.1   The `Fraction-MixedNumber` Hierarchy

The `Fraction` class in `type.lib` encapsulates a fraction, the mathematical entity that we represent as n/d (n is the numerator, and d is the denominator). The `MixedNumber` class extends the `Fraction` class. It encapsulates the mathematical entity

$$\pm \ w \ n/d$$

where w is the whole part, n is the proper numerator, and d is the proper denominator. The class ensures that n<d at all times, hence the qualifier "proper." For example, "five and a half" is a mixed number with a positive sign; w=5, n=1, d=2.

1. Inheritance is an is-a relationship. Is it sensible to say, "A mixed number is a fraction"?
2. Launch your editor, and write the program `Lab9` that contains

   ```
   Fraction x = new MixedNumber(1, 5, 1, 2);
   ```

   Does the program compile? Is this statement legal? Why?
3. Add the following lines to `Lab9`:

   ```
   String secret = x.toString();
   output.println(secret);
   ```

   How will the compiler bind this invocation? The `toString` method appears in both the `Fraction` and the `MixedNumber` classes, and the reference x is declared as one and assigned as another. Do not compile or run your program.
4. How will the virtual machine bind this invocation? Compile and run your program. Determine whether late binding respected or ignored early binding.
5. Add the following lines to `Lab9`:

   ```
   output.println(x.getWhole());
   ```

   How will the compiler bind this invocation? The `getWhole` method appears only in the `MixedNumber` class. Verify your answer by compiling. If it does not compile, comment this statement out.
6. Add the following lines to `Lab9`:

   ```
   Fraction y = new MixedNumber(1, 1, 3, 4);
   x.add(y);
   output.println(x);
   ```

   How will the compiler bind this invocation? The `add` method appears only in the `Fraction` class. Verify your answer by compiling.
7. How will the virtual machine bind this invocation? Compile and run your program. Determine whether late binding respected or ignored early binding.

8. We want to invoke the getWhole method on x. The virtual machine has no problem doing so because x is indeed pointing at a MixedNumber object. If only the compiler would let us reach the virtual machine. Can you convince the compiler to let this invocation through?

9. We want to invoke the Fraction's toString method on x. We will convince the virtual machine to let us do so by casting. Add the following line to Lab9:

```
secret = ((Fraction) x).toString();
output.println(secret);
```

Predict the output, then verify by compiling and running. Explain the behaviour witnessed here in contrast with that of the previous task.

L9.2 The Shape Hierarchy

The Shape interface in java.awt encapsulates a two-dimensional geometric shape that divides the *x-y* plane into two regions: one inside the shape and one outside it. It provides several methods, two of which we focus on:

- boolean contains(double x, double y) This method returns true if the point with the coordinates (x,y) lies inside the shape; otherwise it returns false.
- boolean intersects(double x, double y, double w, double h) This method returns true if the shape intersects with the rectangular area whose upper-left corner is (x, y) and has width w and height h.

This interface is implemented by several concrete classes. We will focus on three:

```
Line2D.Double
Rectangle2D.Double
Ellipse2D.Double
```

It is odd to have a dot in a class name. Technically, this is because the Double class is defined "inside" the Rectangle2D class, but for all practical purposes, you can ignore this and just think of the Rectangle2D.Double class as an odd name.

These classes reside in java.awt.geom. We will demonstrate their constructors through the following examples:

- Line2D.Double(20, 30, 150, 200) This constructor constructs a line segment from (20, 30) to (150, 200).

- Rectangle2D.Double(50, 75, 40, 80) This constructor constructs a rectangle whose upper-left corner is at (50, 75) and has a width of 40 units and a height of 80 units.

- Ellipse2D.Double(50, 75, 40, 80) This constructor constructs an ellipse whose bounding rectangle has (50, 75) as its upper-left corner and has a width of 40 units and a height of 80 units.

1. Launch your editor, and write the program Lab9B that starts off by creating a frame:

```
JFrame frame = new JFrame("My Frame");
frame.setDefaultCloseOperation(JFrame.DISPOSE_ON_CLOSE);
frame.setVisible(true);
frame.pack();
```

If you prefer, start by loading the Paint program of Lab 8 and save it as Lab9B.

2. Create a UniPanel, and add it to the content pane of the frame:

```
Container content = frame.getContentPane();
UniPanel panel = new UniPanel();
content.add(panel)
```

3. Allow the user to size the frame. Once done, obtain a canvas instance:

```
output.println("Resize the frame then press ENTER");
input.nextLine();
Graphics2D canvas = panel.getGraphics2D();
```

4. Now create a Shape object, for example,

```
Rectangle2D.Double r;
r = new Rectangle2D.Double(10, 10, 200, 100);
```

5. Draw the outline of the shape on the canvas:

```
canvas.draw(r);
panel.repaint();
```

6. Create a second rectangle below the first and draw it filled; that is, pass its instance to the fill method instead of the draw method.

```
canvas.fill(r2);
panel.repaint();
```

7. Draw a third rectangle but with a thicker brush:

```
BasicStroke bs = new BasicStroke(20f);
canvas.setStroke(bs);
Shape r3 = new Rectangle2D.Double(250, 10, 200, 100);
canvas.draw(r3);
panel.repaint();
```

8. Generate a drawing similar to that in Fig. 9.12. You can use the rotate method of Lab8 in a loop.

9. Use the setColor method of Lab8 to change the brush's colour.

10. In Lab8 you learned how to draw text in a variety of fonts and sizes. Write your name inside any of the triangles drawn earlier.

11. Repeat the above steps to draw a line or an ellipse instead of a rectangle.

Figure 9.12 A snapshot of the canvas after performing the operations in the Lab.

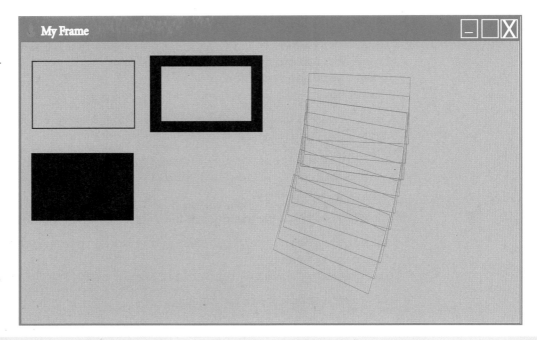

Exercises

Programming exercises are indicated with an asterisk.

9.1 Whenever a program creates an instance of a class, Java automatically creates an instance of its superclass. Use this fact to argue that based on instance count, not feature count, the sub/super nomenclature is justifiable.

9.2 Let A be the target class of an early binding of a method invocation, and let B be the target class of the corresponding late binding. Prove that if the invocation compiles successfully, then class B must be either class A or a subclass of A.

9.3 We claimed that the virtual machine *always* succeeds in finding an exact signature match during late binding. Prove this claim.

9.4 Consider the UML class diagrams shown in Fig. 9.13. Determine the API of class B; that is, produce a diagram similar to Fig. 9.3 and justify your answer.

9.5 For each of the following pairs of statements, determine whether the pair will generate compile-time errors in light of Fig. 9.13:

(a) A a = new B();
     B b = new A();
(b) B b = new B();
     b.beta = 12;
(c) A a = new B();
     a.beta = 12;

Figure 9.13 An inheritance chain for Exercise 9.4

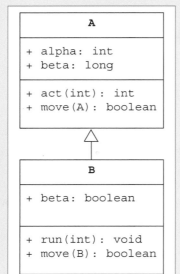

9.6 Based on the inheritance chain in Fig. 9.13, show that the following fragment will lead to compile-time errors:

```
A x = new A();
x.run(5);
```

9.7 The following fragment is meant to fix the compile-time error in Exercise 9.6:

```
A x = new A();
((B) x).run(5);
```

Argue that the modified fragment will successfully compile but that it will now lead to a runtime error.

9.8 Based on the inheritance chain in Fig. 9.13, argue that the following fragment will not lead to compile-time or runtime errors:

```
A x = new B();
((B) x).run(5);
```

Show also that the cast in it is necessary.

9.9 The following fragment uses the inheritance chain in Fig. 9.13:

```
A x = new B();
x.move(x);
```

(a) Write the signature in which early binding culminates.
(b) Argue that late binding will find two methods in the target class, but that since it looks for an exact (rather than a most specific) match, it will bind with the method in A.

9.10 Argue that if an abstract class contains a factory method, then it *must* be a `static` method.

9.11 Consider the interface shown in Fig. 9.14.
Determine whether the following fragment will lead to compile-time errors:

```
X r = new Y();
r.m();
```

9.12 The Omega class contains the following method:

Figure 9.14 A UML diagram for Exercise 9.11

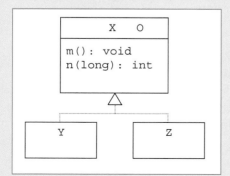

```
public static void shift(X p)
```

where `X` is the interface shown in Fig. 9.14. Argue that all the following invocations are correct:

(a)
```
X r = new Y();
Omega.shift(r);
```
(b)
```
Y r = new Y();
Omega.shift((X) r);
```
(c)
```
Y r = new Y();
Omega.shift(r);
```

9.13 The `GlobalCredit` collection in `type.lib` was designed to be a collection of credit cards. Had it been designed as a generic collection, we could have used it to store objects of type `Fraction` by creating an instance as follows:

```
GlobalCredit<Fraction> gc = new
GlobalCredit<Fraction>();
```

Given this `gc` reference, write a fragment that creates a fraction, stores it in the collection, and then retrieves it without using a single cast.

9.14* Write a program that starts with the following statements:

```
Fraction f = new Fraction(4, 3);
Fraction prod = new Fraction(1, 1);
```

The program must then create a loop that computes f^{10}. Output the result as well as the return of the `Fraction`'s pow method, and compare.

9.15* Modify the program in Exercise 9.14 so that it computes the 10th power of the mixed number 1 1/3 (one and one-third), which has the same value as the fraction 4/3. The challenge is that you may only modify the right-hand side of the two statements shown above.

9.16* Write a program that generates statistics about the return type of the `getRandom` method of the `MixedNumber` class. Specifically, invoke this `static` method 100 times and then output the percentage of times the return was of the type `Fraction` and the percentage of times it was of the type `MixedNumber`. Use the `instanceof` operator. Hint: Since `instanceof` returns `true` even when comparing a class to its superclass, the order of your `else-if` statements is important.

9.17* Repeat Exercise 9.16, but instead of using the `instanceof` operator, use the `getClass` method of Section 9.3.1.

9.18* Write a program that generates statistics about the return type of the `getRandom` method of the `Money` class. Specifically, invoke this `static` method 100 times and then output the percentage of times the return was of the type `Fraction`, the percentage of times it was of the type `MixedNumber`, and the percentage of times it was of the type `Money`.

Hint: Since `instanceof` returns `true` even when comparing a class to its superclass, the order of your `else-if` statements is important.

9.19* Repeat Exercise 9.18, but rather than invoking the `getRandom` method on the class, invoke it on the following instance:

```
Fraction tmp = new Money();
```

(Recall from Section 4.3.3 that static features can be invoked using the class name or a reference.) Explain the output.

Hint: See Section 9.2.3 to determine whether polymorphism is applicable here.

9.20* The following fragment seeks to invoke the `toString` method of the `Object` class in order to determine the memory address of a `Fraction` instance (Section 9.4.2):

```
Object tmp = new Fraction();
output.println(tmp.toString());
output.println(((Object) tmp).toString());
```

Two attempts were made to ensure that the `toString` method in the `Object` class, rather than its overriding version in the `Fraction` class, is invoked. Explain why both attempts fail.

9.21* Consider the following fragment:

```
Fraction xFr = new Fraction(225, 100);
Fraction yFr = new Fraction(227, 100);
output.println(xFr.resembles(yFr));
MixedNumber xMi = new MixedNumber(1, 2, 25, 100);
MixedNumber yMi = new MixedNumber(1, 5, 27, 100);
output.println(xMi.resembles(yMi));
Money xMo = new Money(2.25);
Money yMo = new Money(5.27);
output.println(xMo.resembles(yMo));
```

Write a brief explanation of its output.

9.22* Consider the following fragment:

```
Fraction x = new Money(2.25);
Money y = new Money(5.27);
output.println(x.resembles(y));
output.println(((MixedNumber) x).resembles(y));
output.println(((Money) x).resembles(y));
```

Run the fragment, and write a detailed explanation of its output.

9.23 The web site of this book contains a collection of tests, and you are now in position to take Test C, which covers Chapters 1 to 9. Follow these steps:

- Print and read the outline of the test. It tells you what kind of questions will be on the test, how they are weighted, and what aids are allowed.
- Print the test and take it. Do not use any book or API, and ensure that you do not exceed the allotted time.
- After taking the test, read the answers, and use their marking guidelines to mark your own test.

eCheck

Check09A (TS = 31)

Write the app `Check09A` that starts by finding out whether the user wants to work with a credit card or a reward card. Afterwards, it prompts the user to enter the various transactions that were made on this card. They can be either charge (C) or payment (P) transactions. When all transactions are entered, the app outputs a transaction count, the number of rejected transactions, and the final card balance. Here are two sample runs:

```
Credit or Reward card? [C or R] ... C
Enter the transactions of this card
```

```
(One per line, empty line=sentinel)
C450.00
C30
P100
C75
P200

Transaction Count = 5
Rejected Transactions = 0
Card balance = 255.00

Credit or Reward card? [C or R] ... R
Enter the transactions of this card
(One per line, empty line=sentinel)
C700
C250
C900
Failed!
P200
C70

Transaction Count = 5
Rejected Transactions = 1
Card balance = 820.00
```

Note that when a transaction is rejected (because a charge causes the balance to exceed the credit limit), the app displays the message "Failed!" and then continues reading. Note also that the balance is rounded to the nearest cent.

Your app should start by creating a card with arbitrary number and name. It should then process the transactions by invoking the appropriate method. You can assume, as a pre, that the input is valid; i.e. the first input is indeed C or R and the transactions are all made up of a letter (C or P or c or p) followed by a double.

Develop your app, test it, and then eCheck it.

> **Note:** *If you believe that the first input (C or R) is immaterial then you do understand substitutability!*

Check09B (TS = 36)

Write the app Check09B that behaves as shown in the following sample run:

```
Enter trigger level [1-100]  ... 10
971412-3*    1000    190.86      <
280030-5*    1000    113.46      <
814334-4     5000    17.92
479509-2     5000    72.30
123456-6*    1000    180.52    <
323436-6*    1000    114.24    <
515707-2*    1000    194.95    <
```

```
340463-7     5000    45.90
123734-7     5000    33.45
464703-3     1000    33.00
004134-6     5000    77.82
859717-8     1000    103.63    <
605075-4*    5000    239.63

Number of cards = 13
Percentage of reward cards = 46%
Average balance = 109.05
```

The app starts by prompting for and reading a trigger level, which is interpreted as a percent. You can assume as a pre that the input is an integer between 1 and 100. Next, the app generates a random GlobalCredit instance using its getRandom method. The instance is a collection of cards, some are credit cards and some are rewards cards. The app traverses the cards; determines their average balance; and produces the listing shown above. Each line starts with the card number suffixed with an asterisk if this card's balance is above average, i.e. exceed the average balance of all cards. This is followed by a tab character and the cards credit limit formatted without decimals. The next, tab-delimited, entry is the card's balance formatted with two decimals. If the card's balance divided by the credit limit is less than the indicated trigger, i.e. less than 10% in the above example, then the line ends. Otherwise, the balance is followed by a tab and the "<" character. The listing ends with an empty line followed by the shown stats. The percentage is formatted without decimals while the balance is formatted with two decimals.

Develop your app, test it, and then eCheck it.

Check09C (TS = 31) The Fraction hierarchy consists of three classes: Fraction, MixedNumber, and Money. The base class Fraction encapsulates a mathematical fraction (numerator and denominator) and supports basic arithmetic operations. The MixedNumber subclass encapsulates a mixed number, which is a fraction viewed as a whole part plus a proper fraction (numerator less than denominator). The Money subclass encapsulates an amount of money, which is a mixed number with the denominator being 100, a whole part being the dollar amount, and a numerator being the cent amount. All three classes also handle negative values. See Lab 9 and the API of type.lib for details.

We want to write a program that computes some statistics on the return of the getRandom method of the Money class. Here is a sample run:

```
Sample size?
5
0      $1,477 dollars and 92 cents.
1      - 742 45/148
2      23/19
3      $1,972 dollars and 32 cents.
4      $2,196 dollars and 91 cents.
Sum    34489577/7030
Mixed 20.%
Ptive 80.%
```

The program, Check09B, starts by prompting for and reading a sample size, which you can assume to be positive without validation. It then invokes Money.getRandom that many times and prints the iteration number (starting from 0) and the toString of each return delimited by a tab. In the above example, the loop involves five iterations, and we can see (from the printed values) that the five returned references were of the types Money, MixedNumber, Fraction, Money, and Money. After the loop, the program outputs three lines: the sum of the generated sample (as a fraction), the percentage of references of the type MixedNumber (one of five in the above), and the percentage of positive values (four of five in the above). Note that each of these three lines is also tab-delimited and that the percentages are rounded to zero decimals.

It is very important that you think about the methods that you will need before starting your implementation. A polymorphic method, for example, will be auto-selected by the virtual machine and, hence, does not require if statements. In fact, a properly thought-out program should not have more than five statements in the body of the loop.

Here is a second sample run:

```
Sample size?
15
0        $1,092 dollars and 58 cents.
1        - 998 59/77
2        14/45
3        $2,002 dollars and 51 cents.
4        + 784 23/49
5        + 319 6/35
6        $1,758 dollars and 8 cents.
7        - 155 167/550
8        - 166 58/119
9        $2,633 dollars and 78 cents.
10       $2,086 dollars and 64 cents.
11       - 298 51/638
12       2/773
13       $1,589 dollars and 15 cents.
14       $1,934 dollars and 34 cents.
Sum      581515226966704/46216568475
Mixed    40%
Ptive    73%
```

Develop your app, test it, and then eCheck it.

Technical Note: Do not use the setSeed method of the Fraction class in your program. It is used internally by eCheck to ensure that your program receives the same random sample as the oracle.

Check09D (TS = 31)

Write the app Check09D that starts by obtaining a random `type.lib.Student` instance using the `getRandom` method of that class. It then behaves as shown in this sample run:

```
Student Name: VBIA
Student ID:   200102001
Student GPA:  1.3

1738  D
4203  D
2842  F
Do you think this is a SE student?
Enter y or n ... y
This is in fact a CSEstudent
```

Note that the student GPA is formatted with one decimal. After an empty line, the app displays the courses that the student has taken together with the obtained grades, one course per line. The fields in the line are tab delimited.

The app then asks the user to make a guess as to whether this is a SE student (rather than IT, CE, or CSE). You can assume that the input will be either Y or N (in upper or lower case) If the user answered correctly, the app displays the message "You are right!", otherwise it does not. In both cases, the app continues by displaying the actual type of the student, as shown above.

Here is a second sample run:

```
Student Name: XGGS
Student ID:   200105001
Student GPA:  9.0

1962  B
1106  A
3234  A
4186  B
Do you think this is a SE student?
Enter y or n ... n
You are right!
This is in fact a ITstudent
```

Develop your app, test it, and then eCheck it.

IO

The Collection Framework

A large number of applications store and manage a vast amount of data. In the object world, we always associate data with the code that manipulates it; hence, there is a need for ready-made components that store and manage a vast number of objects. In Chapter 8, you learned about aggregate classes that can hold objects of a specific type; and in Chapter 9, you learned that generics allow components to have types that are set at instantiation time. In this chapter, we study collections that put these two ideas together and, thus, hold objects of any type.

Learning Objectives

1. *Learn about the collection framework*

2. *Use lists, sets, and maps and their associated methods*

3. *Experience generics and become familiar with their notation*

4. *Appreciate the need for iterators, and use the enhanced* `for` *loop*

5. *Explore the polymorphic algorithms of the* `Collections` *utility*

6. *Apply the collection techniques to a variety of problems*

Chapter Outline

10.1 What Is the Collection Framework?

The **collection framework** provides ready-made components in the Java standard library to support applications involving collections. These components consist of interfaces, classes that implement the interfaces, and a collection of polymorphic algorithms. The following sections introduce the most commonly used components in the framework.

10.1.1 The Main Interfaces

Recall from Chapter 8 that a collection is an aggregate that can hold a varying number of elements. But unlike the collections that we used in Chapter 8, which were designed with particular applications in mind, the collections in the framework are meant to be general. They should be general not only in terms of the type of elements they can store (this will be discussed in Section 10.1.3), but also in terms of the views they provide to the client. The framework provides the three main interfaces: List, Set, and Map. See Fig. 10.1.

Each interface provides a distinct view of the elements.

List

The List interface allows the program to view the elements as a **sequence**. The word *sequence* implies that positional order is significant (e.g., [a,b] is not the same as [b,a]). This, in turn, implies that duplicate elements are allowed. (In the list [a,b,a] we can distinguish the two as because they have different positions.) For example, a string can be viewed as a list of characters.

Set

The Set interface allows the app to view the elements as a mathematical set. Recall that in a set order is insignificant (e.g., [a,b] is the same as [b,a]); hence, duplicate elements are not allowed (because they are indistinguishable). For example, the ID numbers of all students registered in a course form a set.

Map

The Map interface allows the program to view the elements as a mapping between a set of so-called **keys** and a set of so-called **values**. Each element in a map is thus a key-value pair. The

Figure 10.1 The main interfaces in the collection framework

```
┌─────────────────────┐  ┌─────────────────────┐  ┌─────────────────────────┐
│    List        ○    │  │    Set        ○     │  │    Map        ○         │
├─────────────────────┤  ├─────────────────────┤  ├─────────────────────────┤
│ add(element)        │  │ add(element)        │  │ add(key, value)         │
│ remove(element)     │  │ remove(element)     │  │ remove(key)             │
│ get(index)          │  │ iterator()          │  │ get(key)                │
│ iterator()          │  │ ...                 │  │ keySet(): Set           │
│ ...                 │  │                     │  │ ...                     │
└─────────────────────┘  └─────────────────────┘  └─────────────────────────┘
```

mapping must be a function (a key cannot map to more than one value) but does not have to be one-to-one (two keys can map to the same value). For example, a phonebook in which an entry contains a telephone number (the key) and its owner (the value) is a map.

In a given application, it should be straightforward to determine whether a list, a set, or a map is the appropriate interface to use. Note, however, that these are simply interfaces; hence, they can be used only for type declaration. To invoke methods, we need to find classes that implement these interfaces, and this is discussed in the next section.

IO.I.2 The Implementing Classes

If you were to ask a developer to make a collection for you, you would probably be bombarded with questions such as the following:

- How often do you insert/delete elements?
- Do you often add elements at the beginning of the list?
- How likely is it that elements in the middle of the list will be deleted?

You might argue that such questions are illegal because they break the encapsulation: why should the implementer know what I, the client, intend to do with a component? The developer might counter by saying that without the answers, performance might suffer significantly. This is precisely why the framework presented the three views as interfaces rather than classes: the client can rely on the stable contract of the interface and at the same time can fine-tune performance by selecting an appropriate implementing class.

To implement an interface, the implementer must decide how the elements of the collection will be stored in memory. Recall from Section 8.2.6 that, depending on how these elements are arranged, one can perform certain operations faster or slower. There are four main storage techniques: **Hash**, **Array**, **Tree**, and **Linked**. As the client, we do not know, and do not want to know, what these techniques mean, but we need to be aware of their names because they are used to name the implementing classes. Specifically, a class that implements the `List` interface using an `Array` is called the `ArrayList` class. Similarly, a class that implements the `Set` interface using a hash is called the `HashSet` class. Since there are three interfaces and four implementation techniques, we can have 12 implementing classes, but some techniques do not serve certain interfaces. For example, the Hash technique does not preserve positional order so it cannot be used for lists. Because of this, only 6 of the 12 possibilities are meaningful:

These classes are shown in Fig. 10.2 on page 379.

Interface	Implementing Classes
List	ArrayList, LinkedList
Set	HashSet, TreeSet
Map	HashMap, TreeMap

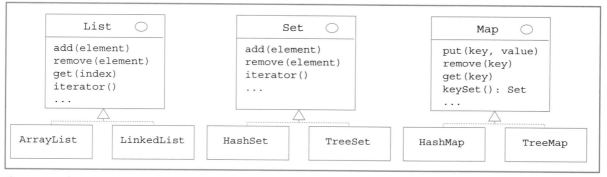

Figure 10.2 The main interfaces in the collection framework and some of the classes that implement them

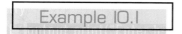

Write a program that prompts for and reads strings from the user, one per line, until the user enters an empty string. The program must store the strings in a collection and then output the returns of the size and toString methods of that collection. Use the List interface first and then re-run using the Set interface. Select any implementing class.

Answer:

The program is shown in Fig. 10.3.

Here is a sample run obtained by un-commenting the List statement:

```
Enter the elements pressing ENTER
after each.  [Empty line = sentinel]
a
b
a
c
Size = 4
[a, b, a, c]
```

And here is a sample run obtained by un-commenting the Set statement:

```
Enter the elements pressing ENTER
after each.  [Empty line = sentinel]
a
b
a
Already present... not added
c
Size = 3
[a, c, b]
```

As expected, the set contract did not allow a duplicate element; its add method returned false. The add method of the list contract, however, always returns true. Note, also, that the list implementation preserved the entry order, whereas the set implementation did not. In fact, there is no rule regarding how the elements of a set will be ordered when they are retrieved from the collection.

Figure 10.3 This program stores the user's entries in a collection named bag. Depending on which statement is uncommented, bag is either a list or a set.

```
// List<String> bag = new ArrayList<String>();
// Set<String> bag = new HashSet<String>();

output.println("Enter the elements pressing ENTER ");
output.println("after each. [Empty line = sentinel] ");

for (String in = input.nextLine(); in.length() != 0; in
   = input.nextLine ())
{
    if (!bag.add(in))
    {    output.println("Not added (already present)");
    }
}
output.println("Size = " + bag.size());
IO.println(bag);
```

The following guidelines will help you select the appropriate class. Keep in mind, however, that this is just a performance issue; if you select the wrong class for your interface, your program will still be correct, but it may be slower than it should be:

- Use ArrayList for the list interface by default (or whenever you are not sure). It is far more efficient than LinkedList except in two scenarios: a program that often adds or deletes elements at the first position in the list and a program that often traverses the list deleting elements or adding new ones as it visits.
- Use HashSet for the set interface by default (or whenever you are not sure). It is far more efficient than TreeSet, but the elements of the set are not sorted.
- Use HashMap for the map interface by default (or whenever you are not sure). It is far more efficient than TreeMap, but the elements of the map are not sorted.

Figure 10.4 This program stores the user's entries in a map. Each entry consists of a key, value pair delimited by a comma.

```
Map<String, String> bag = new HashMap<String, String>();
output.println("Enter the elements pressing ENTER ");
output.println("after each. [Empty line = sentinel] ");
for (String in = input.nextLine(); in.length() != 0; in
   = input.nextLine())
{
    int comma = in.indexOf(",");
    String key = in.substring(0, comma);
    String value = in.substring(comma + 1);
    bag.put(key, value);
}
output.println("Size = " + bag.size());
output.println(bag);
```

> ## Example 10.2
>
> Write a program that prompts for and reads pairs of strings from the user, one comma-delimited pair per line, until the user enters an empty string. The program must store the entries in a map such that the first string of each entered pair is the key and the second is the value. Output the returns of the `size` and `toString` methods of the map. Select any implementing class.
>
> **Answer:**
>
> The program is shown in Fig. 10.4.
>
> Note that the `put` method inserts elements in a map, not add. Here is a sample run:
>
> ```
> Enter the elements pressing ENTER
> after each. [Empty line = sentinel]
> copy,rm
> dir,ls
> copy,cp
> ren,mv
> move,mv
> Size = 4
> {ren=mv, copy=cp, move=mv, dir=ls}
> ```
>
> Note that in order to keep the mapping a function, you cannot have pairs with equal keys. Hence, when `copy,cp` was added, it overwrote the earlier `copy,rm`. It is permissible, however, to have two elements with the same value, as evidenced by the last two entries. Note, also, that entry order was not preserved. Just like a set, there is no rule regarding how the elements of a map will be ordered upon retrieval from the collection.

It is important to declare the collection reference using the interface name, not the name of the implementing class. Hence, instead of writing

```
ArrayList<E> bag = new ArrayList<E>();
```

write

```
List<E> bag = new ArrayList<E>();
```

This ensures that the rest of the program uses only features in the interface, not features peculiar to a particular implementing class. This, in turn, implies that you can change from one implementing class to another by editing one statement only in your program.

10.1.3 Revisiting Generics

To be able to cater to any application, the collections offered by the framework must be general in terms of the type of elements they accept. Unlike `Portfolio`, which can store only `Investment` elements, or `GlobalCredit`, which can store only `CreditCard` elements, the framework's collection must be able to store elements of any type. This can be achieved either by accepting elements of the type `Object` or by allowing the client to specify the object. It was pointed out in Section 9.3.3 that the first approach can lead to unsafe code because it is based on casts that cannot be checked at compile-time. It is used *only* if J2SE 5 (or later) is not available. The second approach is based on generics, and its code is type-safe.

If you instantiate an implementing class without specifying a type (within angle brackets), you are using the unsafe `Object`-based approach:

```
List bag = new ArrayList();
```

You can store *anything* in a collection created this way, even things that were not meant to be stored in it. For example, if you meant to store `Date` objects in this collection but accidentally stored a `String`, the compiler would not detect the mistake, and a runtime error would occur when you later retrieve the string and cast it to `Date`. To select the generics approach, specify the type of elements when the collection is created:

```
List<Date> bag = new ArrayList<Date>();
```

This collection can hold `Date` objects and only `Date` objects. If you attempt to store anything else in it, for example, a string,

```
bag.add("testing");
```

the compiler will issue an error. All classes and interfaces in the collection framework are equipped to handle generics.

In the remainder of this chapter, we will denote the generic element type of a list or a set collection by `<E>` and the types of the key and the value of a map collection by `<K>` and `<V>`, respectively.

It should be noted that types that differ in their generic types are not related in any way. For example, `List<String>` and `List<Integer>` are completely distinct types; neither of them extends the other. Even when the generic types are related by an is-a relationship, no such relationship exists between the types they parameterize; for example, `List<Integer>` is not related to `List<Number>` even though `Integer` is a subclass of `Number`. This point is very important from the client's perspective, because if an API lists a method with a `List<Number>` parameter, we cannot pass to it `List<Integer>` instead.

Most methods specify `<T>` as the generic type, as in `List<T>`; in that case, you can pass a list of any type. Some methods require that the generic type implement some interface or extend some class P, or be a superclass of some class C. In these cases, the API shows the generic type as

```
<? extends P> or <? super C>
```

You can interpret ? as a **type wildcard** that means "any type that." Note that "extends" in this wildcard convention encompasses class extension and interface implementation.

10.2 Using the Framework

The following sections present the most commonly used methods in collection framework.

10.2.1 API Highlights

The classes that implement the framework provide a large number of methods. In this section, we focus on only the key methods and emphasize the similarities and differences among the interfaces.

Constructor

Some classes offer several overloaded constructors to allow you to fine-tune the implementation and, hence, the performance. We will use the default constructor throughout this text.

Adding Elements

As we saw in Section 10.1.2, the `add` method is used for lists and sets, and the `put` method is used for maps. The header of `add` is

```
public boolean add(E o)
```

In lists, the return is always `true`, and the element is added at the end of the list. In sets, the return is `false` if the element to be added is already in the set. For maps, use

```
public V put(K key, V value)
```

The return is typically `null`, but if you attempt to add a mapping of an existing key, the new mapping will overwrite the old one, and the old value will be returned.

By definition, the list view applies to contexts in which the elements' positional order is significant; hence, all classes that implement the list interface have a second, overloaded method for adding elements at a specified position:

```
public void add(int index, E element)
```

This list-only method inserts the element at the specified position and adjusts the indices of all elements at the following positions, if any. As usual, positions are numbered starting from zero; hence, `index` must be in `[0, size()]`. Note that the interval is closed-closed (i.e., includes both ends); this is because there are `size()+1` positions in which the new elements can be added.

Removing Elements

For lists and sets, you can remove an element using the method

```
public boolean remove(Object o)
```

The return is `true` if the specified object was found and was removed, and `false` if the object was not found in the collection.

Note that in the case of a list, the specified element may be present more than once in the list. In this case, its first occurrence is removed. Furthermore, lists get a second, overloaded method that enables removing an element at a given position:

```
public E remove(int index)
```

The position, `index`, must be in the closed-open interval `[0, size())`. This list-only method removes the element at the specified position and returns it. The indices of all the following elements, if any, are adjusted.

Finally, maps use the following method for removing elements:

```
public V remove(K key)
```

If the key is present in the map, this method deletes its pair and returns the value that was associated with it; otherwise `null` is returned.

For example, in the following fragment, we create a mapping between airport codes and their cities. We add three mappings to the map, output the map, and then remove the pair that corresponds to "LHR":

```
Map<String, String> bag = new HashMap<String, String>();
bag.put("YYZ", "Toronto");
bag.put("LHR", "London");
bag.put("JFK", "New York");
output.println(bag);
output.println(bag.remove("LHR"));
output.println(bag);
```

Here is the generated output:

```
{YYZ=Toronto, JFK=New York, LHR=London}
London
{YYZ=Toronto, JFK=New York}
```

Accessing Elements

If you want to traverse all the elements use the iteration mechanism covered in Section 10.2.2. However, if you want to access a particular element (an action that is meaningful only in a list or a map), use the get method. For a list, its header is

```
public E get(int index)
```

If the index is valid (>=0 && < size), the method returns the element at the specified index; otherwise an exception occurs. For a map, the header is

```
public V get(K key)
```

If the specified key is present in the map, its associated value is returned; otherwise the return is null.

Searching for Elements

Lists and sets support the method

```
public boolean contains(E o)
```

If the passed object is an element in the collection, true is returned; otherwise the return is false. A similar method is available in maps:

```
public boolean containsKey(K key)
```

If the passed key is present in one of the map's pairs, true is returned; otherwise the return is false.

10.2.2 The Iterator

It is useful in many algorithms to traverse the elements of a collection such that no element is missed and no element is visited more than once. Such traversals enable us to generate reports (listings) or to search for elements that meet a condition.

List and Set Iterators

The list and set interfaces specify the method

```
public Iterator iterator()
```

It returns an instance of type **Iterator**, an object through which we can traverse the collection. Specifically, it has two methods:

```
public E next()
public boolean hasNext()
```

The next() method returns the next element in the collection or throws an exception if there are no more elements. The hasNext() method tells us whether there are any remaining elements, elements not yet visited in this traversal.

For example, if bag is a reference to any implementation of a list or set, then the following fragment traverses it:

```
Iterator<type> it = bag.iterator();
for (; it.hasNext();)
{
    output.println(it.next());
}
```

The Cursor

When the first statement in the above fragment is executed, an object of type Iterator is created and is set to point to just before the first element of the collection. We say that this object keeps a **cursor**. That cursor is positioned just before the first element.

Figure 10.5 depicts a collection of size n with elements e_0, e_1, ..., e_{n-1}.

When the iterator method is first called, the cursor is positioned to the left of e_0. When the next method is invoked, e_0 is returned, and the cursor is advanced to the position between e_0 and e_1. After the last invocation of next (when e_{n-1} is returned), the cursor is advanced to the right of e_{n-1}. At that point, hasNext will return false.

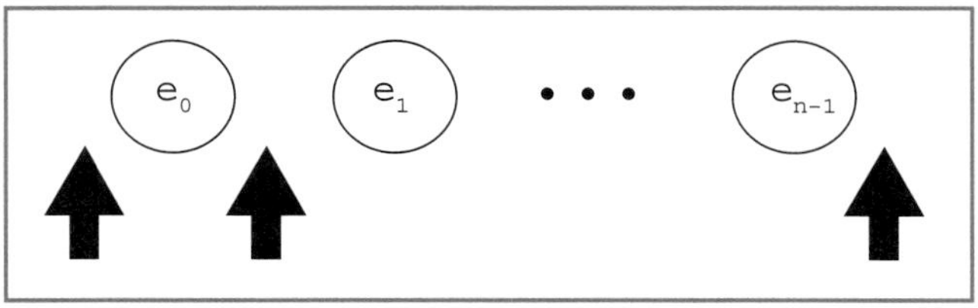

Figure 10.5 The iterator's cursor stays between elements.

An Iterator for Maps

The map interface does not have an iterator, but we can use its `get` method to visit all its values provided we can find a way to visit all its keys. To that end, the method

```
public Set<K> keySet()
```

is used. It returns all the keys present in the map as a set. The following fragment demonstrates using these two methods to visit every mapping pair of a given map bag:

```
Iterator<K> it = bag.keySet().iterator();
for (; it.hasNext();)
{
    K key = it.next();
    V value = bag.get(key);
    output.println(key + " maps to " + value);
}
```

The Enhanced for Loop

Java provides an enhanced version of the `for` loop to enable iterating over any collection regardless of its type. The syntax is as follows:

```
for (T variable : collection)
{
    . . .
}
```

For example, to iterate over a `<String>` list bag, we write

```
for (String x : bag)
{
    output.println(x);
}
```

For a `<String, Integer>` map, we write

```
for (String x : bag.keySet())
{
    output.printf("%s maps to %d%n", x, bag.get(x));
}
```

10.2.3 Searching and Sorting

The `Collections` class provides several algorithms, in the form of `static` methods, for manipulating collections that implement the `List` interface. There are methods for sorting the elements, randomly shuffling or copying them, etc. We will examine two methods: one for sorting and the other for searching.

Sorting

Sorting the elements of a list can be accomplished through the method

```
static void sort(List<T> list)
```

It accepts any instance that implements the list interface and sorts its elements. The word **sort** in computer science refers to arranging the elements in nondescending order. We say "nondescending" rather than the more direct "ascending" so that we can cover the duplicate-element case. Hence, the list of integers [3,6,3,7,0,4] is sorted as [0,3,3,4,6,7].

Given that the elements of the list can be of *any* type, this method needs some mechanism for determining whether an element is greater than, equal to, or less than another. To that end, it requires that the type T define a method:

```
int compareTo(T other)
```

This method is similar to that of the String class: its return is positive (negative) if the element on which it is invoked is greater than (less than) other; and its return is zero if the two are equal. To ensure that T contains such a method, we require that T implement an interface that contains it. The interface

```
java.lang.Comparable
```

has nothing but the above-mentioned compareTo method. Hence, the sort method should require that

```
T extends Comparable<T>
```

But this condition is too strong: if T did not define compareTo, but it extended some class C that implements Comparable<C>, then T would indirectly have compareTo thanks to the substitutability principle. For example, the class GregorianCalendar does not define its own compareTo method, but since it extends Calendar, which implements Comparable, it effectively has a compareTo. Hence, the condition can be relaxed to the following:

```
T extends Comparable<? super T>
```

In other words, the type of the elements of the list must implement Comparable or have a superclass that does.

Since element comparison is based on the elements themselves and not some externally imposed criterion, the resulting order is called the **natural ordering** of elements. For example, the wrapper classes use numeric order; the String class uses lexicographic order; and the Date class uses chronological order. For other classes, it is important that their compareTo method does not throw an exception for any two elements in the list; that is, the list elements must be mutually comparable.

The API of the sort method contains a note that the sort complexity is O(NlgN). This is just a note and is not part of the contract; that is, it is subject to change. It can be shown that no general sorting method can have a better worst-case complexity.

Example 10.3

Write a program that reads a given number of integers from the user, stores them in a list, sorts the list, and then outputs the list.

Answer:
The program is shown in Fig. 10.6.

```
final int SIZE = 5;
List<Integer> bag = new
ArrayList<Integer>();
output.println("Enter the elements");
for (int i = 0; i < SIZE; i++)
{
    int in = input.nextInt();
    bag.add(new Integer(in));
    // bag.add(in) will also work (autobox-
ing)
}
Collections.sort(bag);
output.println(bag);
```

Figure 10.6 This fragment reads integers and outputs them sorted.

```
Enter the elements
7 17 11 7 1
[1, 11, 17, 7, 7]
```

Here is a sample run:

```
Enter the elements
7 17 11 7 1
[1, 7, 7, 11, 17]
```

Note that the program in Example 10.3 used the Integer wrapper class to box the entered numbers. Could it have converted the numbers to strings instead? Such an attempt is shown in Fig. 10.7.

Here is a sample run of the string-based program using the same inputs as before:

The difference between the two outputs is a testimony to the beauty and power of polymorphism. Despite using the same collection and the same method, the computer "knew" that these strings are not numbers and sorted them accordingly.

Searching

In addition to sorting, the Collections class has a method for searching; that is, given an object, either state that it is not in the list or return its position in the list. We can do this by first using contains to determine whether the object is present, and then traverse the list to locate the element. In fact, it is preferable to skip invoking contains and just traverse.

Traversal-based searches were discussed in detail in Section 8.2.5. The techniques found there apply as is to the collection framework. The search loop can be implemented using an indexed traversal (for lists) or an iterator (for an arbitrary collection). And since the enhanced for loop provides an iteration that is independent of the collection type, we can write a generic search algorithm that works for any collection. This is shown in Fig. 10.8.

We saw in Section 8.2.5 that the complexity of any traversal-based search is linear, O(N). If the list is sorted, a faster algorithm is available:

Figure 10.7 This fragment reads integers as strings and outputs them sorted.

```
static int binarySearch(List<? extends T> list, T x)
```

This method searches the passed list for an element equal to x using the so-called binary search algorithm. It returns either the position at which x was found or a negative integer to indicate that the search has failed.

Binary search has an O(lgN) complexity, which is considerably faster than linear search. Note, however, that the method's precondition is that the passed list is sorted. If it is not, one cannot predict what will happen: an exception could be thrown, a wrong result might be returned, etc. By definition, the implementer does not check the precondition; hence, the contract cannot specify what happens when the precondition is false.

```
final int SIZE = 5;
List<String> bag = new
ArrayList<String>();
output.println("Enter the elements");
for (int i = 0; i < SIZE; i++)
{
    int in = input.nextInt();
    bag.add("" + in);
}
Collections.sort(bag);
output.println(bag);
```

```
// Search for x in bag

boolean found = false;
for (E element : bag)
{
    found = found || element.equals(x);
}

// Invariant: found ⇔ "x has been seen in 'bag'"
```

10.2.4 Summary of Features

Figure 10.9 summarizes the commonly used features of the collection framework.

Remember that the shown methods in the `Collections` class apply only to lists and that binary search works only if the list is sorted.

10.3 Applications

The following sections present problems of a general nature and then solve them using a variety of techniques from the collection framework.

10.3.1 Detecting Duplicates

Given a list of integers, determine whether its elements are distinct. For example, if the list is [5, 4, 2, 6, 2], then the program should state that its elements are not distinct because the number 2 appears more than once in it.

Before designing the program, let us write a fragment that generates a list of random integers, and let the list size be random too. To keep the display size manageable, we will keep the integers and the size under 20. The fragment is shown in Fig. 10.10.

After creating the list and printing it, the program declares a flag, `distinct`, and sets it to `true` as a default. We must now add logic that keeps this flag `true` if the elements are indeed distinct, and makes it `false` otherwise. The final output displays the flag's status. Here is a sample run of this program (without the final output):

```
List generated. Size = 18
[6, 15, 9, 5, 5, 9, 2, 8, 13, 1, 13, 7, 2, 1, 15, 11, 3, 7]
```

There are several ways to detect whether an element is repeated, and each has its merit. Let us look at three approaches:

Approach 1

It is easy to spot duplicates if we sort the list because the sorting makes them consecutive. Hence, let us first sort the list and then traverse it. During the traversal, we must compare each element with the one that follows it, and this implies a loop such as the following:

```
for (int i = 0; i < bag.size() - 1; i++)
```

Figure 10.9 A quick reference to the main methods of the collection framework

LIST	SET	MAP
Adding Elements		
`boolean` `add(E e)`		
	`boolean` `add(E e)`	`V` `put(K key, V value)`
`void` `add(int index, E e)`		
Removing Elements		
`boolean` `remove(E e)`		
	`boolean` `remove(E e)`	`V` `remove(K key)`
`E` `remove(int index)`		
Accessing an Element		
`E` `get(int index)`	*none*	`V` `get(K key)`
Searching the Elements		
`boolean` `contains(E o)`	`boolean` `contains(E o)`	`boolean` `containskey(K key)`
Traversing the Elements		

`Iterator`
`iterator()`
 	
invoke on it:
 	
`E next()`
`boolean hasNext()`
	`Iterator`
	`iterator()`
	
	invoke on it:
	
	`E next()`
	`boolean hasNext()`
		`Iterator`
		`keySet().iterator()`
		
		invoke on it:
		
		`E next()`
		`boolean hasNext()`

Other methods (available in all three interfaces)		
`equals, size, toString`		
Algorithms for lists only (`static` methods in the `Collections` class)		
`binarySearch, copy, fill, reverse, shuffle, sort`		

This makes i stop just before the last element, which means the loop's body can compare element i with element i+1. For example, if the list contains 10 elements (indexed 0 through 9), i will stop at 8, which allows the loop's body to compare element 8 with element 9.

Before the loop begins, the value of `distinct` matches the `true`/`false` value of the sentence

    All the elements seen thus far are distinct.

At this stage, both distinct and the sentence are true. Let us design the loop so that these two values are always equal; that is, the loop invariant is

    `distinct` ⇔ *All the elements seen thus far are distinct.*

Figure 10.10
This program
generates a ran-
dom number of
randomly chosen
integers and
stores it in a list.
The fragment
denoted by the
ellipsis (...)
detects duplicates
in the list and
sets -
distinct
accordingly.

```
import java.util.*;
import java.io.PrintStream;

public class Duplicates
{
    public static void main(String[] args)
    {
        Scanner input = new Scanner(System.in);
        PrintStream output = System.out;

        final int SIZE = 20;
        Random rng = new Random();
        int size = rng.nextInt(SIZE);
        List<Integer> bag = new ArrayList<Integer>();
        for (int i = 0; i < size; i++)
        {
            int in = rng.nextInt(size);
            bag.add(new Integer(in));
        }
        output.println("List generated. Size = " + size);
        output.println(bag);

        boolean distinct = true;
        ... // detect duplicates in bag
        output.println("Distinctiveness is " + distinct);
    }
}
```

This requires comparing two elements and updating distinct so that it maintains the above invariant:

```
distinct = distinct && !bag.get(i).equals(bag.get(i+1));
```

As long as the pairs are not equal, distinct remains equal to true. Once an equal pair is encountered, distinct becomes false. Afterward, it remains false regardless of the pairs that follow because "anding" anything with false yields false. This leads us to the code shown in the upper part of Fig. 10.11.

Figure 10.11
This approach
detects duplicates
by sorting then
traversing. The
upper version is
correct because it
maintains a loop
invariant. The
lower version
speeds up the
upper version by
exiting the loop
upon encounter-
ing a duplicate.

```
Collections.sort(bag);
for (int i = 0; i < bag.size() - 1; i++)
{
    distinct = distinct && !bag.get(i).equals(bag.get(i + 1));
}


Collections.sort(bag);
for (int i = 0; i < bag.size() - 1 && distinct; i++)
{
    distinct = !bag.get(i).equals(bag.get(i + 1));
}
```

We can improve the performance of this code by terminating the loop when an equal pair is encountered. This is shown in the lower part of Fig. 10.11.

Example 10.4

Modify the code of Fig. 10.11 so that it also displays the duplicate element if the list contains duplicates. If more than one duplicate exists, display any one of them.

Answer:
Add a variable that remembers the last visited element. Since the loop is exited upon finding a duplicate, the content of that variable after the loop will be the sought duplicate:

```
Integer last;
for (int i = 0; i < bag.size() - 1 && distinct; i++)
{
    last = bag.get(i);
    distinct = !last.equals(bag.get(i + 1));
}
if (!distinct) output.println(last);
```

This program will not compile. The compiler will point to the last statement and claim that `last` may not have been initialized. Indeed, if the list were empty, the loop would be skipped and `last` would be uninitialized. This is not a compiler nuisance; it exposes a weakness in our logic because we need to recognize this possibility and have a value for `last` that corresponds to it. We therefore initialize `last` as follows:

```
Integer last = null;
```

This program will now compile. Running it on the 18-element sample run shown earlier yields 1 for `last` and `false` for `distinct`.

∎

Approach 2

Create an empty set. Traverse the list and attempt to add each visited element to the set. If an element cannot be added, it must be a duplicate. As in the earlier approach, we start with a

Figure 10.12
This approach detects duplicates by using a set. The upper version is readily correct because it maintains a loop invariant. The lower version speeds up the upper version by exiting the loop upon encountering a duplicate.

```
Set<Integer> tmp = new HashSet<Integer>();
for (int i = 0; i < bag.size(); i++)
{
    distinct = distinct && tmp.add(bag.get(i));
}


Set<Integer> tmp = new HashSet<Integer>();
for (int i = 0; i < bag.size() && distinct; i++)
{
    distinct = tmp.add(bag.get(i));
}
```

provable correct loop based on the loop invariant. This is shown in the upper part of Fig. 10.12. We then speed up the loop by not iterating beyond duplicate detection, as shown in the lower part of the figure.

Example 10.5

Modify the code of Fig. 10.12 so that it also displays the duplicate element if the list contains duplicates. If more than one duplicate exists, display all of them.

Answer:

Add a variable that remembers the last visited element:

```
Integer last = null;
for (int i = 0; i < bag.size() && distinct; i++)
{
    last = bag.get(i);
    distinct = tmp.add(last);
}
output.println(last);
```

Running this program on the 18-element sample run shown earlier yields 5 for `last` and `false` for `distinct`.

Approach 3

Traverse the list. Whenever you visit an element, pause the traversal and start a new one. Compare every element you visit in the new traversal with the element you paused at. If equality is detected, abort both traversals and declare the elements not distinct. These two nested traversals allow you to examine every possible pair of elements; with n elements, you will examine n^2 pairs in the worst case. The code is shown in Fig. 10.13.

Two points in the shown logic warrant special attention:

Figure 10.13
This approach detects duplicates using two nested traversals.

- It is important that both traversals be exited upon detecting equality, as in Approaches 1 and 2. This is why both loops contain the `distinct` flag in their headers.
- Even if the elements are truly distinct, there will always be pairs with equal elements. When you generate pairs in all possible ways, n of the n^2 pairs involve pairing an element with itself. For example, the four pairs generated from the list [1,2] are (1,1), (1,2), (2,1), and (2,2). Hence, when we check for equality, we must avoid the trivial case in which the two elements being compared are in fact the same element. The shown code does this by comparing the object references using ==. If found equal in this sense, the two references would be pointing at the same object, which implies self-pairing. In this case, `distinct` must not be set to `false`.

```
Iterator<Integer> outer = bag.iterator();
for (; outer.hasNext() && distinct;)
{
    Integer x = outer.next();
    Iterator<Integer> inner = bag.iterator();
    for (; inner.hasNext() && distinct;)
    {
        Integer y = inner.next();
        distinct = !x.equals(y) || (x == y);
    }
}
```

Example 10.6

It is straightforward to modify the code in Fig. 10.13 so that it also displays the duplicate element if the list contains duplicates. All we need to do is declare x (and initialize it to null) before the outer loop. Running the modified program on the 18-element sample run shown earlier yields 15 for x and false for distinct.

Here is a summary of the results of the three approaches:

```
List generated. Size = 18
[6, 15, 9, 5, 5, 9, 2, 8, 13, 1, 13, 7, 2, 1, 15, 11,
3, 7]
```

1. Sorting Approach: duplicate is 1.
2. Set Approach: duplicate is 5.
3. Nested Traversals Approach: duplicate is 15.

All three approaches correctly detected that the elements are not distinct, but each identified a different element as a duplicate. Explain this difference based on the underlying algorithms.

Answer:

Approach 1 started by sorting the list, and this caused 1 to be the first-encountered duplicate. Approach 2 followed the list's order and inserted its elements one by one in a set. The first offending element in that order was 5. Approach 3 also followed the list's order, but whenever it visited an element, it scanned the entire list searching for duplicates of it. This made 15 the first-encountered duplicate.

Note that the last approach lends itself naturally to the enhanced for loop. We can in fact simplify the code in Fig. 10.13 using this loop, as shown in Fig. 10.14. It is clear from Figure 10.14 that the enhanced for provides a higher level of abstraction because it allows us to see the underlying algorithm unblurred by the details of creating and moving the cursors of each traversal. Note that the third approach does not work if auto-boxing was used to populate the list.

10.3.2 Word Frequencies

Suppose we want to output the distinct words and the number of occurrences of each word in a given text file. The program must be case-insensitive. We can read the file line by line, but

Figure 10.14 This approach uses the same algorithm as Fig. 10.13 but implements it using the enhanced for loop.

```
for (Integer x : bag)
{
    for (Integer y : bag)
    {
        distinct = distinct && (!x.equals(y) || (x == y));
    }
}
```

to be able to extract the words in each, we need a definition as to what constitutes an English word. We will use the following definition (treat it as part of the specification):

An English word is any sequence of nonwhitespace, nonpunctuation characters. (Whitespace characters are listed in Appendix A.) We will take punctuation to mean any character in the string " , ; . : \"\ ' '\\/?! [] () {}<>".

Hence, if we define

```
final String WHITESPACE = " \t\n\f\r";
final String PUNCTUATION = ",;.:\"\''\\/?![](){}<>";
final String WORD_DELIMITER = WHITESPACE + PUNCTUATION;
```

then we can pass WORD_DELIMITER to a tokenizer to extract the words.

Since we need to keep track of two things—the words and the number of times they occur—a map is a natural choice. Whenever we extract a word, we need to determine whether this is its first occurrence. If so, we add it to the map with a count of 1; that is, the key is the word and the value is the integer 1. Otherwise, we need to increment its existing count; that is, keep the existing mapping pair but increase its value by 1. The following pseudo-code captures the key idea:

```
for each word w in the file
if w was not encountered before
{
    put(w, 1)
}
    else
{
    oldCount = get(w)
    oldCount++
    put(w, oldCount) }
```

The full program is shown in Fig. 10.15.

Note that the Integer class was used to wrap the word count, which is an int, but thanks to automatic boxing and unboxing, the program ignored this issue altogether and treated the count as an object when needed and as a primitive type when needed. Note, also, that in order to make the program insensitive to letter case, we capitalized each word upon extracting it.

The output of the program leaves a lot to be desired, but we intentionally kept it basic to avoid distraction from the algorithm. If you supply the following file as input

```
This is a "test case" for this app, which finds
distinct words and outputs, for each, the frequency.
This app demonstrates how a map is used to store
key/value pairs (each with a distinct key), and
how to update the value of an existing pair in it.
```

you will get the following output:

```
{MAP=1, PAIR=1, DISTINCT=2, WHICH=1, OUTPUTS=1, IS=2,
DEMONSTRATES=1, STORE=1, OF=1, UPDATE=1, HOW=2, WORDS=1,
A=3, AN=1, THE=2, VALUE=2, THIS=3, WITH=1, IN=1,
CASE=1, AND=2, TO=2, IT=1, FINDS=1, KEY=2, APP=2,
EXISTING=1, FOR=2, FREQUENCY=1, TEST=1, PAIRS=1,
USED=1, EACH=2}
```

Figure 10.15
This program outputs the distinct words in a file along with their frequencies.

```java
import java.util.*;
import java.io.*;

public class WordFrequency
{   public static void main(String[] args) throws Exception
    {
        Scanner input = new Scanner(System.in);
        PrintStream output = System.out;

        final String WHITESPACE = " \t\n\f\r";
        final String PUNCTUATION = ",;.:\"\'`\\/?![](){}<>";
        final String WORD_DELIMITER = WHITESPACE + PUNCTUATION;

        Map<String, Integer> bag = new HashMap<String, Integer>();
        Scanner fileInput = new Scanner(new File("WordFrequency.txt"));

        for (; fileInput.hasNextLine();)
        {
            String line = fileInput.nextLine();
            StringTokenizer st = new StringTokenizer(line, WORD_DELIMITER);
            for (; st.hasMoreTokens(); )
        {
            String word = st.nextToken().toUpperCase();
            Integer oldCount = bag.get(word);
            if (oldCount == null)
            {   bag.put(word, 1);
            } else
            {   oldCount++;
                    bag.put(word, oldCount);
            }
        }
        }
        output.println(bag);
    }
}
```

10.3.3 Sorting a Map

Let us modify the program of the previous section so that the output is sorted alphabetically on the words. In essence, we need to sort a map based on its keys. Note that we cannot use the sort method in the Collections class because it works only on lists.

Recall that the Map interface has two implementing classes, HashMap and TreeMap. HashMap is efficient, and TreeMap keeps the elements sorted on the keys. Hence, all we need to do is switch to the other implementing class; that is, use TreeMap as shown in Fig. 10.16.

We owe this simplicity to the fact that the collection framework uses interfaces throughout (in parameters, returns, etc.) rather than classes, further evidence of the power of the client abstraction.

We leave it to the reader to beautify the output by iterating over the keys and outputting the word/frequency pairs one per line.

Note: There is a difference between invoking the `sort` method in `Collections` to sort a list and using classes such as `TreeMap` or `TreeSet` to sort maps and sets. `Collections` sorts the list, but it will become unsorted as soon as you add, remove, or modify any of its elements. The tree implementing classes, however, keep their collections sorted at all times. It is thus a difference between a one-time sort for reporting purposes and ongoing order maintenance.

Figure 10.16
This is the only statement that needs to be changed in Fig. 10.15 to make the elements of the map sorted on their keys.

```
Map<String, Integer> bag = new HashMap<String, Integer>();
Map<String, Integer> bag = new TreeMap<String, Integer>();
```

In More Depth   10.1

Arrays versus Collections

We saw in Section 1.2.5 that non-primitive types come in three varieties: the Class Type (such as `String` and `Date`), the Interface Type (such as `Comparable` and `Iterable`), and the Array Type. An array is similar to a list in that it can hold several objects under one roof. For example a `Date[]` array can hold several Date objects and a `Stock[]` array can hold several Stock objects. You can recognize the array type easily by the two brackets suffixing its name.

Even though arrays look like collections, they are extremely primitive compared to collections. For one thing, they cannot grow or shrink automatically, so you have to manage their capacity yourself. Furthermore, they come with no methods whatsoever to help you manipulate them. For example, if you want to add a new item to an array, you must first move things around to make room for it. The same problem arises if you want to remove an item. In other words, building applications with arrays makes you spend more time on the bookkeeping of the array rather than on the application itself. For this reason, arrays play no role in the client world except in few situations, as discussed below. It should be noted, however, that the low level nature of arrays makes them useful in the implementer world.

Most APIs use collections rather than arrays but you will occasionally encounter methods that take or return arrays. This often occurs when you deal with legacy code or with applications that are low-level or time-critical. For example, we saw in Section 6.4.3 that command-line arguments are passed in an array rather than a list. To address these situations, the collection framework has two methods that act as a bridge between collections and arrays:

■ To convert a list to an array, use the `toArray` method in `List`. For example, here is how you convert a list of type `List<String>` to an array:

```
String[] array = list.toArray(new String[0]);
```

■ To convert an array to a list, use the `asList` method in `Arrays`. For example, here is how you convert an array of type `Date[]` to a list:

```
List<Date> list = Arrays.asList(array);
```

Summary of Key Concepts

1. The **collection framework** provides support for applications dealing with collections. It offers interfaces, implementing classes, and polymorphic algorithms.

2. The **List** interface is appropriate when the collection's elements can be thought of as a **sequence**. This implies that duplicates are allowed and that the order in which the elements are inserted is significant.

3. The **Set** interface is appropriate when the collection's elements can be thought of as a mathematical set. This implies that duplicates are not allowed and that the order in which the elements are inserted is irrelevant.

4. The **Map** interface is appropriate when the collection's elements can be thought of as key-value pairs, that is, a mapping between a set of keys and a set of values. The keys of a map must be distinct, but the values need not be. Entry order is irrelevant.

5. The list interface is implemented by two classes: `ArrayList` and `LinkedList`. `ArrayList` is more efficient; hence, it should be used in all situations except applications in which elements are often added near the beginning of the list, or elements are added or deleted during traversals.

6. The set interface is implemented by two classes: `HashSet` and `TreeSet`. `HashSet` is more efficient; hence, it should be used in all situations except applications in which the elements must be kept sorted at all times.

7. The map interface is implemented by two classes: `HashMap` and `TreeMap`. `HashMap` is more efficient; hence, it should be used in all situations except applications in which the elements must be kept sorted at all times.

8. The collection framework uses generics to allow the client to specify the element type upon instantiating the collection. This ensures type safety because the compiler can ensure that only correctly typed elements are added to the collection. It also relieves us from having to case elements upon retrieval.

9. The signature of a generic method may accept any type `<T>` or may impose the condition that `T` must extend (or implement) another type, or that it must be a superclass of another type. This is expressed using the `'?'` **wildcard**.

10. You add elements to lists and sets using `add`. For a map, use `put`. You delete elements using `remove`.

11. Because they are sequence-based, lists also offer `add` and `remove` methods that are index-based.

12. You can access an element of a known index in a list using the `get` method. You can also use `get` to access an element of a known key in a map. Set elements cannot be accessed because set elements are not identifiable by an index or any other mean.

13. An **iterator**, rather than chained `get` methods, is needed to make nested traversals easier. Lists and sets have an `iterator` method that returns an iterator instance positioned at the beginning of the collection. An invocation of `next` on that instance returns the next element in the collection, if any, and advances the iterator's **cursor** one position.

14. Maps do not have an iterator, but the **keySet** method returns a set of all keys in the map. Using the iterator of that set, we can iterate over a map.

15. The **enhanced** `for` loop allows us to iterate over a collection without explicitly manipulating its iterator.

16. The `Collections` utility class offers several polymorphic methods for processing collections. One of them is `sort`. It works only on lists and requires a list whose element type implements the `Comparable` interface or extends a class that does.

17. **Natural order** refers to an ordering that is based on the `compareTo` method of the elements. It is value-based for numbers, lexicographic for strings, and chronological for dates.

18. Linear search can be implemented by adding a loop invariant to a traversal loop, as was done in Chapter 8.

19. Binary search is significantly faster than linear search ($\lg N$ versus N), and there is a method in the `Collections` utility that implements it. The method's precondition, however, is that the list be sorted.

20. The collection framework can be applied in a variety of ways to detect duplicates in a list, to find the distinct words in a file and compute their frequencies of occurrence, and to sort a map.

Review Questions

1. Why do we need the collection framework?
2. What are the three main interfaces in the framework?
3. Name the classes that implement each interface, and state which is used when.
4. Why do we specify a type when creating a collection? Why not leave it `Object`?
5. Consider the types `List<CreditCard>` and `List<RewardCard>`. Is it true that one of them extends the other?
6. A method takes as its parameter `Set<? extends CreditCard>`. Can we pass to it the set `Set<RewardCard>`?
7. How do you add an element to a list? What happens if the element is already present?
8. How do you add an element to a set? What happens if the element is already present?
9. How do you add an element at the end of a list? How about at the beginning?
10. How do you add an element at the end of a set?
11. What happens if you try to remove an element from a set but the element is not in it?
12. Given a reference to a map `<K,V>`, how do you determine whether a given key is in it?
13. Why do we need an iterator?
14. What methods does the iterator have?
15. How do you force an iterator to reset its position back to the first element?
16. How do you iterate over a map?
17. Explain the enhanced `for` loop by giving an example.
18. Given a reference to a map `<K,V>`, how do you determine its elements?
19. What is the syntax for invoking the sort method?
20. What is natural order?
21. Is it possible to sort `List<Equation>`?
22. Is it possible to sort `List<InputStream>`?
23. Explain the loop invariant of linear search.
24. Give an example from everyday life in which we search faster than $O(N)$ when the list being searched is sorted.
25. What is the syntax for invoking the binary search method?
26. What is the complexity of binary search?

A Robot in a Maze

Lab

L10.1 Analysis

Our project is to simulate the movement of a robot in a maze. The maze will be specified by the user relative to a coordinate system in which the origin is at the upper-left corner, and the x and the y axes are as shown in Fig. 10.17.

This coordinate system was chosen because it makes the graphics output simple. The robot, indicated by a circle in the figure, starts at $(1,1)$ and searches for the exit point, which is at $(7,4)$ in the figure.

At any give instance of time, the robot will be at some position (x,y) in the maze. It must decide where it should move next. All that the robot "sees" are the four points around it, that is, the points $(x-1,y)$, $(x+1,y)$, $(x,y-1)$, and $(x,y+1)$. The robot must somehow select one of the points and move to it (without going into a wall).

You can make the following assumptions: the maze is square in shape, the robot's starting point is always $(1,1)$, and the robot's exit point is always at the border of the square. If we

Figure 10.17
A robot in an
8 × 8 maze

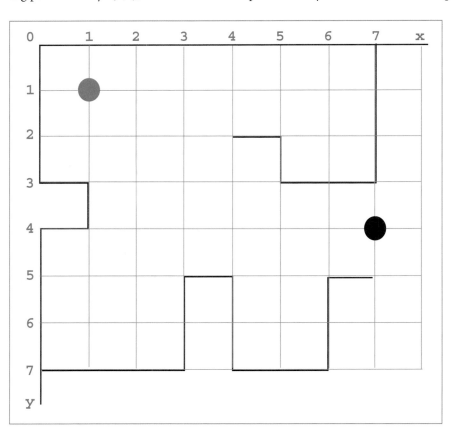

use `size` to denote the size of the maze, then the *x* and *y* coordinates of the robot will be in the open-open interval `(0,size-1)` as long as the robot is in the maze. Once either coordinate becomes `0` or `size-1`, the robot is considered to have exited.

In terms of input, the user will supply the maze size (in this case, 8) and the maze itself (i.e., the coordinates of its walls). This is done through a text file called `maze.txt` in which every record contains the comma-delimited coordinates of a point in which there is a wall. You will find the file for our example maze in your `eCheck` directory.

In terms of output, we want to see the total number of steps needed to exit the maze. The user likes to explore several algorithms for step selection with a view of minimizing the total step count. In addition, we want to see the robot itself as it travels from the starting point to the exit point.

L10.2 Design

We need to address two issues in our design: the step selection algorithm and the data structure that will hold the maze.

We will start by adopting the *Random Algorithm*: whenever the robot reaches a point, it generates a uniformly distributed random number between 0 and 3 (inclusive). These four numbers correspond to the four neighbouring points. If the point suggested by the random number is on a wall, the suggestion is discarded, and a new random number is generated. This process is repeated until a point that is not on a wall is suggested, at which point the robot moves to it. This algorithm corresponds to what we will call a "drunken robot" because it makes choices randomly regardless of previously made choices. Indeed, a drunken robot may travel along a cycle (a closed path) for some time before trying new directions.

The maze must be stored, and this calls for a collection. To determine the ideal collection we ask ourselves: what information does the robot constantly need to retrieve from the collection? The answer comes from the algorithm: given the coordinates of a point, the robot must be able to determine whether or not it is on a wall. We must strive to make this search operation easy (and efficient), so we pick a collection that allows a point to be searched for. A point is specified by two things, its *x* and *y* coordinates, but we can use the class `Point` in `java.awt` to lump these two into one. The collection must therefore be able to store an instance of `Point` together with a string that can be either `"W"`, indicating that the point is on a wall, or the empty string, to indicate that it is not on a wall. A map whose keys are instances of `Point` and whose values are strings is the ideal collection.

You may argue that a `boolean` (wrapped in a `Boolean` instance) would be a better choice for the value since a point is either on a wall or it is not on the wall. This is true for the current algorithm, but to be able to support more complicated algorithms (in which other things need to be remembered per point), we use strings.

Given that reading the maze from the user and creating the corresponding data structure is not trivial, we break this project into two classes: `MazeBuilder` and `Maze`.

■ `MazeBuilder` `MazeBuilder` reads the maze size from the user and processes the `maze.txt` file to create the corresponding map collection. It serializes the map in the file `maze.data`.

■ Maze Maze reads the map from `maze.data` and simulates the steps. This class must also display the maze and the robot's movement in real time.

L10.3 Implementing the Maze Builder

The class must start by reading the maze size:

```
output.print("Maze size? ");
int size = input.nextInt();
ToolBox.crash(size <= 0 "size must be positive");
```

It must then create a map and initialize all its points to "no wall":

```
Map<Point, String> maze = new HashMap<Point, String>();
for (int x = 0; x < size; x++)
{
    for (int y = 0; y < size; y++)
    {
        maze.put(new Point(x,y), "");
    }
}
```

Next, it should read the `maze.txt` and add an element to the map for each record in it. After reading a record and tokenizing its two fields (x and y), we first verify that the maze is consistent by requiring that

```
assert (x >= 0 && x < size);
assert (y >= 0 && y < size);
assert (!(x == 1 && y == 1));
```

The last precondition ensures that the robot does not start inside a wall. The x,y wall point can now be added to the map using

```
maze.put(new Point(x,y), "W");
```

After reading all records and closing the file, we store the maze object in a file:

```
FileOutputStream fos = new FileOutputStream("maze.data");
ObjectOutputStream oos = new ObjectOutputStream(fos);
oos.writeObject(maze);
oos.flush();
fos.close();
output.println("Maze saved in \"maze.data\"");
```

Task 1: Write the `MazeBuilder` program, compile, and run.

L10.4 Implementing the Maze

This program starts by deserializing the map and setting up:

```
int size = (int) Math.sqrt(maze.size());
int a = 1; int b = 1; // starting point
```

Next, it prepares the graphics pane as was done in Lab 9:

```
Create a frame
Create a panel
Add the panel to the content pane of the frame
Allow the user to resize the frame
Graphics2D canvas = panel.getGraphics2D();
```

We will draw each point in the maze as a circle. We will make the circle black if it is on a wall and grey (or whatever the background colour is) if it is not on a wall. Since we need to size such circles in each dimension, we need to space them so that they fill the entire panel. This can be done as follows:

```
double xFactor = panel.getWidth() / size;
double yFactor = panel.getHeight() / size;
double radius = Math.min(xFactor, yFactor) / 2;
```

The two scales may not be equal (depending on how the user sizes the panel), so we set the radius to half the smaller of the two to ensure that the circles do not overlap. We now draw the maze as follows:

```
Ellipse2D.Double circle;
for (int x = 0; x < size; x++)
{
    for (int y = 0; y < size; y++)
    {
        Color shade = Color.black;
        if ((maze.get(new Point(x,y))).length() == 0)
        {
            shade = panel.getBackground();
        }
        canvas.setColor(shade);
        circle = new Ellipse2D.Double(x*xFactor, y*yFactor,
                                      radius, radius);
        canvas.fill(circle);
        panel.repaint();
    }
}
```

Task 2: Write the Maze program, compile, and run.

Even though we have not yet implemented the simulation, it is a good idea to finish and test this iteration of our development process. The program should produce the maze that was built in Task 1. If you do not see the walls where expected, debug either this or the MazeBuilder program.

L10.5 Implementing the Simulation

After drawing the maze, the Maze app must simulate the movement as indicated by the following pseudo-code:

```
int steps = 0;
keep looping as long as a and b are in (0,size-1)
{
    draw a circle at (a,b) in red;
    sleep for 150 ms;
    repeat the following
    {   consider the four neighbors of (a,b) and randomly;
        select one of them. Call it (x,y);
        if (x,y) is not on a wall, exit the loop;
    }
    draw a circle at (a,b) in the background color;
    a = x;
    b = y;
    steps++;
}
output steps;
draw a circle at (a,b) in pink;
```

Notice that you simulate movement by drawing the robot's initial position as a red circle and then sleeping (doing nothing). Once the new position is determined, we redraw the initial position using the background colour. This will, in effect, erase the red circle. When the loop iterates, the new position becomes the initial one, and it will be drawn in red.

You should be able to implement the above algorithm except for one hurdle: how do we sleep for a given number of milliseconds? There is a class called Thread, and it has a static sleep method that takes the sleep duration as parameter.

Task 3: Complete the Maze application, and verify that it correctly simulates the movement of the robot. Note that since the robot's decisions are not coherent in any way, it may take it a few hundred steps before it exits the maze in our 8×8 example.

In your implementation of the step selection algorithm you probably generated a random number between 0 and 3 (inclusive) and updated the robot's position (x,y) accordingly. If the number came out as 0, you would perhaps attempt to move left:

```
x = a - 1;
y = b;
```

Afterward, you consult the map to see whether or not (x,y) is on a wall, and, based on that, you either exit the loop or try again. If this more or less describes your implementation, then you must have used the equivalent of four `if` statements. Is it possible to implement this part of the algorithm without using any `if` statements?

Task 4: Apply the code-handling techniques from Chapter 6 to eliminate `if` statements from the position update part of your program.

Hint: Define two string finals:

```
final String X_SHIFT = "-1 1 0 0";
final String Y_SHIFT = " 0 0-1 1";
```

L10.6 Explore a Different Algorithm (*optional*)

Instead of making decisions in a totally incoherent way, how about maintaining the same direction until we hit a wall? For example, say the robot started by moving right from (1,1) to (2,1). After arriving at (2,1), its first attempt should be to move right again, to (3,1). If this is possible, that is, if (3,1) is not on a wall, then it will make the move, and in this case, it would have made the decision without any random elements. If (3,1) is on a wall, however, then it will revert back to the old algorithm, generating a random number and following whichever path does not lead to a wall.

We will call this the *Straight Algorithm* because the robot tends to follow straight lines until it hits a wall (or exits). The first selection in it (at (1,1)) is arbitrary (since there is no previous direction), and you can make it randomly.

Task 5: Implement the straight algorithm.

You should notice that the straight algorithm results in a significant improvement in the overall step count over the random algorithm. Note, however, that it may lead to cyclic routes in which the robot stays indefinitely in the maze.

Task 6: Implement the following third algorithm, which involves learning: the robot follows the Random Algorithm, but if it revisited the same position, it should try not to make the same decision that it made in its last visit. To implement this, you need to store, in the map, the direction that was taken at each position.

This Lab exposes a class of problems called *Random Walks* and has wide-ranging applications in basic sciences, engineering, and business.

Exercises

Programming exercises are indicated with an asterisk.

10.1 For each of the following collections, determine the interface that should be used. Justify your answer.

    (a) The names of all students registered in a course
    (b) The letter grades obtained in a course
    (c) The names of your contacts and the telephone number of each
    (d) The reserved words in Java

10.2 For each of the following statements, identify the compile-time error:

```
(a) List<int> list = new LinkedList<int>();
(b) Set<Date> set = new HashMap<Date>();
(c) Map<String> map = new TreeMap<String>();
(d) List<Double> list = new LinkedList<Integer>();
```

10.3* Write a program that deletes all but the last element from a given list.

10.4* Write a program that displays every other element of a given list.

10.5* Write a program that determines the largest key in a given map. Assume that the key type K satisfies `K extends Comparable<? super T>`.

10.6* Write a program that inserts elements in an empty list such that the order in the list will end up being the reverse of the entry order.

10.7* Write a program that traverses a given `List<Integer>` and deletes any element that is greater than its predecessor.

10.8* Write a program that deletes all but the last element from a given set.

10.9* Write a program that traverses a given `COLOR<Integer>` and deletes any element that is greater than its predecessor. Assume `COLOR` is a `List`.

10.10* Write a program that determines whether a given map has value duplicates.

10.11* Write a program that sorts a given set.

10.12* Write a program that reads a file name from the user and determines whether it contains a serialization of `Map<Integer, Date>`. If it does, determine and output the earliest date.

10.13* Write a program that reads distinct integers from the user and outputs their median. The program starts by prompting for and reading n, the number of entries to be made. As a precondition, n must be positive and less than 20. If the user enters an integer that was previously entered, an error message is printed, but the input continues.
The median is defined as an entry such that the number of entries greater than it, and the number of entries less than it, are equal (if n is odd) or differ by at most 1 (if n is even). If n is even, there will be two medians. Do not use a list, and do not sort the entries.

10.14* Redo Exercise 10.13, but locate the median(s) by first sorting the entries and then accessing the element(s) in the middle position.

10.15* Write a program that reads integers from the user and outputs their mode (the integer that was repeated the most). If two or more integers repeat a maximal number of times, output all of them. The program starts by prompting for and reading n, the number of entries to be made. As a precondition, n must be positive and less than 20. Do not use a list, and do not sort the entries (use a map with repetition counts as values).

10.16* Redo Exercise 10.15, but this time store the entries in a list and sort them.

10.17* Write a program that reads distinct integers from the user and outputs the two that are closest to each other, that is, the absolute value of their difference is minimal. If two or more pairs of entries have equal minimal difference, output all of them. The program starts by reading n, the number of entries to be made. As a precondition, n must be positive and less than 20. If the user enters an integer that was previously entered, an error message is printed, but the input continues. Do not sort the entries.

10.18* Redo Exercise 10.17, but this time sort the entries before processing them.

10.19* Write a program that generates a random portfolio (using `getRandom` in `Portfolio`) and outputs its content sorted on the stock symbol. Specifically, the program must create a map in which the key of each entry is a stock symbol and its value is an `Investment` object. Using this map, generate a tabular output in which each row contains the stock symbol, name, quantity, and book value.

If the generated portfolio contains two or more investments in the same stock, keep only one of them; that is, ignore stock duplicates.

10.20* Redo Exercise 10.19 but with two variations:

1. Do not generate the portfolio randomly. Do so manually so that you can control its duplicate stocks.
2. If two (or more) investments in the portfolio have the same stock, they should be amalgamated into one investment whose quantity is the sum of the quantities and whose book value is the weighted average of the book values.

For example, 5 shares at book value $5.25 and 10 shares at book value $3.75 become 15 shares with a book value of $(5*5.25 + 10*3.75)/15 = 4.25$.

10.21* Write a program that takes two sorted sets and generates a sorted list containing their union.

Start by writing an auxiliary program that reads a set of, say, 20 integers from the user, stores them in a sorted set, and then serializes the set in a file. Re-run this program supplying a different set of integers in order to create a second file.

Now write a program that deserializes these two files and joins the two sets into a sorted list. If an element is common to the two sets, it must appear twice in the generated list; that is, the list size is the sum of the two set sizes. The program stores the sorted list on disk as an object.

The process involved in this exercise is called a *merge*, and any algorithm that you can think of is acceptable as long as the program is correct. It is worthwhile noting, however, that one algorithm for merging involves no sorting whatsoever.

10.22* Write a program that takes two sorted sets and generates a sorted set containing their intersection, that is, the elements common to both of them. Use an auxiliary program (as in Exercise 10.21) to create and serialize any two input sets.

 eCheck

Check10A (TS = 26)

Write the app `Check10A` that keeps reading integers from the user until a negative integer is entered. It then outputs the average (arithmetic mean) of all entries (excluding the negative sentinel) and outputs all the entries that are above average. Here are two sample runs:

```
Enter your integers
(Negative=sentinel)
30
7
12
45
```

```
6
0
30
8
-6
The average is: 17.25
The sorted, distinct, above-average elements:
30 45

Enter your integers
(Negative=sentinel)
-3
Your list is empty!
```

Note that the average is displayed without any formatting. Note also that the above-average elements are displayed sorted in increasing order, without duplication, and space delimited.

Develop your app, test it, and then eCheck it.

Check10B (TS = 26)

Write the app Check10B that reads a map from the user, inverts it, and outputs the inverted map. The input and the output maps are <Integer,Integer>. Inverting a map makes its values keys and its keys values. If two keys map to the same value in the original map, the value will map back to the smaller of the two keys in the inverted map. Using this rule to break ties ensures that any input map can be inverted. Here is sample run:

```
Enter your map, one key-value pair per line,
comma-separated. Use empty line as sentinel.
12,30
8,4
17,22
6,30
10,4
15,28

The input map is:
{6=30, 8=4, 10=4, 12=30, 15=28, 17=22}
The inverted map [using the smaller key as a tie breaker]:
{4=8, 22=17, 28=15, 30=6}
```

Note that both 8 and 10 map to 4 in the input map. Upon inversion, 4 is mapped to 8 because it is the smaller of the two keys. Similarly, 30 is mapped to 6 rather than 12. You can assume, as a precondition, that the input is valid. To output the maps, simply use their toString method.

The output map must be sorted on its keys.

Develop your app, test it, and then eCheck it.

Check10C (TS = 31)

Write a program that reads a list from the file `lab10data.dat`; that is, the list has already been created and is serialized in that file. Each element in it is a string that represents a DNA strand. The program must examine these strings and identify the two that are closest in length. Here is one sample run:

```
Enter the filename lab10data.dat
The closest two are 3 apart in length.
Their indices are 0,2.
```

The elements of the list contained in the file *lab10data.dat* are the following three strings:

```
ATGTCATGG
ATGCGATGGGGGTCGCCC
ATGTTT
```

In this list, the lengths of the three strings are 9, 18, and 6. Hence, the two to be selected are the one at index 0 and the one at index 2. The program must output the indices of these two strings, the smaller index followed by the larger one, separated by a comma.

In case there are several pairs with the same minimal length difference, the program must select the pair whose indices are closest to each other. If there are several pairs with minimal length difference and minimal index difference, the program must select the pair closest to the beginning of the list (smallest first index). Here is a second example that demonstrates this. A list made up of the following nine elements (indices 0 through 8):

```
ATGGAACTCTGCGGAGGA
ATGACGCACTTTACCCTCCAATCGACGCCCTAC
ATGGAAGATGGCGTACACTTACCTAGTTCAAAGACCAGGCGGAGTGGCCAC
ATGATTGGGATAGCCTTCTAAACCATT
ATGTTGTATATTCCGATTTACGTACATCGGTAACGAGTATCCATTCGT
ATGTAG
ATGAGAACTGCTTCTCTTAAACTATCCTTCTAAGCC
ATGAAATGATGAGAAGACGCGTGAATACTA
ATGTGCCGTTTAAGTTACACATAACTTCTCGATCGGTGC
```

Here, the minimal length difference is 3, but there are several pairs that qualify for this: 1,6; 2,4; 3,7; 6,8; and 1,7. Of these, the program must select 2,4 because it has the smallest index difference (2) and is closer to the top than 6,8. Here is the resulting log:

```
Enter the filename lab10data.dat
The closest two are 3 apart in length.
Their indices are 2,4.
```

Develop your app, test it, and then eCheck it.

Check10D (TS = 31)

The figure depicted in Fig. 10.18 is called a **graph**.

A graph is a set of **vertices** (circles) with a set of **edges** (lines) connecting them. You can think of vertices as locations in a city and of edges as streets. An edge in a graph is either

Figure 10.18 A graph of cities connected by roads. AHGF represents a path whose cost is 10 + 3 + 8 = 21. The path AHB is invalid because there is no road from H to B.

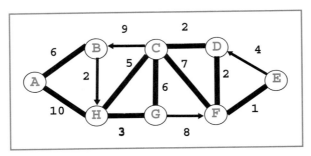

bidirectional (represented by a double line) or unidirectional (an arrow). In Fig. 10.18, and using the city interpretation, we can go from vertex C to B but not from B to C because what connects them is a one-way street.

We associate a label (`String`) with each vertex and a weight (`double`) with each edge. You can think of the label as the name of the location and of the weight as the cost of traversing the edge. The cost could be fuel cost or the time needed for the journey, given the road and traffic conditions. In this app we are going to assume that the label is made up of one character and that all weights are non-negative.

One way of representing a graph in memory is through a "map of maps" (also called a two-dimensional map). We imagine a map whose keys are the vertices of the graph. For the graph in Fig. 10.18, this map would have 8 elements. The value of the element with key X is a map whose keys are the vertices that can be reached from X by traversing a single edge and whose values are the weights of these edges. Here is the map of the graph in Fig. 10.18:

```
{A={B=6,H=10},
B={A=6,H=2},
C={B=9,D=2,F=7,G=6,H=5},
D={C=2,F=2},
E={D=4,F=1},
F={C=7,D=2,E=1},
G={C=6,F=8,H=3},
H={A=10,C=5,G=3}
}
```

Given this map of maps, we can answer any question related to the graph; for example, how many vertices there are, how many (bi/unidirectional) edges there are, and whether there is a path from a given vertex to another. You can assume that the graph has already been represented and that the resulting map has been serialized to a disk file.

A *path* in the graph is defined as any nonempty sequence of edges. In our case (where each vertex label is made up of one letter), we can represent the path by concatenating the labels of the vertices it traverses, that is, by a string. The *cost of the path* is defined as the sum of the costs of its edges. For example, ABHC is a path that takes us from A to C at a cost of 6 + 2 + 5 = 13.

Note that not any string of letters constitutes a path. First of all, it must have at least two characters. Second, any two consecutive vertices in it must correspond to an edge in the graph connecting the first vertex to the second. Based on this, we see that H is not a valid path, and neither are AZ, ABC, and ABF (in our example graph).

The app `Check10B` starts by prompting for and reading the name of the file in which the graph map is stored. It then prompts for and reads a path in the graph. If the entered path is valid, the app outputs its cost; otherwise it outputs: `"Invalid path"` followed by a message indicating why, either "(The path must have more than one vertex)" or "(Edge xx does not exist)", where xx is the first offending vertex pair.

Here are a few sample runs (assuming the file contains our example graph):

```
Filename of the graph... lab10Bdata.dat
Enter the path... ABHCDFE
The cost of this path is: 18.0
Filename of the graph... lab10Bdata.dat
Enter the path... AHCBHG
The cost of this path is: 29.0

Filename of the graph... lab10Bdata.dat
Enter the path... ABCDF
Invalid path (Edge BC does not exist)

Filename of the graph... lab10Bdata.dat
Enter the path... AHD
Invalid path (Edge HD does not exist)

Filename of the graph... lab10Bdata.dat
Enter the path... G
Invalid path (The path must have more than one vertex)

Filename of the graph... lab10Bdata.dat
Enter the path... AHRF
Invalid path (Edge HR does not exist)
```

Develop your app, test it, and then eCheck it.

Exception Handling

tatic void main(String[] args) r h:m:AM or PM >

I t is safe to assume that every component has post-compilation errors, but a carefully implemented component can detect most errors at runtime and throw corresponding exceptions. You must therefore learn how to deal with exceptions thrown by components you use. In this chapter, you will learn how to recognize exceptions in the API of components and how to use try-catch to monitor exceptions, determine what caused them, and select an appropriate course of action. You will also learn how to deal with user input, which is the primary cause of most errors.

Learning Objectives

1. Recognize exceptions in the API

2. Learn language constructs that deal with exceptions

3. Explore the throwable hierarchy

4. Contrast defensive with exception-based programming

Chapter Outline

11.1 What Are Exceptions?

Given a compiled program, we will use the word **error** or **defect** to refer to any program behaviour that is contrary to its specification. There are three possible sources of errors: the programmer, the end-user, and the runtime environment.

1. **The Programmer** The programmer can trigger errors by making mistakes, for example, misinterpreting the postcondition, overstating the precondition, or using an incorrect algorithm.
2. **The End-User** Supplying an invalid input is the main cause of user-triggered errors. The program can limit these errors somewhat through validation, but nothing can prevent a mistyped entry, such as 1.25 instead of 1.52. The phrase "garbage in, garbage out" highlights the role of the end-user as an error source.
3. **The Runtime Environment** The program is executed through several layers of abstractions: virtual machine (VM), operating system, hardware, and network. If any of these layers behave contrary to their specifications, an environment-triggered error will occur.

When an error occurs, the program will perform incorrect operations. If these operations are all valid (albeit incorrect), the program will continue executing normally, and the error will not be detected; it becomes a logic error. But if one of the incorrect operations is invalid, the VM will detect it. Here are examples of invalid operations: dividing an integer by zero, converting a string containing letters to an integer, extracting the fifth character from a string that has only two characters, reading from a file that does not exist, writing to a file that is write-protected, cloning an object when memory is full, and establishing a connection when the network is down. When the VM detects an invalid operation, it reacts to it by throwing an exception. The following sections explore the dynamics of exceptions.

11.1.1 Exception Handling

Consider the program shown in Fig. 11.1 in which the programmer assumed that the end-user would enter two integers, the second of which is not zero.

What if the end-user enters zero for the second integer? In this case, an error will occur, and the operations performed in the program will become incorrect. Moreover, one of them will be invalid; the statement

```
int c = a / b;
```

asks the VM to divide an integer by a zero integer. In response to this, the VM will throw an exception, and the exception will manifest itself in a very ugly way from the end-user's point of view: the program will terminate and a message will appear on the screen. The message, albeit useful to the programmer, is cryptic to the end-user and does not indicate what should be done next. Figure 11.2 depicts what the user sees.

Note that a crash not only looks bad, but it can also lead to serious data loss or file corruption because it prevents a **clean exit**, which is the ability to end the program in a controlled and orderly manner. For example, a clean exit allows the program to flush all output buffers,

Figure 11.1 This program computes and outputs the quotient of two integers. A runtime error will occur if the second input is zero.

```java
import java.util.Scanner; // type.lib.* if Java 1.4
import java.io.PrintStream;

public class Quotient
{
    public static void main(String[] args)
    {
        Scanner input = new Scanner(System.in);
        PrintStream output = System.out;

        output.println("Enter the first integer:");
        int a = input.nextInt();
        output.println("Enter the second:");
        int b = input.nextInt();

        int c = a / b;
        output.println("Their quotient is: " + c);
    }
}
```

commit all pending transactions, close all network connections, and free up all used resources. A clean exit is particularly important in real-time systems in which neither an end-user nor a programmer is present when the program runs (e.g., a rocket navigation system, an autopilot system, and a robot control system). In such systems, the program itself must somehow be able to handle exceptions and prevent them from becoming runtime errors.

We have been using the terms *runtime error* and *crash* to describe situations in which the program is abruptly terminated and an error message, not originating from the program, is

In More Depth   11.1

Exception Terminology

Note that the word *exception* was chosen because of its English meaning—something different—and *not* because of a class in Java called Exception. In fact, the word *exception* and the term *exception handling* are used in many other programming languages. Moreover, we will see later that the main exception class in Java is, in fact, Throwable, not Exception.

Figure 11.2 If the input of the app of Fig. 11.1 is invalid, a runtime error occurs. Depending on your environment, you may get a message that differs slightly from the one shown here.

```
Enter the first integer:
8
Enter the second:
0
Exception in thread "main"
java.lang.ArithmeticException: / by zero
        at Quotient.main(Quotient.java:16)
```

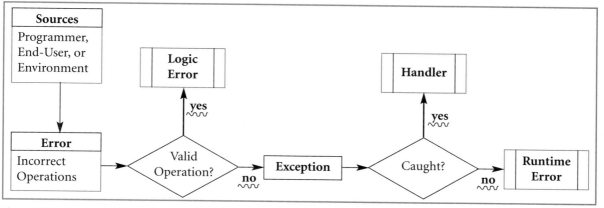

Figure 11.3
Various sources can cause a program to perform incorrect operations. If the VM deems these operations to be valid, the error will become an unnoticed logic error. Otherwise, the VM will throw an exception. If the exception is caught, the handler will be executed. Otherwise, a runtime error will occur.

displayed. We can see now how the terms *exception* and *runtime error* are related: when the VM detects an invalid operation, it **throws** an **exception**. Whether or not this exception leads to a runtime error depends on the program itself: if it contains a **handler** capable of **catching** this exception, the runtime error will be suppressed, and control will remain with the program. Otherwise, a runtime error will occur. If a clean exit is needed, the program must include exception handling. The roles played by these terms are depicted in Fig. 11.3.

The process can be pictured by imagining the VM throwing a ball when it detects an invalid operation. If the program is capable of handling exceptions, it will catch the ball and thus remain in control. Otherwise, the ball will hit the ground, and this will terminate the running program.

11.1.2 The Delegation Model

A typical app performs most of its work by using the services of components, so in addition to exceptions thrown due to an invalid operation in the app itself, we must also think about exceptions thrown while control is in some method invoked by the app. The program in Fig. 11.4 exemplifies this situation. It assumes that the user will enter a string with a slash embedded in it.

What if the input does not contain a slash? In this case, the statement

```
String left = str.substring(0, slash);
```

will cause the `substring` method to extract a substring starting from position 0 up to position −1. This is an invalid operation, but it occurs in the `String` class, not in the app. The Java VM recognizes that errors can occur in methods as well as apps. To accommodate both, Java enforces a **handle or delegate** policy on methods (note that an app is also a method, called `main`): when the VM detects an invalid operation in a method, it throws an exception and searches the method to see if it has a handler that can catch the exception. If it does, control is given to the handler. Otherwise, the search is transferred to the caller of the method, that is, to the method that invoked the current method. If the caller can catch the exception, its handler receives control; otherwise, the search is transferred further up the invocation chain. If no method, including `main`, can handle the thrown exception, a runtime error occurs and the program is terminated. Hence, a method must either handle the exception or delegate its handling to the caller. This behaviour is called the **delegation model** for exception handling.

Figure 11.4
Given a string containing two slash-delimited substrings, this app extracts and outputs the two substrings. For example if the input is "14/9", the outputs would be "14" and "9". If the input does not contain a slash, a runtime error will occur.

```java
import java.util.Scanner; // type.lib.* if Java 1.4
import java.io.PrintStream;

public class Substring
{
    public static void main(String[] args)
    {
        Scanner input = new Scanner(System.in);
        PrintStream output = System.out;

        output.println("Enter a string containing a slash");
        String str = input.nextLine();
        int slash = str.indexOf("/");
        String left = str.substring(0, slash);
        String right = str.substring(slash + 1);
        output.println("Left substring: " + left);
        output.println("Right substring: " + right);
    }
}
```

In the program in Fig. 11.4, neither the substring method nor its caller, the app, is equipped to handle exceptions. Hence, an invalid input should lead to a runtime error, and this is indeed the case as shown in Fig. 11.5.

We mentioned earlier that, while meaningless to the end-user, the message printed after a crash is quite useful to the developer. Now that we understand the delegation model, we can better understand its contents. The first line of Fig. 11.5 indicates the exception type, IndexOutOfBoundsException, its cause, String index out of range, and the offending value of the index, -1. The remaining lines, each of which starts with "at ", are the **stack trace**, and they list all methods in the delegation chain, starting from the one in which the exception was thrown and climbing up all the way to the app. In our example, the trace shows that the statement that led to the exception is at line 1480 in method substring in class String.java and that the caller was line 14 in method main in our app Substring.java.

Note that if a method handles a particular exception, then that exception should not be documented in the method's contract. This is because exception handling is part of the method implementation; any mention of it in the API will thus break the encapsulation. Exceptions that are delegated (not handled), however, are documented in the contract under the Throws section, as we saw in Section 2.3.3. Figure 11.6 shows the API of one of the substring methods of the String class, and you can see that the delegated exception is included along with the conditions that trigger it.

Figure 11.5
When the input of the app of Fig. 11.4 is invalid, a runtime error occurs.

```
Enter a string containing a slash
14-9
java.lang.IndexOutOfBoundsException:
String index out of range: -1
   at java.lang.String.substring(String.java:1480)
   at Substring.main(Substring.java:14)
```

Figure 11.6 The API of this method states that if certain conditions are not met, an exception of a specified type will be thrown. This implies that the method does not handle the exception; it delegates the handling to its caller.

```
public String substring(int beginIndex, int endIndex)
```

Returns a new string that is a substring of this string. The substring begins at the specified `beginIndex` and extends to the character at index `endIndex - 1`.

Parameters:
`beginIndex`—the beginning index, inclusive.
`endIndex`—the ending index, exclusive.

Returns:
the specified substring.

Throws:
`IndexOutOfBoundsException`—if the `beginIndex` is negative, or `endIndex` is larger than the length of this `String` object, or `beginIndex` is larger than `endIndex`.

In More Depth   11.2

Exceptions and Preconditions

If the API of a method specifies that it throws a particular exception when the parameters meet (or do not meet) a certain condition, then this condition is *not* a precondition. Recall from Section 2.3.3 that the API should not specify what happens if the precondition is not met. Doing so breaks the encapsulation. Most methods in the Java standard library include a `Throws` section and, hence, do not have preconditions (their pre is the literal `true`).

 ## 11.2 Java's Exception Constructs

Exception handling is implemented in Java through a special construct that allows you to specify the part of your program in which you want to enable exception handling. It also allows you to specify the types of exceptions that you wish to catch and how each of them is to be handled. The following sections explain this construct and provide examples.

11.2.1 The Basic `try-catch` Construct

The basic construct uses the keywords `try` and `catch`, each of which is followed by a block (and therefore a separate scope), as shown in Fig. 11.7.

Given a code fragment that may trigger an exception, we sandwich it in the `try` block. If the fragment executes without problems, the `catch` block is skipped, and execution continues with the first statement after the closing brace of the `catch` block. But if one of the statements in the fragment throws an exception, execution of the `try` block will be terminated immediately, and the VM will examine the `catch` block header to see if it can handle the exception. The header

Figure 11.7 The basic exception-handling construct

```
try
{    . . .
     code fragment
     . . .
}
catch (SomeType e)
{    . . .
     exception handler
     . . .
}
program continues
```

looks and behaves like that of a method called `catch`, with one parameter of type `SomeType` (an exception type that the programmer chose to handle). If the type of the thrown exception matches the one specified in the header, the VM transfers control to the first statement in the `catch` block; the block is executed, and program execution continues with the first statement after the block. However, if the type of the thrown exception does not match that of the header, then this `catch` cannot handle the exception, and the delegation model is applied.

Example 11.1

Rewrite the program in Fig. 11.4 so that it can handle the exception that the `substring` method delegates.

Answer:
Since we know the type of the exception that is thrown when the input does not contain a slash (see the crash message in Fig. 11.5), we simply specify that type in our `catch` block header. In the body of the block, we print a meaningful error message that explains the problem to the user. The new, clean-exit program is shown in Fig. 11.8.

Figure 11.8 The program in Fig. 11.4 equipped with exception handling

```java
import java.util.Scanner; // type.lib.* if Java 1.4
import java.io.PrintStream;

public class Substring
{
    public static void main(String[] args)
    {
        Scanner input = new Scanner(System.in);
        PrintStream output = System.out;

        output.println("Enter a string containing a slash");
        String str = input.nextLine();
        try
        {
            int slash = str.indexOf("/");
            String left = str.substring(0, slash);
            String right = str.substring(slash + 1);
            output.println("Left substring: " + left);
            output.println("Right substring: " + right);
        }
        catch (IndexOutOfBoundsException e)
        {
            output.println("No slash in input!");
        }
        output.println("Clean Exit."); // closing

    }
}
```

Now if the user makes a valid entry, the app will produce its normal output, skip the `catch` block, and then print the closing statement. And if the input is invalid, the app will print the error message in the `catch` block and then print the closing statement.

◻

11.2.2 Handling Multiple Exceptions

Figure 11.9 The multiple `catch` construct

```
try
{   ...
}
catch (Type-1 e)
{   ...
}
catch (Type-2 e)
{   ...
}
...
catch (Type-n e)
{   ...
}
program continues
```

The basic `try-catch` construct can be extended to support the case in which the fragment can throw more than one type of exception. As shown in Fig. 11.9, we simply add a separate `catch` block for every exception type we wish to handle.

The mechanism is quite similar to that of the single catch: if the fragment does not trigger exceptions, all the `catch` blocks are skipped, and execution continues with the first statement after the last `catch`. If the `try` block does trigger an exception, however, then the VM will examine all the `catch` blocks, one by one, and in the order of their appearance in the program, in search of one that specifies an exception type that is identical to (or, as we shall see later, a superclass of) the type of the thrown exception. If such a block is found, its body is executed, and execution continues with the first statement after the last `catch`. If not, the delegation model is applied.

Note that the specified exception types must be distinct. There is no logical reason for having two identical catch types, but if this is done by mistake, probably due to copy and paste, the compiler will issue a syntax error.

Example 11.2

Write a program that reads a string of two slash-delimited integers, for example, "14/9," extracts the two integers, divides them, and outputs their quotient. Use exception handling to handle the following three input errors: a missing slash, noninteger operands, and division by zero.

Answer:

In a perfect world, where the user's input is always valid, the program can be written along the following pseudo-code:

```
read the string;
left = the left substring;
right = the right substring;
int leftInt = parse an int from left;
int rightInt = parse an int from right;
int answer = leftInt / rightInt;
output answer;
```

But the user's input is not always valid and can be invalid in several ways. For instance, it may not have a slash, and this will lead `substring` to trigger

```
IndexOutOfBoundsException
```

If at least one slash is present, `indexOf` will locate the left-most one, and we can extract the (possibly empty) left and right substrings on its sides. When transforming a string to an integer, the `parseInt` method may throw

```
NumberFormatException
```

because the string is empty or contains characters other than digits and possibly a leading sign. If the two pieces did transform to integers, then the only remaining pitfall is dividing by zero, which triggers

```
ArithmeticException
```

These considerations lead us to the program shown in Fig. 11.10.

Figure 11.10
This program outputs the quotient of two slash-delimited integers. It handles three possible input errors by handling the corresponding exceptions they trigger.

```java
import java.util.Scanner; // type.lib.* if Java 1.4
import java.io.PrintStream;

public class Substring
{
    public static void main(String[] args)
    {
        Scanner input = new Scanner(System.in);
        PrintStream output = System.out;

        try
        {
            output.println("Enter a fraction");
            String str = input.nextLine();
            int slash = str.indexOf("/");
            String left = str.substring(0, slash);
            String right = str.substring(slash + 1);
            int leftInt = Integer.parseInt(left);
            int rightInt = Integer.parseInt(right);
            int answer = leftInt / rightInt;
            output.println("Quotient = " + answer);
        }
        catch (IndexOutOfBoundsException e)
        {   output.println("No slash in input!");
        }
        catch (NumberFormatException e)
        {   output.println("Non-integer operands!");
        }
        catch (ArithmeticException e)
        {   output.println("Cannot divide by zero!");
        }
        output.println("Clean Exit."); // closing
    }
}
```

Note that exception handlers do not have to end the program after catching an exception. For example, the handlers in Fig. 11.10 can allow the user to retry after issuing the error message. Only a minor change is needed to implement this friendlier version:

```
for (boolean retry = true; retry;)
{   try
    {    ... as before
        retry = false;
    }
    catch... as before
}
```

11.2.3 Other Constructs

Java provides two additional extensions of the basic `try-catch` construct—`finally` and the nested `try-catch`—but neither is used in this textbook. We briefly explain them here for completeness and in case you encounter them in code written elsewhere.

■ `finally` As an option, the `try` block can be followed by a `finally` block, either after all the `catch` blocks or without any `catch`. It consists of the keyword `finally` followed by a block. It is guaranteed that once the `try` block receives control, the body of the finally block *will* execute afterward, no matter what. It will execute after the `try` block if no exceptions are thrown, after one of the `catch` blocks if an exception is thrown and caught, or just before delegating to the caller if an exception is thrown (in the `try` block or in one of the `catch` blocks) but was left uncaught. In particular, the block will execute even if a `break` or `return` is present. This construct is most useful when implementing a method, not an app.

■ **Nested** `try-catch` The `try-catch` construct can be nested by placing one construct in the `try` block of another. If an exception is triggered in the innermost `try` block, then its own `catch` blocks are inspected first to see if any can handle the exception. If not, the `catch` blocks of the enclosing construct are inspected next, and so on. If no outer `catch` can handle the exception, the delegation model is applied. If an app has two or more disjoint `try-catch` constructs, then it may be desirable to sandwich them in one outer construct in order to handle exceptions thrown by their `catch` blocks or to unify the handling of one particular exception type.

11.3 Exception Objects

We have been using names such as

```
IndexOutOfBoundsException
```

to specify the exception type in the `catch` header without actually knowing how these names are catalogued. In many programming languages, exceptions are specified using integer codes stored in reserved global variables. In Java, these names are in fact class names because exceptions are instances of these classes. Treating exceptions as objects adds elegance to exception handling and allows us to benefit from the features that objects enjoy. The following sections cover **object-oriented exception handling.**

11.3.1 The Throwable Hierarchy

Java treats exceptions as first-class citizens of the object world. An exception in Java is an object, an instance of a class that has attributes and methods that characterize the exception. And like other classes, exception classes can have a hierarchy in which the superclass contains common features, and subclasses contain specialized features. Also like other classes, exception classes can be grouped in packages, such as `java.util`, based on common usage. The only special thing about these classes is that they all must descend from the class `Throwable`; that is, for a class to be specifiable in a `catch` header, it must inherit from `Throwable` either directly or indirectly. The class `Throwable` is a direct subclass of `Object`; its top-level hierarchy is shown in Fig. 11.11.

`Throwable` has two subclasses: **Error** and **Exception**. Classes in the `Error` family represent conditions that are so abnormal that the reliability of the whole environment is suspect. It is therefore not sensible to specify `Error` (or any of its subclasses) in a `catch` clause because any code you write in the handler may itself not run properly. Classes in the `Exception` family, however, can be caught by programs.

Figure 11.11 The `Throwable` hierarchy. The shaded classes are checked.

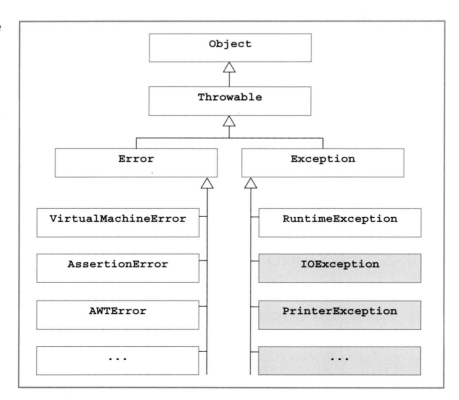

One prominent subclass in that family is **RuntimeException** whose subclasses represent exceptions that the programmer can avoid through validation. In Section 11.3.3 we will see the rationale behind this classification, but for now, let us familiarize ourselves with the most commonly encountered subclasses in this runtime family:

- `IndexOutOfBoundsException` in `java.lang`   This subclass is thrown whenever an index is beyond its legal range. Several methods in the `String` class specify it, but they actually throw a subclass of it (also in `java.lang`) called `StringIndexOutOfBoundsException`. Exceptions of this type are avoidable by index validation.

- `ArithmeticException` in `java.lang` This subclass is thrown when an arithmetic operation fails (e.g., division by zero). Exceptions of this type are avoidable by operand validation.

- `IllegalArgumentException` in `java.lang` `IllegalArgumentException` in is thrown when a method receives an illegal parameter. The parse methods throw a subclass of it (in the same package) called `NumberFormatException`. Exceptions of this type are avoidable (albeit with difficulty) by validating the argument in question.

- `NullPointerException` in `java.lang` This one is thrown when you invoke a method or access a field using a `null` reference. Exceptions of this type are avoidable by comparing with `null`.

- `ClassCastException` in `java.lang` `ClassCastException` is thrown when you attempt to cast an instance of class C to a class P, and C is neither equal to nor a subclass of P. Exceptions of this type are avoidable using `instanceof`.

- `NoSuchElementException` in `java.util` Typically thrown when you request an element from an empty collection. Exceptions of this type are avoidable by querying the collection's size first. For example, you can invoke `hasMoreTokens` before invoking `nextToken`.

Note that if an exception resides in a package other than `java.lang`, then you must either `import` that package or fully qualify the name in the `catch` header.

11.3.2 Object-Oriented Exception Handling

Now that we know that exceptions are actually objects, we can add the following capabilities to our programs:

- The substitutability principle
- The methods in `Throwable`
- Explicit exception creation and `throw`

The Substitutability Principle

We can apply the principle "when a parent is expected, a child is accepted" from Section 9.2.1 when catching exceptions. By specifying a superclass in the `catch` header, we can catch it and all of its descendants. When doing this, pay special attention to the order of your catch blocks, since they are examined in the order of their occurrence in the program (much like a sequence of "`else if`" conditions). If you plan to catch a superclass as well as one of its descendants, then make sure you catch the descendant first. It is generally better to catch specific subclasses because you can then issue specific, rather than generic, messages; it depends on the kind of action that you will take in the handler. An extreme example of this is a program that catches `Throwable`. Such a program can never crash, but the only action that it can take is to retry or shut down, and the only message that it can issue is the ultra-generic "Something Went Wrong!"

Invocation of the Methods in `Throwable`

Since all exception classes descend from `Throwable`, they all inherit its features. Two of the methods listed in its API are `getMessage()` and `printStackTrace()`. `getMessage()` returns a string that contains the error message of this exception, the very string that gets printed if this exception escalated to a crash. `printStackTrace()` is void, and it prints the stack trace, also as if a crash took place. You can use these methods in your handler to access the message or simulate a crash without crashing the system.

Explicit Exception Creation and `throw`

Like any other object, we can create an exception instance ourselves using new. For example, the following statements create a new `ArithmeticException`:

```
ArithmeticException ae = new ArithmeticException();
```

(We did not bother with the actual message but you can supply one.) Once an exception object is created, it can be thrown using the statement

```
throw ae;
```

This has exactly the same effect as triggering a genuine exception. The **throw** statement can trigger any exception you want as long as you supply a reference to an instance of a subclass of `Throwable`. Throwing an exception is admittedly artificial, since no errors/invalid operations are involved, but it can sometimes streamline the handling of exceptions. Example 11.3 demonstrates this.

Example II.3

Rewrite the program in Fig. 11.10 so that it also traps the case when either of the two slash-delimited integers is negative. In this case, the program must output a message indicating that the first (numerator) or the second (denominator) integer is negative.

Answer:
We can of course treat this as a separate validation, but it is far more elegant to treat it like all other violations, that is, by creating and throwing an exception. We can use any exception

in the runtime family as long as it is not already used in our program. Let us use

```
java.lang.UnsupportedOperationException
```

It has a generic name, and we can use its message to convey different types of violation. We add the following to the `try` block after the integers are extracted:

```
if (leftInt < 0)
throw new unsupportedOperationException("Numerator<0!");
}
    else if (rightInt < 0)
{
    throw new
        UnsupportedOperationException("Denominator<0!");
}
```

And to handle this exception, we add the following `catch`:

```
catch (UnsupportedOperationException e)
{
    output.println(e.getMessage());
}
```

As you can see, this approach allows us to treat the added validation like the earlier three.

An Alternative Answer:

We can also use the service of the `type.lib.ToolBox` class whose `crash` method throws a generic `RuntimeException`. We add the following to the `try` block after the integers are extracted:

```
ToolBox.crash(leftInt < 0, "Numerator < 0!");
ToolBox.crash(rightInt < 0, " Denominator < 0!");
```

And to handle the exception that `crash` triggers, we add the following as the *last* `catch` block:

```
catch (RuntimeException e)
{
    output.println(e.getMessage());
}
```

Note that it is imperative that you catch `RuntimeException` last. This is because this exception is the superclass of all other exceptions thrown in this program. If we catch it first, all other exceptions will also be caught and lumped by the same catch. ☐

11.3.3 Checked Exceptions

As shown in Fig. 11.11, exceptions are classified as **checked** or **unchecked**, with all subclasses of `Exception` except `RuntimeException` being checked and all others unchecked. But what does "checked" mean?

Recall that the motivation behind the delegation model is not only to *inform* the caller that an exception has happened, but also to *force* the caller to do something about it. We have seen how the API of a method informs the caller of potential exceptions, but where is the enforcement? What stops a sloppy caller from ignoring the API and thus delivering applications that crash? To mitigate this risk, Java turns it into a compile-time error by using the following **acknowledgment rule:**

> *A program that invokes a method that throws a checked exception must explicitly acknowledge that it is aware of that exception.*

Acknowledgment can be made either by handling the exception or by declaring that the exception is delegated to the caller. For example, suppose we need to write a program that reads data from a disk file. As was done in Section 8.1.5, we create a file input stream and connect it to the file as a data source:

```
FileInputStream fis = new FileInputStream(filename);
```

The API of this constructor states that it throws a `FileNotFoundException`, a checked exception. According to the acknowledgment rule, the above statement cannot compile unless we choose one of two options. The first option is to handle the exception; that is, place the above statement in a try block like this:

```
try
{
    FileInputStream fis = new FileInputStream(filename);
    ...
}
catch (FileNotFoundException e)
{   ...
}
```

The other option is to declare that we are aware of this exception by adding a **throws** to the header of our method:

```
public static void main(...) throws FileNotFoundException
```

If you want to declare several exceptions in the method header, list them separated by commas or specify their common superclass, if any. For example, the above exception can also be declared using

```
public static void main(...) throws IOException
```

This is because `FileNotFoundException` is a subclass of the `IOException` class.

As you can see, some exceptions are labelled *checked* because the compiler *checks* for their acknowledgment. But since checking is important for risk mitigation, why not make all exceptions checked? There are only two unchecked hierarchies: the `Error` and the `RuntimeException` families. We saw in Section 11.3.1 that we should not catch members of the first family; hence, it does not make sense to force programs to acknowledge them. As for the second family, since all of its members can be avoided through validation, it does not make sense to force programs to acknowledge them after having avoided them. For example, consider the following fragment:

```
int a = input.nextInt();
int b = input.nextInt();
if (b != 0)
{
    int c = a / b;
}
```

It would be ridiculous if the compiler refused to compile the above because the exception `ArithmeticException` was not acknowledged. The program has clearly avoided the case of division by zero and should not be required to handle or declare the associated exception. This applies to all members of the runtime exception hierarchy, and that is why all members of this hierarchy are unchecked.

11.4 Building Robust Apps

Our goal is to build applications that are either error-free or at least capable of detecting errors. Thanks to the acknowledgment rule, the compiler will ensure that no checked exception is forgotten. This leaves unchecked exceptions, and in particular, runtime exceptions. These exceptions must either be trapped or avoided, and there are various opinions on which approach is better. The following sections discuss these approaches. They also address, for completeness, logic errors and what can be done to minimize them.

11.4.1 Validation versus Exception

For checked exceptions, the enforcement mechanism guarantees that no exception can go unnoticed; but for the unchecked runtime exceptions, the onus is on the developer. For the app developer, runtime exceptions are caused mainly by entry errors and can be addressed by one of two approaches: defensive programming or exception-based programming.

- **Defensive Programming** This approach relies on validation (`if-else`). It assumes that all inputs are invalid until proven otherwise.
- **Exception-Based Programming** This approach relies on exception handling (`try-catch`). It assumes that all inputs are valid and handles invalidity on an exceptional basis.

In certain situations, you can use either approach, but generally speaking, validation can be so tedious and lengthy that it is likely to miss a case, thus rendering the app not robust. And even if it manages to track every conceivable scenario, it would be redundant and unfair: "redundant" because the methods invoked by the app will probably repeat the same validation and "unfair" because it penalizes the "innocent" cases (by slowing them down) to trap the "guilty" ones.

As a case in point, imagine writing the program in Fig. 11.10 without using exception handling (this is possible because all of its potential exceptions are unchecked). An outline of such an attempt is shown in Fig. 11.12. It is clear that the resulting app is far more involved than that in Fig. 11.10.

Figure 11.12 An attempt at rewriting the program in Fig. 11.10 without using exception handling

```
...
output.println("Enter a fraction");
String str = input.nextLine();
int slash = str.indexOf("/");
if (slash == -1)
{   output.println("No slash in input!");
}else
{   String left = str.substring(0, slash);
    String right = str.substring(slash + 1);
    boolean ok = true;
    /*
    set ok = false if either left or right
    cannot be converted to int
    */
    if (!ok)
    {   output.println("Non-integer operands!");
    }
    else
    {
        int leftInt = Integer.parseInt(left);
        int rightInt = Integer.parseInt(right);
        if (rightInt == 0)
        {   output.println("Cannot divide by zero!");
        }else
        {
            int answer = leftInt / rightInt;
            output.println("Quotient = " + answer);
        }
    }
}
    output.println("Clean Exit."); // closing
}
```

To validate the string-to-integer convertibility, we must ensure for each substring that

- The substring length is at least 1.
- The first character is plus, minus, or neither.
- There is at least one character other than the sign, if there is a sign.
- The remaining characters (aside from the sign, if present) are digits.
- The digits make up an integer that is not bigger than the largest int.

It is clearly a lot easier (and therefore safer) to go ahead and invoke parseInt and deal with the consequences when and if they arise, rather than validate. In other words, we handle input problems on an exception basis.

This example exposes a second advantage to choosing exception handling over defensive programming: it makes the program easier to read and understand because it decouples its computational part, its algorithm, from its input validation; the try block implements the algorithm, while the catch block handles exceptions. With validation, the two parts are jumbled.

II.4.2 Logic Errors

Recall that there are three types of errors: compile-time, runtime, and logic. The compile-time errors are the easiest to handle because the compiler detects all the errors and refuses to produce the ".class" file until they are all corrected. Runtime and logic errors are similar in terms of their sources (end-user, programmer, or environment) and their implication (the software fails to meet its specification), but they differ in how they manifest themselves: a runtime error leads to a crash, whereas a logic error has no visible signature. An app with a logic error behaves normally and produces results, but its results are simply wrong relative to its specification. We learned in this chapter that runtime errors can be avoided by using exception handling and that the compiler enforces such handling for checked exceptions. This leaves logic errors. These are the worst because it is difficult to detect something invisible, let alone demonstrate its absence.

Recall that most software engineering guidelines are themed around mitigation by early exposure (Section 2.3.1). We mitigate potential loss of precision, a logic error, by making it a compile-time error to assign a real value to an integer. Similarly, we use generics to mitigate wrong casting, a runtime error, by making it a compile-time error to put a `Date` object in a `String` collection. We can use this very theme to minimize logic errors by using assertions. Recall from Section 3.2.6 that assertions should be used whenever the programmer has a conviction that some condition is met at a certain point in the code. The `assert` keyword throws

```
java.lang.AssertError
```

As you can tell from the name, this is a subclass of `Error`; hence, it is not meant to be caught. Assertion allows us to expose logic errors early by turning them into uncatchable runtime errors. Other guidelines for minimizing logic errors include using an iterative development process (Section 7.1.2), which exposes analysis or designs misunderstandings early, and a testing methodology (Section 7.2.2), which uncovers algorithmic and implementation errors incrementally throughout the development process.

Summary of Key Concepts

1. A compiled program is said to contain an **error** or a **defect** if it does not behave in accordance with its specification.

2. Errors are caused by **programmer** mistakes, **user** inputs, or abnormalities in the running **environment**. The environment consists of the virtual machine, the operating system, the hardware, and the network, if any.

3. A program with an error will issue incorrect instructions; nevertheless, these instructions may be valid in the eyes of the virtual machine. In this case, the error will go unnoticed, and the program will produce incorrect results. The terms **logic error** and **bug** were used in Section 2.2.3 to describe this situation.

4. If a program with an error issued an instruction that is not only incorrect but invalid, the virtual machine will respond by **throwing** an **exception**. The type of the thrown exception corresponds to the invalid instruction that the program attempted.

5. When an exception is thrown and is not caught, the program is terminated abruptly, and an error message showing the exception type and a stack trace is displayed. The terms **runtime error** and **crash** were used in Section 2.2.3 to describe this situation.

6. A crash prevents a program from performing a **clean exit**, the ability to free up all used resources, close all connections, and end in an orderly fashion. To circumvent this, the program needs to **handle exceptions**. This means it should **monitor** them and **catch** them before they turn into runtime errors.

7. The virtual machine adopts the **delegation model** for exception handling: after throwing an exception, the virtual machine searches the currently executing method (in which the invalid operation was attempted) for a handler that can catch the type of exception that was thrown. If found, it is given control, and the exception is concluded. If not, the method is terminated, and the search is transferred to the caller where, again, the virtual machine looks for a handler. The process continues up the invocation trail (up to the app) until a handler is found. If a handler is not found, the application crashes.

8. The delegation model implies a **handle or delegate** policy because if a method does not handle an exception, it effectively delegates its handling to the caller. Methods document the exceptions they delegate in the *Throws* section of their APIs.

9. The `try-catch` construct allows us to handle exceptions as follows: We place code to be monitored for exceptions in the `try` block. For each exception type we want to trap, we use a `catch` block. The block header specifies the exception type, and the block body contains the handler.

10. Exceptions in Java are in fact objects. They are instances of a hierarchy of classes with a common superclass: **Throwable**. This class has two subclasses: `Error` and `Exception`.

11. Classes in the **Error** hierarchy correspond to exceptions triggered by hardware, the virtual machine, or other abnormalities that cannot possibly be handled by the running program. These exceptions should not be caught.

12. One of the hierarchies within the **Exception** hierarchy has `RuntimeException` as its root. Classes in this hierarchy correspond to exceptions that can be avoided by the program.

13. Six classes in the `RuntimeException` hierarchy occur often, and it is worthwhile to familiarize yourself with their names and the invalid operations that trigger them.

14. As with other objects, you can substitute a subclass when a superclass is expected. Hence, by specifying a superclass in a catch block, it and all of its descendants can be caught. This can be used to adjust the level of granularity in the handler.

15. You can use the methods in `Throwable`, such as `getMessage` and `printStackTrace`, in any exception handler because they are inherited from the superclass.

16. The **throw** keyword can be used to throw any exception class after instantiating it. This can help streamline the handling of exceptions.

17. If your program invokes a method that throws a **checked** exception, then you must either `catch` that exception or declare (in the `main` method header) that your app `throws` that exception. This **acknowledgment rule** confirms that you are aware of the exception.

18. All exceptions other than descendants of the `Error` and `RuntimeException` are checked. The `Error` classes are **unchecked** because you are not supposed to catch them. The `RuntimeException` classes are **unchecked** because you can avoid them.

19. Input validation can be done either through **defensive programming**, in which you check for each possible error, or through **exception handling**, in which you assume the input is valid but do so in a `try` block. The disadvantages of defensive programming are, first, that it can be difficult or lengthy, and thus prone to errors, to check for every possible error; second, its code is more

difficult to read because validation is muddled with processing.

20. Assertions, testing, and an iterative methodology can minimize logic errors.

Review Questions

1. When do we say that a compiled program is defective or that it has an error?

2. What are the sources of program errors?

3. Argue that the end-user can introduce an error into a program no matter how well written the program is.

4. How can an instruction be incorrect yet valid?

5. What is an exception, and how is it generated?

6. What is a clean exit, and why is it desirable?

7. Is it possible that a program with an error will execute without any exception being thrown?

8. Is it possible for an exception to be thrown without a crash?

9. Explain the delegation model by giving an example.

10. The API of a method states that it throws a particular exception if a certain condition is not met. Does this method handle or delegate this exception?

11. What statements should be included in the `try` block?

12. How many `catch` blocks can follow a `try` block? On what does this depend?

13. What is the root of the exception tree? Name its two children.

14. Explain why we are not expected to catch classes in the `Error` family.

15. What is special about members of the `RuntimeException` family?

16. Name six classes in the `RuntimeException` family, and explain the circumstances that lead to throwing each of them.

17. Is it possible to catch two exceptions using one `catch`?

18. Explain why it is imperative that we place `catch` that specifies a superclass after the one that specifies its subclass.

19. Show how the `getMessage` method can be used in a `catch` block.

20. Write a program that instantiates any exception you want and then throws it. Run the program, and examine the resulting crash.

21. What is the **acknowledgment rule**, and what is its purpose?

22. What makes checked exceptions special?

23. Compare and contrast defensive programming with exception-based programming.

24. Argue that the Java compiler can eliminate runtime errors due to checked exceptions just like it eliminates syntax errors in a program.

25. Explain through an example how an implicit assumption can lead to a logic error, then show how assertions can mitigate this risk.

26. Explain using an example how a misunderstanding between the client and analysts or between analysts and other members of the development team can lead to a logic error, then show how an iterative methodology can mitigate this risk.

Socket Programming

◢ L11.1 A Networking Primer

In this Lab you will learn how to make two programs running on two different machines communicate with each other. The two machines must of course be connected through a network of some sort. To understand how such a communication is possible, we must first understand three key concepts: **IP addresses**, **ports**, and **sockets**.

- ■ **IP Addresses** Every computer on a network must have a unique address, called its IP address (IP stands for the Internet protocol). The address is expressed either as four dot-delimited numbers, for example, `130.63.92.157`, or as several dot-delimited names, for example, `cs.yorku.ca`. The class `InetAddress` in `java.net` allows us to convert back and forth between numeric and name-based addresses.
- ■ **Ports** If a program plans to communicate over a network, it must first register itself with the operating system (O/S) of the machine on which it is running. Upon registration, the O/S assigns a unique port number (an integer) to the program. The program is said to *speak through that port* because all messages transmitted by it will specify its port number as the sender. Similarly, the program is said to *listen on that port* because all incoming messages that specify its port number will be routed to it. Note that it is possible for a program to request a specific port number, but the request may be denied if the requested port has already been assigned to a different program.
- ■ **Sockets** A socket is a virtual conduit that connects a program running on one machine with one running on another. It is thus uniquely identified by two IP/port pairs: the IP address of the first machine and the port number of the first program, and a similar pair at the other end. Sockets enable two-way traffic by allowing the program at either end to create an output stream (through which it sends) and an input stream (through which it receives).

The communication can thus be established by creating a socket that connects the two programs as depicted in Fig. 11.13.

The term **server** is used to designate the program that runs first and waits to be contacted by the other program, the **client**. The server requests that a specific port number be assigned to it and then listens on that port.

Given the IP address of the server's machine and the server's port number, the client can create a socket by using the `Socket` class in `java.net`. The class constructor

```
public Socket(String host, int port)
```

creates an instance connected to the indicated server. As you can see, the client provides the IP address of the server's machine as a name, `host`, and the port on which the server is listening as an `int`, `port`. Upon invocation, this constructor determines the IP address of the client's

CLIENT

IP: cs.uiuc.edu

Input Stream
Output Stream

Port: 1225

SERVER

IP: cs.yorku.ca

Input Stream
Output Stream

Port: 5005

Figure 11.13
Two applications running on two networked machines can communicate through a socket. A socket consists of two IP/port pairs, one at the server's end and one at the client's end. Once the socket is connected at both ends, the apps can communicate using input/output streams.

Figure 11.14
Some of the methods in the Socket class are shown in this class diagram.

java::net::Socket
+ close()
+ getLocalAddress(): InetAddress + getInetAddress(): InetAddress
+ getLocalPort(): int + getPort(): int
+ getInputStream(): InputStream + getOutputStream(): OutputStream

machine and assigns a port number to the client. These two items, together with the two parameters passed in the invocation, form the four items necessary to create a socket connected from both ends. Note that the constructor throws exceptions if the port number is invalid, the host does not exist, or no server is listening on the indicated port in the indicated host. The API of the Socket class is captured, in part, in the class diagram shown in Fig. 11.14. In the following two sections, you write the client and the server. Note that the client program will not successfully establish a connection until the server program is running.

LII.2 Writing a Client

Carry out the following tasks:

1. Launch your editor, and write the program Lab11Client, which starts with the following:

```
final String HOST = "localhost"; //replace by server's IP
final int PORT = 4413;
```

The HOST string should contain the IP address of the server machine expressed as dot-delimited numbers or names. If you do not have access to two networked machines, keep HOST set as above. (In that case, your lab will demonstrate how two programs can communicate across virtual machines on the same computer.) The PORT integer should contain the port number on which the server is listening. Keep the above-chosen number. (Any integer between 1024 and 2^{16} will do.)

2. Create a socket:

```
Socket socket = new Socket(HOST, PORT);
```

Since this constructor can throw exceptions, sandwich the above statement in a `try-catch` block, and trap the exceptions indicated in the API. For each, output a clear message. The entire app will be created in this `try-catch` block.

3. Add statements to output the four characteristics of the created socket: the local and the remote IP/port pairs. See Fig. 11.14 for the needed accessors.

4. Add a statement to extract the output stream from the created socket: `OutputStream os =...`

5. Since we will be outputting full strings to the socket, not one byte at a time, bundle the output stream in a print stream:

```
PrintStream out = new PrintStream(os, true);
```

The `true` parameter causes auto-flushing. Without it, we would have had to flush the stream after each output operation.

6. Add statements to extract the input stream from the created socket and bundle it in an input stream reader bundled in a buffered reader:

```
BufferedReader in = new BufferedReader(...
```

7. Add the following statements:

```
output.println("Enter an integer [ENTER=sentinel]");
output.print("> ");
String request = input.readLine();
```

Our client program prompts its user to enter an integer. It should then read the input as a string and send it to the server. The server should compute the square root of the integer and return the result to the client. The client should display the square root and then reprompt. The cycle continues until the client's user enters a zero-length string:

```
for (; request.length() != 0; request = input.readLine())
{
    ... // send request to the server
    ... // read the server's response line
    ... // display the server's response
    output.print("> ");
}
```

8. Add the following statement to terminate the connection and close all of its underlying streams:

```
socket.close();
```

Compile your program and handle any reported compile-time errors. Run the program, and examine the exceptions that were caught. Try to trigger the various exceptions by changing the port number to an invalid one (e.g., −1) or by using a nonexistent host. Note that the IP address assigned to `"localhost"` is `127.0.0.1`. Also note that the client program will not successfully establish a connection until you run the server first.

LII.3 Writing a Server

Carry out the following tasks:

1. Launch your editor, and write the program `Lab11Server`, which starts with the following:

```
final int PORT = 4413;
```

Note the absence of a host constant. This is because a server can have many clients and is created before them, so it cannot be expected to specify an IP address.

2. Note that the `Socket` class assumes that the other end of the socket has already been connected. But if each end insisted that the other end must be connected first, we would have a deadlock. To overcome this, a second class is provided to allow the server to create "half a socket," one that is connected only at the server end:

```
ServerSocket serverSocket = new ServerSocket(PORT);
```

Since this constructor can throw exceptions, sandwich the above statement in a `try-catch` block, and trap the exceptions indicated in the API. For each, output a clear message. The entire app will be created in this `try-catch` block.

3. Add the following statements:

```
output.println("Waiting for a client...");
Socket socket = serverSocket.accept();
```

The `accept` method will block until a connection from a client is received. At that point, the other half of the socket will become known, and a full `Socket` instance is returned.

4. Add statements to output the four characteristics of the created socket: the local and the remote IP/port pairs. You can copy and paste the exact same statements written in the client program.

5. Extract input and output streams from the created socket as was done in the client:

```
PrintStream out =...
BufferedReader in =...
```

6. The server must read the client's request, turn it into an integer, compute its square root, and send the result to the client. The process repeats until the client closes its end of the socket (signalled by receiving a `null`):

```
String request = in.readLine();
for (; request != null; request = in.readLine())
{
    ... // convert the request to an integer
    ... // compute its square root
    ... // send the root back to the client
}
```

7. Add the following statement to terminate the connection and close all of its underlying streams:

```
socket.close();
output.println("Connection closed by client.");
```

Compile your program, and handle any reported compile-time errors. If you will be using two different machines to test the system, transfer your server application to the server machine. Otherwise, store both client and server on the same machine.

LII.4   Testing the Client-Server System

Carry out the following tasks:

1. Create two terminal windows, one for the client and one for the server. If you are using `localhost` (client and server on the same machine), the windows will be separate instances of the command prompt. Otherwise, the client window will be the command prompt, and the server window will be your `telnet` session with the server machine.
2. Run the server. You should see the following message:

   ```
   Waiting for a client...
   ```

3. Switch to the client window and run the client. It should display the socket data and then prompt you to enter an integer. The server window at this stage should indicate that a connection has been established, and it should show the socket data.
4. Enter 25 at the client, and verify that 5 will be returned.
5. End the session by pressing ENTER. Verify that the server has detected that the client has closed its end of the socket.
6. Modify the server program so that it detects invalid requests. If the received string is not an integer, the response should be a message. This implies you should trap this exception within the loop and change the response accordingly. Recompile and redeploy the server. Test by entering AAA at the client and examine the response.

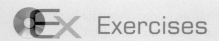 Exercises

Programming exercises are indicated with an asterisk.

11.1 We have been using the `crash` method in `type.lib.ToolBox` to terminate apps and display a message, for example,

```
ToolBox.crash(amount < 0, "A negative Amount!");
```

Write a code fragment that performs the same function as above without using the `crash` method.

11.2 Locate the error in the following fragment, and specify whether it is a compile-time, runtime, or logic error.

```
try
{
    ... // some code
}
catch (java.io.IOException e)
{
    ... // some code
}
catch (java.io.FileNotFoundException e)
{
    ... // some code
}
```

11.3 The following fragment is said to squelch exceptions and is considered very bad (and dangerous) programming practice. Explain what is wrong with it.

```
try
{
    ... // some code
}
catch (Exception e)
{
}
```

11.4 Some app programmers prefer not to trap any exceptions. Instead, they always qualify the main method as follows:

```
public static void main(String[] args) throws Exception
```

Provide a critique of this approach. In particular, do you consider it similar, better, or worse than exception squelching (see Exercise 11.3)?

11.5 The following code fragment attempts to read one byte from a disk file. It handles the two exceptions that may get thrown and then closes the file:

```
try
{
    FileInputStream fis = new FileInputStream("test");
    int x = fis.read();
    output.println("Data: " + x);
}
catch (FileNotFoundException e)
{
    output.println("File Not found!");
}
catch (IOException e)
{
    output.println("Could not read the data!");
}
fis.close();
```

Explain why this fragment will not compile, then suggest a fix.

11.6* Write a program that reads a string consisting of a name and a value separated by a slash for example, `Adam/25`. The program must use exception handling to examine the input and then output one of the following messages:

- `Invalid entry format` Generated if the input is not made up of two slash-delimited tokens

- `Non-integer value` Generated if the value is not an `int`

- `OK` If none of the above exceptions occurred

Note that the contract for "value" implies that it should be made up of digits, possibly with a leading sign, and has the `int` range.

11.7* Redo Exercise 11.6, but change the "value" contract to the following:

- `Value is out of range` Generated if the value is not an `int` in the range [0, 100)

(Recall that a square bracket in an interval includes its end, whereas a parenthesis excludes it.) You can handle the range check either by throwing your own runtime exceptions or by using `crash` in `type.lib.ToolBox` and trapping its exception.

11.8* Write a program that reads a string consisting of a name, an amount, and a file name, all separated by commas, for example, `Eve,1215.75,trx.txt`. It then uses exception handling to examine the input and accordingly outputs one of the following messages:

- `Invalid entry format` Generated if the input is not made up of three comma-delimited tokens

- `The name is too short` Generated if the name has less than four characters

- `Value is out of range` Generated if the value is not a non-negative double

- `Could not open the file` If the file could not be opened for any reason, for example, does not exist or is read-protected

- `OK` If none of the above exceptions occurred

11.9* Write a program that reads the content of the file `trx.txt`. Each record in the file contains a transaction made up of three tab-delimited fields: an account number (8 digits), a code (`C` or `c` or `D` or `d`), and an amount (a positive `double`). The program computes the sum of all the amounts in the records after multiplying each by 1 if its code is `d` or `D`, and by −1 if its code is `c` or `C`. If all the records in the file are as specified, the program outputs this sum, but if any of the records are malformed, the program outputs the record number (starts at 0) and a message indicating the problem. Afterward, the program continues reading records, but it no longer outputs the sum; that is, it either outputs the sum or a log of malformed records (one per line). The message can be as follows:

- `Invalid record format` Generated if a record is not made up of three tab-delimited fields

- `Invalid account number` Generated if the account is not an 8-digit string

- `Invalid transaction code` Generated if the code is not in `"DdCc"`

- `Invalid amount` Generated if the amount is not a positive `double`

11.10* Write a program that reads time from the user in the 24-hour time format and outputs it in the 12-hour time format. For example, if the input is `"15:45"`, the output will be `"3:45 pm"`. The program must use exception handling to ensure the entry is a valid time; otherwise, it must output a message that indicates the entry error.

11.11* An ISBN (International Standard Book Number) is a 10-character code that identifies books. The first 9 characters are digits. The 10th character is represented as a digit if its value is in [0,9] and as an X if its value is 10. It acts as a check digit that ensures that the weighted sum of all digits, including it, is divisible by 11 (sum MOD 11 = 0). The weights, from left to right, are 10, 9, 8,..., 1.

For example, the ISBN 0131211447 leads to the sum: $0*10 + 1*9 + 3*8 +... + 7*1 = 88$, which is divisible by 11. This ISBN is thus valid.

Write a program that reads an ISBN number from the user and outputs a message regarding the validity of the input. The message can be as follows:

- `Illegal ISBN` Generated if the entry is not made up of 9 digits followed by a digit or an X

- `Invalid ISBN` Generated if the ISBN does not satisfy the MOD-11 check

- `OK` If none of the above exceptions occurred

11.12* Write a program that reads a file name from the user and verifies that the file exists and can be read without using exception handling.

Hint: Use `java.io.File`.

11.13* Write a program that reads a file name from the user and verifies that it is indeed a file and not a directory.

11.14* Write a program that does not use `java.io.File` to write the current date and time on a user-specified file. After reading the file name from the user, the program must check to see if such a file already exists. If it does not, the file is created as specified. Otherwise, the program must warn the user and prompt for confirmation before overwriting the file. Here is a log:

```
Enter the name of the file:
trx.txt
This file already exists. Overwrite? [y/n]
y
File created.
```

Hint: Try to read the file.

11.15* Rewrite the program from Exercise 11.14 using a more elegant approach, one that relies on the method `createNewFile` in `java.io.File`.

11.16* Write a program that determines the IP address of your favourite web site and displays it in the dot-delimited-numbers format. Make the program read the web site from the user, and output either an error message or the IP address. As a test, provide `localhost` as the web site and verify that `127.0.0.1` is displayed.

11.17* Write a program that scans all ports below 1024 in your computer and lists those that are in use.

Hint: Try to create a server socket on each.

11.18* Create a client-server system on the same machine (`localhost`) such that when the client sends one byte to the server, the server echoes it back, that is, sends the same byte back. Note that you do not need to wrap a reader (or a buffer) on the input stream of the socket since data is exchanged one byte at a time. Use an auto-flushing print stream for output.

11.19* Redo Exercise 11.18 without auto-flushing. Do you have to manually flush the buffer after each output?

11.20* It is possible to implement Exercise 11.19 without a print stream, that is, by directly using the output stream of the socket? Rewrite the program accordingly.

11.21 Consider the following scenario: Your program invokes a method m, and m invokes a method w, which throws the exception E. The developers of m decide not to handle E. They argue that the acknowledgment rule gives them the right to choose between handling and delegating, and they choose delegating. Argue that they do not have the right to delegate in this case; that is, they *must* handle E.

11.22 The fragment

```
try
{
    ... // some code that throws E1
}
catch (E1 e)
{
    throw new E2("Message", e)
}
```

monitors an exception of one type and throws an exception of another type. The one it throws is called a **wrapped exception** because its constructor takes another exception as a parameter. The second exception is said to **wrap** the first; the first is said to be the **cause** of the second. You can get the cause of any exception by using the `getCause` method.

Show that wrapped exceptions can solve the problem posed in Exercise 11.21 in which the developers of *m* do not want to handle *E* but they have to.

eCheck

Check11A (TS = 26) We want to write a program that reads the time of day and outputs the number of minutes that have passed since midnight. The program reads the user's input as the string *h:m:ind*, where *h* is the hour (must be >0 and <=12), *m* is the minute (must be >=0 and <60), and *ind* is either AM or PM (case-insensitive). Ten sample runs are shown below:

```
Enter h:m:AM or PM > test
Non-numeric Data!

Enter h:m:AM or PM > 15:5:AM
Values out of range!

Enter h:m:AM or PM > 1:15:am
75

Enter h:m:AM or PM > 12:10:am
10

Enter h:m:AM or PM > 1:5:tm
Invalid AM/PM indicator!

Enter h:m:AM or PM > 11:50:am
710

Enter h:m:AM or PM > 12:10:pm
730

Enter h:m:AM or PM > 1:25:PM
805

Enter h:m:AM or PM > 11:50:pm
1430

Enter h:m:AM or PM > 12:55:am
55
```

If the entry is valid, the program outputs the number of minutes and ends. Otherwise, it outputs one of four error messages and then ends. The messages are the following:

"Values out of range!"	if *h* or *m* is outside its legal range
"Missing colon!"	if a colon is missing
"Non-numeric data!"	if *h* or *m* is not an integer
"Invalid AM/PM indicator!"	if the indicator is neither AM nor PM (upper or lower)

The program must perform the computation without doing any validation whatsoever and without using any `if` statements, `switch` statements, or similar constructs. Instead, it should rely on exception handling as it implements the following algorithm:

1. Read the user's entry.

2. Extract the three tokens.

3. Convert the first token to an integer h.

4. Assign `h = h % 12`.

5. Convert the second token to an integer m.

6. Capitalize the last token.

7. Look up the last token in the string `"00AM12PM"` and extract the two-digit integer a before it.

8. Compute and output 60 * (h + a) + m.

For example, if the entry is `12:10:pm`, step 3 leads to h = 12, step 4 leads to h = 0; step 5 leads to m = 10; and step 6 leads to PM. Upon searching for "PM" in the string of step 7, we find it preceded by the two digits "12," which leads to a = 12. The final computation is thus 60*(0 + 12) + 10 = 730.

Develop and eCheck Check11A.

Check11B (TS = 31)

Write the app Check11B that reads a string of the form n/x from the user, where n is a month number and x is an arbitrary string, and outputs the `double` stored in the first record of the file MMM.txt, where MMM is the three-character month name that corresponds to n; e.g. if the user entered 2/York then the file is Feb.txt.

Your app implement follow the following algorithm:

1. Locate the slash or issue the error message "Invalid Input"

2. Interpret n as a number or issue the error message "Non-numeric Entry"

3. Convert n to a 3-letter month name or issue the error message "Invalid Input"

4. Print the name of the file and then open it or issue the error message "File not found"

5. Read the first record or issue the error message "File Empty"

6. Interpret the record as a double or issue the error message "Non-numeric Record"

7. Output the balance.

Here are a few sample runs:

```
Entry ... hello
Invalid Input

Entry ... a/b
Non-numeric Entry
```

```
        Entry ...  77/Canada
        Invalid Input

        Entry ...  2/YYZ
        The Filename is: Feb.txt
        File not found

        Entry ...  3/Toronto
        The Filename is: Mar.txt
        File Empty

        Entry ...  12/York
        The Filename is: Dec.txt
        Non-numeric Record

        Entry ...  6/Ontario
        The Filename is: Jun.txt
        The double # is: 450.75
```

Develop your app, test it, and then eCheck it.

Check11C (TS = 26)

When a form is submitted to a web application, the http protocol requires that the browser packs all its data in one string, known as the query string. The string consists of several *variable=value* substrings delimited by the '&' character, as shown in this example:

id=575&place=Toronto%2C%20Ontario&name=Adam

At the server, the web app must parse this string in order to determine the values. Note that if the value contains reserved characters then the browser replaces these characters with %nn, where nn is the character code in hex. This replacement is known as *URL encoding* and must be undone by the server through a *URL decoding*. In the above query string, for example, the place variable has the value "Toronto, Ontario" so the browser replaced the comma with %2C and the space with %20 (the ASCII code of comma is 42 decimal or 2C hex and that of space is 32 decimal or 20 hex). There is a class in the Java library that does this replacement: URLDecoder in the java.net package. We will delegate to it to decode the value.

Write the app Check11C that prompts for and read a query string and a variable name and output the *decoded* value of the indicated variable (or a message if the variable is not in the string). Here are two sample runs:

```
        Enter the query string:
        id=575&content=75%3aF%2fG&name=Adam
        Enter the variable name:
        content
        Before decoding:
        75%3aF%2fG
        After decoding:
        75:F/G
```

```
Enter the query string:
id=575&content=75%3aF%2fG&name=Adam
Enter the variable name:
test
No such variable "test"!
```

As you can see from the first run, the decoder replaced %3a with a colon. The decoding class requires that you specify a supported character encoding or else it throws an exception. Hence, your app must supply the correct character encoding (which can be obtained from the default of the Charset class) and must handle the exception.

You can assume that the supplied query string is valid. Make sure your app handles boundary cases in which the sought variable is the very first or the very last. You may want to use the split method, and to that end you may want to prepend the query string with '&' so you can handle all cases in a uniform way.

Develop your app, test it, and then eCheck it.

Check11D (TS = 26)

Write a program that reads from the user a mathematical expression that may contain nested *precedence characters*, which are the following: parentheses "( )," brackets "[ ]," and braces "{ }." For example, the input string can be

```
{a-b*[c/(d+e)]+f*[g-h*{i+j*k}]-m/(n+1)+((p/[r/t]-u)-v)/w}
```

The program should ignore operators and operands and focus only on the above precedence characters. Specifically, it should determine whether these characters are "OK," "Imbalanced," "Overlapping," or "Too Deeply Nested" and accordingly output one of the above four messages. Here are five sample runs:

```
Enter expression
[a+b*(c-d])
Overlapping

Enter expression
(a+(b-[c/d])
Imbalanced

Enter expression
(a+b)]-c
Imbalanced

Enter expression
{a-[b/(c+d)]}
OK

Enter expression
(((([[a + b] / c] + d) + e) + f)
Too Deeply Nested
```

Your program must implement the following algorithm and handle exceptions:

1. Create an instance of the `type.lib.CharStack` class, an ordered collection of `chars`, using its default constructor.

2. Scan the input string character by character, left to right.

3. Ignore nonprecedence characters.

4. If an open precedence character is encountered (i.e., (or [or {), store it in the stack.

5. If a closed precedence character x is encountered, remove from the stack the character y that was stored last. If x and y correspond, for example, x is] and y is [, then continue scanning; otherwise, end the program with the "Overlapping" message.

6. If you need to remove a character from the stack but find it empty, or you complete scanning the string but find the stack not empty, then end the program with the "Imbalanced" message.

7. If you need to store something in the stack but find it full, then end the program with the "Too Deeply Nested" message.

8. If the program did not end in one of the above cases, print "OK."

The last sample run, which shows that six levels of nesting is considered too deep, is just an example. Your program must *not* assume that five (or any other number) is the maximum number of levels. Instead, it must rely on the stack becoming full to detect this case. And since the stack's maximum size is subject to change (by the maker of the `CharStack` class), our program must not assume any particular size. Instead, it should rely on the exception thrown by the add method in order to detect that the stack is full. Develop your app, test it, and then eCheck it.

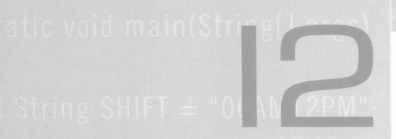

12

A Multiclass Application

Learning Objectives

1. *Apply concepts and techniques to a real-life example*

2. *Experience the complexity of an integrated system*

n this chapter, you will apply the concepts learned in this book to applications that use a system of inter-related classes.

12.1 Introduction

We can now put together and apply all the concepts that we have learned so far to confront the complexity of a multiclass application. Not only will this help strengthen your understanding of these concepts, but it will give you a glimpse into real-life, integrated applications. The following two sections describe the general features of integrated, multiclass applications and introduce the application that will be examined in-depth in this chapter.

12.1.1 Multiclass Applications

Recall that there are three types of interclass relationships: dependency, aggregation, and inheritance. All the applications that we have written so far involve dependency, and a few of them also involve aggregation or inheritance. There is no standard definition for a **multiclass application**, but we can define it informally as one that involves all three relationships and several classes. You need at least three classes (plus the app) to have inheritance and aggregation, but a typical multiclass application involves tens of classes.

The multiclass application that we study in this chapter involves inventory and sales, but it is actually far more general in terms of the issues it brings to bear: inheritance through specialization and through abstract generalization; aggregation through maps and lists; compositions; transaction processing through various architectures (interactive, batched, and multitiered); report generation; persistence of objects; and more.

The classes involved in this application are all members of the SDK or the `type.lib` package; hence, you can easily write applications to test different aspects of the system. Furthermore, you can obtain a snapshot of the system, one containing randomly generated data and transactions, in the form of a serialized object stored in a binary file. This means you can write several independent applications that focus on different aspects of the system, and they will all share the same set of objects.

12.1.2 The Abstract Foods Company

The Abstract Foods Company is in the business of buying food products from manufacturers and selling them wholesale to clients. Its clients are supermarket and convenience store owners. Abstract Foods uses many software systems to automate and conduct its business, including inventory control, warehouse management, invoicing, order processing, payroll, and accounting. The systems run on several hardware platforms at different locations, but they are all linked. To understand these systems, we will ignore the links and focus on one system at a time. We will look only at the **inventory** subsystem (the one that manages stocked food items) and the **contacts** subsystem (the one that manages the clients and suppliers). The links between these two subsystems and others (e.g., accounting) are therefore irrelevant to us. Figure 12.1 depicts the UML diagram of these two subsystems.

Figure 12.1 may look intimidating at first, but once you look at the pieces one by one, it becomes a simple and natural depiction of relationships. The left part of the diagram shows the inventory subsystem. It is characterized by classes that encapsulate food items (the `Item` class and its `Fresh` subclass) and culminates in a collection, the `Inventory` map. The right

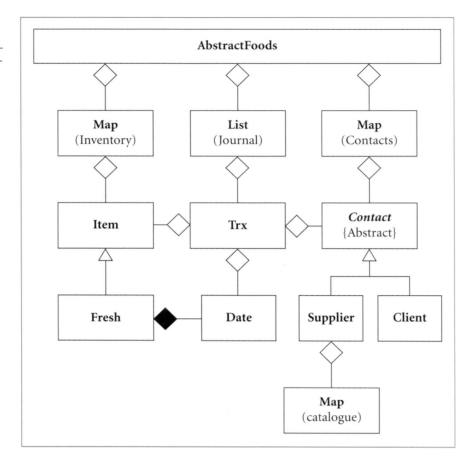

part of the diagram shows the contacts subsystem. It is characterized by classes that encapsulate contacts (`Client` and `Supplier`) and culminates in a collection, the `Contacts` map. The middle part of the diagram shows transactions that involve these two subsystems. It also culminates in a collection, the `Journal` list. These parts are discussed in detail in the following sections.

12.2 Inventory Control

Classes in the inventory control subsystem encapsulate the items that the company stocks. They provide attributes that hold information about these items and methods to make buying and selling easier. The following sections examine the inventory classes.

12.2.1 The Items

Every **item** that the company buys or sells is encapsulated by an instance of the `Item` class, which is in `type.lib`. An `Item` object maintains two types of data about the item it represents: basic (unchanging) information, such as the item's number and name, and dynamic data (information that changes with every sale and purchase), such as number of units sold. We create an item by using the constructor

```
Item milk = new Item("2001M071", "Java Milk 1%", 4.75);
```

The first parameter is the item number. In this example, we used a structured number: the first five characters, 2001M, indicate the item's group (e.g., "bagged dairy milk"), and the remaining three characters, 071, identify the item within the group. We will always use an 8-character, 5 + 3, number for our items, but note that this is not a class requirement. The above constructor accepts any non-null string as the first parameter. Note also that we are not concerned whether the item number is unique. It is a concern for the collection that holds instances of this class. The second parameter is the name of the item, and the third, a double, is its sale price.

At this stage (i.e., immediately after instantiation), the stock quantity of milk is zero; hence, we cannot sell any of it. What can do is to buy some of it:

```
milk.purchase(100, 325.00);
```

In this example, we purchased 100 units (bags) of milk at an overall cost of $325. If you now invoke accessors on milk, you will get the returns shown in Fig. 12.2.

Let us purchase 50 additional bags of milk before conducting any sale. We will buy these bags from a supplier who has a promotion on milk, 50 bags for $100:

```
milk.purchase(50, 100.00);
```

If you now invoke accessors on milk, you will get the returns shown in Fig. 12.3.

The API of the getUnitCost method states that it divides the total dollar amount paid toward purchasing (i.e., total of all purchases since the item was created) by the total number of units purchased since the item was created; that is, it is a convenience method that returns the result of dividing getPurchases() by getPurchasedQty(). Indeed, $425/150 \approx$ $2.83 is the average of the two purchases weighted by their quantities.

To process a sales transaction, you invoke the sell method and pass the quantity to be sold. If you try to sell 500 bags of milk while you have only 150 in stock, the sale will be rejected. Indeed, the sell method is boolean, and it processes the sale (and returns true) only if there are enough units in stock. The statement

```
boolean ok = milk.sell(10);
```

will succeed (ok will be true) and will lead to the returns shown in Fig. 12.4.

Accessor		Return
int	getStock()	100
int	getPurchasedQty()	100
double	getPurchases()	325.00
double	getUnitCost()	3.25

Figure 12.2 The status of milk after the first purchase

Accessor		Return
int	getStock()	150
int	getPurchasedQty()	150
double	getPurchases()	425.00
double	getUnitCost()	2.83

Figure 12.3 The status of milk after the second purchase

Accessor		Return
int	getStock()	140
int	getPurchasedQty()	150
double	getPurchases()	425.00
double	getUnitCost()	2.83
int	getSoldQty()	10
double	getSales()	47.50

Figure 12.4 The status of `milk` after the sale

Notice that the in-stock quantity has been reduced to `140`. In fact, this quantity can be obtained by subtracting the total sold quantity (`getSoldQty`) from the total purchased quantity (`getPurchasedQty`). Note the two sales accessors: one is for the total quantity, and the other is for the total dollar amount of all sales made since the item was first created. In our case, they indicate that 10 bags of milk were sold for $47.50. The dollar figure was computed by the `sell` method by multiplying the sold quantity by the sale price of a bag of milk (set to $4.75 by the constructor).

Abstract Foods Company may sometimes sell a bag of milk for more or less than the posted sale price. For example, a special discount may be given to preferred customers or to high-volume sales; in this case, the sale price is less than $4.75 per bag. Or perhaps certain sales involve delivery charges, leading to an effective sale price of more than $4.75 per bag. To accommodate these situations, the class offers a second, overloaded method that allows specifying the sales amount. The statement

```
boolean ok = milk.sell(10, 40.00);
```

indicates the sale of 10 bags of milk for a total of $40 (i.e., effectively $4 per bag). The method behaves exactly as the earlier method, but it uses 40 rather than 47.50 (10*4.75) to update the total sales amount.

12.2.2 The Fresh Items

Fresh items are products that spoil relatively quickly; hence, their expiration dates must be closely monitored. Fresh meat and produce are examples. The `Fresh` class is a subclass of the `Item` class, and it inherits and retains all of its functionality except for a minor override to the `toString` method (see the API). To support an expiry date, an aggregation is used to make one of the attributes of the `Fresh` class a `Date` object. This aggregation is in fact a composition because without the `Date` attribute, the `Fresh` object cannot exist.

The class expects us to pass the expiry date to the constructor:

```
Calendar cal = Calendar.getInstance();
cal.set(2006, 0, 15);
Fresh meat = new Fresh("0905A071", "Top Sirloin",4.75,
cal.getTime());
```

The first three parameters are the same as in the superclass. The fourth is the expiry date, which we have set to Jan. 15, 2006. The class provides an accessor to retrieve the expiry date. If you write

```
output.println(meat.getExpiry());
```

you should get `Sun Jan 15 15:12:52 EST 2006` expressed in local time zone.

12.2.3 The Inventory Map

Figure 12.5 The inventory control subsystem

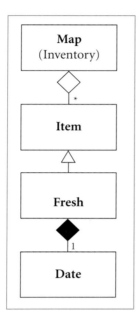

To accommodate a large number of items and fresh items, we need a collection to hold them, one that is easy to access and to search. The guidelines in Chapter 10 make it clear that Map is the ideal choice. It is very important for our application that no two items share the same number. Hence, if we set up a map such that the first element of each pair (the key) is the item number (a string), and the second element (the value) is the item itself (an object reference), we will ensure a unique item number (because a map views its keys as a set). We create the **inventory map** using the following:

```
Map<String, Item> inventory = new
    HashMap<String, Item>();
```

We can then add an element, for example, meat:

```
inventory.put(meat.getNumber(), meat);
```

Figure 12.5 reproduces the part of Fig. 12.1 that relates to inventory control and shows the classes discussed in this and the previous sections.

12.3 Contacts

The main business of the Abstract Foods Company is the purchase and sale of food products; hence, its main **contacts** are **suppliers** and **clients**. Therefore, we need classes to encapsulate these two types of contacts. The following sections examine the design of these classes.

12.3.1 The Need for an Abstract Class

For each contact, we need a unique identifying number, perhaps a serial number (e.g., 10001, 10002,...), and the contact's name and address. For clients, we also need the credit rating that helps assess risk when we extend credit (sell and bill later). For suppliers, we also need to know the items that each supplier supplies and their prices, that is, we need the catalogue from each supplier.

At first glance, you may think you should treat the client/supplier classification as you did the item/fresh pair; that is, imagine a supplier as a subclass of client. This would be incorrect because you cannot say, "A supplier is a client." A supplier is not a special kind of client, even though it shares with it several attributes (e.g., name) and methods (e.g., the getNumber method). We can correctly capture this relationship by having both of them inherit from a third class that encapsulates their common features. This way, we can still consolidate their types (under the type of their parent) yet maintain their distinctiveness.

Let us therefore imagine a class called Contact that maintains the contact (serial) number, name, and address and that provides methods such as accessors/mutators, toString,

Figure 12.6 The `Contact` class, the superclass of `Client` and `Supplier`, must be made abstract.

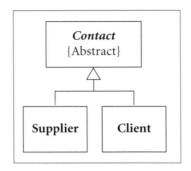

and `equals`. Given this class, it is easy to imagine a subclass `Client` that adds the credit rating functionality, and a subclass `Supplier` that adds the catalogue functionality.

This design has only one problem: what if an app created an instance of `Contact`? This instance would be neither a client nor a supplier, yet it is a valid contact. To avoid the ramifications of such a meaningless instance, we imagine `Contact` as an abstract class. Recall that such a class behaves like any class but it cannot be instantiated. Hence, we will assume the structure depicted in Fig. 12.6. Recall that an abstract class is flagged in UML by writing its name in italics and adding {Abstract} to its title box.

12.3.2 The Clients

The `Client` subclass adds only one thing to its superclass: support for credit rating. The constructor has a parameter that specifies the rating, for example,

```
Client c = new Client("Corner Mart", "17 Elm", "B++");
```

In addition to specifying the name and address, we specified B++ as the credit rating for this client. The class has an accessor and a mutator that allow us to inspect, and possibly change, this rating after creation. The class does not enforce any particular rating system; any non-null string is accepted as a rating.

Assignment of numbers is handled by the superclass and is thus the same for clients and suppliers. It is done serially starting at 10000 (a field, FIRST_NUMBER, in `Contact`), so if the above client were the very first contact, its number would be 10001. This can be verified using

```
output.println(c.getNumber());
```

Note that if a supplier is created next, its number will be 10002. In other words, the contact number does not indicate whether the contact is a client or a supplier.

12.3.3 The Suppliers

The `Supplier` subclass provides support for a new feature: a **catalogue** of all items that we can purchase from this supplier as well as the purchase price for each. Some suppliers do not have catalogues, and some do. Hence, the catalogue aggregation in the supplier class is not a composition.

The catalogue itself is a two-column table. One column contains the numbers of the items that the supplier supplies (using our numbering scheme); the other column contains the corresponding prices. This makes Map the ideal collection for representing the catalogue; indeed, the `Supplier` class has an attribute of the type Map. You can provide the map as part of creating a supplier object, by passing it to the constructor, or you can create a supplier with an empty map and set the map later. The class offers two overloaded constructors to support this flexibility.

The statement

```
Supplier s = new Supplier("The ABC Group", "4700 Finch");
```

creates a supplier with the passed name and address, assigns it the next free number, and sets its catalogue to an empty map. By default, the class creates the map as HashMap; that is, it creates the object

```
new HashMap<Item, Double>()
```

If you prefer to use a different map, then either supply it as a parameter in the three-parameter constructor or use the catalogue mutator, setCatalog. These two methods are demonstrated in the following example.

Let us create a new supplier that supplies two types of milk: Java milk (item# 2001M071) at $3.65 per bag, and Abstract milk (item# 2001M088) at $3.50 per bag:

```
Supplier s = new Supplier("The ABC Group", "4700 Finch");
Map<String, Double> c = new HashMap<String, Double>();
c.put("2001M071", new Double(3.65));
c.put("2001M088", new Double(3.50));
s.setCatalog(c);
```

Note that the above Double instances are optional thanks to auto-boxing; that is, we could have written the third statement as

```
c.put("2001M071", 3.65);
```

Instead of creating the supplier and then the catalogue, we could also start by creating the catalogue and then the supplier:

```
Map<String, Double> c = new HashMap<String, Double>();
c.put("2001M071", new Double(3.65));
c.put("2001M088", new Double(3.50));
Supplier s = new Supplier ("The ABC Group", "4700 Finch", c);
```

Either way, if you output the catalogue (output.println(c)), you should get

```
{2001M088=3.5, 2001M071=3.65}
```

Given a supplier reference, the traversal and search methods of the Map collection can be used to determine whether it supplies a given item and, if it does, for how much.

12.3.4 The Contacts Map

To accommodate the creation of a large number of clients and suppliers, we need a collection to hold them, a collection that is easy to access and to search. The guidelines in Chapter 10 make it clear that Map is the ideal choice, as it was for the inventory subsystem and for the same reason: in our application, it is important that no two contacts share the same number. Hence, we set up a map with the contact number as key and the contact object itself as value. For example, we start by creating a map:

```
Map<String, Supplier> contacts = new HashMap<String, Supplier>();
```

Given a supplier s, we add it to the map as follows:

```
contacts.put("" + s.getNumber(), s);
```

Figure 12.7 reproduces the part of Fig. 12.1 that relates to contact management and shows the classes discussed in this and the previous sections.

Figure 12.7 The contacts sub-system

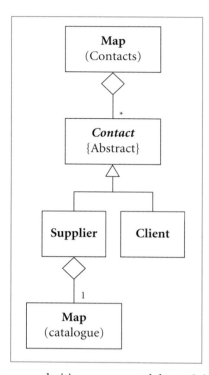

12.4 Transactions

The classes we have met so far represent the back end of the system, the part that maintains the data and enforces all the business rules. To conduct its business, the company will also need several apps that act as front ends; they interact with the user (often through a GUI) and then pass the user requests to the back end classes as **transactions**. One app, for example, would be for invoicing, and it would culminate in sales transactions; another would be for order processing, and it would generate purchase transactions. These apps could be running on the same machine as the back-end classes and directly invoking their methods, or they could be running on remote machines and communicating with the back-end classes using XML (for on-line processing) or plain tab-delimited text files (for batch processing).

It is clear from the above discussion that we still need one more class in our system: a collection that holds all the transactions that were processed. These transactions have already been posted, but they must be kept because many decision-support and data-mining applications will need to inspect them. For example, our back-end classes can readily determine the stock quantity of an item, its total sales, or its profitability, but it cannot possibly discover a correlation between the sales of two items (whenever one is sold, the other is also sold in the same invoice). Discovering such patterns requires access to all posted transactions, and since extensive processing is involved, we prefer to store these transactions as objects in a collection, rather than archiving them on some backup tape.

12.4.1 The `Trx` Class

Every instance of `Trx` (also in `type.lib`) represents one posted transaction ("posted" means it has already been processed, and the appropriate back-end methods have already been invoked). The API of the `Trx` constructor reveals that each transaction has seven elements:

- **Transaction Date** This is the date on which the transaction occurred. It is a `Date` instance.

- **Transaction Code** This is a string that identifies this transaction; for example, S means sales, and P means purchases.

■ **Transaction Reference** The transaction reference is a string that identifies the document of the transaction, for example, invoice number.

■ **Contact** The involved party, for example, a client or a supplier, is a `Contact` instance.

■ **Item** This is the involved item; it is an `Item` instance.

■ **Transaction Quantity** Transaction quantity is an `int` that indicates the number of units involved in the transaction.

■ **Transaction Amount** The transaction amount is a `double` that indicates the dollar amount of the transaction.

In addition to the constructor, the class provides accessors for these fields but no other behaviour. The class acts as a mere aggregate (a bag) that makes storage and addressing of its attributes easy.

12.4.2 The Journal List

To accommodate the creation of a large number of transactions, we need an easily accessible and searchable collection to hold them. The guidelines in Chapter 10 in this case—unlike the inventory and contact cases—argue against a map or a set. Looking at the attributes of each transaction, and unless we introduce a new one that is unique per transaction, it is clear that we can easily have duplicates. Hence, `List` is the only interface we can use. We create such a list using, for example,

```
List<Trx> journal = new ArrayList<Trx>();
```

Let us assume that we want to sell 20 bags of milk to client c for $80. Let the transaction date be now, and let its reference number be 114. The program may proceed like this:

```
if (milk.sell(20, 80.0))
{
    Date now = new Date();
    Trx trx = new Trx(now, "S", "114", c, milk, 20, 80.0);
    journal.add(trx);
}
```

Figure 12.8 reproduces the part of Fig. 12.1 that relates to transaction processing and shows the classes discussed in this and the previous sections.

Figure 12.8 The transaction sub-system

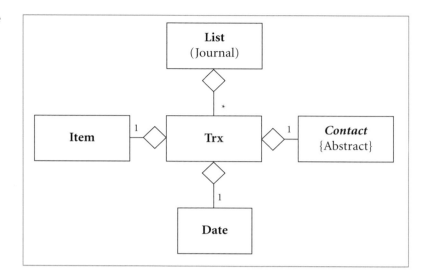

Summary of Key Concepts

1. A **multiclass application** is an application made up of an app and several (typically many) component classes. The classes participate in inheritance, aggregation, and dependency relationships.

2. The **inventory subsystem** handles the items that the company buys and sells. Its main classes are the Item and Fresh classes.

3. The Item class encapsulates a stock item. Its attributes hold the item's basic data (number, name, etc.) as well as its transactional data (sold quantity, sales, etc.).

4. The Fresh class extends Item, and its instances represent items that spoil quickly, such as meat and milk. It inherits all the features of the Item class and adds features to handle expiry date.

5. The **inventory map** is a collection of all items that the company handles. Its keys are the item numbers, and its values are the items themselves.

6. The **contacts subsystem** handles the contacts that are essential for the company's business. Its main classes are the Supplier and Client classes.

7. The two contact classes share many features but do not exhibit an is-a relationship. A third class, Contact, was therefore added to act as their superclass. It was made abstract because it would be meaningless to instantiate it.

8. The Client subclass encapsulates a client.

9. The Supplier subclass encapsulates a supplier and aggregates a **catalogue** that lists all items supplied by this supplier.

10. The **contact map** is a collection of all contacts that the company has. Its keys are the contact numbers, and its values are the contact objects themselves.

11. The inventory and contact subsystems represent (in part) the **back end** of the system. For each business activity, such as ordering and invoicing, there is a **front end** that interacts with the end-user and transmits **transactions** to the back end.

12. The Trx class encapsulates a transaction. Its attributes hold the transaction fields, which include the transaction date, type, and the contact/item involved.

13. A transaction is said to be **posted** when its data has been reflected in the back end; that is, when it is used to update the inventory or contact subsystems.

14. The **transaction list**, also called the **journal**, is a collection of all the posted transactions. It is a list whose elements are the transaction objects.

Review Questions

1. Describe the role of the Abstract Foods Company in the supply chain.
2. What is the function of the inventory subsystem, and what are its main classes?
3. Name three attributes of the Item class that do not change when the item is bought or sold.
4. Name three attributes of the Item class that do change when the item is bought or sold.
5. How is the Fresh class related to the Item class?
6. Argue that the Fresh class must be an aggregate.
7. Describe the collection that holds all the company's items.
8. What is the function of the contacts subsystem, and what are its main classes?
9. What is wrong with making Supplier a subclass of Client or vice versa?
10. Why is the Contact class abstract?
11. Name one attribute that is present in the Client class but not in the Supplier class.
12. Name one attribute that is present in the Supplier class but not in the Client class.
13. Name one attribute that is shared by the Supplier and Client classes.
14. Is the Supplier class an aggregate?
15. Describe the collection that holds a supplier's catalogue.
16. Describe the collection that holds all the company's contacts.
17. What is the difference between a back-end and a front-end piece of software?
18. What is a transaction, and which class encapsulates it?
19. What does it mean that a transaction is posted?
20. Describe the collection that holds all the company's posted transactions.

Inventory, Contacts, and Transactions

LI2.I The Inventory Collection

Carry out the following tasks:

1. Launch your editor, and write the program `Lab12Inv`, which starts with

```
AbstractFoods af = AbstractFoods.getRandom();
Map<String, Item> inv = af.getInventory();
output.println(inv.size());
```

Compile and run. Confirm that the randomly generated instance contains approximately 100 different items.

2. We want to list the numbers of these items. To that end, we must browse the keys of the map. Add the following lines:

```
for (String itemNumber: inv.keyset())
{
```

Add code to the loop so that the item numbers are displayed delimited by a space.

3. We want to know which of the listed items is `Fresh`. Add the following lines:

```
Item item = inv.get(itemNumber);
if (item instanceof Fresh)
{
```

Add code to the loop so that the fresh item numbers are displayed with an asterisk as a suffix. In addition, compute and output a count of the fresh items. They should constitute approximately 25% of the total number of items.

4. Add code to generate a listing that shows the item number, an asterisk if `Fresh`, the stock quantity, the price, and the name. It should look like this:

```
2910h335    1544 4.05   Honey Oat Cereal by ZB
2002H804    3286 4.58   Semi-Hard Gouda Cheese by NR
2910h771    3989 5.92   U8 Oat Cereal
0905A737*   1861 6.12   Side Veal Meat by IT
1409S004    3363 3.52   S8 Brownie Ice Cream
0905A015*   3298 5.63   T9 Lamb Meat
1409S992    2951 7.02   K5 Praline Ice Cream
```

You can use tabs (`"\t"`) or spaces to separate the columns, but they should end up aligned. You can safely assume that the stock quantity is at most seven digits and that the unit price can be formatted in "7.2."

LI2.2 The Contacts Collection

Carry out the following tasks:

1. Launch your editor, and write the program `Lab12Con`, which starts with

```
AbstractFoods af = AbstractFoods.getRandom();
Map<String, Contact> con = af.getContacts();
output.println(con.size());
```

   Compile and run. Confirm that the randomly generated instance contains approximately 100 different contacts.

2. We want to list the numbers of these contacts. To that end, we must browse the keys of the map. Create a loop that displays the contact numbers delimited by a space.

3. We want to know which of the listed contacts is a Supplier. Add code to the loop so that supplier numbers are displayed with an asterisk suffix. In addition, compute and output a count of the supplier contacts. They should constitute approximately 50% of the total number of contacts.

4. Add code to generate a listing that shows the contact number in the first column and the contact name in the third. The second column depends on the contact type: for a client, show the credit rating; for a supplier, show the number of items in its catalogue (get the catalogue, and invoke its size method). The listing should look like this:

```
10097    4       UK Mart
10007    6       The A4 Ltd. Group
10029    B++     HH Ltd.
10098    C++     VX Limited
10041    B+      VJ Limited
10069    6       MZ Limited
10026    5       TK Company
10047    3       The H5 Enterprise Group
10033    3       The J1 Mart Group
10027    7       NB Mart
10038    A+      The D0 Company Group
```

   You can see that the first contact is a supplier and that it supplies four different items. The third contact, however, is a client with a B++ credit rating.

LI2.3 The Journal Collection

Carry out the following tasks:

1. Launch your editor, and write the program `Lab12Trx`, which starts with

```
AbstractFoods af = AbstractFoods.getRandom();
List<Trx> jour = af.getJournal();
output.println(jour.size());
```

Compile and run. Confirm that the randomly generated instance contains anywhere between 500 and 1000 transactions.

2. We can traverse a list using indexed or chained (maplike) access. Let us use the first:

```
for (int i = 0; i < jour.size(); i++)
{
    Trx trx = jour.get(i);
```

Add code to the loop to output the date, code, and reference of each transaction. The output should look like this:

```
Thu Jun 19 17:18:42 EDT 2003 P 1
Thu Jun 19 17:18:42 EDT 2003 P 1
Thu Jun 19 17:18:42 EDT 2003 P 2
Thu Jun 19 17:18:42 EDT 2003 P 3
Thu Jun 19 17:18:42 EDT 2003 P 3
Thu Jun 19 21:18:42 EDT 2003 P 4
Thu Jun 19 21:18:42 EDT 2003 P 4
Thu Jun 19 21:18:42 EDT 2003 P 4
```

3. Compute the output of the number of sales transactions (code S) and the number of purchase transactions (code P).

4. Modify the output so that it becomes a listing of the transaction code, the item number, the contact number, the quantity (formatted to 7), and the amount (formatted to "7.2"). It should look like this:

```
P 2910h597 10005  316   1403.19
P 1409S535 10005 1219   3412.19
P 2002H848 10005  780   3959.36
P 0905A052 10005  890   2969.73
P 0905A864 10005 1798   7931.81
P 2910h884 10010 1452   4283.49
P 0905A112 10010 1134   5407.50
S 0905A039 10011   35    189.70
S 2910h960 10011    2      4.94
S 2910h597 10011   19    117.99
```

 ## Exercises

Programming exercises are indicated with an asterisk.

12.1* The text claims that the Fresh/Date aggregation is a composition. Prove (by writing a program) that the expiry date of a Fresh item is created in the Fresh constructor, not in a Fresh client.

12.2* Write a program that performs the following tasks in the order shown:

■   Create an Item instance named Tuna with price $2.45.

- Purchase 200 units for a total of $250.
- Sell 50 units.
- Sell 25 units for a total of $30.
- Purchase 100 units for a total of $175.
- Output the returns of all accessors.

Predict the unit cost price, and compare your answer with the program's output. Does the answer change if the tasks are executed in a different order?

12.3* Write a program that performs the following tasks:

- Create a `Fresh` instance named "Pacific Salmon" with any item number, a price of $20, and an expiry date three weeks from now.
- Create a `Fresh` instance named "Atlantic Salmon" with the same item number as above, a price of $25, and an expiry date 20 days from now.
- Output the return of the `equals` method invoked on one passing the other of the above two items.
- Output the returns of the `toString` methods invoked on the above two items.

12.4* The object reference x was declared and assigned as follows:

```
Contact x = new Client("Adam", "Toronto", "AA-");
```

Write a code fragment that changes the credit rating to AA.

12.5* The text claims that `Supplier` aggregates a catalogue and that the aggregation is *not* a composition. Prove (by writing a program) that this is not a composition.

12.6* Write a program that performs the following tasks:

- Create an `Item` instance named Tuna with price $2.45.
- Create a `Supplier` instance named "Adam" with any address such that it supplies the above item at $1.75 a unit.

12.7 Argue that the relation between suppliers and items is many-to-many. To do that, show that the map catalogue does not preclude the possibility of two suppliers supplying the same item, or of one supplier supplying two different items.

12.8* Write a program that creates two `Trx` instances using data values of your choosing. Let your program output the returns of the `toString` methods as well as that of `equals` invoked on one passing the other. Predict the output, then verify.

12.9* Starting from a randomly chosen inventory collection, that is,

```
AbstractFoods af = AbstractFoods.getRandom();
Map<String, Item> inventory = af.getInventory();
```

write a program that lists the fresh items and their expiry dates. Show only the item number, year and month of expiry, and the name of the item.

12.10 Starting from a randomly chosen inventory collection, write a program that lists all items that will expire within a week from today.

12.11 Starting from a randomly chosen inventory collection, write a program that computes the value of the inventory at cost; that is, if we were to liquidate and sell all items at cost, what would be the total value?

12.12*Starting from a randomly chosen inventory collection, write a program that identifies the item that is generating the most revenue for the company.

12.13*Starting from a randomly chosen inventory collection, write a program that identifies the item that is generating the most profit for the company. Note that the item that sells the most is not necessarily the one that generates the most profit.

12.14*Starting from a randomly chosen inventory collection, write a program that generates a sorted list of all item numbers.

Hint: `ArrayList` has a constructor that takes a `Collection`; `Set` is a `Collection`.

12.15*Starting from a randomly chosen contacts collection, write a program that identifies the client with the highest credit rating. The rating is A, B, or C possibly suffixed by one or two plus signs.

12.16*Starting from a randomly chosen contacts collection, write a program that identifies the supplier with no catalogues. For such suppliers, the catalogue is either null or contains zero items (i.e., is empty). The program must also output the supplier with the thickest catalogue (one whose catalogue has more items than any other). If you find more than one such supplier, output any of them.

12.17*Starting from a randomly chosen contacts collection, write a program that determines whether any item has more than one supplier.

12.18*Starting from a randomly chosen transaction collection, write a program that counts the number of invoices involved in sales transactions. Sales transactions have an S code, and the invoice number appears in them as the transaction reference.

12.19*Starting from a randomly chosen transaction collection, write a program that identifies a client that made more than one purchase in the same month. If more than one such client is found, output any of them.

12.20*Starting from a randomly chosen company, write a program that reads an item number from the user and lists all suppliers that supply this item.

12.21*Starting from a randomly chosen company, write a program that reads an item number, a client number, and a quantity from the user. If the item and the client exist, sell the indicated quantity to the client. Output the item's stock before and after the transaction. Remember to also add an entry to the transaction journal.

12.22*Starting from a randomly chosen company, write a program that posts the following file:

```
 1 S 10001   0905A447    14      62.86
 1 S 10001   2910h131    40     159.2
 1 S 10001   0905A236    44     201.52
 1 P 10010   2910h207    1133   5174.15
 1 P 10010   1409S086    700    2139.38
 1 P 10010   2910h303    553    1044.89
16 S 10070   1409S887    13      79.95
16 S 10070   0905A950    5       32.85
16 S 10070   2002H394    41     167.69
```

It is a tab-delimited text file. Each record contains the transaction reference, transaction code, contact number, item number, quantity, and amount. For each, attempt to post the transaction by invoking the `purchase` or `sell` method in the `Item` class. If the posting fails, output the offending record number. Otherwise, add an entry to the `Trx` journal using today's date as the transaction date.

Once posting is done, it is a good idea to persist the company instance in a file; that is, serialize it. This allows you to write a second general-purpose program that deserializes the instance and verifies that the text file was indeed posted.

12.23 The web site for this book contains a collection of tests. You are now in position to take Test D, which covers Chapters 1 to 12. Follow these steps:

- Print and read the outline of the test. It tells you what kind of questions will be on the test, how they are weighted, and what aids are allowed.
- Print the test and take it. Do not use any book or API, and ensure that you do not exceed the allotted time.
- After taking the test, read the answers, and use their marking guidelines to mark your own test.

eCheck

Check12A (TS = 31)

Write the app `Check12A` that starts by obtaining an instance of the Abstract Foods Company using its `getRandom` method. It then prompts the user for a year range and outputs all inventory items that will expire within that range, i.e. items whose expiry date is less than that many years from today. Here is a sample run generated on May 28, 2010:

```
Enter range ... 3
Items expiring within your range:
0905A032  10/07/2011
0905A123  17/06/2012
0905A374  24/01/2012
0905A384  03/07/2010
0905A457  13/10/2010
0905A458  05/05/2011
0905A593  29/05/2012
0905A623  03/06/2012
0905A716  22/05/2011
0905A743  03/12/2012
0905A932  10/01/2012
count = 11
```

As you can see, the report displays all items whose expiry dates are before May 28, 2013. For each (Fresh) item displayed, the app outputs its item number and expiry date separated by one space. The date is formatted with a zero fill for the day and month. The listing ends with a count of the displayed items.

Develop your app, test it, and then eCheck it.

Check12B (TS = 31)

Write the app `Check12B` that starts by obtaining an instance of the Abstract Foods Company using its `getRandom` method. It then prompts the user for an item number. If the item exists, the app outputs some of its data including the supplier(s) who supply it. Otherwise, an error message is displayed. Here are *two* sample runs:

```
Enter item number ...  0910A447
No such item!

Enter item number ...  1409S123
Item Details:
Description:     Praline Ice Cream with Raspberry by EF
Qty in stock:    1800
Sale Price:      2.93
Sold Quantity:   97
Sales [in $]:    284.21
Supplier:        NK Ltd.
Supplier:        The J6 Mart Group
Supplier:        PX Enterprise
Supplier:        PS Incorp.
```

Note that detail lines use a tab to separate the data from the headers; i.e. the colon is followed by a tab character. Note also that the dollar amounts are rounded to two decimals. To find the supplier(s) of an item, you need to get the contact map and search the suppliers in it for those who have this item in their catalogs.

Develop your app, test it, and then eCheck it.

Check12C (TS = 36)

We want to write a program that allows us to drill down the sales figures of a given item.

After obtaining a random instance (using `getRandom`) of the Abstract Foods Company, the program prompts for and reads an item number from the user. If the item is not found in the company's inventory, a message is printed and the program ends. If the item is found, its sales figures (quantity sold and the corresponding dollar amount) are shown. This is then followed by a listing of all sales transactions that led to these figures. The program must traverse the transaction journal looking for S-type transactions involving this item. When one is found, its reference (the invoice number), quantity, and amount are displayed with a tab delimiter. Here is a sample run:

```
Enter item number:0905A112
Sold Qty =     146
Sales $$ = 778.18
Drill-down:
12    48     255.84
```

```
23      7      37.31
39     24     127.92
59     12      63.96
81     20     106.60
87     19     101.27
90      2      10.66
93     14      74.62
```

The output shows that the 146 units ($778.18) were sold in total. It also shows the individual transactions that led to these figures. In terms of formatting, all quantity figures are formatted using "7," and all dollar amounts are formatted "7.2." The columns in the table are separated by tabs.

Here is a second sample run:

```
Enter item number: 0912W450
No such item!
```

Develop your app, test it, and then eCheck it.

Check12D (TS = 46)

Our client needs a sales report for a given month. The report must list every item that was sold in the indicated month, its total dollar sales amount, and the percentage it contributed to the overall sales amount of all items in that month. It must also identify the item that was sold the most (in terms of dollars, not quantity) in that month.

For example, suppose the journal of the Abstract Foods Company indicates that a particular item, "M2 Stew Meat", was sold three times in November and that the corresponding transaction amounts were $50.50, $60.00, and $62.30. The report will reflect these sales by including one line in its listing showing the item name and the amount $172.80 (being the sum of the above three sales transactions):

```
Generate report for the month [1,12] ... 11
 172.80      8.57%  M2 Stew Meat
 184.86      9.17%  Thick Cut Stew Meat by RT
 256.71     12.73%  D7 Fudge Ice Cream
 390.96     19.39%  H1 Raspberry Ice Cream
 642.00     31.83%  G0 Chocolate Ice Cream
  11.16      0.55%  Semi-Soft Swiss Cheese by LK
   6.49      0.32%  Semi-Edam Cheese by WD
 277.38     13.75%  Semi-Soft Monterey Cheese by ZJ
  74.36      3.69%  Raisin Maple Cereal by JY
----------
2,016.72
==========
 642.00     31.83%  G0 Chocolate Ice Cream
```

Each item sold in the month must appear in one and only one line in the listing. The line contains three tab-delimited fields: the item's total sales amount in that month (formatted as 12.2), the item's percent contribution to the total sales in the month (formatted as 6.2 and followed by a % sign), and the item's name. The listing ends with a footer, as shown, that outputs the total sales in the month (also 12.2) and identifies the item that sold the most by relisting its sales line. The generated listing must be sorted on the item. Hence, you must ensure (perhaps by using a `TreeMap`) that the output you generate is ordered based on the item's `compareTo/` method.

Your program must start by prompting for and reading the month from the user (no validation is necessary). It must then use the `getRandom` method of the `AbstractFoods` class to obtain an instance. You may want to read the API of the `getRandom` method to better understand the returned instance, which, while random, does exhibit certain properties.

Develop your app, test it, and then eCheck it.

Appendix A
UCS, Unicode, and ASCII

The International Organization for Standardization (abbreviated as ISO, from the Greek *isos*, which means "equal") has a standard (ISO-10646) that defines a Universal Character Set (UCS). This set includes virtually every character used on this planet. Characters from all modern and historic languages are included, as well as those used in certain scripts and in a number of specialized fields, such as math, science, character recognition, and publishing. The UCS has room for over one billion characters. Of these, only around one million are currently defined, and of these, only around 64K are widely used. Of these 64K characters, the first 128 (code 0 to 127) are the ones used every day in the English-speaking world. They make up what is called the Basic Latin set, which is also called the ASCII code.

Even though ISO-10646 assigns a code to every character in the UCS, it does not define a corresponding representation. It is clear from the above counts that you will need 1 byte per code if your app is limited to Basic Latin, 2 bytes per code if it is limited to the most widely used 64K set, and 4 bytes per code if the app is to use any UCS code. Using 4 bytes per code is certainly the most regular and, thus, the simplest solution, but it comes at a high price: it uses a lot of memory and processing time. This is especially true for applications in which Basic Latin is the predominant character subset. At the other extreme, using only 1 byte per code is unacceptable in today's globalization climate.

Unicode, a consortium of business and research institutions, came up with a solution that sacrifices regularity for efficiency: instead of storing all codes in 4 bytes, store codes between 0 and 127 in 1 byte, and store bigger codes in 2, 3, or 4 bytes as needed. This variable-length representation is called UTF-8 (Universal Transformation Format in 8 bits). Unicode also endorses UTF-16 (which uses 2 bytes to represent the first 64K codes and 4 bytes to represent bigger codes) and UTF-32 (which uses 4 bytes to represent all codes in UCS, a fixed-length representation). See www.unicode.org for more details.

The `char` data type and the `String` class in Java use 2 bytes per character (as in UTF-16), thereby enabling the representation of any of first 64K codes in UCS. Note, however, that while your Java app can store and manipulate these characters, their input and output are controlled by the operating system.

The codes of the Basic Latin subset have certain features, which are depicted in Fig. A.1.

There is no need to memorize any of the codes; however, it is helpful to keep the following in mind: the code for space is 32, digits start at 48, uppercase letters start at 65, and lowercase

Figure A.1
The main character groups in the Basic Latin (ASCII) subset

Decimal	Unicode (U + hex)	Content
0–31	\u0000 - \u001f	control characters
32	\u0020	space
48–57	\u0030 - \u0039	the digits 0 to 9
65–90	\u0041 - \u005a	uppercase letters A–Z
97–122	\u0061 - \u007a	lowercase letters a–z

letters start at 97. Note that the codes for uppercase and lowercase letters differ by 32.

Five of the characters in the Basic Latin subset are called whitespace, and they are shown in Fig. A.2. They play an important role in parsing strings.

Decimal	Unicode	Escape Sequence	Character
9	\u0009	\t	HT: horizontal tab
10	\u000a	\n	LF: line feed
12	\u000c	\f	FF: form feed
13	\u000d	\r	CR: carriage return
32	\u0020		SP: space

Figure A.3 lists all characters in the Basic Latin subset except for control characters, which are the first 32 characters (codes 0 to 31) and the last character (code 127).

Figure A.2 The whitespace characters in Java

Figure A.3 The Basic Latin subset (excluding the first 32 control characters)

Decimal	Unicode	Char	Decimal	Unicode	Char	Decimal	Unicode	Char
32	\u0020	SP	64	\u0040	@	96	\u0060	`
33	\u0021	!	65	\u0041	A	97	\u0061	a
34	\u0022	"	66	\u0042	B	98	\u0062	b
35	\u0023	#	67	\u0043	C	99	\u0063	c
36	\u0024	$	68	\u0044	D	100	\u0064	d
37	\u0025	%	69	\u0045	E	101	\u0065	e
38	\u0026	&	70	\u0046	F	102	\u0066	f
39	\u0027	'	71	\u0047	G	103	\u0067	g
40	\u0028	(	72	\u0048	H	104	\u0068	h
41	\u0029	)	73	\u0049	I	105	\u0069	i
42	\u002a	*	74	\u004a	J	106	\u006a	j
43	\u002b	+	75	\u004b	K	107	\u006b	k
44	\u002c	,	76	\u004c	L	108	\u006c	l
45	\u002d	-	77	\u004d	M	109	\u006d	m
46	\u002e	.	78	\u004e	N	110	\u006e	n
47	\u002f	/	79	\u004f	O	111	\u006f	o
48	\u0030	0	80	\u0050	P	112	\u0070	p
49	\u0031	1	81	\u0051	Q	113	\u0071	q
50	\u0032	2	82	\u0052	R	114	\u0072	r
51	\u0033	3	83	\u0053	S	115	\u0073	s
52	\u0034	4	84	\u0054	T	116	\u0074	t
53	\u0035	5	85	\u0055	U	117	\u0075	u
54	\u0036	6	86	\u0056	V	118	\u0076	v
55	\u0037	7	87	\u0057	W	119	\u0077	w
56	\u0038	8	88	\u0058	X	120	\u0078	x
57	\u0039	9	89	\u0059	Y	121	\u0079	y
58	\u003a	:	90	\u005a	Z	122	\u007a	z
59	\u003b	;	91	\u005b	[	123	\u007b	{
60	\u003c	<	92	\u005c	\	124	\u007c		
61	\u003d	=	93	\u005d	]	125	\u007d	}
62	\u003e	>	94	\u005e	^	126	\u007e	~
63	\u003f	?	95	\u005f	_	127	\u007f	

Appendix B · Operators and Precedence

All the operators that are referenced in this book are listed in Figure B.1. The operator symbol appears in the second column and its operation (or action) appears in the fourth column.

The third column in the figure, "Kind", indicates the placement of the operands with respect to the operator. For unary operators (ones that take one operand), the kind is either prefix (the operator appears before its operand) or postfix (the operator appears before its operand). For binary operators (ones that take two operands), the kind is always infix in Java; i.e. the operator appears in between its two operands. One operator in Java is neither unary nor binary; it is the ? operator and it is ternary (it takes three operands).

The first column in the figure specifies precedence and association. When an expression involving several operators is evaluated, operators with a higher precedence are evaluated before ones with a lower precedence. Precedence is a negative integer, and hence, an operator with precedence −1 has the highest precedence and is evaluated before any other. If an expression involves two or more operators of equal precedence, they are evaluated left-to-right or right-to-left based on their association rule. This rule is indicated in the figure by an arrow that points either to the right or to the left.

Figure B.1
Some of Java's operators. (The arrows indicate association.)

Precedence	Operator	Kind	Operation
-15 ←	*op=*	infix	operate then assign
	=	infix	assign
-14 ←	? :	ternary	if-else
-13 →	||	infix	logical OR
-12 →	&&	infix	logical AND
-8 →	==	infix	equal
	!=	infix	not equal
-7 →	<	infix	less than
	<=	infix	less than or equal
	>	infix	greater than
	>=	infix	greater than or equal
	instanceof	infix	instance of
-5 →	+	infix	add
	-	infix	subtract
-4 →	*	infix	multiply
	/	infix	divide
	%	infix	remainder
-3 ←	new	prefix	instantiate
	(type)	prefix	cast
-2 ←	+	prefix	plus sign
	-	prefix	minus sign
	++	prefix	increment
	--	prefix	decrement
	!	prefix	negation
-1 →	++	postfix	increment
	--	postfix	decrement
	.	infix	invoke/access

Appendix C Coding Style

Although the compiler ignores style, experience has shown that code that adheres to a simple and consistent style will actually contain fewer errors. Furthermore, such code is easier to read, and this makes modifying and debugging it much faster.

◼ C.1 Naming Convention

Choose names that are meaningful and of reasonable length. Avoid using abbreviations unless they are standard, and avoid using generic names unless the context is generic. In terms of letter case, use the following widely adopted conventions:

1. **Packages**

   Use lowercase throughout, even for acronyms. For example, `java.util` and `java.io`.

2. **Classes**

   Use title case, that is, capitalize the first letter as in `Math`, but if the name is made up of more than one word, then capitalize the first letter of each, as in `StringBuffer`. If the name is an acronym, then capitalize all letters, for example, `IO` and `URL`.

3. **Variables, methods, and packages**

   Use lowercase characters, for example, `length`. If the name is made up of more than one word, capitalize the first letter of each subsequent word, for example, `indexOf`.

4. **Constants**

   Use uppercase characters, for example, `LIMIT`. If the name is made up of more than one word, separate the words by an underscore, for example, `UPPER_LIMIT`.

◢ C.2 Statement Layout

1. Editor

Use a nonproportional font such as Courier, with a point size of 10. Optionally, set the tab size to 3; that is, a tab should skip two positions.

2. One statement per line

Write only one statement per line. If a statement is longer than 80 characters, then break it (ideally after a comma) and continue it indented on the next line.

3. Token spacing

Leave exactly one space between otherwise-touching keywords and identifiers. In addition, leave exactly one space around operators and after commas.

4. Indentation

Indent each block by one tab relative to its braces.

◢ C.3 Braces

1. Usage

Always use braces in control structures, even if the block contains only one statement.

2. Placement

Corresponding opening and closing braces must be vertically aligned.

◢ C.4 Magic Numbers

Aside from zero, ±1, and ±2, no hard-coded literal numbers (also called *magic numbers*) may appear in code except in a `final` statement.

◢ C.5 Examples

■ Declaration

```
int counter;
final int PORT = 80;
final char CODE = '';
final char TAB = '\t';
double costPrice;
final double ELECTRON_CHARGE = 1.60219E-19;
```

- Expression

```
double z = Math.sqrt(x * x + y * y);
boolean isValid = (address > 0) && (address % size == 0);
```

- Selection

```
if (x % y == 0)
{
    z = x + y;
}
else if (x / 2 * 2 == x)
{
    z = y;
}
else
{
    z = x;
}
```

- Iteration

```
int sum = 0;
for (int i = 0; i < name.length(); i++)
{
    sum = sum + name.charAt(i);
}
```

- Exception handling

```
try
{
    int colon = entry.indexOf(":");
    output.println(entry.substring(0, colon);
}
catch (IndexOutOfBoundsException e)
{
    output.println("No colon in input!");
}
```

Throughout this textbook we have adopted the client view. Given the API of a class, we learned how to *use* it in our app. The implementer also starts with a given API but seeks to *implement* it, that is, to develop a class whose fields and methods are as specified in the API. In this appendix, we see how a class is implemented.

Consider the API of `type.lib.Rectangle`. This class encapsulates a rectangle with integer width and height and provides constructors and a number of methods. We will implement a subset of this API in a class named `MyRectangle`. Here is how the implementation looks like:

```java
public class MyRectangle
{
    //attributes
    private int width;
    private int height;

    //constructor
    public MyRectangle(int width, int height)

    {
        this.width = width;
        this.height = height;
    }

    // accessors
    public int getWidth()
    {
        return this.width;
    }
    public int getHeight()
    {
        return this.height;
    }
}
```

The above code is saved in a file named `MyRectangle.java` and then compiled, as usual, to a file named `MyRectangle.class`. You do not run the resulting class file; you use it in apps.

Note that the internal structure of the class is not very different from an app. You will observe the class header and body and recognize the syntax of all statements.

The attributes are declared at the top and their scope encompasses the entire class. Constructors and methods appear as blocks. The implementer's view emphasizes the role of the constructor as a state initializer. You can see that it sets the state (the two attributes) based on the parameters it received from the client. The attributes are accessed using the "this" keyword, which is an object reference that points at the object being constructed.

To better expose the mechanics by which methods work let us add the getArea method:

```
public int getArea()
{
    return this.width * this.height;
}
```

You can see the mechanics by which methods work. The getArea method computes the area (by multiplying the width and height attributes) and then uses the return keyword to literally return the product to the client.

To get a feel for life in the implementer's world, create this file and compile it. If you get compile-time errors, you should be able to handle them. After wards, put back your client's hat and build an app that creates MyRectangle objects and uses them.

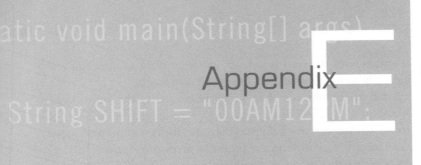

Appendix E — The TYPE API

TYPE refers to several subpackages and applications written especially for this textbook and bundled into one file called `type.jar`. As shown in Lab 2, this file installs as a Java extension, which means you can use its services from any directory as if they were part of the standard Java library. This appendix provides an overview of the services provided by TYPE and how to use them.

Using the type Services

You can use a class C in subpackage S of TYPE by including the following statement in the imports of your program:

```
import type.S.C;
```

To launch a TYPE application A, issue the following command from a console while in any directory:

```
java A
```

This is the same command you use to launch your own applications. Assuming you do not have an application named A, the virtual machine "knows" that it should find the application in the TYPE jar file.

The lib Subpackage

This subpackage contains a set of carefully designed classes that demonstrate the basic concepts of object-oriented programming (OOP) and software engineering. Some of the classes are stand-alone, some participate in a single relation, and some are involved in multiple relations. The UML class diagrams of these classes are shown in Fig. E.1, along with the interclass relationships.

The top pane in Fig. E.1 shows stand-alone classes. Each class can be used without worrying about other classes; that is, the client does not need to be concerned with any inheritance, aggregation, or dependency of any kind. All exceptions thrown by these classes are

Figure E.1 These UML diagrams depict the inter-class relationships between the main `type.lib` classes.

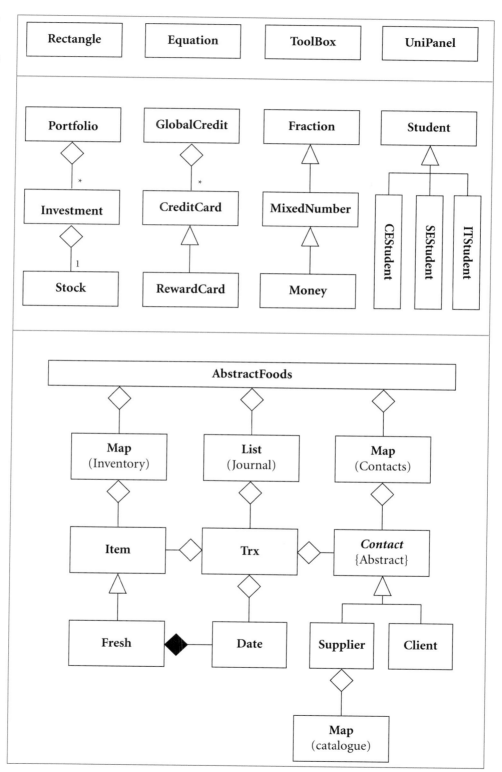

unchecked and, hence, do not need to be caught. Classes in the middle pane of the figure, however, involve a single relationship, aggregation or inheritance. The lower pane shows classes that are corrected by more than one relation. This gradual exposure of complexity is ideal for studying OOP because it allows us to focus on one concept at a time.

The classes in this subpackage span several application areas and have contexts that are familiar to most. Figure E.2 provides an overview of each class; refer to the API for details.

For pedagogical purposes, however, a few features have intentional guideline violations, for example, a public attribute that should have been made private or a mutator that changes the state without validation. Such violations are clearly indicated in the API.

The `util` Subpackage

Aside from `lib`, all subpackages in `TYPE` are auxiliary and are of no direct interest to application developers. The only exception is `util`, which is meant for those who have not installed release 5.0 (or later) of J2SE but who like to use the enhanced input/output that was introduced in that release. As was shown in Chapters 2 and 3, this subpackage allows you to use `Scanner` and `printf` even if you are using J2SE 1.4.

The `TYPE` Applications

There are three applications: `eCheck`, `Options`, and `UniCon`.

- ■ `eCheck` This is a testing and marking program. It is meant to help you learn programming by checking the correctness and length of your programs. It can also be used to contact the `eCheck` server in your school to record that your program has passed all tests.
- ■ `Options` `Options` is used to configure `eCheck`. You can use it, for example, to set your ID and password and to specify your school's URL.
- ■ `UniCon` This program provides a platform-independent console. It acts like a command prompt window. Its main advantage over the operating system console is that it does not require a `path` or `classpath` setting.

The web site for this book contains further information on installing and using `TYPE`. It also maintains the latest version of `type.jar`.

Class Summary	
AbstractFoods	This class encapsulates the inventory/sales businesses of the Abstract Foods Company.
CEstudent	Provides services to maintain information about a CE (computer engineering) student.
CharStack	This class encapsulates a stack (last-in, first-out) of characters.
Client	This class encapsulates a client.
Contact	This class encapsulates a contact.
CreditCard	This class encapsulates a credit card and maintains information about it.
Equation	Encapsulates an algebraic equation of the second degree.
Fraction	This class encapsulates a fraction.
FractionNS	This class is identical to Fraction except for two nonstandard (NS) features.
Fresh	This class encapsulates a fresh item.
GlobalCredit	This class encapsulates the credit card operations of a Global Credit Centre (GCC).
Investment	This class encapsulates a stock investment.
Item	This class encapsulates a stock item.
ITstudent	Provides services to maintain information about an IT (information technology) student.
MixedNumber	This class encapsulates a mixed number.
Money	This class encapsulates an amount of money.
Portfolio	This class encapsulates a portfolio of investments.
Rectangle	An object-oriented nonutility class for encapsulating a rectangle.
RewardCard	This class encapsulates a CreditCard that offers reward points.
SEstudent	Provides services to maintain information about an SE (software engineering) student.
Stock	This class encapsulates a stock.
StockNS	This class is identical to Stock except for two nonstandard (NS) features.
Student	Provides services to maintain information about a computer science (COSC) student.
Supplier	This class encapsulates a supplier.
ToolBox	This class contains various utilities.
Trx	This class encapsulates a transaction.
UniPanel	This class encapsulates a (JPanel) with buffered (rather than callback) graphics.

Figure E.2 This figure highlights the classes of type.lib.

Index

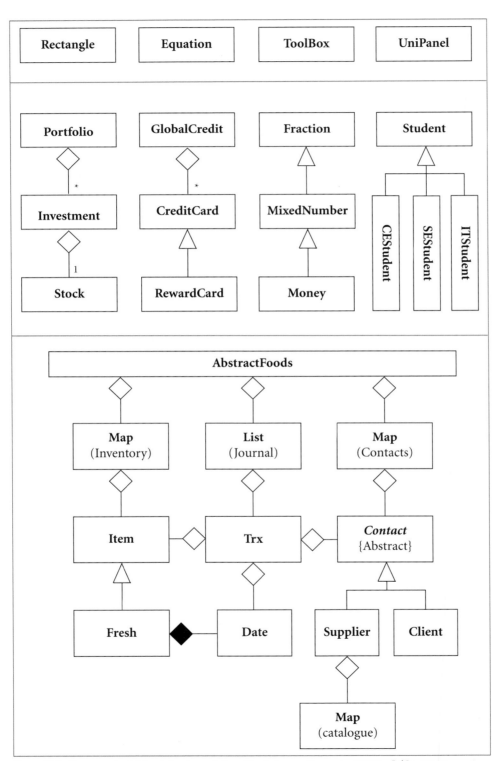

These UML diagrams depict the interclass relationships between the main `type.lib` classes.